Case Studies in
International Marketing

OTHER TITLES IN THE SERIES

Case Studies in International Marketing

Edited by

PETER DOYLE and NORMAN A. HART
BA (Econ) MA MS PhD   MSc McAM FIPR

Published on behalf of the CAM Foundation
and The Institute of Marketing

HEINEMANN : LONDON

William Heinemann Ltd
10 Upper Grosvenor Street, London W1X 9PA
LONDON MELBOURNE TORONTO
JOHANNESBURG AUCKLAND

First published 1982

434 90370 1

Typeset by Supreme Litho Typesetting, Goodmayes, Ilford, Essex.
Printed in Great Britain by Redwood Burn Limited, Trowbridge, Wiltshire.

Preface

The objective of this book is to provide a series of case problems as a basis for class discussion, with the student placed in the role of decision-maker. Each case describes a real managerial situation, often in a well-known company. Dealing with these cases is not unlike working with the problems that men and women encounter in their jobs as managers.

The case study method has proved to be an effective and increasingly popular approach to teaching marketing management. The great majority of cases so far have been based on the experiences of US companies and many of the best cases have been written by professors at the Harvard Business School. We aimed to produce cases of comparable quality as teaching vehicles which looked at the decisions of European companies. Such cases are found to be more immediate and relevant to British and European students. In addition, all of the cases are new and reflect the significant changes in the marketing environment which have occurred since the mid-1970s.

All the cases are written by teachers of marketing. They have tried to put together problem situations which are real, relevant and stimulating to discuss. All the cases have been extensively tested in the class.

Certain points about the case study method of learning are worth noting. First, unlike lectures and textbooks the case method of instruction does not present students with a technique or comprehensive methodology about how to market goods and services successfully. Instead, it provides an opportunity to 'learn by doing'. As a teaching device, it can be successful only if the student is encouraged to accept the role of involved participant or decision-maker rather than disinterested observer. Second, students learn about the uncertainties of the real world management environment. Rarely is information available in a form which is sufficient, precise and unambiguous. Managers often have to proceed on the basis of judgment or inprecise information. Finally, there is rarely a 'correct' answer to a case. Instead there may be a number of feasible strategies that management might adopt, each with somewhat different implications for the future of the organization.

It is hoped that these case studies will be of value on graduate programmes at universities and polytechnics, as well as those studying for professional examinations. They are particularly relevant to those studying for the Diplomas of the CAM Foundation, the Institute of Marketing, and for the International Advertising Association.

The project of writing these case studies was financed by the Foundation for Management Education. We would like to express our gratitude to the Foundation and to its director, Philip F. Nind, for their support. In addition we would like to thank the companies that have worked with us and helped us write these case studies about their international strategies. It must be emphasized that the studies are not intended to provide examples of either effective or ineffective handling of management problems but rather to provide a vehicle for discussion and learning about the issues involved.

Most of all we would like to thank our colleagues: Professor M. J. Baker, Dr M. F. Bradley, D. Cook, Dr G. Hooley, J. Lynch, C. McIver, G. A. Randall, J. Saunders, Dr J. Ward, R. Willsmer and J. Wilmshurst for contributing to this book. Writing good case studies is a time-consuming, complex and at times frustrating task. Finally, we would like to thank Mrs Anne Denby who typed the manuscript for this book at great speed and with her usual professionalism.

P. Doyle
N. Hart

Note. Companion to this volume is the *Teachers' Manual for Case Studies in International Marketing*, written by the same contributors and following the same sequence of topics. The *Teachers' Manual* highlights key issues in the case studies as a guide to teachers and for the benefit of students working on their own: it also suggests ways of handling class discussions.

Contents

Part A

Environment of International Marketing

Marketing strategies are successful when they match the opportunities existing in the environment. Strategies which are successful in one environment (e.g. the home market) can be disastrous if they are pursued in environments which are different (e.g. overseas markets). The starting point of developing any marketing plan is to analyse the nature of the environment where it has to operate.

International marketing is complex because overseas markets are usually different in significant ways from the home market and because it is more difficult for managers to understand and learn about markets in other countries, due to differences in language, culture, life-styles and economic structures. The complexity of the task increases exponentially when the company is trying to develop positions in many overseas markets.

Various components of the environment impact on marketing performance including economic, social, cultural, regional and financial variables. On the *economic* environment the marketer needs to analyse the country's income and *per capita* distribution, its population size and structure, consumption patterns, and stage of economic development. Such factors have major effects on market potential and marketing strategies. In general, data on economic variables are available, in some form at least, from well-known national and international sources. More difficult to learn about and evaluate are the *social and cultural* elements of the international market environment. The values, ideas, attitudes and symbols of a nation shape the behaviour and aspirations of its people, creating exciting opportunities but also, frequently, unexpected problems for the international marketing firm.

Regional market characteristics are having increasing impacts on world trade. The growth and development of such associations as the European Economic Community and the Latin American Free Trade Association have significant economic, political and regulatory implications for businesses. Finally, the international marketer operates within a more complex and risky *financial framework* than a company operating within only one country. Unless the manager has the knowledge of how to deal with the uncertainties of operating in fluctuating currencies, the profits he earns from overseas ventures are likely to be short-lived.

The following cases and exercises explore the problems of working in this type of complex international marketing environment.

I
Hawker Siddeley Aviation Ltd

J. Sanders

The Initial Request

On 14th April 1972, Bob Lomas, Sales Administration Manager at Hawker Siddeley Aviation's (HSA), Manchester Division, received a telephone call from Wing Commander Weir, the Air Attaché for the United Kingdom in a European Nation. The Wing Commander had found out that the National Air Force (NAF) were looking for an aircraft to replace their ageing freight/transport aircraft which it used primarily on intra European operations. The requirement was for equipment to fit between the large Lockheed C-130 Hercules that the air force had already decided to buy and lighter, utility/transport aircraft. An additional requirement was that the aircraft should be capable of being maintained and serviced by an outside organization. It was felt that the Hawker Siddeley 748 Series 2a (HS.748), produced at Manchester, was a suitable candidate for the role specified. (See Exhibit 1.4 and Appendix 1.3.)

Hawker Siddeley Aviation Ltd

In 1972 Hawker Aviation Ltd was the largest subsidiary owned by Hawker Siddeley Group Ltd, a United Kingdom based company with worldwide interests in aerospace, transport, mechanical, electrical

This case was prepared by John Saunders, Lecturer in Marketing at the University of Bradford Management Centre, and was financed by the Foundation for Management Education. At the request of Hawker Siddeley Aviation, the actual names of customer organizations and personnel are not used. Throughout the case the country whose air force is concerned is referred to as the Country or the Nation.

and civil engineering. Hawker Siddeley Group Ltd and Hawker Siddeley International Ltd, a subsidiary responsible for the group's international operation, including de Havilland Canada, were based in London. The head office of HSA was at Kingston, south London, which was also the centre for the company's military sales organization. The Manchester division of HSA had two large sites. Chadderton, in north Manchester housed most of the division's commercial departments. The main machine shop, light assembly and main assembly bays were also located there. Large airframe parts such as wings and fuselage were fabricated at Chadderton then moved, by road, to the second factory at Woodford, which is south of Manchester. There, final assembly took place and the aircraft were fitted out for delivery to customers. In addition to having an airfield and aircraft servicing facilities, Woodford was the centre for the division's technical departments.

Locally the Manchester division was called Avro, a name which was officially dropped in 1963 although HSA had owned the facilities since before the Second World War. As Avro the company had designed and built many famous aircraft. These included the 504 in the First World War and the Lancaster bomber in World War II. More recently, the Shackleton maritime patrol aircraft and the Vulcan strategic bomber had occupied most of the company's manufacturing capacity. In 1972 two aircraft were in production, the Nimrod maritime patrol aircraft and the HS.748.

The Hawker Siddeley 748 Series 2a

The HS.748 entered production a few years after the Dutch Fokker F.27 Friendship (see Appendix 1.3) and the British Handley Page Herald which were its main competitors. The three aircraft were similar in many ways, all using variants of the same Rolls Royce Dart turbo-prop power plant.

After intensive engineering and market research the HS.748 was designed to become a DC.3 replacement. Over 10,000 Douglas DC.3s had been constructed between 1936 and 1946 with over 1,200 remaining in service by 1972 as the 'workhorse' of many small airlines and air forces. The DC.3 replacement market had been active for a number of years with several 'replacements' having come and gone. Unlike the F.27 and Herald, the HS.748 was a low winged monoplane. Besides giving an unobstructed passenger area it was claimed that this also gave the aircraft aerodynamic, structural and maintenance advantages. During the initial design stage a primary objective was set to develop an aircraft that would have low maintenance costs and allow high utilization by operators. To achieve this all components used on auxiliary services were selected on the basis of proven reliability, long overhaul life and ease of provisioning. Several primary components were also adapted from aircraft already in service. Another design feature was that the aircraft was to be fully fail-safe. This meant that in the event of a failure of any part of the structure, sufficient members were available to allow redirection of loads. The result was a robust aircraft, where any failure due to fatigue develops sufficiently slowly for it to be detected during routine inspection before becoming dangerous. A further feature necessary if the HS.748 was to become a DC.3 replacement was short take-off and landing performance from semi-prepared runways. This capability was particularly needed by operators in underdeveloped parts of the world. Eventually the HS.748 was to become well known for its outstanding performance out of hot and high air strips. To quote from the company's sales literature; 'the 748 represents no great technological "breakthrough". It is instead a classical example of the application of "state of the art" technology in achieving highly satisfactory performance, reliability and comfort'. The original design aims for the aircraft were to become the main selling features of the aircraft in the years to come.

By 1972 the HS.748 had become one of the most successful commercial aircraft ever manufactured in the UK (see Appendix 1.1). One of the original competitors had disappeared with the demise of Handley Page but several new manufacturers were now in the market. The Japanese NAMC YS-11A was very similar in configuration to the HS.748, although significantly larger. HSA had been closely involved with NAMC during the project stage of the aircraft. The original hope was that the company would take on a large share of the work associated with the venture but this never came to fruition. Less competitive and aimed at the military market were the Russian Antonov AN-26 and the de Havilland of Canada DHC.5 Buffalo. Fokker, the strongest competitor, besides making the F.27 had become involved in the manufacture and marketing of two pure jet aircraft. These were the Dutch-built Fokker F.28 Fellowship and the VFW-Fokker VFW 614, made in the Federal Republic of Germany.

Sales Organization

The sales organization of HSA Manchester (see Exhibit 1.2), was responsible for selling the HS.748 and Nimrod.   Each year the potential markets were analysed and a list made of the most likely sales prospects for the coming twelve months.   Area Sales Managers were then given 'designated areas' that comprised of a number of prospective customers.   These were usually grouped geographically, although there were exceptions due to special relationships a sales-man had developed in the past.   As the year progressed new pros-pects would be added to the designated areas which would also be changed to balance the workload that developed.

Doug Watts was the Area Sales Manager who would eventually be responsible for the National Air Force prospect.   Until then, his designated area included the Air Forces of Malaysia, Thailand and Zaire together with Germany.   Like several other Area Sales Mana-gers he had joined HSA after a distinguished career in the Royal Air Force.   Immediately before joining the company in 1970 he was Group Captain, Air Plans RAF Germany.   Three of the Area Sales Managers had no RAF experience but had previously worked in one or more of the company's technical departments.   One had been in the Sales Engineering Department for a number of years before being promoted to the Sales Department.   In the company the Sales Department had high status, occupying a series of offices on the ground floor at the front of the Chadderton works.

The Sales Engineers were all technically qualified, a number having post-graduate degrees.   Most had become Sales Engineers directly after completing a technical apprenticeship with the com-pany although some had been recruited from other technical depart-ments.   They were responsible for providing technical support to the Sales Department but also did much routine work associated with the sales effort.   Although the Sales Engineers were not working directly for the Area Sales Managers, the work of each Sales Engineer usually related to one part of the world necessitating frequent contact with one or two people in the Sales Department.   The Sales Engineering Department was close to the Sales Department and could be reached by a corridor which led from the 'front corridor', where the Sales Department was located, to the corner of the design office occupied by the Sales Engineers.

Ian Crawford, the Marketing Director of the whole of HSA, was based in London.   He had overall responsibility for marketing in all the British and overseas subsidiaries — together with the HSA Regional Executives (see Exhibit 1.3).

The Opening Phase

After receiving the telephone call from Wing Commander Weir, Bob Lomas circulated news of the prospective sale while Doug Watts was given responsibility for the new prospect. Although HSA Manchester had agents in the Country, these either had not heard of the NAF requirement or had failed to communicate news of it to the company. As the agents seemed to be dormant, direct contact was made with the National authorities. Following a visit to Herr Hans Schülter, the Defence Secretary, Bob Lomas was asked to send copies of the standard HS.748 military brochure directly to the Ministry of Defence where they would be passed on to the Minister. A few days later, Lieutenant Colonel Schemann, Junior Defence Secretary, wrote thanking Bob Lomas for the material.

The next contact made was with Lieutenant General Baron von Forster, Defence Attaché to the Country's Embassy in London, whom Bob Lomas met at the Hanover Air Show. The General confirmed the Air Force's interest in new equipment and asked for details of the HS.748 so he could pass them on to the authorities.

On 6th July, Air Commodore Netherton informed John Upton of HSI that the NAF probably had a requirement for an aircraft that could be used as a State transport. The Air Commodore had lived in the Capital of the Country for eight years since retiring from the Royal Air Force where he had been responsible for the Queen's Flight. After completing his military career he had become a founder member of EILLUFT AG, a group which dominated civil aircraft maintenance and light aircraft operations in the Country. He had later been used by HSA Kingston, as an agent on an *ad hoc* basis in connection with the prospective sale of fighter aircraft. Having become an accredited agent for HSA Kingston, it was proposed that he should act as an agent in the Country for HSA Manchester.

Besides the HS.748, HSA made another aircraft which could be sold for VIP purposes. This was the HS.125, a small, twin-jet aircraft manufactured and marketed by HSA Hatfield. The sales organizations of both the Manchester and Hatfield divisions were told of the sales opportunity.

In response, Geoff Lancaster, Deputy Sales Manager of HSA

Manchester sent copies of the HS.748 brochure to Air Commodore Netherton requesting that they be passed on to the prospective customer. As the Air Commodore was not familiar with the HS.748, a letter was enclosed with the brochures outlining some of the selling points that he could use. The following is an extract:

> 'Although the HS.748 does not have the glamour of a fast jet aircraft, it has many other advantages which make it perhaps the most suitable choice for a State Aircraft ... the size of the accommodation coupled with reasonably low purchase price. Most VIP layouts consist of a large rear state room with seats for four or five persons. These would be of the fully reclining and swivelling type. The forward part of the cabin would accommodate anything up to 20 attendants. The large size of the HS.748 also allows full galley and toilet facilities to be placed if need be both forward and aft in the aircraft, so that the VIP party could have complete privacy.
> ... use all airfields currently used by the DC.3 ...
> credit terms are available.'

It was also mentioned that the Country's Minister of Defence had recently flown in an Andover of the Queen's Flight and was said to have been favourably impressed. (The Queen's Flight Andovers are a special variant of the HS.748.)

On July 10th, Air Commodore Netherton met the officer in charge of the Operations Requirements Branch of the NAF and confirmed that a study into the replacement of several types of transport aircraft was being undertaken. Simultaneously, Wing Commander Weir contacted Ron Hill, the Executive Director, Marketing, HSA Manchester saying that it was imperative that the company made direct contact with the Long Term Planning Department of the National Air Force concerning their requirement. Major Gräf was suggested as the best contact although Colonel Brauers and Lieutenant Colonel Horton were given as alternatives if he was not available. Since Doug Watts was out of the country, Brian Cowley, the 748 Sales Manager, was asked to arrange a meeting. A first exploratory meeting was arranged for the 26th July to be followed by another on the 7th August when Ron Hill would be able to meet the senior personnel responsible for aircraft procurement.

Work in Iran prevented Ron Hill from attending the meeting so his place was taken by Steve Williams, his executive assistant. The discussions between Steve Williams, Air Commodore Netherton,

Major Gräf and Lieutenant Colonel Horten, went well. Lieutenant Colonel Horten, the second in command of the Planning Department, outlined the need for the Air Force to completely re-equip their tactical and transport squadrons before 1976. Large Lockheed C.130 Hercules had already been ordered but they were still looking for a small, more flexible aircraft to replace their piston engined DC.3s and DC.4s. Major Gräf, the officer in command of re-equipment evaluations, explained that he had already completed preliminary analysis of suitable replacements which had included the HS.748. Fokker had given a demonstration of the F.27, an aircraft very much favoured by many in the Air Force, partly because a large proportion of the air frame was constructed in the Country. The final requirement would be for two or three general transport aircraft plus possibly a third for the paratroop training school at NAF-Graz. A Short Skyvan had already given a demonstration as a paradrop aircraft and de Havilland Canada had been asked to demonstrate their aircraft.

It was proposed that the HS.748 be formally demonstrated to a team from the National Air Force on 19th/20th October, and the schedule presented in Appendix 1.2 was agreed. Major Gräf asked for further evidence to support the HS.748. In response, certain advantages of the HS.748 were highlighted. These were lack of bonding and spot welding, no pneumatics, fail-safe design, progressive maintenance and rough-airfield performance. Since C.130s had already been ordered it would also be an advantage if commonality of avionics could be achieved.

During the visit they met briefly with Colonel Brauers, the officer commanding the Long Range Planning Department. Air Commodore Netherton had known him well for a number of years but was disturbed to find that Colonel Brauers was soon to be moved to NATO HQ and replaced by an officer who he did not know.

After the meeting the Air Commodore expressed the hope that, provided the presentation in October went well and the Air Force wanted the aircraft, the political people would most likely agree to the purchase. He added that the sale of the paradrop aircraft would depend upon support from Colonel Smit, the Commanding Officer of NAF-Graz. The main issue, he thought, would be the ability to operate safely, fully loaded for a parachute training mission, from the airstrip which was grass and only 650 metres long.

Following the visit, Ernie Wise, a Senior Sales Engineer, was asked to manage the technical selling effort. Through the Sales Department Customer Specifications Engineer, the Production Planning

Department were asked for a delivery schedule and the Estimating Department were asked to cost the aircraft. Numerous other technical departments also became involved in supply cost and performance evaluations. Eventually it would be the responsibility of the Contracts Department to negotiate a price for the package of aircraft, spares, guarantees, and after-sales services required.

Glynn Wills, a Sales Engineer who worked closely with Ernie Wise in the specification and requisitioning of art work for the demonstration, became particularly involved with the avionics requirements. Several requests for detailed information were received from Major Gräf, including details of the take-off and landing performance of the HS.748 at NAF-Graz. Since it was found to be marginal, Air Commodore Netherton concluded that the only course of action available was to convince the airfield's commanding officer of the desirability of extending the runway.

Before the scheduled demonstration, the biennial Farnborough Air Show took place. Invitations to attend were sent to a number of National Air Force personnel, several of whom visited the show and were entertained by HSA. The guests were:

Lt. Col. Horten	Chief of Plans and Studies	5—6 September
Lt. Col. Wabber	Chief of Pilot Training	5—6 September
Maj. Bayer	Plans and Studies	6—7 September
Maj. Gräf	Plans and Studies	7—8 September

The meetings with these personnel were thought to have progressed well, providing a useful prelude to the full demonstration. Nine National Air Force officers visited Woodford for the demonstration of the HS.748 in October:

Col. Zvinek	Planning
Lt. Col. Horten	Plans and Studies
Lt. Col. Schmidt	Technical Section
Maj. Holtmann	Avionics
Maj. Vorfeld	Avionics
Maj. Winkels	Supply/Spares
Maj. von Betterei	HQ Transport
Maj. Kochem	Plans and Studies
Maj. Gräf	Plans and Studies

During the visit each was looked after by an appropriate technical specialist from HSA Manchester while the men from the Long Range Planning Department were kept together to discuss contractual considerations. Prices for the aircraft in three configurations were presented, £900,000 the basic version, £950,000 the basic version with strengthened floor for cargo operations and £1,125,000 with strenthened floor and large freight door. (All prices quoted in this case are fictional although they do reflect the relative magnitudes involved.) To these basic prices there needed to be added the cost of avionics, spares and other equipment which allowed the aircraft to perform a wide variety of roles.

On the whole, the demonstration and presentation went down very well although Major von Betterei 'from whom it was difficult even to wring a smile', was identified as 'F.27 oriented'. Steve Williams reported that Air Commodore Netherton and he had been able to talk separately with the senior officer present with whom they had a 'long and useful discussion about compensation'.

The Second Phase

In 1972 compensation or offset was becoming an increasingly common part of large international sales. The arrangement usually involved a provision being made, in a contract, for the vendor or the vendor's country to purchase a specified quantity of goods from the customer's country. The magnitude of the offset varied a lot, ranging from a fraction of the contracted price to, on rare occasions, more than the contracted price. The discussion with Colonel Zvinek at Woodford marked the first occasion when offset was mentioned in connection with the NAF's procurement of transport aircraft.

HSA Manchester conducted investigations to determine the importance of offset arrangements to the National Government. The first news from HSA Hatfield suggested offset was critical. They had been attempting to sell two executive jet aircraft to the NAF. It was reported that 'sales of the HS.125 failed mainly due to offset being ignored'. Two French-built Falcon 10 aircraft were eventually supplied as VIP transports as part of a deal with very high offset involved. This had been easy for Dassault-Breguet to arrange as the aircraft were partly built in the Country. While continuing internal studies into offset, HSA Kingston warned HSA Manchester not to try to use any of the compensation which was already in the process of being arranged by a team working on the possible sale of HS.1127 and HS.1182 trainer aircraft to the Country. To clarify the situation Air Commodore Netherton visited Herr Maximilian, an undersecretary in the Ministry of Economic Affairs, who was responsible for advising the Ministerial Committee on such matters.

Herr Maximilian stated that recently offset had been set at between 60% and 70% of the value of a contract and had to be completed by delivery date of the last aircraft. He felt that ideally the work should be related directly to the major project being considered and should involve the manufacture of main sub-assemblies such as wings, air frames or engines. He concluded by saying that negotiations were the responsibility of the vendor alone who was not expected to increase prices as a result of the required activities.

Soon after his visit to Herr Maximilian, the Air Commodore had obtained some encouraging information about the prospective sale. The Air Force had given the replacement top priority with a schedule for action defined. This gave:

March 1973	Finalized requirements
Mid—1973	Signing of letter of intent
Late 1973	Signing of contract and deposit payment
1974	Delivery and full payment.

Colonel Zvinek, who had originally been doubtful about the HS.748, had been firmly converted since the demonstration together with all the other important Air Force officers concerned. Also, since the government had already earmarked funds for the procurement of three aircraft, all that was necessary was to assemble an acceptable offset.

Some time passed with little further progress being made with the sale but it was becoming evident that although the Air Force staff officers were still in favour of the HS.748, Fokker were offering a very substantial offset. It was thought that one reason for Fokker being able to do this was their shareholdings in Baden GmbH who owned Nationale Flugzeugwerke AG (NFW), the largest National airframe manufacturer. Since NFW were already manufacturers of F.27 parts it was easy for them to show an advantageous offset capability.

Early in 1973 Kevin Murphy, the Contracts Manager for HSA Manchester, sent a firm proposal to Colonel Zvinek. Simultaneously members of the Sales Engineering Department were attempting to persuade the Air Force to accept performance and weight information which showed the HS.748 in a better light. The original figures they had been asked to provide were chosen by the NAF to allow direct comparison with the F.27. Unfortunately, the conditions for the 'paper comparison' had been set by Fokker and not surprisingly they were chosen to favour their own aircraft.

Some days later an urgent telex was received from Roger Woods of HSI who had met Colonel Horten at a cocktail party in the Capital. He said that Fokker's exceptional offset looked like losing HSA the deal. Panic was averted when Air Commodore Netherton talked to Colonel Horten and confirmed that the offset was 'not big business'. Further, Messrs Jones and Bedwell of HSA Kingston, who were in the Capital at the time negotiating a large offset deal with the Ministry of Economic Affairs, asked about the HS.748 and were told, 'offset would not really be involved on such a small order'.

Major Gräf and Air Commodore Netherton visited Manchester on 11th April, 1973 to discuss the contract. Major Gräf said there was a feeling that the HS.748 was inferior to the F.27 on several technical grounds. Also the price of £1,393,000, being asked for an aircraft with large cargo door and the required equipment, compared unfavourably with a comparable F.27. In addition, when the price of spares was added to the aircraft cost, the total was more than the amount budgeted for the purchase. Negotiations centred around reducing the number of roles the aircraft would be required to perform, so reducing the amount of optional equipment supplied. By eliminating paradropping, supply-dropping, and aeromedical capabilities the price was reduced to a more acceptable £1,323,000. A new formal offer was taken to the Capital before the end of April. This included details of an increased 'all up weight' of the aircraft, which would allow an extra 2,000 lb of fuel to be carried, thereby increasing performance over some of the longer sectors the aircraft would be required to fly.

At the Paris Air Show on 13th June Doug Watts again met Major Gräf. Two issues were discussed. After careful consideration the Air Force desired to change the specifications of the aircraft to such an extent that a new quotation would be necessary. He also emphasized the importance of offset. Since by this time Steve Williams had left HSA, Geoff Lancaster took over negotiations. Wing Commander Weir, the Air Attaché in the Capital, was contacted and questioned about the sale. He said he would probably be able to help in arranging some offset deal but added that it was generally felt in diplomatic circles that it was 'Britain's turn' to obtain a contract.

On 16th July Geoff Lancaster, Major Gräf and Air Commodore Netherton visited Herr Maximilian at the Ministry of Economic Affairs to discuss alternative offset arrangements that the company could provide. Four were put forward:

1 Bought out equipment for the HS.748 could be purchased from the country's firms.
2 Basic aircraft could be flown to the Country where they would be finished and new avionics fitted by an NAF contractor.
3 HSA's own vendors could be asked to sub-contract work into the Country.
4 The Country's industry could be given part of a future batch of HS.748 to build.

The Civil Servant's response to the suggestions was not enthusiastic. His main point was that offset should not be related directly to the main contract in question, nor should it involve the NAF or Government. He explained how critical offset arrangements were to the Nation's aerospace industry, which designed and marketed few aircraft and was almost totally dependent upon outside work. To underline his Government's concern he quoted the offset associated with the recent sale of two Boeing 737 to the country's national airline. Boeing had agreed to place £3,000,000 of work with the Country's industry in the first year and £15,000,000 over the next ten years. The figures suggested that the offset was far more than the price of the two aircraft.

After leaving the ministry Geoff Lancaster told Major Gräf the possible consequence of further delay in placing a firm order. The three aircraft set aside for the NAF would have to be sold to other customers and eventually be supplied from a later batch of aircraft. Since each batch was costed separately the price per aircraft could increase to almost £1,800,000. The longer the delay, the less likely would HSA be able to supply at the original price. As several customers were on the verge of signing contracts, there was need for a quick decision.

Major Gräf was concerned about the delay but said there was little he could do. His recommendations for purchase would be passed on to General Petsch when they would become the official NAF requirements. They would then go to the Air Force Advisor to the Defence Secretary, who would examine the report closely but would not be concerned about offset. The Defence Secretary, General Keil, would then receive the documents and pass them to the Minister of Defence. He, together with the Prime Minister and the Minister for Economic Affairs, would make the final decision.

Before leaving the Capital it was agreed that arrangements would be made for a group of NAF officers to visit Schiller Aviation, an independent airline who had recently purchased some HS.748s. As the visitors were mainly concerned with the operation and maintenance of the aircraft, Chris Dyer was asked to help. As an Assistant Customer Liaison Manager he had been working closely with Schiller Aviation during the early stages of them operating the aircraft. Air Commodore Netherton escorted the group on the visit and later reported that the airline was 'very complimentary' about the aircraft and HSA support.

The Offset

In an attempt to arrange the necessary offset, several channels were investigated. One of the main problems facing the company was the large part of a completed aircraft being accounted for by very specialized equipment which was bought out. There was little chance of this being purchased from anyone other than the normal vendor. The largest bought-out items were the Rolls-Royce Dart turboprop engines. One source for the offset was for Rolls-Royce to place work with Baden GmbH, who had been undertaking subcontract work for a number of years. Although there was a chance that Rolls-Royce would help, since they supplied the same Dart engines for the F.27, the offset work could be of equal value to Fokker.

A team of HSA design and production engineers were asked to investigate what work could be 'put out' to National subcontractors. Three types were identified:

1 Design work on the HS.146, a small jet transport aircraft still at the project stage.
2 Machining of components which were required in small quantities but were difficult and heavy.
3 Sheet metal work construction.

Negotiations with NFW were initiated with a view to their doing work valued at approximately £1,000,000. Several exchanges of personnel, specifications, and estimates took place but little progress was made towards achieving a satisfactory agreement.

Meanwhile Geoff Lancaster contacted Coles and Turf Ltd, a London-based company who had previously helped the company with offset associated with the attempted sales of HS.748 to Yugoslavia. They indicated a willingness to accept £4,500,000 worth of the Country's goods for a commission of 10%. Within days the company again contacted HSA saying they had £1,500,000 worth of lard which was available for use as part of an offset. The feeling at HSA was that the commission rate being requested was far too high, leaving no room for them to make a profit on the contract. They wrote to Coles and Turf Ltd saying this and explaining there was only need for £1,500,000 of offset rather than £4,500,000. The company's response was to suggest that 10% commission on £1,500,000 would leave plenty of room for HSA to make a profit and subsequently offered alternative products for offset.

Finally Roden AG, a subsidiary of The Roden Co. Ltd was contacted. After initial talks, packages of parts and drawings were sent to the company so that prices for manufacture and assembly could be estimated.

The situation became critical on 9th October when Air Commodore Netherton requested an urgent meeting with Geoff Lancaster at the NAF HQ. It seemed possible that a letter of intent could be signed by 1st November, with the final contract being signed before 1st April 1974. To achieve this, however, a global level for the offset would have to be presented together with details of how it would be broken down. Negotiations with NFW, Coles and Turf, and Roden intensified as the deadline approached.

On 16th October a contract for six aircraft was signed with a Brazilian operator. This meant that the NAF aircraft would have to be supplied from the more expensive batch 15 rather than the original batch 14. The aircraft would also be of slightly different specifications. The new price estimated for an aircraft with strengthened floor and large freight door was £1,470,000. The price increase was reluctantly accepted by the customer and a letter of intent was signed. It was also agreed with Roden AG that they would do £450,000 worth of specified subcontract work. With this development it looked as though future activities would be mainly the responsibility of the Contracts Department.

As April approached a team at HSA were preparing to make a trip to the Capital for final negotiation and contract signing. A day before they were to leave Dick Drake, the Commercial Director, received a telex from the National authorities. It read:

'DEPARTMENT OF ECONOMIC AFFAIRS URGENTLY EXPECT MORE PRECISION ABOUT YOUR COMMITMENT AND ALSO SENSIBLE INCREASE OF WORK FOR NATIONAL INDUSTRY. IT IS QUITE OBVIOUS THAT THE 10% OFFSET IS ABSOLUTELY UNSATISFACTORY. A REPLY IS EXPECTED BY AT LEAST FOR APRIL 29TH.'

A copy of the message was sent to Air Commodore Netherton by telex to which Dick Drake added:

'IT IS VIRTUALLY CERTAIN THAT IT WILL BE NECESSARY FOR ME TO REPLY ON FRIDAY THAT WE REGRET WE ARE UNABLE TO INCREASE OUR COMMITMENT AND THAT THE ONLY OTHER OFFSET IS THAT WHICH THEY ALREADY KNOW ABOUT FROM ROLLS-ROYCE. HOWEVER BEFORE REPLYING I WOULD LIKE TO KNOW WHETHER WEIR STILL BELIEVES IT IS BRITAIN'S TURN.'

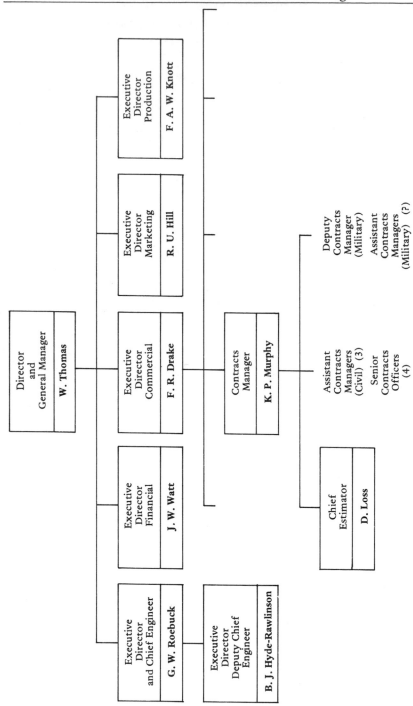

Exhibit 1.1: Main Board, HSA Manchester plus Contracts Department HSA Manchester

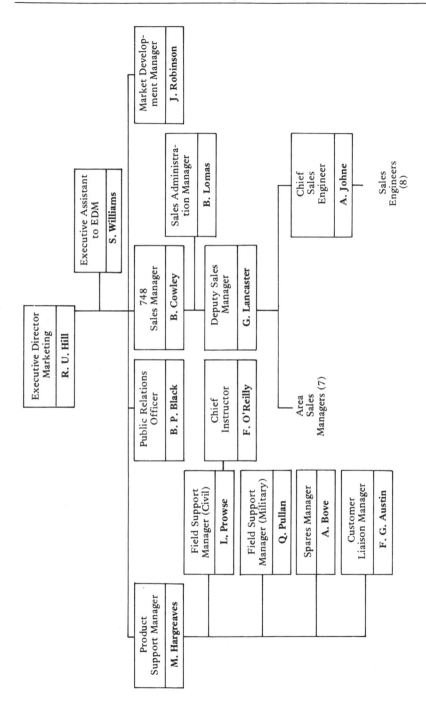

Exhibit 1.2: Marketing Organization, HSA Manchester

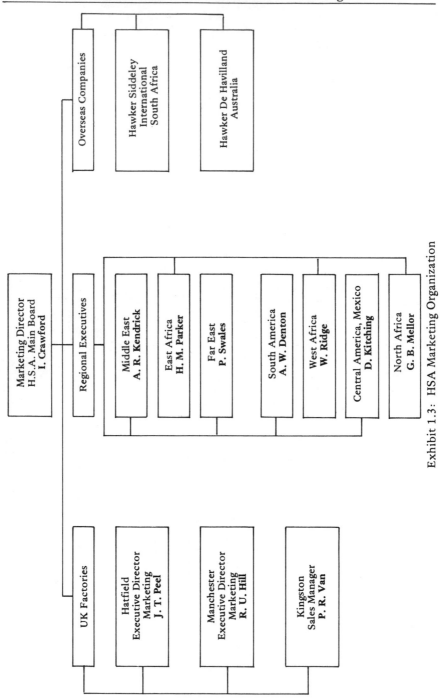

Exhibit 1.3: HSA Marketing Organization

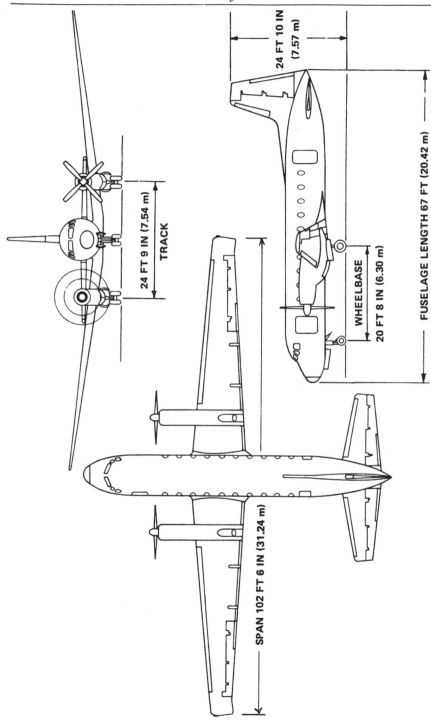

Exhibit 1.4: The Hawker Siddeley 748

Appendix 1.1

HS.748 Deliveries to 1971

	Owner	Country	Quantity
1962	Skyways Coach Air	UK	2
	Aerolineas Argentinas	Argentine	9
	Forca Aerea Brasileira	Brazil	1
1963	Skyways Coach Air	UK	1
	BKS	UK	1
	Forca Aerea Brasileira	Brazil	5
	Aerolineas Argentinas	Argentine	3
	Smiths Aviation Division	UK	1
1964	BKS	UK	1
	RAF (The Queens Flight)	UK	3
	RAF	UK	3
	Thai Airways Company	Thailand	3
	Royal Thai Air Force	Thailand	1
	Air Ceylon	Ceylon	1
1965	BKS	UK	1
	Linea Aeropostal Venezolana	Venezuela	4
	Leeward Island Air Transport	Leeward Islands	1
	Channel Airways	UK	2
1966	Linea Aeropostal Venezolana	Venezuela	2
	Leeward Island Air Transport	Leeward Islands	1
	Channel Airways	UK	2
	Austrian Airways	Austria	2
	Venezuelan M.O.D.	Venezuela	1
	Autair International	UK	2
	Compania Panamena de Aviacion	Panama	1
	Argentinian M.O.D.	Argentine	1
	AerO Maya	Mexico	1
	Bahamas Airways	Bahamas	1
	Royal Australian Air Force	Australia	2
	Zambian Air Force	Zambia	1
1967	Royal Australian Air Force	Australia	8
	Falcks Flyvetjeveste	Denmark	1
	AerO Maya	Mexico	1
	Bahamas Airways	Bahamas	3
	Fiji Airways	Fiji	1
	LAN Chile	Chile	4
	VARIG	Brazil	1
	Philippine Airlines	Philippines	4

	Owner	Country	Quantity
1968	LAN Chile	Chile	3
	VARIG	Brazil	9
	Philippine Airlines	Philippines	4
	Thai Airways Company	Thailand	3
	Mount Cook Airlines	New Zealand	1
	Avianca	Colombia	2
	Fiji Airways	Fiji	1
1969	Civil Aviation Flying Unit (BOT)	UK	2
	BFS	Germany	1
	Philippine Airlines	Philippines	1
	Compania Panamena de Aviacion	Panama	1
	Fiji Airways	Fiji	1
	Air Malawi	Malawi	2
	Midwest Airlines	Canada	1
	Amoco Canada Petroleum Co. Ltd	Canada	1
	Leeward Island Air Transport	Leeward Island	1
1970	Royal Nepal Airlines	Nepal	2
	Saesa	Mexico	3
	Zambia Airways	Zambia	3
	Rousseau Aviation	France	2
	Ecuadorean Air Force	Ecuador	3
	Chevron Standard Oil	Canada	1
	Ghana Airways	Ghana	1
	Thai Airways	Thailand	1
1971	Ghana Airways	Ghana	1
	Zambia Air Force	Zambia	1
	South African Airways	South Africa	3
	Mount Cook Airlines	New Zealand	1
	Sultan of Brunei	Brunei	1
	Merrati Airlines	Indonesia	2
	Air Gaspe	Canada	1

Since delivery to the original buyer several aircraft had been resold to other operators to 1971.

Original Buyer	Agreement	Quantity	New Operator/Country	Year
BKS	sale	2	Skyways/UK	1967
Channel Airways	sale	2	Leeward Island Air Transport	1968
Channel Airways	sale	1	Midwest/Canada	1967
Skyways	sale	1	Dan Air/UK	1968
Austrian A/L	sale	1	Skyways/UK	1970
AerOmaya	sale	2	Saesa/Mexico	1970
Austrian A/L	sale	1	Philippine A/L	1971
Bahamas A/W	sale	1	Philippine A/L	1971

HS.748 manufactured in India under Licence

Owner	Country	Quantity	Owner	Country	Quantity
1967 Indian Airlines	India	2	1969 Indian Airlines	India	4
1968 Indian Airlines	India	5	1970 Indian Airlines	India	2

Classified number to the Indian Air Force.

Appendix 1.2

HS.748 Demonstration

18th October	p.m.	(a) Position demonstrator aircraft at NAF Kevelaer
		(b) Check out presentation room facilities

19th October	08.30	Comprehensive HS.748 briefing

Inspection schedule: Airframe
         : Engine
         : Main components
Technical documentation
Spares support
Ground service equipment (G.S.E.)
Training: Aircrew
     : Technicians
Recommended initial stock of spares and GSE with prices for:
   4 aircraft – per 500 hrs/aircraft/year
   3 aircraft – per 500 hrs/aircraft/year
   2 aircraft – per 500 hrs/aircraft/year
Maintenance and overhaul costs
Price of basic aircraft including avionics
Price of different options

	10.30	Presentation of aircraft on ground
	11.15	Presentation/Information flight
	12.30	Lunch
	14.00	Evaluation flight – general performance at NAF Schraveln followed by flight to Woodford with NAF party.

20th October	09.30	NAF party visit Woodford
		(a) Product support/customer training
		(b) Production line
	11.00	Discussion and further evaluation flight with specialist transport evaluation pilots.
	p.m.	Return flight to Kevelaer.

Appendix 1.3

HAWKER SIDDELEY 748 SERIES 2A

Country of Origin: United Kingdom.

Type: Short- to medium-range commercial transport.

Power Plant: Two 2,280 ehp Rolls-Royce Dart R.Da.7 Mk. 532-2L turboprops.

Performance: Max. speed at 40,000 lb (18 145 kg), 312 mph (502 km/h at 16,000 ft (4 875 m); max. cruise, 287 mph (462 km/h) at 15,000 ft (4 570 m); econ. cruise, 267 mph (430 km/h) at 20,000 ft (6 095 m); range cruise, 259 mph (418 km/hl at 25,000 ft (7 620 m); range with max. fuel and reserves for 45 min. hold and 230-mile (370-km) diversion, 1,862 mls (2 996 km), with max. payload and same reserves, 690 mls (1 110 km).

Weights: Basic operational, 25,361 lb (11 504 kg); max. take-off, 44,495 lb (20 182 kg).

Accommodation: Normal flight crew of two and standard cabin arrangement for 40 passengers in paired seats. Alternative high-density arrangement for 58 passengers.

Status: First prototype flown June 24, 1960, and first production model (Srs. 1) on August 30, 1961. Srs. 1 superseded by Srs. 2 in 1962, this being in turn superseded by current Srs. 2A from mid-1967. Total of 258 ordered by beginning of 1972.

Notes: Manufactured under licence in India by HAL for Indian Airlines (24) and Indian Air Force (five Srs. 1 and 22 Srs. 2) at rate of nine per year.

Dimensions: Span, 98 ft 6 in (30,02 m); length, 67 ft 0 in (20,42 m); height, 24 ft 10 in (7,57 m); wing area, 810·75 sq ft (75,35 m²).

FOKKER F.27 FRIENDSHIP SRS. 500

Country of Origin: Netherlands.

Type: Short- to medium-range commercial transport.

Power Plant: Two 2,250 eshp Rolls-Royce Dart 532-7 turboprops.

Performance: Max. cruise, 322 mph (518 km/h) at 20,000 ft (6 095 m); normal cruise at 38,000 lb (17 237 kg), 292 mph (470 km/h) at 20,000 ft (6 095 m); range with max. payload, 667 mls (1 075 km), with max. fuel and 9,680-lb (4 390-kg) payload, 1,099 mls (1 805 km); initial climb at max. take-off weight. 1,200 ft/min. (6.1 m/sec); service ceiling at 38,000 lb (17 237 kg), 28,500 ft (8 690 m).

Weights: Empty, 25,300 lb (11 475 kg); operational empty, 26,190 lb (11 879 kg); max. take-off, 45,000 lb (20 411 kg).

Accommodation: Basic flight crew of two or three and standard seating for 52 passengers. Alternative arrangements for up to 56 passengers.

Status: First Srs. 500 flown November 15, 1967. Production currently standardising on Srs. 500 and 600. Orders for the Friendship (including those licence-built in the USA by Fairchild) totalled 580 by beginning of 1972.

Notes: By comparison with basic Srs. 200 (see 1968 edition), the Srs. 500 has a 4 ft 11 in (1.5 m) fuselage stretch. The Srs. 400 'Combiplane' (see 1966 edition) and the equivalent military Srs. 400M are convertible cargo or combined cargo-passenger versions of the Srs. 200, and the current Srs. 600 is similar to the Srs. 400 but lacks the reinforced and watertight cargo floor.

Dimensions: Span. 95 ft 1¼ in (29 00 m); length 82 ft 2½ in (25 06 m); height, 28 ft 7¼ in (8 71 m); wing area, 753·47 sq ft (70 m²).

II
Arthur Guinness Son & Co. Ltd

G. Hooley

In July 1977 Guinness Management were considering the results of marketing efforts in its new markets on the Continent of Europe. Results in Italy had been very encouraging whereas performance in West Germany had not come up to expectations. In developing future marketing plans for West Germany they were faced with the questions: 'Why the poor performance?' and 'What can Guinness do about it?'.

Company Background

Arthur Guinness had first started brewing in Dublin, Ireland, in 1759. The product, Guinness stout, was a dark, top-fermented beer essentially the same as is available throughout the UK to the present day. Current brewing practice follows very closely the original methods developed in Dublin, even to the extent that the same strain of yeast used in the original 1759 brews is cultivated and still used today.

During the 1800s the fame of Guinness spread along the trade routes and Guinness supplied these markets by exporting from Dublin. The product was adapted for export by an increase in alcoholic strength so as to facilitate better keeping qualities on the often long journeys around Cape Horn.

This case was prepared by Graham Hooley, Lecturer in Marketing at Bradford University Management Centre, using material supplied by M. G. Vineall on behalf of Arthur Guinness Son & Co. (Park Royal) Limited. The case was financed by the Foundation for Management Education, 1978.

With the growth of these export markets 1930 saw the formation of Guinness Export Ltd (G.E.L.). This subsidiary was concerned exclusively with bottling and forwarding and based in Liverpool. Guinness stout, brewed in Dublin, was shipped to Liverpool, where it was bottled for distribution to export markets.

International Expansion

1936 saw the first overseas brewery opened at Park Royal, London. This brewery, closely following the Dublin plant in design, was used to supply the southern half of England, while the north was supplied from Dublin via Liverpool.

By the early 1950s the export markets of the Commonwealth represented a large proportion of the trade of Guinness (Dublin). However, with the growing trend towards independence these markets became threatened. As former Commonwealth countries became independent, often facing balance of payments difficulties, so tariff barriers to imports sprang up. In an effort to protect its overseas markets Guinness Overseas Ltd (G.O.L.) was formed with the objective of converting the export markets into local production markets. Breweries were built in such places as Nigeria, Malaysia, Jamaica and Seychelles to satisfy the local markets. By 1977 Guinness had fourteen breweries around the world supplying local markets. Contracts were also negotiated to brew Guinness under licence in local breweries. The product, though uniform throughout these export markets, is different to the home-sold Guinness. It is again stronger, in terms of alcoholic content, resembling the original export version.

Expansion into Europe

Guinness Overseas Ltd had been formed in the early 1950s with the express objective of converting export markets, threatened by independence, into local production markets. As a consequence little attention had been given to the development of new markets. In particular the potential of the continent of Europe had never been explored to the full.

In an effort to redress this situation somewhat, in 1968 a European Sales Manager was appointed with the task of exploring the potential of European markets. Executives were stationed in Italy,

Holland and West Germany with the task of investigating, and starting to fulfil, local demand. Because of the more immediate needs of protection of export markets, however, little support was given to these efforts.

In 1973 responsibility for Europe was transferred from Guinness Overseas Ltd to Arthur Guinness (Park Royal) Ltd. The London-based Park Royal brewery had seen steady growth throughout the 1960s, particularly from the introduction of draught Guinness. By the early 1970s this growth was slowing down as distribution had reached near saturation levels*. While production was at a near optimum level, the slow down in growth meant an excess of management capacity. This excess management capacity was used to look for development markets, particularly in Europe.

In 1974 the Continental Division of the Park Royal company was formed, with its own marketing department, to take charge of Guinness' interests in Europe. Immediately the new division set about assessment and evaluation of possible European markets for Guinness. Of particular interest were West Germany and Italy.

The West German Beer Market

The Federal Republic of Germany, or West Germany, consists of 248,571 square kilometres (the area of the UK is 244,014 square kilometres) divided into 11 Länder, or provinces. In 1972 the population of West Germany was 61,500,000 (the population of the UK being 55,790,000).

West Germany is the largest beer producer in Europe, and the second largest in the world behind the United States. From the point of view of *per capita* consumption of beer, Germany came first in the world (see Exhibit 2.1). Coupled with the vast size of the West German beer market (92,500,000 hectolitres in 1973) is a high level of consumer interest in beer. Customers believe that they know what they want from a beer and take immense local and national pride in their brews.

The brewing industry is very fragmented and regionalized with

---

* Distribution of Guinness in the on-licence trade in the UK is particularly interesting. While other brewing groups have pursued a policy of tied-houses, i.e. owning pubs which sell their own beers, Guinness have achieved distribution throughout the UK without owning licenced premises. Guinness can be bought in nearly all licenced premises, irrespective of the brewing group that holds the deeds. This extensive distribution had been achieved primarily through very strong national advertising (approximately 20% of all press and TV expenditure by breweries in 1969).

no brews being able to claim to be truly national. At the end of 1971 there were 1770 breweries and an estimated 1730 brewing companies brewing approximately 6,000 brands of beer. This is the largest number in a European country, the closest rival being Belgium with 187 breweries. In the UK in 1970 there were approximately 3,000 brands of beer brewed by 98 brewery companies, seven of which produced about 80% of total beer output. Rationalization of the industry had, however, been one of the main considerations of previous years. The number of breweries decreased by 45 during 1971, and over the period between 1960 and 1971 nearly 450 breweries had been closed. In 1971 nearly 70% of breweries were in Bavaria where the traditions of localized brewing are seen at their strongest. The average production per brewery in 1971 was 51,000 hectolitres, and per brewing company 52,000 hectolitres, by far the lowest average in Europe (see Exhibit 2.2).

Approximately one-third of trade is on-licence and two thirds off-licence. These basic divisions also represent the split between draught beers, which are sold almost exclusively in the on-licence situation (98% of the on-licence trade is draught) and bottled and canned beer for home consumption. In 1972, 69.3% of the beer market was bottled or canned while 30.7% was draught.

Distribution is achieved through the beer wholesaler. Each beer wholesaler is contracted almost exclusively to a brewery. Many of the licenced premises for the on-licence trade are tied financially, usually by loan, to either the local brewery or to the wholesalers. In the past this has tended to mean that one brewery would dominate the sales of a particular outlet. By current European law, however, at least 10% of sales by volume must be other than by tie. Acceptance in the take-home trade has in the past necessitated prior establishment in the on-licence trade. The take-home trade is through supermarkets, department stores, and drink cash-and-carry specialist stores. Here the majority of beer is bought as a cheap commodity item by the crate.

The type of beer drunk varies from region to region. Southern beers, notably from Bavaria, tend to be the lighter, sweeter beers. As one goes northwards through Germany, the beers become darker and more bitter.

The basic beer divisions are between the bottom-fermented (untergäriges bier), pale, lager beers, accounting for 90% of the market, and the top-fermented (obergäriges bier), darker, 'alt' beers. The share of top-fermented beers is expected to continue in a steady rise. Alt beers started in the Düsseldorf area and became something of a cult. Now most of the major breweries have an alt beer among their range of brews. The strength of beers does not vary to any great extent.

Because of the fragmentation of the industry the market is essentially segmented regionally with nearly all beers using a similar advertising theme. The advertising stresses the pure and natural nature of the beer, brewed from perfect ingredients by local brewers with centuries of experience. In fact German brewers place great store by the 1506 Purity Laws (Rheinheitsgebot) to which they adhere rigidly. Over the period 1962—72 the beer market had seen a steady growth of over 6% per annum but that was tailing off and predicted to slow down to 2—3%. In fact the actual growth rate from 1974 was lower still.

Guinness in Germany

Guinness was represented in Germany by an ex-Procter and Gamble area manager, who by 1974 had built up a network of twenty four wholesalers. During his five years in Germany he had built up a detailed understanding and knowledge of the German beer market, a source of information for Guinness that was to prove invaluable. The Guinness share of market was small but growing steadily (see Exhibit 2.3).

With the formation of the Continental Division in 1974 a market appreciation study was compiled from secondary sources and two pieces of primary research undertaken.

Market Research in Germany

In 1974 Makrotest Ltd were engaged to estimate the incidence of Guinness drinkers among the population of West Germany and to profile these drinkers in demographic terms. This was approached through the use of an omnibus survey.

A sample of 1975 adults (over the age of 16) was interviewed. The sample was selected by a three stage sampling scheme.

1 400 districts were chosen from a listing of districts which was stratified by Bundesland and by community size.
2 Households were selected by random walk method: interviewers were given starting points within the district selected and a random walk scheme.
3 Within each household the selection of person to be interviewed was done by a random method. The interviewer had to interview

the person within the household whose birthday fell nearest to a particular date. The interviewer had to make three attempts to interview that person.

Results of the survey are shown in Exhibits 2.5 and 2.6. Of particular interest was the discovery that over 50% of Guinness drinkers had finished upper school or been to university, compared with less than 10% of the total sample. Also of interest was the age distribution of Guinness drinkers, 50% being below the age of 30, compared to 20% of the sample.

Once a demographic picture of Guinness drinkers in Germany had been obtained, attention was shifted to the question of consumer attitudes towards Guinness. Consequently Market Behaviour Ltd (M.B.L.) were retained to conduct a qualitative research study of Guinness drinkers. Their brief was to gain a broad and as detailed an understanding as possible of the position of Guinness within the German beer market, of consumer attitudes towards Guinness, and of brand and user imagery.

The research design consisted of twelve group discussions conducted amongst Guinness drinkers. Three group discussions, two with male and one with female drinkers of Guinness, were held in each of four locations: Düsseldorf, Hamburg, Berlin and Münich. The groups were conducted by a bi-lingual German/English psychologist with four years' research experience and with another full-time MBL staff psychologist with fluent German in attendance. The groups were conducted between Monday 1st and Friday 12th July 1974. For a summary of findings see Appendix 2.1.

Guinness Marketing in Germany

As a result of the two pieces of primary research together with the less formalized information gained by the management of the division, the target market was established as up-market, young, affluent Germans who were looking for a beer that was different.

Promotions were to stress the traditional values of a pure, wholesome beer, brewed with centuries of tradition but with the added bonus of being different and of being Irish. Ireland had a very favourable image, the Ireland of the tourist brochures, 'rural charm and brown eggs'. Guinness was promoted as a sophisticated beer for the connoisseur that would demonstrate affluence and knowledge of good beers. In the UK the advertising agency for Guinness was J. Walter Thompson (J.W.T.) who were retained for advertising throughout Europe through their local offices. The one exception was in Germany where J.W.T. acted for a competitor to Guinness and therefore could not accept the account. Heumann, Ogilvy and Mather were appointed for Germany. The advertising appropriation was set at £80,000, much of that being spent in Der Spiegel — an up-market, intellectual, colour newspaper with a readership profile very similar to Guinness drinkers (based on the 1974 omnibus survey). For an example of the advertisements see Exhibit 2.7. For the on-licence trade, point of sale material was developed including glassware (see Exhibit 2.4) and licencees were introduced to Guinness through trade literature, Irish evenings and sampling at exhibitions. In the off-licence outlets special offers were made including display competitions and an 'Irish week'.

In line with the promotional strategy the price of Guinness was at a premium. This was largely set by the retail outlets through which Guinness was sold. In many on-licence premises local beers were sold at one price and foreign beers at another. Wholesaler and retailer mark-ups varied considerably, the latter often being as high as 300%. Management, however, did not believe sales to be price elastic. Certainly in the on-licence trade there was a marked lack of price consciousness due partly to the fact that individual drinks were not paid for as they were ordered but the bill was settled at the end of a drinking session. There were signs, however, that the off-licence trade was much more price elastic — in particular the emergence of discount 'drink markets' as competitors to supermarkets was noted. Prices in off- and on-licence outlets varied greatly. Typically on-sales could be up to three times the price of the off-sales.

The product sold in Germany was the same beer as sold throughout the rest of Europe, with the sole exception of Belgium. Draught beer was sold in on-licence premises together with some bottled. One of the problems of selling draught Guinness was the relatively short shelf-life once a barrel was opened. To ensure good quality Guinness required a fairly rapid throughput.

Distribution had, in the past, proved the most difficult problem in getting Guinness accepted into the German beer market. The local manager had built up a successful chain of twenty four wholesalers but without additional salesmen it seemed unlikely that this figure could increase or distribution begin to approach a national basis. Coupled with this were the strong ties between local breweries, wholesalers and retail outlets. To break into those chains would be very difficult. Consequently it was decided to use local breweries for distribution where possible.   Contracts were negotiated with several leading regional breweries to carry Guinness, essentially as an additional brand in their ranges.   These local breweries had exclusive marketing rights for Guinness in their localities, and of the original twenty four wholesalers, twenty one of the smallest had to obtain deliveries from their 'local brewery'.   One field assistant was added to the staff early in 1976.

Results in Germany

By 1977 it had become clear that the sales of Guinness were not approaching expected levels.

The growth had gone out of the West German beer market.   Total consumption of beer for 1976 was put at 91.5 million hectolitres (a decrease of 1% on 1975).   Consequently the contracted brewers had been more concerned with defending their own brews than with promoting Guinness.   Because of the small volumes of Guinness sold, trade incentives had not proved successful in pushing Guinness through the distribution system, and lack of availability, in both on- and off-licence premises, had prevented significant pull through by consumers.   In particular the association with the brewers had failed to effectively get Guinness established in the off-licence retail outlets.   The Continental marketing department set about interpreting these results and developing marketing tactics and strategy for 1978 and beyond.

The Italian Beer Market

In contrast to the problems encountered in attempting to enter more fully into the West German beer market, introduction of Guinness into Italy was a more immediately successful venture.

Italy is roughly the same size as the UK in terms of area and population.   The distribution of the population and wealth is also similar.   Northern Italy is like Southern England with a higher density of population and higher *per capita* income.   Southern Italy is poor and undeveloped in spite of recent efforts by the Italian Government to industrialize the South.   Generally speaking the Italians are conservative with regard to food and drink, prefering strong tastes and having a bitter palate.   They tend to have extrovert personalities and are very concerned with the image they create of themselves for other people. It is interesting to note that in spite of the apparent difficult financial situation of the country in 1976 Italy was still the world's largest importer, outside the USA, of Whisky, Champagne, Russian Caviar and Rolls Royce cars.

Italy is one of the world's two major producers of wine and in recent years has even produced more than France. Wine is the predominantly drunk alcoholic beverage, in 1974 amounting to 57,160,000 hectolitres, compared with 8,580,000 hectolitres of beer. Consumption of beer per capita rose steadily from a 1963 level of 8.3 litres to a 1973 level of 15.7 litres (see Exhibit 2.8).

As with the rest of Europe, approximately 60% of beer sales were off-sales and 40% on-sales. Very little draught beer is sold in Italy, even in the on-licence trade. Draught beer accounts for only 7% of total beer consumption while 80% of beer is sold in bottled form.

Partly as a result of the size of the Italian beer market, and because of agreements between brewers restricting advertising prior to 1964, there was little or no 'beer culture' in Italy, no established brands with loyal followings or strong reputations. Beer had grown out of an extension of the soft drinks trade and was seen very much as a thirst-quenching, summertime drink. Heavy advertising throughout the year had not managed to change the seasonal nature of the market. 50% of annual sales are consumed between June and September.

Virtually all Italian beers are light, both in colour and in taste; the very few so-called dark beers are still considerably lighter than brown ale.

Beer in Italy is divided into three categories:

1 Normal light beers. They have a gravity of between 11 and 13 saccharometric degrees (4° proof) and still retain a 'soft drink' image. They represent 80% of total national production.
2 Special beers with a gravity of between 13 and 15 saccharometric degrees (5° proof). These are gaining an increasing share of the market.
3 Double malt beers with a gravity over 15 saccharometric degrees (6° proof).

Imported beers, including Guinness, fall into the special beers category above. As a consequence they are not as heavily seasonal as the light beers. Imported beers made up 7% of total consumption in 1974 and were still increasing their share. They sold at a premium price, often one price being established in an outlet for all foreign beers.

Italian brewers achieved distribution to retailers predominantly through a system of tied concessionaires. A concessionaire would hold only one line of beer, usually representing 30—40% of his turnover, although he might carry many lines of other drinks. Importers of foreign beer tend to sell direct to wholesale and retail outlets through a sales force of commission agents. Generally speaking none of the outlets, on or off sale, are tied.

Guinness in Italy

Since 1970 Guinness had enjoyed considerable success in Italy. Sales had risen from 738 hectolitres in 1970 to 2,210 hectolitres in 1973.

Distribution had been achieved through the services of a local importing company in Milan who specialized in importing alcoholic beverages including brandy, whisky, champagne and other beers. This importing company employed freelance commission agents. High labour costs and strict laws governing the dismissal of personnel make it very difficult for a company to employ salesmen. The commission agents were paid high commissions (10% of sales). In 1975 Guinness acquired a 75% holding in the importing company, renamed Stout SpA.

Successful selling and distribution, guided by Guinness' man in Italy, meant that sales had increased well until 1973. But they had then levelled off and the expected take-off of sales had not been achieved.

Market Research in Italy

In 1974 the Continental Division conducted research of both a quantitative (through the use of an omnibus survey) and qualitative nature.

The qualitative research consisted of a series of twenty five depth interviews amongst Guinness drinkers conducted by System Three (Communications) Ltd and their Italian company Sistema Tre (Italia) based in Milan. The method, sample, interviewing brief and summary of findings are presented in Appendix 2.2.

The image of Guinness was found to be generally positive and favourable, a masculine, up-market 'English' drink for the connoisseur. The major problem identified, however, was that of lack of availability or awareness of availability. Sales information was monitored by the use of a computer service bureau for all ordering, invoicing, sales reporting etc.

Guinness Marketing in Italy

Further analysis showed that a very high proportion of sales were to new commission agents and it became apparent that the company was being very successful at filling the distribution pipe lines but that the Guinness was not being sold to consumers. All previous marketing effort had been below the line, in the form of commission agents' incentives. As a consequence of this failure to pull sales through the retail outlets, Guinness embarked on an advertising test in three towns in Northern Italy experimenting with different media. The appropriation was £25,000 and the agency JWT Milan. The target market considered was wider than in West Germany, being concentrated, however, on men, young, up-market, from the north of Italy. Advertising copy stressed again the Irishness of the product. For an example of the advertisements see Exhibit 2.9. It was presented as a unique beer that appealed to the open-minded, knowledgeable and discriminating drinker. Its Irish origin and British character were stressed as were its strength, bitterness, black colour, and fullness of flavour. Media used were weekly colour magazines such as Espresso and Panorama and the monthly Playboy. Cinema was used as a support medium.

The advertising test proved successful in increasing sales significantly above the overall national increase in Guinness sales. Consequently more money was made available for advertising until by 1977 Guinness advertising represented 5% of all beer advertising.

Results in Italy

By 1977 Guinness represented 1.5% of beer imports and 0.1% of total Italian beer consumption and was available in an estimated 12,000 outlets throughout Italy. 1976—77 sales showed an increase of 33% over the previous twelve months and prospects for continued growth appeared good (see Exhibit 2.10). Stout SpA now had 104 commission agents on the selling side for whom Guinness now represented a sizeable proportion of turnover. They were all highly motivated to achieve higher sales with a commission rate higher than other areas of the beer market (see Exhibit 2.11). Significantly, 85% of sales of Stout SpA were to existing customers, indicating that Guinness was being pulled through the distribution pipe-line as well as being pushed into it. An Omnibus survey conducted in 1977 by Makrotest Ltd showed Guinness drinkers to be male, young, and up-market (see Exhibit 2.12).

The margins achieved by Stout SpA were, however, disappointing and the company was considering alterations to the price structure. This would mean either a lowering of retail margins or an increase in retail price. At the same time Guinness was actively exploring the possibilities of importing other premium beers through Stout SpA now that Guinness was becoming well established.

European Marketing Plans

In July 1977 the Continental Director and his staff were studying the contrasting results in the two European markets. In the beer drinking culture of West Germany results had been disappointing whereas in wine-drinking Italy sales were progressing well. Future marketing plans needed to solve the problems of the German market and to consolidate, and further capitalize on, the success of the Italian venture.

		Litres per capita per annum	Total Hectolitres ('000)
1	West Germany	146.7	92,500
2	Czechoslovakia	146.4	21,210
3	Belgium	142.5	13,909
4	Australia (1972)	128.2	16,643
5	Luxembourg	127.1	449
6	Ireland	126.0	3,753
7	Denmark	125.4	6,270
8	New Zealand	121.1	3,532
9	East Germany	112.7	19,136
10	United Kingdom	112.1	62,635
11	Austria	110.1	8,223
12	Canada	84.5	18,657
13	USA	75.9	160,514
14	Switzerland	75.3	4,880
15	Netherlands	73.5	9,879
16	Sweden	54.8	4,451
17	Finland	54.5	2,544
18	France	44.5	23,288
19	Spain	43.0	14,562
20	Norway	41.9	1,662
21	Italy	15.7	8,580

Source: The Brewers' Society Ltd

Exhibit 2.1: The World Beer-Drinking League (1973) Top Twenty and Italy
(Based on per capita consumption)

	1970 (HL per year)	1972 (HL per year)
Ireland	726,400	791,400
Holland	513,200	448,900
UK	312,000	354,100
France	177,700	205,600
Italy	160,400	176,800
Denmark	108,900	149,500
Luxembourg	67,700	81,600
Belgium	56,100	68,100
West Germany	48,000	53,000

Source: Guinness Market Appreciation of Germany 1974

Exhibit 2.2: Average Beer Production of European Breweries

	Total Mkt (HL)	Total Imports (HL)	Share (%)	Guinness (HL)	Guinness Share of Imports (%)	Guinness Share of Total Mkt (%)
1968	79,126,000	418,000	0.54	1,200	0.29	0.0015
1969	83,981,000	401,000	0.48	1,600	0.40	0.0019
1970	87,051,000	446,000	0.52	2,100	0.47	0.0024
1971	90,035,000	468,000	0.53	2,700	0.58	0.0030
1972	91,044,000	500,000	0.55	3,300	0.66	0.0036
1973	92,500,000	606,000	0.66	4,100	0.68	0.0044

Source: Guinness Market Appreciation of Germany 1974

Exhibit 2.3: Guinness's Share of the German Beer Market

Exhibit 2.4

	Total	Male	Female
Base of %: All respondents	1,975	925	1,050
	%	%	%
Guinness	1.5	2.3	0.8
Köenig Pilsner	14.6	21.3	8.8
'Alt Bier' (any brand)	12.7	16.0	9.8
Pilsener Urquell	12.5	16.8	8.8
Bitburger Pils	8.9	12.4	5.7
Veltins	3.8	5.5	2.3
Total drinking any of these beers	33.7	44.5	24.2
None of these beers drunk	66.3	55.5	75.8

Source: Omnibus Study in Germany, August 1974

Exhibit 2.5: Drinking of Certain Beers in Previous Four Weeks

	The Sample	Guinness Drinkers	
		Percent	Numbers
Base of %: All respondents	1975	29	
	%	%	
Sex			
Male	46.8	72.4	21
Female	53.2	27.6	8
Monthly Income			
Up to 999 DM	14.4	13.8	4
1000–1499 DM	28.6	17.2	5
1500–1999 DM	25.5	17.2	5
2000–2499 DM	14.0	13.8	4
2500–2999 DM	6.6	13.8	4
3000 + DM	7.1	24.1	7
(No answer)	(3.7)	—	—
Terminal Educational Establishment*			
Primary School — no trade learnt (aged c. 14 years)	25.7	3.5	1
Primary School — trade learnt (aged c. 17–18 years)	45.5	17.2	5
Middle School (aged c. 16 years)	14.2	10.3	3
Upper School — Unfinished (aged c. 16 years)	5.5	17.2	5
Upper School — Finished (aged c. 18–20 years)	3.8	10.3	3
University	5.5	41.4	12
Occupational Group			
Unskilled manual worker	12.2	—	—
Skilled manual worker	28.7	13.8	4
Other employees in industry or commerce	29.2	37.9	11
Officials	13.1	17.2	5
Professional people and other self-employed	11.2	6.9	2
Landholders	2.8	—	—
Others	2.7	24.1	7

Exhibit 2.6: Profile of Guinness Drinkers in Germany

Continued

	The Sample	Guinness Drinkers	
		Percent	Numbers
Base of %: All respondents	1975	29	
	%	%	
Bundesland			
Schleswig-Holstein	5.0	13.8	4
Hamburg	4.1	24.1	7
Lower Saxony/Bremen	13.2	3.5	1
North Rhine/Westphalia	30.3	20.7	6
Hesse	5.9	6.9	2
Rhineland Palatinate/Saar	6.5	3.5	1
Bavaria	17.3	3.5	1
Baden Wurttemberg	13.9	3.5	1
West Berlin	3.8	20.7	6
Age			
16—19 years	5.4	6.9	2
20—29 years	15.9	44.8	13
30—39 years	23.7	27.6	8
40—49 years	17.6	3.5	1
50—59 years	15.8	6.9	2
60 or over	21.5	10.3	3
Town Size			
Over 500,000	21.3	44.8	13
100,000—499,999	15.5	13.8	4
20,000—99,999	20.5	17.2	5
10,000—19,999	7.5	—	—
2,000—9,999	19.5	6.9	2
Less than 2,000	15.5	17.2	5

* The ages given are approximate ages when pupils would normally leave the establishment specified.

Source: Omnibus Study in Germany, August 1974

Exhibit 2.6: Profile of Guinness Drinkers in Germany

Continued

Drittes Inserat für den Freundeskreis der deutschen Guinness-Trinker

Wenn Sie Guinness lieben,
sagen Sie bitte nichts gegen gewöhnliches deutsches Bier.

1. Deutsches Bier ist mindestens so gut wie sein Ruf.

2. Da sich ca. 4.732 Sorten auf dem deutschen Markt tummeln, ist man auf zugkräftige Unterstützung dringend angewiesen.

3. Der deutsche Biertrinker fühlt sich mit Recht als Experte.

4. Erst im Vergleich mit anderen Biersorten erlebt man die absolute Ein-

Jedem das Seine.

maligkeit des Guinness-Geschmacks.

5. Wird unser Guinness bereits ausreichend anerkannt: Täglich werden auf der Welt ca. 8 Millionen Gläser getrunken, das ergibt im Jahr 11,5 Millionen Hektoliter.

Lediglich in Deutschland haben wir unsere besondere Freude an einer besonders kleinen, feinen Position:

Die Deutschen trinken pro Kopf und Jahr 150 Liter Bier und exakt nur 0,016 Liter unseres ungezähmten samtschwarzen Guinness.

Das bedeutet, daß Guinness in Deutschland das mit Abstand exclusivste Bier ist. Wenigstens in einem Land wird es offenbar nur zu den wirklich erlesenen Anlässen (frische Austern, neue Kaviarernte, Ernennung zum Staatssekretär etc.) gereicht. Was uns sehr befriedigt.

Schweigen über Irland.

Lassen Sie also weder etwas über die länger haltende sahnige Schaumkrone verlauten, noch über das nur bei Guinness verwendete, geröstete Gerstenmalz, noch über die unerreichte

männlich-herbe Note, noch über die besonders geduldige, seit zwei Jahrhunderten unverändert natürliche irische Brauweise, die sich fast noch strengere Gebote auferlegt, als das deutsche Reinheitsgebot.

Viele Deutsche wissen anscheinend gar nicht, daß Guinness aus dem grünen urwüchsigen Irland kommt, sondern halten es für irgendein englisches Bier.

Gut so, daran sollte man nicht rühren.

Wenn Sie sich also in Zukunft wieder einmal öffentlich profilieren müssen, dann tun Sie es nicht mit Guinness, sondern mit Veuve Clicquot, Laurent Perrier, Heidsieck Gold Top oder Pommery Brut.

Das ist zwar nicht ganz so exclusiv. Aber auch nicht übel.

Some like it black.

Bitte haben Sie Verständnis, daß unser weltberühmter Slogan „GUINNESS IS GOOD FOR YOU" aus den hier zitierten Gründen nicht in deutschen Anzeigen verwendet wird.

GN 4/77

Exhibit 2.7

Year	Output (x 1000 Hl)	1963 = 100 Index	Imports (x 1000 Hl)	Index	Consumption litres per capita
1963	3753	100	164.9	100	8.3
1964	4208	112	161.8	98	9.2
1965	4558	122	165.5	100	9.9
1966	5179	138	200.6	122	11.2
1967	5544	148	208.3	126	11.9
1968	5391	144	211.3	128	11.7
1970	5949	158	294.8	179	12.6
1971	6280	167	330.7	201	13.3
1972	6542	174	361.3	219	13.7
1973	8621	229	449.0	272	15.7

Source: Guinness Market Appreciation of Italy, August 1977

Exhibit 2.8: Growth of the Italian Beer Market

Prima di berla, conviene conoscerla.

6. Cosa pensare mentre bevi una Guinness.

Probabilmente non hai mai bevuto nulla di simile a una Guinness. Perciò ti conviene fare la cosa con calma.

Trovati un posto piacevole, dove ti puoi concentrare. Poi, lentamente, versa la tua Guinness. Vedrai subito che non è soltanto scura,

è proprio nera. Ti renderai conto che sopra, non ha le solite bollicine, ma una vera e propria "testa".

Ora, bevi. Ma lentamente. Pensa al piacevole gusto amaro (si tratta dell'orzo tostato).

Assapora l'aroma forte e gradevole (viene

dalla delicata miscela di luppolo e malto).

A questo punto, forse ti verranno in mente immagini della quieta e verde campagna irlandese. Se è così, è un buon segno. Vuol dire che sei pronto per pensare alla tua seconda bottiglia di Guinness.

Guinness, Birra Scura, Amara, Forte, Irlandese.

Exhibit 2.9

Year End August		Cartons	Hls.
1970		12295	738
1971		22223	1333
1972		27492	1649
1973		36837	2210
1974		34427	2065
1975	§§	34021	2694
1976		55257	4375
1977		70000 Est.	5542

§§ Change from 25 cl. bottle to 33 cl. bottle.

Source: Guinness Market Appreciation, Italy, August 1977

Exhibit 2.10: Guinness Sales in Italy

Per Bottle *(Italian lire)*

Price F.O.B. Liverpool	
Bottle at Lit 4.000 per carton (24 bottles)	
Cans at Lit 4.300 per carton (24 bottles)	166.67
Transport Liverpool — Milan	27.79
Import Duty at 4.8%	9.33
Excise Duty	23.40
Clearance Charges	1.15
Warehousing Charges	8.15
Miscellaneous — samples, breakages, etc.	1.90
Cost C.I.F. Cleared	238.39
Delivery note	1.50
Transport to Customer	20.00 (Estimate)
Commission to Agent 10.70% of selling price minus	
discount	37.56
Average discount 10%	39.00
Total cost to Stout SpA	336.45
Stout SpA Margin	16%
Selling Price to Retailer	390.00
On-licence selling price	700 — 1000
On-licence margin	79% — 156%
Off-licence selling price	450 — 600
Off-licence margin	15% — 54%
Supermarket selling price	440 — 490
Supermarket margin	13% — 26%

Source: Guinness Market Appreciation, Italy 1977

Exhibit 2.11: Guinness Breakdown of Costs in Italy

	Guinness	*Population*
Sex		
Male	71%	48%
Female	39%	52%
Age		
15–24	30%	19%
25–34	27%	18%
35–44	7%	17%
45–54	18%	17%
55 +	12%	29%
Social class		
Upper/Upper Middle	27%	12%
Middle	48%	47%
Lower Middle	21%	32%
Lower	4%	9%
Area		
North West	27%	29%
North East	29%	19%
Centre	17%	20%
South	27%	33%
Town size		
Up to 10,000	19%	35%
10,000–30,000	29%	19%
30,000–100,000	24%	17%
100,000 +	29%	29%

Source: Makrotest, October 1977

(Total Guinness drinkers in sample = 32)

Exhibit 2.12: Profile of Guinness Drinkers in Italy

GEBRAUT IN DER GUINNESS
BRAUEREI DUBLIN, IRLAND

CONTENUTO 33cl.
BIRRA PRODOTTA NELLA BIRRERIA DI DUBLINO IRLANDA
IMPORTATA DA STOUT CO. LTD. SPA. MILANO

Exhibit 2.13: German and Italian Bottle Dressings

Appendix 2.1
Extracts from Report Presented Sept. 1974

Introduction and Background

Currently there is practically no quantified information on the position of Guinness within the German market, and very little on the German beer market as a whole.

Germany, however, represents the largest *per capita* market for beer in Europe. Whereas France has a very low *per capita* annual consumption of beer:

40 litres per person compared with a UK figure of
106 litres per person.

Germany has a very high *per capita* annual consumption:

145 litres per person, compared with a UK figure of
106 litres.

The German market however, is rich with indigenous beers, some 6000 brands in total — and the competitive situation facing Guinness is a tough one.

Arthur Guinness Son & Co. Ltd is interested in increasing sales of Guinness in West Germany. Current Guinness sales are predominantly bottled, with some backing from draught outlets. The company, however, has very little information about consumer attitudes towards, and perception of, Guinness in Germany, and knows little or nothing about the German Guinness drinker.

Prior to further marketing or advertising action in Germany, Arthur Guinness Son & Co. Ltd wish to improve their understanding of the position of Guinness in the German beer market. Consequently, MBL International has been commissioned to carry out research into the German beer market in several different German towns.

Research Objectives

The primary objective of the research was very simply to gain as broad and as detailed an understanding as possible of the position of Guinness within the German beer market, of consumer attitudes towards Guinness, and of brand and user imagery.

More specifically, the research was intended to provide information which would ensure a better understanding of Guinness' position in Germany, and of its future potential. Some key areas which required investigating were:

Beer generally:
Drinking occasions for different types of beer; when and where Guinness is drunk — home, bar, keller, hotel, restaurant, etc.

Guinness drinkers:
What sort of person is the German Guinness drinker? How did he/she begin drinking Guinness? Why does he/she drink it now — medicinal reasons, pleasure?

The Image of Guinness:
What sort of product is Guinness seen as? What is known about it? Is it thought of as English or Irish? What sorts of occasions is it thought to be appropriate for, and when would it be inappropriate? What are felt to be its advantages/disadvantages?

When would it be drunk and when not — and why? How does it compare with, and how is it different from, German beers?

Drinker Imagery:
What sort of people generally would like to drink dark beers? What sort of people would be likely to drink Guinness — older/younger; poor/wealthy; middle-class/working class; modern/traditional; fashionable/old-fashioned; etc.

Is it seen as an appropriate drink for women?

Product Presentation/Advertising:
Are there any spontaneous remarks about the product's presentation? What do people think of the bottle and label? Of the new Guinness glass? What impression of the product do they create? What advertising, if any, is recalled for Guinness? What impression/image did it create? What did it say about the product? Etc.

Method and Sample

The research had been intended to take the form of a series of twelve group discussions with an agreed quota sample of male and female drinkers of Guinness. The choice of location was governed to a large extent by the pattern of Guinness sales within Germany. Three group discussions, two with male and one with female drinkers of Guinness, were held in each of four locations: Düsseldorf, Hamburg, Berlin and München.

In view of the very low incidence of Guinness drinking in Germany, it was felt that no age or drinking frequency controls could be imposed on the quota. Respondents consequently, were to be recruited purely on the basis of having had *some* experience of Guinness; however, given that it is customary in Germany to over-recruit, the German recruiting agency was asked to ensure where possible a spread of ages and drinking frequency within and across groups.

Due to mis-recruiting and the late arrival of addresses of pubs and shops stocking Guinness, respondents in two of the Hamburg groups (one male, one female) were predominantly non-Guinness drinkers. Two further group discussions were, therefore, held with a correct quota sample at the end of the research, and results from the two 'incorrect' groups were kept as a useful yardstick against which to compare the Guinness-drinking market.

The three Düsseldorf groups were carried out by a bi-lingual German/English psychologist with four years' research experience. These groups were also attended by another full-time MBL staff psychologist with fluent German, and by an additional German/English interpreter.

All other groups — that is, groups in Hamburg, Berlin and München — were carried out jointly by the latter two.

Locations for the groups varied. In Düsseldorf, all three groups were held at the head offices of Makrotest, the recruitment agency. The last two groups in Berlin were held in a private house. For all other groups rooms had been hired in 'snackbar-cum-pub'-like premises.

Groups were provided with snacks: cheese cubes and cheese/salted biscuits, *or* a selection of open sandwiches.

The same approach was used for all groups, with topics for discussion being explored in much the same order. Respondents were given a glass of Guinness to sample only once they had discussed the broader aspects of Guinness, and its appearance and presentation. Unfortunately, it was not possible to provide similar glasses from which to sample the Guinness at all groups.

The Guinness was served out of sight so as not to influence respondents' recall of the Guinness bottle. A larger Pils bottle with a silver and white label was used in each group to compare and contrast with the Guinness bottle — in terms of both presentation and imagery.

Two specimens and the new Guinness glass format were shown at each group. Respondents were encouraged to hold them and even to drink out of them.

At the end of each discussion group, respondents were asked to complete a brief questionnaire with reference to their Guinness and other beer-drinking habits.

Fieldwork

The groups were carried out between Monday, 1st and Friday, 12th July, 1974.

Verbal Presentation

A verbal presentation of findings from the research was made to the Client at a meeting of MBL, Guinness, and J. Walter Thompson personnel on Wednesday, 14th August, 1974. A summary report of the main findings from the research was prepared for this meeting.

This Document

This document is the full and final report on this research project and contains a full analysis of results as well as our conclusions and recommendations concerning the Client's present and future line of action.

NB: We would like to remind the Reader that this was a small-scale qualitative project — 112 respondents in total — and while we remain confident that findings from the research are replicable, they lack quantitative validity.

NBB: For the purposes of this report, respondents will be referred to as being in a Lower Income Bracket (under 2500 DM per month) and in a Higher Income Bracket (over 2500 DM per month).

Summary and Conclusions

The overall objective of the research was to gain as full and as broad an understanding of the German beer market as possible, in order to better the position of Guinness within it, and to suggest ways and means of improving Guinness sales and the product-image in Germany.

Some general information relating to current and possible trends on the German drink market would seem a necessary background to assessing marketing possibilities for Guinness. Some of this information will already be known to the Client, but we include it nevertheless to ensure the 'good fit' of the total picture that emerged from the research.

Germany is currently the largest consumer of beer in the world. The national annual *per capita* consumption of beer is now 145 litres, and it has reached 230 litres in Bavaria. Stagnation has set in, and in an effort to counteract it breweries have followed the European example of joint enterprise. As a result, small breweries have been, and are being, forced into liquidation and the leading breweries are amalgamating. The German beer market features some 6,000 brands — the great majority of which are light beers. Pils and Export are still league leaders, but some breweries have taken further precautions against stagnation by diversifying into special brews. Despite the complexity and diversity of the German beer market, brewers have succeeded in maintaining high production standards, and have strictly abided by the Purity Law since 1506. Germany expected other EEC members to introduce similar measures of quality control for their own beers, but the Purity Law was in fact revoked by EEC legislation. This provoked leading German breweries to attack foreign beers in the national press. The quality and ingredients of Belgian beers in particular were under attack but foreign beers generally need to regain the confidence of many German beer consumers.

Southern and Northern Germany are the stronghold of light beer and we gathered that few dark beers remaining in Germany are now being bottled only for export. The research has confirmed the fact that regional brands are beginning to gain ground further afield. Alt seems to have spread to Berlin and Pils to Western regions of Germany. Leading breweries now have to face strong competition from cheap cut-price brands. These have a relatively short shelf-life and the quick turnover of unfamiliar brands appears to be corroding consumer brand loyalty in the shop-buying situation.

Other factors appeared to be contributing to greater brand-promiscuity generally. Apparently, there is little difference in taste between national light beers, especially in the South, so that consumers are not particular about which brand they order.   Moreover, most pubs are tied-houses and even regionally there are so many different brands available that tied-houses serving the same brand are unlikely to be in close geographical proximity.   Most consumers do not seem prepared to plan ahead or travel further afield in order to buy a particular brand, and the general attitude is that any brand will do as long as it is well cared for — 'gutgepflegte'.   This brings us to a very interesting finding from the research, namely, that the German beer drinker does not seem to be brand-conscious nor knowledgeable about the German beer market generally.   We cannot say whether this is the cause or result of the brand promiscuity observed generally, but respondents' grasp of the total market appeared to be very primitive indeed.   6,000 odd brands were casually classified as 'light and dark', 'Pils and Bock'.   Brands per se — their ingredients, place of origin, and histories — had very little, if any, gossip value.   Perhaps, this is not too surprising in the light of the difficulties apparently inherent in remaining brand loyal, and which were mentioned above.

The German beer drinker appears to more than compensate for his lackadaisical interest in brand differences by the importance he attaches to all beer being correctly served.   All light beers seem to be expected to have a stiff, white head, and the sight of the pale liquid in a cool and misted glass, topped by the creamy head, was described as giving almost as much pleasure as drinking it.   Dark beers were not thought to produce as much, or as stiff, a head.   Consumer expectations in this area appear to have been influenced, and supported, by a recent and concentrated spate of advertising promoting 'das kühle Blonde'. The concept of 'gutgepflegtes Bier' appears to have particular significance in Germany.   The freshness of the beer, the correct temperature, a good head and the appropriate beer-glass could be said to serve the function of a gauge against which the German beer drinker accepts with good nature whatever brand is available.   Respondents all preferred draught beer and saw it as the 'original' beer, fresher, livelier, earthier and more vital than bottled beer, not least because of the ritual involved in serving it and the more lively atmosphere in the pub. Nevertheless, bottled beer might apparently be chosen despite a preference for draught, in pubs which do not look after their draught beer or where the bartender cheats on the 0.4 litre limit.

Beer generally appears to be very little associated with health in Germany. Beer seems to have become such a common quantity that it may in essence have been devalued in consumers' minds.   Respondents appeared to nurture few illusions about the health-giving properties of beer and the general opinion was that if breweries made any such claims these would be dismissed as sales talk.

As a general comment, we would point out that beer brands varied across localities, but that attitudes to drinking and favourite beverages were remarkably homogeneous across localities.   The drinks most frequently consumed were beer and wine, followed by mineral water, fruit juices and the occasional long drink or liqueur.

The research suggests that Guinness is thought by German consumers to be oily, thick, spicy and bitter, in sharp contrast to the sweeter, dark German beers. It was also perceived to be very filling — though not nutritious or potent — and for this reason only two or three glasses would be drunk at a single drinking session.   This fullness was not felt to be compatible with Guinness being drunk with meals or mixed with other flavours, and Guinness emerged as a 'real' and 'concrete' beer, an 'intensive' beer which is not a refreshing nor an easy drink.

The colour of Guinness appeared to be liked generally, but it was thought to be more dense than all other beers, light and dark.   Whether Guinness is drunk at home or out of the home depends largely on consumer knowledge of outlets that sell Guinness.   Some respondents claimed never to have seen a shop selling Guinness, others never to have seen a pub selling Guinness.   Respondents who had drunk Guinness first in the UK attached great importance to a pub setting for Guinness, and disliked home drinking.   Respondents with no experience of UK pubs were not particular about where they drank Guinness, except if they were badly off — in which case they tended to drink Guinness, and beer generally, at home — or if they fell in with the current craze in Germany for UK pubs and UK music, in which case they tried to drink Guinness out even if it was felt to be beyond their means to do so.

Guinness' main appeal appears to lie in what it is felt to do for the consumer at an intra- and interpersonal level.   We would hypothesize that this varies considerably from consumer to consumer.   The high premium price of Guinness confers considerable snob-value to the product, and some consumers seem simply to like being seen to drink it, or being known to like it.   A second aspect to Guinness is that it is closely associated with the UK overall, and England and Ireland are very much in vogue currently in Germany.   Again, some consumers probably like to be seen drinking Guinness because they hope for some transference of its trendy image.

Nostalgia for the UK seems to be a very strong motivator for sustaining one's Guinness-drinking career, and it is likely that the current popularity of England and Ireland is positively reinforcing holiday memories of the UK.   Respondents who had visited the UK were mostly young, mostly comfortably off, and mostly consumed a fair amount of Guinness.   UK holiday memories seem to confer existential validity to the product, and an English pub atmosphere in Germany is apparently a source of welcome escapism for Anglophiles.

Major findings from the research would indicate that the problems immediately facing Guinness are likely to have some solution in better distribution and concentrated promotional backing.   Briefly, the situation seems to us to be as follows:

1   Consumer level of awareness of Guinness is either very low or nil.   Respondents claimed very few shops or pubs sell Guinness, and advertising recall for Guinness was nil.   In shops that do sell Guinness, shelf-display for it is, apparently, often very poor and some consumers waste a lot of time looking for the product.   This is not helped by the fact that Guinness is thought in its presentation to resemble closely German sauce and fruit juice products.

2   Recruitment to the product seems to be almost exclusively by personal

recommendation and its reputation to rely on word-of-mouth advertising.

3 A fair number of consumers will have first drunk Guinness when visiting the UK. English beers seem to have a poor reputation in Germany as being weak, warm and headless. Experimentation in search of an acceptable English beer eventually leads the German tourist to try Guinness, usually at the recommendation of English friends or strangers − the barman, etc. − who are anxious to re-establish a foreigner's faith in English beers. Such circumstances appear to be favourable to Guinness as Guinness will be judged against other English beers.

4 Other consumers will have drunk Guinness for the first time in Germany, mostly in company and at the instigation of friends. Some will already have heard of the beer, others will have seen strangers drinking it. Such circumstances appear to be less favourable to Guinness initially. German dark beers are generally sweet-tasting, and the unsuspecting novice is in for a shock when he realizes Guinness is a bitter dark beer.

5 The habituation period for Guinness appears to be protracted but painless. Some time elapses before Guinness is tried again, but the second time round the consumer is prepared for the bitterness and his threshold for disappointment is much lower. This time, the beer comes over as less bitter than anticipated.

6 After the second and third trial, loyalty to Guinness seems to be very much a matter of luck. If the consumer lives near a shop or pub which he knows to stock Guinness, the likelihood is that he will re-purchase Guinness if he likes sharp beers. If he has to rely on luck and other people to find new outlets, he may well give up Guinness completely, or drink it only spasmodically because of having to go further afield than would be convenient on a regular basis.

We therefore suggest that Guinness owes its current success in Germany to the fact that it is unusual for a dark beer to be bitter, and/or to consumer-perception of Guinness as being 'More than just a beer', as being a beer that can do things for rather than to the consumer. Nevertheless, we believe that Guinness is at a considerable disadvantage in relation to other beers in Germany − in the consumer's mind.

We believe that any future marketing strategy for Guinness in Germany needs to take into account and counteract the handicaps attributed to Guinness by the consumer, and these seem to be the following:

1 Guinness is a dark beer, and the majority of beer drunk in Germany is light.
2 German beer-drinkers appear to be concerned currently with the possibility that beer is fattening. The decline in popularity of dark beers in the South was at least in part attributed to the widespread belief that light beer is less fattening than dark beer.
3 The perceived fullness and oiliness of Guinness are not thought to be compatible with 'capacity' drinking and with summertime drinking.

4 Very few German beer-drinkers know that Guinness is a beer. Many respondents did not appear to have fully internalized its identity and referred to it
in contrast to beers. Moreover, other beer brands were referred to in the
masculine, suggesting respondents had personalized them, whereas Guinness
was talked about in the neutral form.
5 The product-presentation may be adding to the confusion concerning the
product-identity. As noted earlier, the Guinness bottle was said to resemble
sauce and juice products. Germans not familiar with the brand name would
not have their attention drawn to the fact that Guinness is a beer in the
shop-buying situation.
6 The majority of respondents felt that the product-presentation conflicts
with the product-image. The beer itself comes across as being vital, rural,
earthy and yet elegant. The product presentation appears to suggest an
effete and unisex image for Guinness.

Appendix 2.2
System Three Attitudinal Research in Italy: Extracts from Report Presented Dec. 1974

A. Objectives

1 To find out how Guinness is regarded in Italy in comparison with other
Italian and foreign beers, and other alcoholic drinks.
2. To find out why those who have tried it do not consume it more often in
spite of its excellent distribution.
3 Specifically, to find out what role Guinness plays in Italy, when and why
it is drunk, and what characteristics of product and image are valued.

B. Method and Sample

Individual depth interviews lasting 1½ hours upwards were used, because of
previous experience with up-market Italian drinkers.

Respondents were recruited; partly around pubs and bars which were on a
list provided by Guinness in Italy; partly by cold canvassing to locate those with
past experience of Guinness. They were screened by a question listing Guinness
among the names of all major imported beers, and asking 'have you ever drunk

any of these?'. If they claimed to have drunk Guinness, they were subsequently interviewed. Only two were mistaken due to confusion with other dark English beers. Respondents were easier to recruit in Bologna than in Milan.

There were twenty-five interviews: twenty men and five women. The original intention was to have sixteen AB and ten Cl: this proved absolutely impossible to recruit, as all drinkers found proved to be ABs. The age of respondents spread evenly from twenty to fifty-eight.

All the interviews were in October.

All respondents were found to have visited Britain, and almost all had first drunk Guinness there.

This survey was, of course, a pilot study based on a relatively limited sample, but the close unanimity of the comments suggest that the findings are broadly accurate in so far as they concern drinkers with some past experience of Guinness in Northern Italy. They do not, of course, cover the views of Italian beer drinkers who have not yet tried Guinness, but might.

This report was prepared in several stages: the Italian interviewers wrote up each interview; a first report was written in Italian by the Italian director of the project and this was discussed in detail in Milan; certain aspects were then expanded further; and the final report is a consensus of all these stages and the conclusions that can be drawn from this research.

C. Summary of Findings

This is a summary of the detailed findings — inevitably it oversimplifies certain aspects. (It should be remembered that this sample was usually up-market.)

1 Beer means clear light beer in Italy. It is drunk as a refreshing drink, and increasingly with lighter meals and snacks, particularly in summer, mostly by men, but increasingly by younger women.
2 Foreign beers have greater prestige than Italian, but are drunk on similar occasions. (A minority, however, are beginning to see Italian beers as an acceptable alternative to 'normal' German beers.)

   Germany is seen as the beer-drinking country, but Tuborg and Oranjeboom are the widest known and most respected foreign beers.

   Branding is weak: normally a 'beer' or a 'foreign beer' are ordered.

   British beers are not as well known in Italy, nor expected to be on sale there.
3 Dark beers are not expected to be found on the Italian market, though most drinkers are aware that they exist in England, Germany, and some other countries.
4 The majority of these exclusively up-market drinkers are not aware that Guinness, (which most respondents positively liked) is on sale in Italy, and few drink it often, or at all.

(a)   Approximately a quarter of those interviewed were drinking Guinness in Italy, but rather infrequently (not more often than once a quarter).

Some of the others had drunk once or twice in Italy, but the majority had assumed it was not on sale, and had only drunk in Britain.

(b) Approximately 40% really seemed to like the taste very much (and around 60% claimed to) — with only two disliking it — in spite of initial reservations at the time of their first experience. The bitterness suited their tastes.

(c) It was almost invariably drunk outside the home in the evenings, in small groups of men.

(d) It was invariably drunk one bottle per person at a time, sip by sip like the better wines, which it was often seen to resemble.

(e) Drinkers were not aware of Guinness's 'excellent distribution'.

5 Guinness is seen as a connoisseurs' drink, valued for:
  — its bitter taste
  — its highly distinctive, dark colour
  — the creaminess of the foaming head
  — natural, farmhouse 'barley' taste
  — it is seen as a traditional and honest product
  — it is a unique drink not another imported beer
  — alone of beers, it is not seen exclusively as a summer drink.

6 It is seen by men (and by the women who drink it) as an exclusively masculine drink, and valued for this — by both sexes.

7 England and Ireland are inextricably confused by the majority of Italians and seen as the one same source of Guinness.

As far as Italians see it, it does not, at this moment, matter whether the origin is Irish or English: possibly a campaign to emphasize the 'more special' Irish origin could give Guinness an even more distinctive background.

8 The unique product qualities of Guinness enable it to be used as a prestige symbol in a social situation by Italians, as a sign of connoisseurship and as a connection with the distinguished and exotic life of Britain as they see it — London pubs and the high society of Edwardian Britain — which they all felt they had at one time shared in.

9 The old label is decisively preferred to the new one.

The old one is old-fashioned, genuine, special, like a connoisseurs' estate-bottled wine, and highly distinctive in a bar: the only drawback to a minority is the green with its superstitions; to the majority, green symbolizes the green fields of England or Ireland, and makes it more noticeable.

The new label by contrast is ordinary, banal, and, to most, rather ugly in colour, and much more easily confused with ordinary beers.

But the label is much less important to the Guinness drinker than the image and the distinctive, pleasingly bitter taste.

10 The image of the Guinness drinker is entirely masculine: up-market 'English', a man in vigorous, early middle age, a sea captain, a farmer, a man in the open air, and above all a connoisseur.

11 Guinness is almost invariably seen as being drunk in bars, and only sometimes at home with TV, and never as a drink to be drunk with food or in mixed company.

Lines of Interviewing — Brief

These were informal and unstructured, but covered:

1 **Warm-up discussion**
   When beer is drunk: in Summer and Winter. What beers are drunk: which foreign beers. What other foreign beers are known. Attitudes to foreign beers. Images of different foreign countries as producers of different types of beer. When beer and when other alcoholic drinks — by time of day, social occasion, by time of year. What type of person drinks.

2 **First impressions of unidentified Guinness**
   Trial glass of Guinness. What is it: how well liked/disliked. Why. Previous experience. What caused you to try it then. Describe occasion in detail: sensations around drink: pleasure or otherwise. Subsequent consumption of 'it' (if any).
   Who does drink dark beer like this in Italy. Male/female. Upper class/everyone. Modern/traditional. For what purpose. What makes them drink this kind of beer. How often do they drink it and when?

3 **Feelings about Guinness**
   Produce labelled bottle and offer another glass. 'The drink was Guinness' and note immediate reactions.
   Which country makes Guinness. How does it differ from Italian beers. What qualities does it have that Italian beers do not.
   Then repeat (2) using Guinness name, and probing more into why and the type of occasion.
   Probe any recall of advertising. Probe reactions to label. What impressions do/did they give you of the product. How accurately do they put over the real nature.

4 **Guinness in the context of other beers**
   Show Guinness with two leading local Italian beers, two German and any other major imported beer (briefing needed).
   Re-examine experience of each, by type of occasion, and by role of each (refreshment, prestige, nourishment, gourmandise, etc.).
   Compare believed prices in shops and bars. Compare likely future use. How does Guinness fit in with these beers, or have a very different role. Which would be particularly good for you/under which conditions. What price is each, and what price should each be if you were to drink more often.
   What changes would make Italians drink Guinness more often. Why don't Italians drink Guinness more often: men and women. Should product be stronger/less strong: darker/less dark: different taste, etc. (NB: Not to suggest product modification, but to disclose any barriers to drinking more often.) On what sort of occasion is Guinness at its best. Examine effect of pricing. Awareness of any publicity.

5 Re-examine 3/4 in light of any areas of doubt or discrepancy.

III
Finnish Tourist Board

G. Hooley

Late in 1979 the Finnish Tourist Board were considering the results of several marketing research studies amongst tourists. They were concerned about the slower than expected growth in tourism from outside Finland. Prior to the studies conducted in 1979 they knew little about how tourists and potential tourists viewed a holiday in Finland and what they were looking for when considering a holiday destination. The several studies conducted provided a mass of information for the Tourist Board. Their main concern was that they should fully appreciate that information and make full use of it.

Background

Before 1979 Finland had failed to attract the numbers of tourists it had hoped for from aborad. While net receipts from travel had increased up to 1973 the middle and end of the 70s showed a marked decline (see Exhibit 3.1). Receipts had increased by 250% since 1971 but expenditure by Finns abroad had increased by nearly 350%. Since 1974 the positive contribution of travel to the current balance of payments had greatly decreased, 1977 even providing a net loss. Results for 1978 had been somewhat improved, however. During the same period (1971—1978) trade had increased

---

This case study was prepared by A. Haahti, Helsinki School of Economics, Finland, R. R. van den Heuvel, Groningen University, The Netherlands, and G. J. Hooley, University of Bradford Management Centre, UK. Results have been disguised for the purpose of confidentiality.

virtually fourfold (see Exhibit 3.2). Travel receipts provided a small but important contribution to the country's balance of payments.

Visitors to Finland came from a wide number of countries though there was a marked preponderance of Scandinavians, Sweden accounting for 78% of foreign tourists and Norway 11% in 1978 (see Exhibit 3.3). Interestingly, however, this high proportion of visiting Scandinavians is not so marked when considering holiday accommodation used (see Exhibit 3.4). Swedes, for example, tend to stay with families and friends very often and Danes tend to camp more than other nationalities. Contribution to the nation's travel account is therefore not directly proportional to the numbers of visitors. In 1978 53% of receipts were in Swedish crowns, 15% in Deutschmarks, 10% in US dollars and 22% in other currencies.

In order to shed more light on why tourists came to Finland, two marketing research studies were undertaken.

1 Research among tourists in Finland

A sample of 681 holiday makers in Finland was selected and interviewed concerning their background and reasons for selecting Finland for their holidays. The sample was selected in the three major tourist regions: Helsinki, the capital (approximately 300 interviews), Saimaa, an area of natural beauty not unlike the English Lake District (200 interviews) and Lapland (150 interviews). Sampling was conducted by two-stage, random sampling. Initially hotels/motels were selected and subsequently tourists within accommodations selected.

As a consequence of interviewing in accommodation a lower proportion of Scandinavians was reached than represented the population of holiday makers (many Scandinavians, as noted above, stay with relatives or friends). Appendix 3.1 gives information on the characteristics of the sample and the main survey findings.

2 Research among tourists at home

While the research in Finland gave valuable insights into the tourists that had chosen Finland as a holiday destination it did not paint a full picture of tourists in general. In particular the tourist board were concerned to know more about the 'European' tourists other than those who specifically chose Finland. It was therefore decided to draw samples of tourists in their home countries to determine their reasons for choice of a variety of holiday destinations of which Finland would represent only one. This it was hoped would put Finland into perspective amongst other potential choices.

This research was conducted by local marketing research agencies and was often part of a random omnibus survey. A summary of the main results is presented in Appendix 3.2. The survey design and selected results from the Netherlands are presented in Appendix 3.3.

On the basis of the evaluations of alternative holiday destinations on the set of ten attributes (presented in Table 3A.10) a perceptual map of holiday destinations was obtained (see Exhibit 3.5).

The perceptual map was developed using the PREFMAP multi-dimensional scaling package to generate a configuration of destinations and simultaneously an interpretation of the dimensions of that configuration. Technically the procedure is termed internal property fitting analysis. The map thus produced can be used to summarize the images of each destination and, of particular importance, to demonstrate the destinations that are perceived as similar to each other and hence are likely to be in direct competition.

Respondents had also been asked to evaluate their 'ideal' holiday locations on the basis of the ten attributes. Using these evaluations, four clear segments were identified relating to the location of the 'ideal' holiday on the perceptual map. These four segments (termed A to D on the map) represented 92% of respondents in the sample, the remaining 8% produced diverse ideals. The main characteristics of each segment were as follows:

Segment A

Segment A represented 40% of the sample. Respondents wanted a cheap, sunshine holiday and were predisposed to choose Spain. They came from a wide variety of age groups and from all over Europe but tended to be the lower education and income groups. They tended also to be families, rather than individuals, and to prefer package tours to individually organized holidays.

Segment B

This segment represented 15% of the sample and contained both students on low-budget travel holidays, and the middle-aged, middle-income holiday maker. Great Britain and Ireland particularly appealed. There was a predominance towards individually organized tours and the middle age groups often brought their own car for these purposes. Accommodation tended to be in guest houses offering bed and breakfast facilities. This segment was dominated by the Dutch, Germans and French.

Segment C

Representing 15% of the sample, Segment C wanted peaceful, quite holidays with beautiful scenery. They tended to be couples on their own or with only one child. They also stemmed from the higher income groups and chose to organize their holidays themselves, taking their own car, rather than join package tours. This segment consisted primarily of the Dutch, Germans and Scandinavians. Interestingly, only about half of the respondents in this segment had visited Finland.

Segment D

The final segment accounted for 22% of the sample. This was a fairly heterogeneous group with few distinguishing characteristics. They tended to be high income, to go for both individual and package tours, and to be Scandinavians.

Strategic Planning

By late 1979, the results from the marketing research were available to the Tourist Board. There was a large amount of information and they were concerned that they should fully understand and utilize the results in their strategic planning.

	Receipts from Travel	Expenditure on Travel	Net Surplus
1971	724	477	247
1972	985	649	336
1973	1162	822	340
1974	1178	852	326
1975	1215	1110	105
1976	1307	1285	22
1977	1519	1522	−3
1978	1814	1648	166

Source: Bank of Finland

Exhibit 3.1: Travel Trends (Finnish marks millions)

	1971	1972	1973	1974	1975	1976	1977	1978
Exports	2344	2930	3802	5473	5500	6321	7652	8529
Imports	2800	3192	4335	6799	7614	7384	7617	7852
Trade Balance	−456	− 262	− 533	−1326	−2114	−1063	35	677
Transportation (Net)	157	178	261	285	268	309	346	410
Travel (Net)	59	82	89	87	29	6	−1	40
Other Services (Net)	16	18	8	28	59	64	102	233
Investment (Net)	−114	−133	−212	−286	−415	−484	−642	−746
Current Balance	−339	−177	−387	−1212	−2173	−1169	−159	+615

1 $ US   4 Finnish Marks

Source: OECD Surveys of Finland. Bank of Finland Monthly Bulletin.

Exhibit 3.2: Finland Balance of Payments ($ US millions)

Arrivals

	Tourism		Business		Total	
	'000s	%	'000s	%	'000s	%
Sweden	2306	78.0	337	60.6	2643	75.3
West Germany	125	4.2	50	9.0	175	5.0
Soviet Union	19	0.6	11	2.0	30	0.9
USA	46	1.6	15	2.7	61	1.7
Norway	329	11.1	48	8.6	377	10.7
Great Britain	14	0.5	18	3.2	32	0.9
Switzerland	16	0.5	5	0.9	21	0.6
Netherlands	18	0.6	8	1.4	26	0.7
Denmark	14	0.5	15	2.7	29	0.8
France	15	0.5	11	2.0	26	0.7
Italy	7	0.2	3	0.5	10	0.3
Austria	6	0.2	5	0.9	11	0.3
Japan	7	0.2	4	0.7	11	0.3
Canada	8	0.3	3	0.5	11	0.3
Belgium and Luxemburg	5	0.2	3	0.5	8	0.2
Spain	3	0.1	2	0.4	5	0.1
Other	18	0.6	18	3.2	36	1.0
TOTAL	2956	100	556	100	3512	100

Source: Finnish Tourist Board Marketing Plan 1979

Exhibit 3.3: Number of Visitors to Finland by Country of Domicile 1978

Country of Domicile	1972	1973	1974	1975	1976	1977	1978	1978 %	Non-Finland 1978 %
Finland	3,084,683	3,184,481	3,824,583	4,232,855	4,174,048	4,060,683	4,186,045	72.5	—
Sweden	536,211	590,574	582,335	556,348	470,412	452,643	486,403	8.4	30.7
West Germany	213,629	263,762	292,730	269,198	235,672	249,370	257,993	4.5	16.3
Soviet Union	108,050	116,791	129,468	143,270	152,526	143,287	144,237	2.5	9.1
Norway	47,619	55,491	66,068	77,671	74,042	75,105	90,933	1.6	5.7
USA	158,159	144,455	122,597	120,966	103,446	108,488	121,876	2.1	7.7
Great Britain	74,427	74,505	68,833	74,701	74,030	68,204	73,290	1.3	4.6
Switzerland	42,257	53,665	62,092	55,504	51,779	52,828	55,661	1.0	3.5
Netherlands	31,426	40,531	51,931	46,988	44,912	39,486	39,416	0.7	2.5
Denmark	39,244	37,708	37,023	42,791	40,038	38,148	43,091	0.7	2.7
France	32,422	32,076	35,384	37,880	38,568	33,933	37,670	0.7	2.4
Other countries	170,198	212,417	208,529	221,793	228,411	224,763	235,489	4.1	14.8
Total Non-Finland	1,453,642	1,621,975	1,656,990	1,647,110	1,513,836	1,486,228	1,586,059	27.5	100
TOTAL	4,538,325	4,806,456	5,481,573	5,879,965	5,687,884	5,546,911	5,772,104	100	—

Source: Central Statistical Office of Finland

Exhibit 3.4: Number of Nights in Accommodation (Hotels, motels, boarding houses, motor inns) by Country of Domicile of Traveller

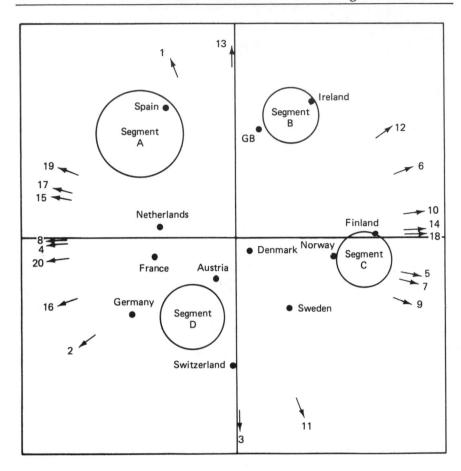

Exhibit 3.5: Internal Property Fitting Analysis Using PREFMAP

Attribute Key

1	Good value for money	11	Poor value for money
2	Accessible	12	Inaccessible
3	Good facilities	13	Poor facilities
4	Good entertainments	14	Poor entertainments
5	Peaceful and quiet	15	Not quiet
6	Friendly and hospitable	16	Unfriendly
7	Wild areas	17	No wild areas
8	Good cultural experience	18	Poor cultural experience
9	Beautiful scenery	19	Not scenic
10	Unique and different	20	Similar to others

Appendix 3.1
Results of the Survey of Tourists in Finland

Summary of Main Findings

The majority of those sampled were on a tour of the Scandinavian countries. Most did not have children with them. Reasons for choosing Finland as a holiday destination varied across nationalities but the most important were the scenery, nature and the Finnish people and their way of life. To a large extent holiday expectations of tourists were met by the Finnish experience and most would recommend Finland to friends and relations.

Some differences in perceptions of Finland were observed between respondents in the different regions. Respondents in Lappland, for example, regarded Finland as a cultural experience but with poor sports and other activity facilities. Respondents in Saimaa regarded Finland as peaceful, with wild and beautiful scenery but with difficult accessibility.

Table 3A.1. Respondents by Nationality

	Number	%
Germans	299	44
Dutch and Benelux	84	12
Swiss and Austrian	116	17
French and Spaniards	28	4
British	19	3
Norwegian	22	3
Danes	10	2
Swedes	43	6
Others (inc. USA)	60	9
	681	100

Table 3A.2. Average Number of Holiday Trips per Year

	Number	%
Less than 1	101	15
One	246	37
Two	234	36
More than 2	77	12
	658	100
No reply	23	

Table 3A.3. Number of Children on the Trip

	Number	%
None	500	80
One	34	5
Two	56	9
Three	33	5
Four	8	1
More than Four	2	—
	633	100
No reply	48	

Table 3A.4. Means of Transport Used in Finland

	Number	%
Car	185	27
'Bus	100	15
Train	309	45
Boat	327	48
Aeroplane	118	17

(Many respondents used more than one means of transport)

Table 3A.5. Type of Accommodation in Finland

	Number	%
Hotel	209	30
Motel	31	5
Caravan	81	12
Pension	97	14
Tent	260	37
Other	13	2
	681	100

Table 3A.6. Main Reason for Coming to Finland

	Number	%
On a round trip in Scandinavia	351	54
On the way to USSR	15	2
On holiday only in Finland	287	44
	653	100
No reply	28	

Table 3A.7. Most Important Reason for Coming to Finland (an open-ended question) by Nationality of Respondent

	Total Sample	Germans	Dutch & Benelux	Swiss & Austrian	Scandinavians	Others
	%	%	%	%	%	%
1 Nature: scenery, summer sights, lakes and woods.	34	36	33	38	28	29
2 Finnish People: the way of life.	23	23	27	28	22	30
3 Peaceful: quiet tranquil holiday.	18	22	51	16	11	4
4 Hobbies: adventure, camping, canoeing, active sports.	10	13	8	12	12	14
5 Friends: visiting friends and relatives.	6	3	4	2	5	13
6 Part of a longer trip	2	1	2	2	17	9
7 Other	7	2	—	2	5	1
	100	100	100	100	100	100

Table 3A.8. Degree of Realization of Expectations by Nationality

Measured on a scale 1 to 9
where 1 = expectations not realized
9 = expectations fully realized
Figures are % of each nationality

Nationality	1–5	6	Scale Values 7	8	9	%	Total
German	12	8	23	22	34	100	286
Dutch & Benelux	3	6	31	25	35	100	80
Swiss & Austrian	16	10	21	23	31	100	112
French & Spanish	31	8	23	15	23	100	26
British	29	12	24	18	18	100	17
Norwegian	14	9	18	18	41	100	22
Danes	20	20	20	40	0	100	10
Swedes	5	8	28	15	44	100	39
Others	12	15	27	22	25	100	56
Total	12	8	25	22	33	100	648
No reply							33

Table 3A.9. Overall Perception of a Finnish Holiday by Nationality

Scale values 1 to 5
1 = least favourable
5 = most favourable
Figures are % of each nationality

Nationality	1	2	Scale 3	4	5	%
German	12	23	22	18	25	100
Dutch & Benelux	6	14	20	30	30	100
Swiss & Austrian	11	23	15	24	27	100
Scandinavians	10	29	15	20	26	100
Other	9	23	21	20	27	100

This measure of overall perception was based on responses to the following attributes:

1 Value for money
2 Ease of access
3 Facilities for sports etc.
4 Night life & entertainment
5 Peace and quiet

6 Friendly & hospitable people
7 Wilderness, treking & camping
8 Cultural experience
9 Beauty of scenery
10 Uniqueness

Appendix 3.2
Summary of results from the In-Country Research (From the report to the Finnish Tourist Board)

Profiles of The Individual Countries

These results are based on the ratings of each country on the ten attributes from Table 3A.10 and the summary provided by the perceptual map in Exhibit 3.5.

Table 3A.10. Ratings of Holiday Destinations on Ten Key Attributes

	Finland	Gt Britain	Ireland	Austria	Sweden	Switzerland	Norway	France	Spain	Netherlands	Germany	Denmark
Value for Money	5.7	6.5	6.2	5.5	4.4	4.4	4.7	5.8	6.6	5.6	5.4	4.8
Accessibility	4.7	5.5	4.1	6.8	5.4	7.0	5.1	7.0	5.3	7.1	7.6	6.6
Facilities	6.7	5.8	5.6	6.6	6.4	6.6	6.2	6.2	5.7	6.3	6.7	6.2
Entertainment	4.8	6.0	4.7	6.3	5.2	5.8	4.7	6.9	6.8	7.0	7.0	5.7
Peace and quiet	8.0	6.3	7.0	6.5	7.2	6.6	7.5	6.2	5.0	5.7	5.5	6.7
Friendliness and hospitality	7.2	6.7	6.6	6.4	6.4	5.9	6.7	5.8	6.0	6.3	5.4	6.7
Wilderness	8.2	5.3	7.1	6.6	7.5	6.6	7.7	5.7	4.8	4.7	5.1	6.2
Culture	4.5	7.0	5.6	6.2	5.7	6.1	5.6	6.8	5.8	5.7	6.3	5.5
Beautiful Scenery	8.1	6.5	7.3	7.5	7.5	7.8	7.9	6.8	6.2	5.6	6.2	6.4
Uniqueness	7.7	6.2	7.1	5.4	5.7	5.5	7.3	5.0	4.6	5.2	4.9	6.2

Based on a Scale of 1 to 10

Finland

Wilderness, peacefulness and beautiful scenery were almost unanimously regarded as the really strongly appealing features of Finland. The weaknesses of Finland seem to be accessibility, entertainment opportunities, chances for cultural experience, and, to some degree, the value for money the tourists seemed to receive.

Sweden

The strengths of Sweden were the beautiful scenery, wilderness — camping and trekking possibilities — and the peaceful and quiet holiday opportunities the country offers. Its weaknesses are: poor value for money, poor entertainment facilities and to a lesser degree, accessibility, cultural experience and change from previous experiences.

Norway

The strengths of Norway were: peace and quiet, wilderness — camping and trekking possibilities — beautiful scenery and the change it offers from previous experiences. The weaknesses of Norway are: poor value for money, poor accessibility, poor entertainment facilities and cultural experiences.

Denmark

Denmark did not seem to have distinguishing strengths on these dimensions. It fared well on accessibility, was peaceful and quiet, and friendly and hospitable. It was not regarded as good value for money nor as a cultural experience, but on the other dimensions the results were average.

Germany

Germany fared well on accessibility, activities — sports etc. — and on the entertainment dimension. It was not perceived as a change from usual destinations, or as good for wilderness experience, peace and quiet, friendliness and hospitability.

The Netherlands

The strengths of Holland were accessibility and entertainment. Its weaknesses were wilderness and change from the usual destinations. The other dimensions scored average.

Switzerland

Switzerland had one clear advantage and that was its beautiful scenery. It was also accessible, good for activities such as sports, trekking and camping and peaceful. It was perceived as poor value for money.

Austria

Austria was perceived positively on most of the dimensions except two, which were good value for money and change from the usual destinations. Its strength was the beautiful scenery and its accessibility.

Great Britain

Great Britain was perceived not to have distinguished strengths on these dimensions; on the other hand neither did it have any weaknesses for that matter. To profile Great Britain meaningfully one would use other dimensions.

Ireland

Ireland scored high on beautiful scenery, camping and trekking possibilities, change from the usual destinations, peace and quiet and on friendliness and hospitability. It was perceived as inaccessible and short of entertainment possibilities.

France

France scored well on accessibility, entertainment, cultural experience and beautiful scenery. It did not score so well on change from other holiday destinations.

Spain

Spain was seen as good value for money and high on entertainment value. Its relative weak points were accessibility, peace and quiet, camping and trekking, and it was not perceived as a change from other destinations.

Appendix 3.3
Finland Through Dutch Eyes

The results of the study of Dutch tourists conducted in November 1978 on behalf of the Finnish Tourist Board.

Introduction

Preface

On behalf of the Finnish Tourist Board a survey was carried out into the image of Finland as a holiday destination. The objective of the survey was to determine how Dutch holidaymakers considered Finland as a possible holiday destination and what are the reasons for not wishing to spend a holiday in Finland.

Method of Research

The questionnaire for this study was incorporated in a weekly Omnibus survey in the last three weeks of November 1978. For the purpose of this survey, interviews were held in 3720 households. This large sample was drawn at random from the dwelling files of Dutch municipalities and may be considered representative for the total number of households in the Netherlands.

Tabulations

The percentages in the tables are calculated vertically, that is to say, the total number of respondents (consistently reported at the bottom of each table) is set at 100%. At the bottom of these tables two totals can appear:

1 Total respondents. This total is reported on every table and reflects the number of persons represented in the specific sub-group in the vertical column.
2 Total answers. This total is reported only in those cases where multiple answers to the question are possible and it should be considered as the sum total of the answers.

Summary

A. General Description

Holiday participation

Of all people aged 18 years or older 37% had been on holiday *abroad* during the period from October 1977 up to September 1978.

	Total Sample	
	Abs	%
Didn't take a holiday abroad	2350	63
Spent one holiday abroad	823	22
Spent two holidays abroad	460	13
Spent three or more holidays abroad	87	2
	3720	100

37% (for the latter three rows)

Holiday-taking abroad occurs more among people belonging to the higher and middle social classes than among people in the lower social classes. There is also a relatively lower participation among people in the older age categories and among people living in the northern region of this country.

The questions intended for the Finnish Tourist Board were only put to the 1370 who spent their holidays abroad.

Means of transportation and type of accommodation used

Results were analysed both for the main holiday and for second holidays taken abroad as shown in Table 3A.11.

Table 3A.11

	Transportation	
	Main Holiday	Second Holiday
	%	%
Car	61	61
Bus	11	7
Aeroplane	20	20
Train	7	10
Boat	7	4
Others	2	3
No answer	3	2
(m)	110	107

(m) = multiple answers

	Type of Accommodation	
	Main Holiday	Second Holiday
	%	%
Friends/family	9	12
Hotel/motel	37	41
Pension	8	9
Apartment/bungalow/cottage	17	18
Camping site	18	8
Caravan	11	9
Boat	1	1
Others	3	4
No answer	3	3
(m)	107	105

(m) = multiple answers

Countries

The following questions were asked of ten holiday destinations:

To which have you been on holiday in the past 12 months?
To which have you ever been on holiday?
Which would you like to visit in the future?
Which would you like to visit for a winter holiday (1 week or shorter)?
Which would you like to visit for a summer holiday (2 weeks or longer)?
Which would you NOT consider for a holiday?

The results of those questions are as shown in Table 3A.12.

Table 3A.12

	Last Year's Holiday	Has ever Been There	Would Like to Visit	Consider for Winter Holiday	Consider for Summer Holiday	Would NOT Consider for Holiday
	%	%	%	%	%	%
Switzerland/ Austria	22	63	18	45	22	6
Spain/Italy	24	57	18	7	28	23
Great Britain	9	33	17	2	14	19
Greece	3	9	24	2	24	21
Yugoslavia	3	19	15	2	17	24
Ireland	1	4	14	1	10	29
Finland	1	3	13	3	10	31
Sweden	2	8	18	3	14	26
Norway	1	8	21	5	16	26
Denmark	1	10	13	1	11	28
Other country	56	73	19	6	18	8
Not interested/ No answer	—	—	18	42	21	32
(m)	122	288	208	118	204	273

(m) = multiple answers

More than half of the respondents spent their holidays in countries other than the countries explicitly mentioned in the questionnaire. In this group of 56% the main countries were:

France	19%
West Germany	18%
Belgium, Luxemburg	9%

With regard to Finland, only 3% out of the 1370 respondents spent their holidays in this country, i.e. only 39 respondents have ever been there. For a winter holiday Finland is judged less popular than Switzerland and Austria. For a summer holiday the attraction of Finland is higher; about one of each ten holiday-takers would like to visit for a summer holiday, but on the other hand 31% would not like to visit Finland for holidays.

Attractions of Holiday Destinations

The main attractions of holiday destinations were as shown in Table 3A.13.

Table 3A.13

	Important for	
	Main Holiday	*Second Holiday*
	%	%
To experience a different culture and way of life	37	13
To enjoy an exciting night life, dancing and entertainment	11	6
To enjoy good restaurants, good food	36	17
To visit places of significant historical interest	40	17
To see beautiful scenery	64	26
To meet interesting new people	33	13
To learn new things that would be helpful in one's business or social life	10	6
To get a bargain-priced vacation	21	13
To bring back interesting gifts and souvenirs	11	5
To participate in warm weather sports and activities	42	13
To participate in winter sport and activities	8	20
To experience a relaxing atmosphere	33	14
To participate in out-door activities like hiking and camping	24	7
There should not be any language problems	15	6
(m)	385	176

(m) = multiple answers

To see beautiful scenery, to participate in warm weather sports (including bathing and swimming), to visit places of historical interest and to experience a different culture and way of life are the most important reasons for choosing a destination for the *main* holiday. For a *second* holiday an important reason is to participate in winter sports and activities. The reasons mentioned above for the main holiday are also important for a second holiday but they all appear on a lower level.

It is interesting to see how each of the countries is considered on the various attractions. This has been analysed by means of the question: 'Please tell me now for each of the reasons one or more suitable countries'.

The results are shown in Table 3A.14.

Table 3A.14

	Diff. way of life %	Night life %	Good food %	Places of hist. int. %	Beautiful scenery %	Int. new people %	New things %	Bargain priced vacation %	Gifts souvenirs %	Warm weather sports %	Winter sports %	Relaxing atmosphere %	Outdoor activities %	No language problems %	Country not mentioned for one of these reasons %
Switzerland/Austria	17	14	30	13	62	20	11	6	14	11	60	19	25	31	17
Spain/Italy	24	37	22	25	23	21	10	28	19	64	6	50	31	11	19
Great Britain	16	8	9	28	22	20	10	14	12	4	1	11	16	27	37
Greece	39	6	12	42	21	23	12	9	13	28	1	19	17	4	35
Yugoslavia	34	5	14	12	22	20	11	16	11	23	2	19	18	5	39
Ireland	12	2	4	8	20	13	7	4	6	1	1	10	15	10	56
Finland	20	2	5	4	22	15	10	1	7	1	7	10	13	4	54
Sweden	17	5	8	5	25	15	11	1	7	1	10	11	16	5	50
Norway	17	2	8	5	32	16	10	1	8	1	14	10	17	5	47
Denmark	13	3	7	5	18	14	9	1	6	1	4	10	16	5	55
Other country	16	10	25	15	19	16	12	12	10	11	6	17	18	19	45

In sequence of the most important attractions, the most suitable holiday countries are:

to see beautiful scenery	— Switzerland/Austria and Norway
to participate in warm weather sports and activities	— Spain/Italy and the other sun-countries
to visit places of significant historical interest	— Greece and Great Britain
to experience a different culture and way of life	— Greece and Yugoslavia

Finland scores relatively high on 'to experience a different culture and way of life' and on 'beautiful scenery', but for both attractions the competition of other holiday countries is strong. It is evident, however, that there is an enormous lack of practical knowledge and experience about Finland: more than half of the respondents didn't mention Finland for one or more of these holiday reasons.

B. *Opinions about Finland*

Attitudes

The introductory question about this subject was:

(INT.: Show card with words 'Holiday in Finland'). On this card it says: 'Holiday in Finland'. Could you tell me in your own words what enters your mind, reading this?

Many spontaneous remarks were registered:

- beautiful nature, woods and lakes, pure country, bays, clear and clean woody landscape, birches and pine trees, many isles, thousand lakes 41%
- cold weather, much rain and snow, too cold for a holiday, no sun, low temperature 22%
- probably suitable for langlauf, wintersport and also for watersport (except swimming) e.g. sailing, making boat trips, fishing 6%
- too far away for a holiday and too expensive. Life is expensive in Finland, too expensive for me 15%
- not attractive, too monotonous, lonely, not comfortable, dull 13%
- much space, big empty country, quiet, no tourists, no density of population 10%
- interested in visiting, should like to go there 10%
- sauna 4%
- don't go anymore on holiday abroad 5%
- pleasant country, pleasant people, hospitality 5%
- other remarks 25%
- no idea 21%

(m) 176%

(m) = multiple answers

About half of the holidaymakers seemed to be positive about the country. In general the attitudes towards Finland are more or less ambivalent. The attitudes are clearer in the answers on the more specific question about the attractiveness of Finland as a holiday destination: 'Does it look very attractive, attractive, less attractive or not attractive at all to spend a holiday in Finland'.

very attractive	14% ⎫ 45%
attractive	31% ⎭
less attractive	15%
not attractive	35%
don't know	4%
	100%

45% of all Dutch holiday-takers, especially among the youngsters and among people from the upper and middle social levels, see a holiday in Finland as attractive. Fewer, however, had considered spending a holiday in Finland.

ever considered spending a holiday in Finland	28%
never considered spending a holiday in Finland	72%
	100%

Again, more interest was shown among younger and more prosperous people. Of all people who never considered spending a holiday in Finland the reasons given were:

bad weather	31%
too far away	48%
hard to reach	19%
too expensive	28%
language problems	31%

The distance and the possibility that bad weather spoils the holiday are very important reasons. Also language problems and the high prices are hindering factors.

To all holiday takers questions were put about the most pleasant and less pleasant aspects they have in their mind about Finland as a holiday destination.

	pleasant aspects %		*less pleasant aspects* %
peaceful and quiet	51	expensive	34
not too expensive	3	monotony in landscape	6
possibility to use your own car	13	hardly any camping	5
different way of life	30	only a few hotels	5

Continued

	pleasant aspects %		less pleasant aspects %
beautiful lakes	59	no package tours available	3
beautiful woods	55	often bad weather	27
interesting cities	8	far away and hard to reach	38
good camping	4	same landscape as (nearer)	
good hotels, apartments,		Sweden	6
cottages	5	too quiet	7
a chance to see a lot	22	no recreation possibilities	7
long summer (mid-		no beaches	8
summer night)	14	language problems	37
other aspects	6	nothing for children	9
don't know	13	gloomy	5
		other aspects	8
		don't know	12
(m)	283	(m)	217

(m) = multiple answers

With regard to the less attractive aspects of Finland as a holiday destination the same motives arise as we have seen before: the country is hard to reach, the weather is — in the opinion of the respondents — not so good, standard of life is expensive and it is difficult to communicate with the inhabitants. Positive aspects are the attractiveness of the landscape (lakes and woods), the peacefulness and quietness and the different way of life.

Information seeking

The following two questions were put about the information seeking behaviour:

'Suppose you would like to go to Finland for holidays. How would you acquire information?'

'And which source of information do you consider as most important?'

	acquire information %	most important %
discuss it with family/friends	16	7
look for magazines/brochures about Finland	32	7
go to a travel agency	40	19
to contact/to write to Finnish Tourist Board	36	18
to contact/to write to Finnair	2	—
to contact/to write to Finnlines	2	—
acquire information from ANWB	48	26
elsewhere	6	3
don't know	5	19
(m)	186	100

Most holiday-takers would be informed by the ANWB, the Dutch organization that gives information about all kinds of holidays in the various countries. Travel agencies and the Finnish Tourist Board are second and third in line.

Details about a possible visit

Respondents were asked how they would prefer to go about a holiday in Finland:

package tour or own transport:	package tour	34%
	own transport	50%
	don't know	16%
		100%

means of transportation:	car/boat	44%
	train/boat	3%
	aeroplane	25%
	bus/touring car	5%
	boat	10%
	others	1%
	don't know	20%
		108%

combination with other countries:	Finland exclusively	36%
	also other countries	35%
	don't know	29%
		100%

To visit Finland using own transport is more popular than booking a package tour. Especially among the younger people and in the higher social levels, people prefer to go at their own convenience. This is not peculiar to Finland; in other surveys the same results appeared for all the other holiday countries.

The car is seen as the most appropriate means of transport. Of all people who prefer to go at their own convenience 87% want to make use of their own car.

If the boat was chosen 10% of all holiday takers couldn't say if they should make use of the car or the train.

C. Visits made to Finland

Only 39 of all 1370 people who have been on holidays abroad have ever visited Finland for holidays. 10 of them have been there in the last two years; for the other 29 it happened longer than two years ago.

The interview has been continued with the 10 people who have been there in 1977 or 1978. It is obvious that this number is too small for analysis.

In the tables below the absolute figures are shown.

holidays in Finland:	in 1978	7
	in 1977	3
		10
number of times visited Finland:	once	3
	twice	6
	three times	—
	four times	1
	five times	—
		10
length of stay last time:	up to 4 days	7
	5 up to 9 days	2
	10 up to 12 days	—
	2 weeks	—
	3 weeks	—
	4 weeks or longer	1
		10
main or second holiday:	main holiday	8
	second holiday	2
		10
if second holiday, where have you been for your main holiday?:	Germany	2
		2

accommodation:	friends/family	—
	hotel/motel	7
	cottage/stuga	1
	caravan	—
	tent	2
		10

means of transport:	plane	—
	train/boat	2
	car/boat	7
	bus/boat	1
		10

- Only one of them would consider Finland for a winter holiday.
- 8 of them would consider Finland for a summer holiday.
- None of them would *not* consider Finland for holidays.
- Motives don't differ very much from the other holiday-takers'.
- For 27 of them a holiday in Finland is (very) attractive.
- 22 of them want to go again to Finland for holidays.

IV
Halifax Exhaust Systems Ltd
P. Doyle

HES manufacture car exhaust systems. Purchasers of exhausts include car manufacturers, garages and large fleet operators. Currently HES sell 350,000 units in the UK, largely through distributors to garages. In recent years it had also built up a small export business in Holland and France accounting for another 50,000 units. Its ex-factory price averages £3 per unit both to UK and overseas distributors.

After a visit to Sweden by the Marketing Director, HES received an enquiry from Volvo on whether they would deliver 50,000 units at an f.o.b. price currently equivalent to £2.20 sterling. The Managing Director was totally against taking this order since the price left no margin for profit. Unit cost of goods sold, he pointed out in the income statement, amounted to £2.25. The Marketing Director, on the other hand, argued that the financial press were almost unanimous that sterling was overvalued, and that a 10% slide in the pound against the kroner would make the order highly profitable and fill up the unused capacity in the factory.

Assess HES current financial position and make a recommendation on the Volvo order.

Prepared by Professor Peter Doyle, Bradford University.

		£000	
Net Sales (400,000 units at £3)		£1,200	
Cost of goods sold			
Direct Materials	£250		
Direct Labour	350		
Manufacture Overhead	300		
		900	
Gross Profit Margin		£ 300	(25%)
Less: Operating Expenses			
Selling Expenses	£128		
General and Administration	100		
Net Profit before Taxes		£ 72	(6%)

Exhibit 4.1: HES Income Statement

£000

Current Assets			Current Liabilities		
Inventory	£250		Accounts		
Accounts			Payable	£110	
Receivable	100		Notes Payable	100	
Other	50		Other	90	
		£ 400			£ 300
Fixed Assets			Long Term Liabilities		£ 300
Buildings	£300		Net worth:		
Equipment	300		Common Stock	£200	
			Retained earnings	200	
		£ 600			£ 400
TOTAL		£1,000	TOTAL		£1,000

Exhibit 4.2: HES Balance Sheet

	£000	
	£000	
Sales (400,000 at £3)	£1,200	
Variable costs:		
Trade discounts	15	
Commissions	10	
Labour	350	
Materials	250	
Manufacturing O/H	35	
Total Variable Costs	660	
PROFIT CONTRIBUTION	540	45%
Specific Product Expenses		
Programme costs:		
Advertising	10	
Promotion	13	
Selling	80	
Standby costs:		
Product Management	100	
Overhead	165	
Total Specific Expenses	368	
PRODUCT EARNINGS	172	14%
General Expenses		
Programme	20	
Standby	80	
Total General Expenses	100	
Total Fixed Costs	468	
NET PROFIT	72	6%

Exhibit 4.3: HES Variable Budget

Problems on HES

1   How many units does it have to sell to break even?
2   How much (£ sales) does it have to sell to break even?
3   What is the safety-factor?
4   Next year inflation is expected to push up variable labour and materials costs by 15%. What impact will this have on the safety factor?
5   What is break-even in units and sales if HES drops its average price by 10%?
6   What is it at a price up by 10%?
7   How many units does it have to sell at £3.30 to make the same budgeted profit?
8   How much sales (£) does it have to make at a price of £2.70 to make the same profit as budget?
9   HES has as a long-run profit objective to improve the net profit margin to 10%. What turnover is necessary to achieve that result?
10   Adding a top salesman would cost £15,000. You estimate he could increase sales by 5%. Should you hire him?
11   Is there a case for doubling the advertising and promotional budget?
12   What level of sales is needed to maintain budgeted profits if the following changes are introduced simultaneously:

(a)   advertising and promotion increased by £20,000
(b)   variable labour costs are cut by 10%
(c)   a new salesman is hired for £15,000?

13   Should you take the Volvo order?

V
Causeway Engineering Ltd
P. Doyle

Causeway Engineering had an annual turnover of £38 million generated from four product lines. Each line contained a number of closely related products.

Line A was the company's original product line. This was a group of standard non-differentiated electric components. Over the years, the market for this type of component had been declining as technologically more advanced systems had been introduced. Causeway was now left with a small and declining core of traditional buyers.

Line B, a specialist line of cable fittings, was the next oldest group of products. Although growth in this market too was now negligible, Causeway held a leading position with most of the larger buyers in this field.

Line C was an advanced engineering device developed by Causeway some six years ago. Sales had built up rapidly and though there was increasing competition, a volume expansion of 15% was anticipated over the coming year.

Line D was the most recent introduction. A high value product developed by the Company's own research staff, it was regarded as a potential 'real winner' for the Company. The market was expected to be large, perhaps £60 million per annum, and Causeway were encouraged by early buying interest.

Management kept the profitability of all products under review. Exhibit 5.1 shows the data presented to management by the Chief Accountant. Here the cost of goods sold included manufacturing overheads allocated in proportion to direct labour costs. Selling expenses were allocated at 10% of sales. Exhibits 5.2 and 5.3 show

Prepared by Professor Peter Doyle, Bradford University.

the profitability of the product mix using a variable budget system. Currently, all sales are in the UK, but recently a Dutch distributor had offered to buy £1.5 million of line D, over a 12 month period, at Causeway's current trade price (c.i.f.). However when Causeway looked at shipping and insurance costs, these amounted to £300,000, completely eliminating the gross profit on the business.

1 Discuss the limitations of Exhibit 5.1 as a control system.
2 Evaluate the product mix.
3 Assess the Dutch proposition.

Product		Sales	Cost of goods sold	Gross Profit	Selling & Admin. Expenses	Net Profit
	A1	2,200	1,829	371	371	0
	A2	2,000	1,666	334	374	−40
	A3	500	555	−55	25	−80
	A4	200	200	0	20	−20
	A5	100	100	0	10	−10
Total	A	5,000	4,350	650	800	−150
	B1	6,500	4,784	1,716	929	787
	B2	6,000	4,623	1,377	856	521
	B3	1,300	1,260	40	186	−146
	B4	200	133	67	29	38
Total	B	14,000	10,800	3,200	2,000	1,200
	C1	8,000	5,694	2,306	1,333	973
	C2	2,000	1,580	420	333	87
	C3	1,500	1,386	114	250	−136
	C4	500	340	160	84	76
Total	C	12,000	9,000	3,000	2,000	1,000
	D1	4,000	3,184	816	697	119
	D2	2,000	1,684	316	349	−33
	D3	1,000	732	268	174	94
Total	D	7,000	5,600	1,400	1,220	180
Total		38,000	29,750	8,250	6,020	2,230

Exhibit 5.1: Summary of Product Profitability (£000)

Product	A	B	C	D	Total
Sales	5,000	14,000	12,000	7,000	38,000
Variable costs:					
Labour	1,200	1,800	1,680	600	5,280
Materials	2,600	5,920	4,150	1,500	14,170
Manuf. and comm. OH	200	400	410	700	1,710
Total variable costs	4,000	8,120	6,240	2,800	21,160
Profit Contribution	1,000	5,880	5,760	4,200	16,840
% of Sales (PV)	20%	42%	48%	60%	44%
Specific programme costs:					
Advertising	200	560	480	400	1,640
Selling	280	380	400	300	1,360
Specific standby costs:					
Labour	600	2,680	2,360	1,700	7,340
Line management	50	60	60	30	200
Depreciation	20	500	610	670	1,800
Total specific costs	1,150	4,180	3,910	3,100	12,340
Product Earnings	−150	1,700	1,850	1,100	4,500
% of Sales	−3%	12%	15%	16%	12%
General programme costs					960
General standby costs					1,310
Total specific and general fixed costs					14,610
Net Profit					2,230
% of Sales					6%
Specific investment	4,000	12,000	9,000	11,000	36,000
Earnings of investment	−3.8%	14%	20%	10%	12%

(ROI = 6%)

Exhibit 5.2: Variable Line Budget (£000)

Product		Sales	Variable Costs	Contribution	PV	CFH* (£)
	A1	2,200	1,670	530	24.1	540
	A2	2,000	1,626	374	18.7	260
	A3	500	443	57	11.4	24
	A4	200	165	35	17.5	28
	A5	100	96	4	4.0	40
Total	A	5,000	4,000	1,000	20.0	200
	B1	6,500	3,616	2,884	44.4	1,545
	B2	6,000	3,624	2,376	39.6	1,034
	B3	1,300	752	548	42.2	400
	B4	200	128	72	36.0	40
Total	B	14,000	8,120	5,880	42.0	932
	C1	8,000	4,124	3,876	48.4	4,610
	C2	2,000	1,087	913	45.7	520
	C3	1,500	768	732	48.8	610
	C4	500	261	239	47.8	140
Total	C	12,000	6,240	5,760	48.0	980
	D1	4,000	1,587	2,413	60.3	2,810
	D2	2,000	840	1,160	58.0	1,276
	D3	1,000	373	627	62.7	800
Total	D	7,000	2,800	4,200	60.0	1,604
Total		38,000	21,160	16,840	44.3	920

* Contribution per hour of scarce facility

Exhibit 5.3: Summary of Product Contributions (£000)

Part B
Identifying International Marketing Opportunities

A company identifies a marketing opportunity when it sees a means of matching the actual or potential wants of buyers more effectively than competitors. It capitalizes on this opportunity by developing a marketing mix — product, price, promotion and method of distribution, which offers a differential advantage. That is, when it presents buyers with an offer which they will prefer to those of competitors.

There are three basic steps in this marketing process. First the business has to be able to appraise the market and segment it to determine which customer groups offer the most potential. Most markets are very heterogeneous and a central element in marketing success is the ability to. select target segments and develop strategies which match their requirements with precision. The second task is to research the needs and decision-making processes of buyers within the chosen target segment. Analysis of these features together with the structure of competition and distribution within the market forms the basis for developing a company's differential advantage. The final step is the organization of the business's total resources and skills to develop a marketing mix which incorporates this differential advantage and communicates it effectively to the target segment.

In international marketing these tasks are particularly difficult and therefore require thorough research and planning. One problem is that top management at head office have, generally, a much weaker understanding of overseas markets and their buying characteristics. This makes formal market research and the development of comprehensive market information systems especially important. Overseas markets are also very heterogeneous: a few may appear quite similar to the home market, but most will be very different. Such differences arise from the totally different economic, cultural and socio-political environments of these countries. They imply different types of market segmentation criteria, different customer wants and decision-making patterns, and different competitive and distribution structures. Sometimes different countries appear as snapshots taken at points of time over the product's life cycle. A company introducing a new product may find the market at the earliest stage of development in some countries, at the growth stage in others, while in affluent countries the market might have reached the maturity or decline stage. In such situations the company will obviously have to pursue quite different strategies for the product if it is going to be launched successfully.

Such international diversity and complexity mean that the international marketing executive must know what information is required for identifying problems and opportunities, where it can be obtained and how to analyse it. Long-term success in foreign markets is based upon thorough market research, comprehensive planning and decisive implementation and control.

VI
J. W. Thornton Ltd
P. Doyle

Developing a Retail Marketing Strategy

'Business is going great — I wish I knew why' laughed Peter Thornton, joint managing director of J. W. Thornton a leading manufacturer and retailer of high quality confectionery. Certainly there appeared reasons for his good humour; while the dismal economic situation in the United Kingdom was causing most retailers to show little volume growth and declining margins, four months into the financial year, Thornton's sales from their 148 shops were 4% up on budget and profits were even further ahead.

Nevertheless there were many decisions that needed to be taken on how to move the business forward. In particular, it was not obvious how many new stores the company should aim to open, whether franchising offered an effective method of long-term growth, or whether the company should seek to manufacture confectionery for a broader range of retailers at home and overseas. Further, while the current situation looked satisfactory, in the recent past it had appeared much less rosy and the directors felt that major mistakes had been made on pricing policy, advertising and overhead cost control which had significantly curtailed profit performance. The board of directors, in discussing these issues, had identified the need for a corporate strategy to provide a longer-term perspective than that of the annual budget. Mr Peter, as he was known in the company, had agreed and had offered to present

Prepared by Professor Peter Doyle, Bradford University. Some details on the company are disguised.

a paper for the next meeting outlining his ideas about the strategic direction for the business.

Company Background

The company was founded in 1911 by J. W. Thornton, who began making hard-boiled sweets in the coke stove in the basement of his shop in Sheffield. He was soon joined by his two sons, Norman and Stanley, who remain on the board to this day. In the years that followed, the company opened more shops and gradually expanded its product range. In 1925 the company's Special Toffee was developed; this is still the shops' best selling product. Another milestone was Stanley and Norman's decision to develop a really high quality range of chocolates. During a Continental holiday in 1953 the brothers visited the Basle school for Swiss Chocolatiers and recruited one of the top students. The result was the Thornton range of Continental Chocolates which now sells 600 tons annually. By 1939 Thorntons had expanded to 35 shops in the Midlands and North of England. Further rapid growth followed the end of confectionery rationing in 1952 and advertising and seasonal promotions gradually increased consumer awareness of the Thornton name. By 1980 the company had over 1,000 employees, two factories and 148 shops.

The company had always emphasized certain features. Most important was the commitment to product freshness and quality. Unwillingness to hazard the business's hard-won reputation in these areas accounted for management's long reluctance to sell confectionery outside their own shops despite many requests from interested retailers. This philosophy together with the desire to develop a distinctive specialist confectioner image also made them increasingly reluctant to buy products for their shops other than those produced from their factories. Bought-in goods (mainly greeting cards) now account for only 5% of shop turnover. A consequence was that the shops continued with a narrow range of products — three basic lines: chocolate, toffee and hard-boiled sweets account for over 90% of sales.

The company has continued to emphasize traditional values. The shops have changed relatively little over the years and there has been no major product introduction since the range of Continental Chocolates over twenty five years earlier. Advertising made much of the products being 'all made in the good old-fashioned way'. Finally, it remained very much a family business, all the shareholders and all eight members of the Board including president, chairman, the two managing directors and the company secretary were Thorntons. Hence the practice within the company of calling the directors Mr Tony, Mr Peter etc. was not just quaint; it was necessary.

After the mid-60s, Mr Norman's three sons Tony, Peter and John together with Mr Stanley's son Michael took an increasingly large part in running the business. In 1979, Peter and John became joint managing directors when Tony moved up from managing director to chairman. Previously both Peter and John had shared responsibility for the manufacturing side of the business. Under the new structure Peter's main sphere of responsibility covered marketing and retail, and John looked after manufacturing and product development. Stanley and Norman remained on the board as president and consultant respectively.

Until the mid-70s the company had seen almost uninterrupted progress (see Exhibit 6.2). Probably the peak year was 1973, when the company earned a pre-tax margin of 16% and a return on net worth of 44%. Then, as for many other retailers, business became more difficult as the slower growth of consumer expenditure and the rapid rise in inflation hit margins and cash flow.

Retailing in the United Kingdom

The postwar years saw remarkable changes in the pattern of retailing in the UK. A number of forces created the stimuli for change. Car registrations grew from 2¼ million in 1950 to 13½ million in 1973, when the majority of households had a car which both increased their mobility and enabled them to carry more shopping in one trip. A second feature was the dispersal of population from major towns. While the drift to the suburbs was less dramatic than in the USA, it did result in a noticeable shift in retail buying power from the inner urban areas to the outer suburbs.

A third factor was the rise in female employment, which increased the pressure for longer shop opening hours and for facilities for shopping with the family. Finally, the overall level of spending rose sharply as a result of both a larger population and, more importantly, rising income levels. Real disposable income doubled between 1950 and 1980.

The most important responses to these stimuli were:

1 The growth of self service across many sectors of retailing. Self

service offered savings both to the retailer and the shopper. In food, for example, supermarkets increased from only 500 in 1950 to over 30,000 in 1973.

2 A trend towards fewer, larger shops. The total number of food shops, for example, fell by over a half between 1960–80 but the development of self service in particular meant that on average the newer shops had much larger floorspace.

3 Economies of scale in buying and marketing led to increased concentration in retailing. The major multiples increased their share of trade at the expense of independent shops in all sectors of retailing.

4 A consequence of this greater retailing concentration was increasing bargaining power over manufacturers. Manufacturers' margins were squeezed as the larger retailers demanded own brands and larger discounts.

5 The extension of intertype retailing competition or 'scrambled merchandising'. Retailers sought to strengthen their margins by broadening their merchandise assortments. Food retailers diversified into non-foods, and non-food businesses added on food lines.

6 The development of out-of-town retailing and the growth of new types of shops such as superstores, hypermarkets, discount stores and catalogue showrooms. Many innovations took place during this period and grew rapidly at the expense of retailers which had reached the maturity stage of the institutional life cycle.

7 Working wives, greater car ownership and new types of mass merchandising encouraged the trend towards once weekly one-stop shopping, increasingly at the large suburban superstore with ample parking.

After 1973, competition in retailing toughened noticeably and retailers' profit margins halved between 1973 and 1980. The causes were the stagnation in consumer spending after 1973 and the rapid escalation in inflation. Larger retailers responded to the lack of market growth by price cutting to expand or maintain market shares, pressuring manufacturers even further for discounts and financial support, and boosting advertising budgets in an effort to strengthen the competitive position of their shops. During this period, independent retailers had great difficulty in surviving and several major retail groups ran into difficulties as they were squeezed by newer and more aggressive forms of retailing.

The Confectionery Market

British confectionery consumption per capita at almost 8½ ounces per week is the highest in the world. The British eat twice as much as the Americans and French and four times as much as the Italians. Retail sales in 1980 exceeded £2000 million and amounted to over 700,000 tons. The market is divided about equally in tonnage terms between chocolate and sugar confectionery though chocolate's price makes that sector twice as valuable. Since 1960 there has been little difference in the volume or value growth rates between the two sectors. A more detailed breakdown is given in Exhibit 6.3.

While the market has trebled in money terms between 1970 and 1980 there has been little volume growth, volume in 1980 is still marginally below the 1973 peak of 717 thousand tons. This lack of growth is blamed on the recession, the sharp rise in cocoa and sugar prices and the imposition of Value Added Tax (VAT) of 8% in 1974 rising to 15% in 1979. Unlike the US, where consumption had been declining for many years, there was little evidence that diet or dental concerns were significantly affecting the market.

Confectionery manufacturing is fairly concentrated. Seven companies account for 52% of sales strongly biased towards chocolate, while over 200 companies fight for the remaining 48% biased towards sugar. Cadburys, Rowntree Mackintosh and Mars are the three leading groups. Competition is fierce in advertising and brand development especially in the filled chocolate bar/count line segment, the most buoyant and valuable sector of the whole confectionery market in recent years. Around £40 million was spent on advertising in 1980, making confectionery the most highly advertising of all product groups. There are many brands – the top forty account for about 40% of the market. Other than Thorntons (which ranks about 16th) no major manufacturer is integrated foward into retailing.

Distribution of confectionery is extremely wide through a great variety of retailing outlets. The main channel, however, is still the mass of largely independent small confectioner/tobacconist/ newsagents (CTNs). Around 45,000 of these account for 38% of confectionery sales. But the number of CTNs has declined sharply in recent years and their share of confectionery sales has dropped from 55% in 1960. Increasingly important are the large grocery supermarkets and superstores which have expanded their confectionery share from 20 to 32% since 1960. Other important outlets are cinemas, department stores and variety chains.

Women are the main purchasers of confectionery, although children are the largest *per capita* consumers especially in sugar. Women buy about 67%, men 20% and children 13%. 50% of purchases are made on Fridays and Saturdays. The average amount spent on each purchase occasion was about 33p in 1980. The gift market is very important, especially for Christmas, Easter and Mother's Day. About 40% of spending is for gifts, mainly women for children and secondly by men for women. A recent survey shows that among adult 'heavy users' of confectionery women consume more than men and that they are predominantly in the lower (C2D) income groups. (Survey researchers classify households and adults by social class. Broadly, A refers to upper middle class households — 3% of all households; B middle class — 13%; Cl lower middle — 22%; C2 skilled working class — 33%; D working class — 21%; E lowest levels of income — 8%.)

Thorntons' Channels and Products

The company now had 148 shops controlled by a sales manager supervising sixteen area manageresses. While in recent years shops had been opened in Scotland and the South of England, the majority of them were in the Midlands and North of England. Virtually all shops were in the town centre shopping areas. Most of the shops were very small, the majority having under 300 square feet of selling space although the company had tried to open somewhat larger units in recent years. The shops were not self service and queuing was a significant problem at peak periods. In 1980 the average turnover per shop was £110,000, though some of the better shops were doing two or three times this figure.

After 1974, under Mr Tony's lead, the company began to sell its confectionery through other shops. The real stimulus for this change in direction was the alarming rise in high street shop rents which, if continued, threatened to make many of Thornton's shops unprofitable. The most significant move was the decision to allow other shops (generally small CTNs) to sell Thornton's confectionery as part of their range on a franchise basis. In return for a small fee, franchisees could buy from Thorntons at 25% off retail price. During its first five years, franchising showed considerable growth (see Exhibit 6.4). Currently there were 45 shops with a Thornton franchise. The second important development was the request by Marks and Spencer, Britain's most successful variety store group, to sell Thornton's chocolate under its own private label. Currently this exceeded £800,000 in sales. Besides franchising and Marks and Spencer, small amounts were sold to a few other UK multiples and some £167,000 worth was exported to distributors in fourteen countries overseas.

Thorntons were represented in product groups representing only about one-third of the chocolate market (mainly assortments, straight lines and Easter eggs etc.) and about two-thirds of the sugar market (boiled, toffee and jellies etc.). In particular, they were not represented in 'count lines' and filled chocolate bars which made up the most valuable segment of the chocolate market. Besides confectionery the shops sold small amounts of bought-in greeting cards (£500,000 in 1979–80) and ice cream (£200,000). Percentage value added averaged 60 for sugar confectionery, 57 for chocolate, 50 for cards and 30 for ice cream.

The Thorntons Consumer

When Mr Peter took over responsibility for the marketing operation in 1979 his lack of experience was balanced by an enthusiasm to get the business moving ahead again. He was critical that many important decisions had been neglected in the past due to differences of opinion and priorities on the board. In an early memorandum he said that product standards had dropped, production convenience was taking precedence over marketing needs, shortages at peak times were losing business, and shop display, hygiene and stock control standards were all declining due to insufficient investment in shop-fitting and management.

Peter inherited Tucker Advertising, a Manchester advertising agency appointed by Mr Tony some months earlier. The agency convinced Peter of the need to undertake some research into Thorntons consumers and the confectionery market before a marketing strategy could be developed. Until then the company had undertaken little market research. But from Tucker's research and that conducted by the two agencies succeeding it, a fairly complete picture had been developed.

The main research findings were:

1 In socioeconomic terms, the Thorntons shopper profile was close to the average profile of confectionery buyers: AB 15%, C1 26%, C2 38%, D 18%, E 3%.

2 In areas where Thorntons have shops, 71% of confectionery eaters shop at Thorntons at least occasionally. The average expenditure per shopper was 70—99 pence in October 1978, rather higher for the AB socioeconomic group.

3 Thorntons' shoppers have very positive attitudes to the shops. A sample of 544 Thornton shoppers found 42% mentioning product quality as the most attractive feature, 21% good service and 11% window displays. Only 20% of respondents could think of anything unattractive about the shops.   Of the negative responses 'too small' and 'queueing' were most frequently mentioned.

4 Price did not appear a problem. Respondents thought generally that Thorntons were a little more expensive but they believed the products to be of higher quality and good value for money. This was especially true of chocolate, but boiled sweets were seen as neither more expensive nor of better quality than elsewhere. Chocolate and toffee were seen as of very good value by over 90% of Thornton shoppers.

5 Most Thornton customers buy more confectionery from other outlets than Thorntons. As the agency noted this is not surprising. 'However good the product and reputation, however conveniently located the outlets, Thorntons account for a tiny proportion of confectionery distribution. When heavily advertised, well-established products are available at the checkout of a supermarket that Thornton's customers have to visit to buy groceries, it is not surprising that they purchase competitive brands. Customers typically buy a wide range of confectionery from a variety of outlets.' Thorntons 148 shops compete with 127,000 other outlets selling confectionery!

6 Non-Thornton customers appeared to be much younger, often to be heavy confectionery eaters, especially of count lines (i.e. market leaders like Mars Bars, Kit-Kat, Yorkie), and to be more down-market. Thorntons products appeared to appeal to older consumers, especially women.

7 Gift purchasing is very important in confectionery, especially for boxes of chocolates. The majority of boxed chocolates are bought for family or friends. Self-consumption is more frequently the purchase motive for loose chocolates, toffee and boiled sweets. Toffees and boiled sweets are the most favoured purchases for children.

The advertising agencies came up with various proposals from their research findings. Tucker Advertising recommended targeting

on ClC2D housewives aged over 25, focusing on increasing awareness of Thornton's traditional product quality. Penelope Keith,
a well-known television comedy actress, was used in humorous TV
and radio commercials to communicate the product benefits. Beau-
mont, Robock and King (BRK), a leading London agency which
won the account early in 1979 defined the primary target as the
'heavy confectionery purchaser' who was female, aged 16—34,
in the (C2DE) groups with 2—3 children and whose life-style might
be summarized as 'laugh and grow fat'. Their creative approach was
again humorous and traditional, based around singing confectionery
workers at Thornton's factory. The creative proposition was aimed
at expressing Thornton's shop as a 'treasure trove' of high quality
confectionery and 'a family firm making your family favourites'.
The Cundiff Partnership, a small London agency which gained the
account in mid-1980 decided to target on 'medium' confectionery
buyers who were younger and more up-market (ABClC2) than the
typical Thornton consumer. Creatively they concentrated on telling
straightforward product quality stories about the brands and linking
with main gift-giving occasions such as Christmas and Easter.

Thornton's Marketing Organization

In 1978 Mr Tony asked Dr John Riley, a professor of business
administration at a local university, to take an overall look at the
company's operation. In his report he showed that profitability had
declined significantly since 1970. He argued that this was due
mainly to external factors: little market growth; the changing pattern
of retailing and high rates of inflation eroding margins. But he also
suggested the problem had been worsened by management cutting
back on marketing investments, falling shop volume and a switch
in the product mix towards less profitable items. On the positive
side he noted the remarkable growth of franchising, the success of
continental chocolates, good cost control and the margin protection
the shops offered ('unlike other manufacturers, Thorntons are not
easily squeezed by the buying power of the major retail groups').
Mr Peter accepted most of the points in the Riley report and
was intent to attack these problems quickly. One difficulty he
faced immediately was the lack of retail experience of his two
senior managers, Joe Royston, the marketing manager, and Len
Andrews, the sales manager. After much exasperation with his

inability to get information and implementation from his marketing and sales people he hired a retail manager, Colin Shaw, in June 1980. The new man was not a retailer but Peter felt that he was young and bright and that his experience in brand management would be very valuable. Andrews resigned around the same time and Peter was hoping to find an experienced successor quickly.

Dr Riley also drew attention to the need to improve the management information and planning procedures. Peter agreed that most of the information the directors receive is still production-oriented. A vast amount of information was available on manufacturing costs and standards but it was not easy to determine the sales and profit performance trends of the products, channels of distribution, and shops. Evaluating price and promotional changes on different parts of the business was virtually impossible. One of the problems, he felt, was forcing the accounting department to give a greater priority to providing better information.

Thorntons had never undertaken formal, longer-term planning. In recent years however the accountant had developed a useful, annual budget for them, although it often did not appear until a few months into the financial year (beginning June 1st). Another problem was that sales appeared as a residual rather than an output from a marketing forecast. Generally, overhead costs for the forthcoming year were taken as 'given', target net and gross profits were then agreed by the board, and turnover was subsequently defined as that level needed to balance these assumptions. It was perhaps not surprising that the sales volume figures generally proved optimistic. In the 1979–80 financial year this budgeting procedure had, however, produced more serious consequences (see Exhibit 6.5). Overhead costs in the budget had been allowed to escalate by a heavy commitment to advertising and a decision to introduce a new layer of management to strengthen the manufacturing team, but the level of sales needed to meet these costs proved to be much too high and net profit suffered severely. The directors were determined not to let this mistake be repeated and in future they were sure that budgeted cost increases would be checked by realistic or even pessimistic budget sales forecasts.

Marketing Policy

In thinking about the longer term, Peter felt that there were a number of areas where fundamental decisions needed to be made. Getting these choices right would determine whether the business would have a successful future or not.

Shop Policy

This was perhaps the area where the most crucial decisions were needed. There were a number of obvious questions. Should Thorntons continue to see the shops as providing the vast majority of sales and profits? How many shops should they have? Where should the shops be located? What 'image' should the shops aim to present to the public? Peter initially concluded that their own shops should be the dominant form of growth rather than outside sales. He argued, 'in this age of the superstore and self-service with impersonal indifference, there is a demand for a specialist with a unique proposition. We are in a position to fill this role with our unique business. We have a fine manufacturing plant, involved people, high street sites and quality products to build on'. He argued for opening as many shops as the company could afford, probably 10–20 a year.

Another area of concern was the shop image. Several observers believed that the stores were not right and that their appearance was confusing, lacking in impact and old fashioned. Over the years the board had experimented with various piecemeal modifications to layout and window display but there had been no real fundamental changes for many years. Worse, many of the older shops were now much in need of refitting and modernization. Peter, influenced by the successful remodelling ventures of a number of leading British retailers, became convinced that Thornton's shops needed a comprehensive repositioning guided by experts. After interviewing all the top retail designers he commissioned Fitch and Company, the largest and most experienced of these organizations, to develop a complete shop redesign and corporate identity programme for the group. Fitch's past clients included many of Britain's largest and most successful retail organizations. In October 1979 Fitch produced their models which proposed to completely redesign the shops, merchandising methods, packaging and company image. A programme for implementing these changes at a cost of about £25,000 per shop was also defined in detail.

During the following six months, experience and changed circumstances led to some rethinking. One problem was that sales and profit were less buoyant than expected. Another was that rising costs of rents and staff, and the failure of the advertising campaign to boost shop volume, made the race to open new shops look very risky. In particular, the shops opened in new types of off-centre locations — at the Tesco, Carrefour and Fine Fare hypermarket complexes for example — proved highly disappointing. Finally, there was the view on the board that while the Fitch proposals contained some good ideas, the complete shop redesign they proposed was really not the type of atmosphere that would appeal to Thornton's traditional customers.

Franchise

Both Tony and Peter were less than enthusiastic about the Thornton franchise operation and in 1978 they agreed to halt further growth despite many requests for franchises. All the franchisees were independent CTN shops which sold Thorntons lines as a part of their general ranges of tobacco, newspapers, other confectionery and miscellaneous merchandise. The board felt these outlets generally failed to display the products properly and kept stock for too long, so threatening Thornton's quality image as well as losing its exclusivity. Finally franchised confectionery offered a lower gross margin than that through their own shops.

But both felt that now this attitude should be reconsidered. Average shop volume was slipping marginally nearly every year. Further, Dr Riley had pointed out that while the gross margin was higher from throughput in their own shops, when average shop operating costs were allowed for the margin on franchise sales appeared to be at least as good. A report the directors had received the previous week from Mr Michael and the company accountant supported this analysis. Their analysis estimated the gross and net trading margins as follows:

	Gross Margin (%)	Trading Profit (%)
Thornton shops	55	6
Franchise sales	45	14

Continued

	Gross Margin (%)	Trading Profit (%)
Marks and Spencer	37	7
Other home sales	35	3
Export sales	33	−6

Two other points also counted. First, their franchise operation had developed too fast and without proper understanding of the problems involved. The directors felt they now had the experience to develop a much better control system which would overcome many of the past weaknesses. Second, with only 45 franchises there was undoubtedly vast sales growth potential.

Marks and Spencer

With 255 stores in the UK and a turnover approaching £2,000 million, Marks and Spencer is generally regarded as one of Britain's best-managed retailers. Since 1975 its business had become very important to Thorntons. M & S merchandising policy was based on developing very close, durable relationships with a small number of high quality British manufacturers in each product field. Manufacturers produced, to M & S's exacting quality standards, exclusive products sold under the 'St Michael' brand name. Thorntons were approached when M & S diversified into food and confectionery in the mid-1970s. In 1979—80 M & S purchased around £870,000 of Thornton's boxed chocolates and was also beginning to take Special Toffee and fudge on a trial basis.

Tony and Peter had always been hesitant about the M & S business. One reason was that the mark-up M & S required, exceeding 25%, meant it was a lower gross margin business for Thorntons. The profitability of the whole business was affected too, they believed, because M & S were reluctant to accept price increases not justified by corresponding manufacturers' cost increases. This was making it difficult to increase margins and since Thorntons were not willing to be undercut in prices by M & S the whole of Thornton's margin was held back. There were also strategic issues. M & S offered such large potential that Thorntons might risk becoming too dependent upon them in the future. In addition, the directors asked, what is the differential advantage of a Thornton shop if the customer can buy its confectionery at Marks? M & S also interfered with Thornton's flexibility in other directions. They were unwilling to allow it to sell the products M & S bought to competitive retailers, severely limiting diversification options, although it was possible this objection could be overcome by introducing minor product differences which could differentiate the M & S range.   Finally M & S made life difficult for the factory: they could cancel or significantly increase orders with little notice. For example, 1978—79, M & S purchases dropped substantially when for tax reasons they ceased to supply their Canadian stores with Thorntons confectionery.   Finally, M & S orders were generally at peak times when capacity was already fully stretched. Nevertheless, in 1980—81 M & S orders were expected to top £1 million.

Export and Other Commercial Sales

The board believed there were many other exciting growth opportunities.   In 1979—80 they exported some £167,000 of products to fourteen countries mainly through overseas distributors.   While the volume was small, with sufficient management attention they felt it was possible to achieve major expansion, perhaps through overseas franchising.   Thorntons toffee and chocolate had gained much favourable comment, many enquiries from interested buyers, and a number of prizes for quality at international confectionery exhibitions over the years.   The board felt that in many overseas markets Thorntons confectionery could offer a unique combination of very high quality at prices which were affordable by the average consumer.

   At home too, many enquiries came into Thorntons from department stores, supermarkets and other retailers interested in the lines.   In recent years small businesses had been built up with a few retail groups, the largest being the Waitrose supermarket group which in the last year had bought £70,000 of fudge and chocolates for sale under the Waitrose label.   The Marks and Spencer constraint and the board's doubts about whether this was the right direction had restricted growth in this direction.   Finally in the last year, mainly under the enthusiastic direction of Joe Royston, Thorntons had begun selling by mail order, sales reaching around £4,000 over the period.

Product Policy

On reflection Peter admitted that what Thorntons sold was largely based on tradition ('what we have always sold') and what the factory people thought they could produce, rather than on much considera-tion of market opportunities. But even without a changed strategy the market was shifting the nature of Thornton's business. In recent years it had become much more a chocolate and gift retailer. Volume sales of chocolate through the shops had increased by 40% since 1970 while sugar confectionery had dropped by over 10%. The highest growth was in boxed chocolates which had almost doubled over the decade; the weakest area was the traditional boiled sweet which had almost halved (Exhibit 6.6). Chocolate now repre-sented 43% of retail volume and over 61% of sterling value.

This change had not helped profits. Hard-boiled sweets in parti-cular had high profit margins and a relatively low cost of sales. Further, the new growth areas that had compensated (i.e. chocolate boxes) had required additional investment which adversely affected return on assets and net profit. But there was probably little that could be done since Thorntons hard-boiled, unlike its chocolate, had few distinctive features and the factory could not compete in unit cost with the large modern facilities of the major competitors.

Tony and Peter spent considerable time thinking about what products the shops should carry and 'what business are we in'. But defining the customer 'need' or 'want' Thorntons served in opera-tional terms was not easy. The shops had sold at various times cigarettes, lemonade and more recently greeting cards and ice cream. But the current view was that such extensions were inconsistent with the image of a unique specialist that Thorntons wished to create. However, they did not rule out certain complementary lines (e.g. cakes) in the future. Another possibility was broadening the confectionery lines carried by adding bought-in ranges to com-plement their own products. This had not been done in the past, Peter said, partly because there was a tendency in the company for the shops to be seen as an outlet for the factory.

Mr John Thornton had a committee which met on a regular basis to consider new product development in the factory. Thornton's past advertising agencies had been eager to push the company into producing a count line or filled chocolate bar like Yorkie or Cad-bury's Fruit and Nut to compete in those sectors representing up to 50% of the chocolate market and where Thorntons were unrepresented. But Thorntons felt this was unrealistic since these often massively advertised products relied for their sales on virtually universal distribution and impulse purchasing. However, Thorntons were thinking about new lines. Additions and replacement items to the basic ranges of boiled sweets, toffee and chocolates were being made continually. Up to twelve different centres or flavours might be introduced in a year. Four years ago 'Traditional Assortment' had been introduced on a trial basis. This was a new range of super quality, hand-finished chocolates selling at almost twice the price per pound of the Continental range. This was now in some 40 shops and generated a turnover last year of around £100,000. Other items on trial included additions to the children's confectionery lines and a small range of confectionery for diabetics.

Price Policy

Like other retailers, Thornton's margins had been hit by the acceleration of inflation after 1973 and government price controls. But now they believed margins were under much better control. Peter said pricing strategy was based on the recognition that Thorntons were high-priced shops (e.g. a half pound box of Continental was around 20% more expensive than a box of best selling Cadbury's Dairy Milk) but that the consumer recognized their superior quality and this allowed them to be perceived as good value for money. On the other hand, he believed that where their products were not unique they must be priced competitively. Recent experience, he believed, had proved this view. Continentals had been unaffected by fairly steep price increases whereas boiled sweets had shown impressive volume gains after a price cut. Although he admitted that fudge had not shown a similar increase after the same policy had been applied.

Advertising and Promotion

During his first twelve months as managing director, Peter had spent an enormous amount of time with the advertising agency attempting to formulate a decisive marketing and advertising campaign. Between 1975 and 1978 Thorntons had tried to hold up net profit margins by restricting the growth of advertising and promotional expenditures. On taking over, Peter had felt this lack of investment had been a material cause of Thorntons recent sluggish performance.

In 1979 Peter appointed BRK a large London advertising agency to handle the account. The advertising budget was trebled to over £500,000 and BRK developed a campaign employing television and a wide range of media to boost Thorntons image as a traditional and special type of confectionery shop. But the results were disappointing and net profit was severely affected. In 1980 Peter began a serious reconsideration of advertising's role in the business.

He felt that a business of Thornton's size could not compete in advertising terms with Cadburys or Rowntrees which spent over £1 million supporting an individual brand. He also felt that broad 'image' advertising for Thorntons was not the way. Instead he believed that advertising should be tailored to support Thornton's brands with the strongest identity — Special Toffee and Continental Chocolates — and to help build new ones.

A new agency, the Cundiff Partnership, was appointed in mid-1980 with a much reduced budget. Local radio was chosen as the prime medium on cost efficiency grounds with local press as a 'top up'. Advertising was targeted around the main gift seasons — Christmas, St Valentines Day, Mother's Day and Easter. In addition a Special Toffee promotion was scheduled for October 1980 to re-stimulate volume. (Examples of Cundiff's advertising are shown in Exhibits 6.8 and 6.9.)

With his new retail manager, Colin Shaw, Peter was also seeking to strengthen Thornton's public relations. They had retained the services of a local PR consultant at a reasonable fee and they were also considering retaining Harry Shepherd's new PR consultancy in London. Mr Shepherd had worked for thirty years as head of PR at Marks and Spencer and had recently resigned to start his own business. Peter felt that they were now on the right track as far as advertising and PR were concerned.

Marketing and Organization

The directors were fairly happy with the current situation. Important decisions were being taken and there were some favourable features in the environment. For example, while in the late 70s they had been squeezed by rising commodity prices, cocoa was now trading at record lows. This year the price had dropped by £400 a ton and since Thorntons were buying 1,000 tons annually, this was having a significant effect on profitability.

Besides changes in marketing strategy, Tony and Peter knew that changes in marketing organization were also needed. Currently,

Colin Shaw was retail manager looking after advertising and promotion, Joe Royston was now responsible for exports, Marks and Spencer, franchise and other home sales, and a new sales manager responsible for the shops was to be appointed. The last was felt to be particularly important since there was much to do in the area of sales control and supervision. Training was poor and the manuals detailing expected behaviour from retail staff were now out of date and not used. Peter knew from experience that strategy would never be implemented properly without the right people and organization.

Year	Retail Sales	Sales of CTNs[1]	Company Profits[2]	Cost of Living Index
1970	100	100	100	100
1971	108	107	113	109
1972	133	121	126	117
1973	151	131	150	128
1974	175	155	160	148
1975	208	191	171	184
1976	238	223	219	213
1977	271	257	265	251
1978	310	285	300	274
1979	345	297	379	311
1980	389	351	468	360

[1] Retail sales of confectioners, tobacconists and newspaper shops.
[2] Before providing for depreciation and stock appreciation.

Source: UK Annual Abstract of Statistics

Exhibit 6.1: Some General UK Economic Indicators 1970–1980

Financial Year	Sales £000 (ex VAT)	Gross Profit	Pretax Net Profit	Total Assets[1]	Stockholders' Funds	No. of Shops
1969/70	2,262	1,240	237	1,218	809	107
1970/71	2,222	1,177	270	1,305	885	110
1971/72	2,783	1,517	336	1,503	1,043	122
1972/73	3,461	1,869	544	1,896	1,241	126
1973/74	4,270	2,263	581	2,373	1,488	130
1974/75	5,653	2,802	576	2,931	1,735	128
1975/76	7,091	3,824	709	3,425	2,002	130
1976/77	8,821	4,455	552	4,228	2,217	130
1977/78	10,887	5,532	704	4,749	2,661	132
1978/79	12,826	6,714	946	6,201	2,594	138
1979/80	15,551	8,360	668	7,515	3,113	148

[1] Assets valued on historic cost basis

Source: Annual Reports

Exhibit 6.2: J. W. Thornton Ltd Selected Performance Data (£000)

| | 000 tons | | |
	1974	1977	1979
Chocolate			
Milk chocolate bars with fruit, nuts etc.	27	15	18
Plain chocolate bars	47	40	38
Filled bars with various centres[1]	153	159	186
Chocolate assortments (inc. boxes)	65	51	51
Straight lines	51	47	47
Easter eggs/novelties	18	20	21
Total	361	332	361
Sugar			
Hard boiled	95	87	75
Toffee, caramel and fudge	66	75	68
Gums, jellies, pastilles	41	42	41
Liquorice	20	18	16
Chewing gum	15	16	14
Medicated	13	12	8
Other	78	71	72
Total	328	328	294

[1] Including count lines (items sold for individual consumption rather than by weight or quantity e.g. Kit Kat, Mars Bar).

[2] UK sales by UK manufacturers only. Approximately an additional 50 tons of confectionery were imported in 1979.

Source: Cocoa, Chocolate and Confectionery Alliance

Exhibit 6.3: UK Confectionery Tonnage by Product Group 1974–9[2]

Financial Year	Thornton Shops	Franchise	Marks & Spencer	Other Chains	Export
1974/75	6,049	1	3	3	3
1975/76	7,203	92	255	136	11
1976/77	8,351	392	661	167	24
1977/78	9,933	1,002	636	172	149
1978/79	11,845	1,303	462	205	184
1979/80	14,753	1,259	868	205	167

Exhibit 6.4: J. W. Thornton Ltd Sales by Selected Channels of Distribution (inc. VAT) (£000)

	Actual 1978/79	Actual 1979/80	Budget 1980/81
Sales (ex. VAT)	12,826	15,551	18,250
Direct costs	6,112	7,191	8,760
Gross profit	6,714	8,360	9,490
Wages and salaries	2,947	3,942	4,335
Pension scheme	94	116	125
Distribution	266	321	404
Repairs	354	405	460
Rent and rates	625	821	1,000
Post, telephone, travel	166	240	267
Power	225	294	343
Legal and finance charges	242	307	284
Advertising	153	503	253
Display	48	52	53
Miscellaneous	90	147	149
Depreciation	508	553	650
Total trading overheads	5,718	7,701	8,323
Trading profit	996	659	1,167
Non-trading net income (expense)	(50)	9	(26)
Pre Tax profit	946	668	1,141

Exhibit 6.5: J. W. Thornton Ltd Income Statement and
Budget 1980—81 (£000)

	tons			
	1974	1977	1979	1980
Chocolate				
Boxed chocolates	523	566	704	773
Continental — loose	241	250	282	279
Other chocolate — loose	567	458	489	491
Easter eggs, novelties	79	74	94	127
Mis-shapes	124	159	99	78
Total	1,534	1,507	1,668	1,748
Average price per ton	£1,850	£2,603	£3,884	£4,660
Sugar				
Hard boiled	620	529	421	409
Toffee	1,619	1,481	1,551	1,396
Fudge	185	190	219	179
Jellies	92	75	67	80
Total	2,516	2,275	2,258	2,064
Average price per ton	£1,031	£1,473	£1,862	£2,141

[1] Thornton shops only. Sales through other outlets amounted to 927 tons in 1980 (see Table 6.7).

Exhibit 6.6: Thornton Shops: Confectionery Tonnage by Product Groups 1974–80[1]

	tons				
	Shops	*Franchise*	*M & S*	*Other*	*Export*
Chocolates					
boxed	773	145	183	25	28
other	975	115	50	15	16
Hard Boiled	409	80	0	16	13
Toffee and miscellaneous	1655	127	70	24	20

Exhibit 6.7: Summary: Sales by Product and Channel 1980

Exhibit 6.8:
Newspaper
Advertisement

VII
Big Ben Sports
D. Cook

Company Background

Martin Alden and Colin Hardy met whilst studying for an MBA at the Management Centre, Bradford University, in October 1976. Throughout the year they got to know each other pretty well and on discussing what they were going to do when the course finished, they realized that ideally they would both like to start a business of their own. The problem was, of course, what to do. Certainly neither of them wished to return to working for medium to large-sized companies. Both would much prefer, almost as a last resort, to join a small-sized company.

Martin, who had graduated with a degree in Sciences and Wildlife Management (Cantab), had, after a short spell on a wildlife park in Africa, worked for Asda as a management trainee and then for a couple of years in brand management with Fisons. Colin Hardy, (BSc. Econ.), had, on graduating, first joined British Rail and then moved into corporate planning with BAT (British American Tobacco).

In many ways the catalyst for their venture was sown by Martin Alden's MBA thesis — 'the US Market for Golf Equipment'. With the financial support of a Scottish manufacturer, Martin was able to conduct a limited amount of fieldwork in the USA. His respondents included importers and retailers. He quickly became aware of the cultural, economic and social differences between the USA and the UK. Although most chary of using clichés, he did not think it was too unreasonable to accept the description of the USA as the

Prepared by David Cook, Bradford University.

'land of opportunity' in as much as there seemed to be more opportunities for someone to set up successfully their own business venture.
His thinking was coloured by the fact that he had heard of a pine/
antiques exporting business that had successfully been established at
Addingham, near Bradford, which was shipping regularly to the
States container loads of stripped pine and antique furniture. In
some instances the goods were being sold direct from the container
both to the trade and on occasions to the house/flat owner.

Once the germ of an idea had been decided, it was necessary to
find a suitable product and to arrange a source of supply for the
product(s) concerned. Particular problems envisaged at this stage
included:

1 suppliers being unwilling to take on an unknown quantity and
   offer practical help in the form of stock financing and credit;
2 buyers being unwilling to shift to a new completely unknown
   supplier;
3 a limited self-financing ability and relatively high overheads;
4 the difficulty of obtaining financial support from the traditional
   institutions, e.g. banks.

Market Research

Because of their own interests and a general belief in the future of
the leisure market, the potential partners selected sporting goods as
the first area of enquiry. They managed to persuade a small manufacturer, who did not export any of their output, Spall Sports Ltd,
that should a viable export market be demonstrated then they would
be happy to supply the product.

Armed with this knowledge Big Ben Sports, the name selected by
Martin and Colin for their partnership, requested assistance from
the British Overseas Trade Board under the Export Marketing
Research Scheme to study the market for a limited number of
sporting goods in the USA, Canada, Holland and Belgium. A grant
of approximately £1,500 was made and a research programme,
involving a limited amount of fieldwork, was conducted intermit-
tently throughout the period April—July 1977. The major part of
the field research programme was spent obtaining reaction from
American wholesalers and retailers to samples of Spall Sports
clothing.

Articles of Association

As stated in the Company's Memorandum and Articles of Association, dated 25th January 1978, the major object of the Company is:

'to carry on business as manufacturers of the wholesale and retail dealers on sporting goods and apparel of all kinds and as manufacturers of and retail dealers in equipment, accessories, implements, supplies, clothing and articles of every description used for and in connection with sports, games, athletics, games, pastimes, exercises, recreations and entertainments of every description and to act as managers of sporting and other celebrities and to arrange for and deal with contracts in connection with sports meetings, stage, radio, television broadcast and similar activities and to carry on business as travel agents in connection therewith and to act as trainers and advisers to sports and sportsmen of every kind ...'

Product/Market Selection

A quote from Martin Alden explains the reasons behind the product and market selection:

'On the basis of our own interests and research findings, confidence in the long term future of the leisure consumer markets, and to some although lesser extent what we were offered, we chose to establish ourselves in the US sporting goods market and we plumped for soccer as our number one. The market was in a period of rapid growth, soccer was something we ourselves knew a lot about,[1] — both equipment and, especially, the game — and our footballers (see Exhibit 7.1) and to a lesser extent, equipment, had, we knew, a good reputation in America. Obviously we would try to sell the attributes (quality more than price) of the equipment, but perhaps above all we would have expertise at the game itself. Our market research before we set up the US office had told us that we had a high quality product and also one or two useful technical product advantages, particularly a

---

[1] Both partners are interested in sport in general, and have participated in rugby, soccer and squash at representative level. Colin Hardy, in addition to being an F.A. trained coach, had played a number of football league games for Barnsley.

highly flexible jersey 'Special Designs' (see Exhibit 7.2) and a more or less unique shin and ankle guard in one. The high level of duty[1] on imported clothing into the US was very much against us, but overall we felt we had enough plus points to set up our office from scratch.'

Big Ben Sports Ltd decided to concentrate on Texas and in particular Dallas and Houston because of:

- a relative lack of competition
- the strength of soccer in Texas, particularly at the schoolboy level
- the intention of a Houston-based team participating in the professional North American Soccer League (NASL).

Exhibit 7.2 shows the Big Ben Product Range.

Distribution

Because of the problems of cash flow it was decided to hold a minimum stock level but to guarantee delivery of orders within 5—6 weeks of receipt. It was vital that the company did not promise anything, particularly delivery dates and designs, that it could not satisfy.

From the point of view of the buying process it is important to make the distiction between supplying a retailer for subsequent resale or selling direct to a team or league. Because the latter represent a major market for the retailer it was not thought appropriate to attempt to satisfy both markets in one geographic area. Hence Texas was divided into a North and South sales territory roughly as defined by the North and South Texas Soccer Associations. In the South (mainly in Houston) Big Ben supplies teams and leagues direct, while in the North, because of the lack of manpower, the company uses retailers. The implication is that soccer teams will pay 20—30% more in the North than in the South of the State for the same strip.

Despite this implication, both markets were thought to be price conscious. The buying situation was complicated by the fact that in the South soccer leagues tended to act as 'central buying points' for all teams in the league whereas in the North, particularly in

---

[1]   Soccer jerseys and socks 35%. Shorts 30%. Darts 10%. Pub paraphernalia 0—10%.

Dallas, there was a preference for buying for a team, even for one player individually, and mainly from retailers. Martin Alden estimates that the North Texas market is about double the size of that in the South and that company sales by type of outlet are roughly as shown in Exhibit 7.3.

Big Ben's main competition in Texas comes from cheap 'off the rack' clothing (notably multi purpose Addidas T shirts) and from cheap American and Far East manufactured clothing supplied to teams and leagues direct. A few British and other European competitors are attempting to cultivate the market but less so than in New York or California. Approximately 90% of players prefer cheaper equipment than that supplied by the UK manufacturers but on quality, particularly design, washability, durability, and fastness of colour, British equipment is superior.

The price gap can be seen from the following prices (in Texas) for shirts:

1 cheap polyester Taiwan or California manufactured
   soccer jersey retail $10—13 each
2 Addidas T shirt retail $5—6 each
3 Big Ben nylon jersey direct to team or league price
   depending on design $12—22 each

Colin Hardy is permanently based in Houston, concentrating on direct sales, while Martin Alden is based in Bradford, mainly concerned with the problems of supply although making frequent trips to Houston and there concentrating on sales to retailers.

Finance

As well as the supply problem, the other major difficulty faced by Big Ben Sports was financial. Apart from £13,000 of self-financed capital, the only financial backing in the first two years of operation was from the company's UK bank (£3,000 overdraft) and a substantial loan over two years (to a maximum of £23,000) under the MEGS scheme to help towards the cost of certain clearly defined 'setting up' costs, e.g. office in Houston, travel, printing and telephone, etc.

The general attitude of the company's UK bank was initially unhelpful and it took two years to negotiate the overdraft facilities. USA banks, too, much to the partners surprise, were not prepared to loan money because Big Ben was completely unknown in Texas and there was no USA ownership. However it was anticipated that after some 12—18 months of operating it will become easier to borrow from both UK and USA banks because:

1 Big Ben will be better known and will be able to supply audited accounts
2 once the company is incorporated in the USA and has ownership there, the USA banks will be more interested — in general they lend money to business, on the basis of items such as stock, vehicles and debtors, more readily than do UK banks.

Exhibit 7.4, prepared before the approval of the MEGS loan, shows a cash flow forecast indicating a positive flow of £43,000 by year 5.

1978 NASL Season

On 5th January, 1978 Commissioner Phil Woosnam (ex Wales and West Ham) announced the programme for the 1978 NASL (North American Soccer League) season. Six new teams will be participating — Boston, Colorado (Denver), Detroit, Houston, Memphis and Philadelphia.

The 12th season of NASL competition, it was announced, would last for 18 weeks ending with the Soccer Bowl final on Sunday August 27th at Grants Stadium, E. Rutherford, New Jersey. Each of the 24 participating teams would play 30 matches with the resulting 360 matches being the most wide-ranging major league soccer schedule ever in North America. The teams were allocated to Conferences and Divisions, as follows:

National Conference

Eastern	*Central*	*Western*
Toronto Metros	Minnesota Kicks	Vancouver Whitecaps
Rochester Lancers	Colorado Caribous	Seattle Sounders
New York Cosmos	Tulsa Roughnecks	Portland Timbers
Washington Diplomats	Dallas Tornado	Los Angeles Aztecs

American Conference

Eastern	*Central*	*Western*
New England Teamen	Detroit Express	Oakland Stompers
Philadelphia Fury	Chicago Sting	San Jose Earthquakes
Tampa Bay Rowdies	Memphis Rogues	California Surf
Ft. Lauderdale Strikers	Houston Hurricane	San Diego Sockers

Commenting on the detailed 1978 programme, Phil Woosnam has been reported as saying 'Our new format will provide the NASL with a schedule that emphasizes both regional and conference games while also providing inter-conference competition during the regular season, an exciting playoff format using the wild card system, and excellent television and marketing opportunities'.

The Houston Hurricane home matches, it was announced, would be played at the 50,000 seat Astrodome. The ownership of the team includes:

Gerald D. Hines	— real estate developer
Ben Woodsen	— president and chief executive of American General Insurance Co.
Hans van Mende	— lawyer
Joe Wood	— president of Bayly Corp., a casual wear manufacturer and sporting goods store chain.

Van Mende, the Hurricane's general manager, has been quoted as saying:

'We hope to bring a world class team to Houston. With the active and sizeable number of youth soccer players in the area, the fact that soccer is the fastest growing youth sport in Houston, and the world class facilities available in the Astrodome, we feel there is a sound base for soccer in the community.'

Exhibits 7.5 to 7.8 and Appendix 7.1 present a range of data on the US sporting goods market. Despite the fact that soccer is not as yet reported separately in the statistics, NASL officials are confident that the sport is now at the take-off point in America, and fully expect it to be a major growth area. They expect the sport to be especially successful in high schools and universities because of the current difficulties being experienced with American football:

- American football is a sport only suitable for physically large men whereas soccer is a game everyone can play successfully at varying levels of skill.
- American football involves the institutions (high schools etc.) in high costs because firstly the individual cannot afford to buy the equipment, and secondly, an increasing number of injured players are suing the team for defective coaching and the institution for defective equipment.
- Soccer equipment is relatively cheap with the institution only having to provide balls, goal posts and nets, and to remark the pitch.

Performance

In early September 1978 the company's accountants prepared an Income and Expenditure Account for the six months since the opening of the USA office in Houston (Exhibit 7.9). The account was at some variance with the cash flow forecast, showing an excess of expenditure over income of £3,500.

Martin Alden, who was due to fly to Houston in mid-September, was actually considering alternative marketing plan options for the next twelve months. He wanted to have his ideas clearly worked out before he left so that he could discuss them with Colin. Particular opportunities that had arisen in the preceding six month period were to:

1 extend the product range to include soccer and rugby boots and training shoes. A Wakefield manufacturer had been contacted and had expressed a willingness to supply the product at £2.50 per pair for a minimum order size of 2,500.
2 diversify the product range to include darts and dart boards and 'pub paraphernalia', e.g. hand-carved signs, hand-painted sporting pictures depicting English scenes.

   Again suppliers had been contacted and shown a willingness to supply. The major problem with the pub paraphernalia was that being a craft-based product supply was limited,
3 enter a joint venture/piggy back relationship with a Hull-based chess set manufacturer, who was already established in the USA with an office in Houston and thirteen commission-only salesmen selling throughout the USA.

UK	134
USA	120
Canada	21
Mexico	14
Yugoslavia	12
West Indies	9
Portugal	8
Ireland	6
Argentina	3
Brazil	3
S. Africa	3
Italy	2
Ghana	2
Hungary	2
Peru	2
Poland	2
W. Germany	2
Austria	1
Bolivia	1
Chile	1
Croatia	1
Guatemala	1
Haiti	1
Holland	1
Israel	1
Sweden	1
Uruguay	1
	355

Source: 1977 North American Soccer League Guide

Exhibit 7.1: North American League-Registered Players
by Citizenship 1976

Item	Material	Type	Size	Colour
Footballs				
Spall Ball 'Gold Cup'	laceless chrome leather	Super Tan 18 panel	5	Tan
		Standard White 18 panel	5;4	White
		Standard Tan 18 panel	5;4;3	Tan
Monarch	laceless laminated leather	Diamond 32 panel	5;4	Black/White
		Diamond 32 panel	5	Yellow/Black
		Diamond 32 panel	5	Red/White
		Diamond 32 panel	5	Black/White
		White 18 panel	5;4	White
		Tan 18 panel	5;4	Tan
Shorts				
Standard	Nylon	Playtex waistband	waist SB — 24" B — 26/8" Y — 30/2" S — 34" M — 36" LM — 38/40"	Scarlet/Yellow, Royal/Emerald, Navy/Amber, Black/Maroon, White/Tangerine, Sky Blue, Scarlet/Black, Yellow/Royal, Royal/White, Emerald/Yellow, Amber/Black, Navy/White, Sky Blue/White, Tangerine/ Black, White/Scarlet, Maroon/ White, Black/White *
Tie Cord	Nylon	Elasticated waist and tie cord		
Hose	Nylon	Min. order 6 doz. in any one size	Shoe size B 12–5 Y 6–8 M 9 up	Scarlet, Yellow, Royal, Emerald, Amber, Sky Blue, Tangerine, White, Maroon, Black, Navy, Black/Scarlet, Scarlet/White, Royal/White, Emerald/White, Amber/Black, Sky Blue/White, Black/White + 12 standard ring patterns all various colours *

Jerseys †			
Crew Neck long sleeves	med. weight nylon heavy weight nylon med. weight interlock cotton		Chest SB – 26/8" B – 30/2" Y – 34/6" M – 38/40" LM – 42" Scarlet, Yellow, Royal, Emerald, Amber, Navy, Sky Blue, Tangerine, White, Maroon, Scarlet/White, Yellow/Royal, Yellow/Green, Royal/Yellow, Royal/White, Amber/Black, Navy/White, Sky Blue/White
V insert with collar long sleeves	med. weight nylon heavy weight nylon med. weight interlock cotton		
Striped crew neck or V insert with collar	med. weight nylon	horizontal or vertical in 2" regular alternate stripes	as above — Scarlet/White, Scarlet/Black, Royal/White, Emerald/White, Emerald/Black, Amber/Black, White/Black, Amber/Royal
Continental Goalkeeper Jerseys V insert with collar	heavy weight nylon		as above — Scarlet, Royal, Emerald, Amber, Black, Yellow, Scarlet/Black, Royal/Black, Emerald/Black, Yellow/Black, Amber/Black
Special Design Jerseys	med weight nylon heavy weight nylon cotton	manufactured to client's own design with delivery 5/6 weeks from receipt of order	
Skin and Ankle Guard			Black, White, Red

Notes

* denotes any combination of colours/styles available on request.

† on all jerseys a number and letter service is available viz. – 9", – 6", 8", 9" nylon and cotton numerals available in sets of 1–12 – individual numerals also available – 2½", 3", 4", 6", 8", 9" letters available in nylon or cotton – colours for both numerals and letters, white, black, maroon, royal, scarlet, emerald, sky blue, tangerine, yellow, navy.

The company also carries in its product line a range of ancillary equipment and accessories, e.g. sports bags, training shoes, dart board, track suits, darts equipment, 'pub paraphernalia', table tennis bats and tennis, squash and badminton rackets, tennis clothing – dresses, shorts, shirts, socks.

Exhibit 7.2: Big Ben Sports Ltd Product Range

Outlet	%
Direct particularly in South	40 – 60
Soccer specialist particularly in North	40 – 60
General sporting goods	30 – 40
Department stores	10 – 20
	100

Source: Company estimate

7.3: Sales by Outlet of Soccer Equipment in Texas (%)

			Sales Receipts	Gross Margin	Overhead	Net Cash Flow
Year 1	(i)	case (a)	95,000	18,200	16,340	1,860
	(ii)	case (b)	175,000	33,000	38,000	(5,000)
Year 2	(i)		260,000	49,000	43,000	6,000
	(ii)		350,000	66,000	63,000	(3,000)
Year 3	(ii)		475,000	90,000	85,000	5,000
Year 4	(ii)		600,000	114,000	90,000	24,000
Year 5	(ii)		725,000	138,000	95,000	43,000

(i) provisional forecast presented to Bank possessing built in element of limited sales because not at present consider financing all anticipated orders.
(ii) more realistic forecast based upon what orders can be anticipated.

Exhibit 7.4: Big Ben Sports Ltd Cash Flow Forecast (£)

		Total	Games Played	Average	Highest Gate
1	CHICAGO STING Chicago, Illinois	75,062	13	5,774	28,000
2	CONNECTICUT BICENTENNIALS Hamden, Connecticut	41,037	12	3,419	8,933
3	THE COSMOS New York	241,417	13	18,570	28,436
4	DALLAS TORNADO Dallas, Texas	178,526	13	13,732	20,418
5	FORT LAUDERDALE STRIKERS Ft Lauderdale, Florida	36,843	12	3,070	9,457
6	TEAM HAWAII Honolulu	57,522	12	4,793	6,789
7	LAS VEGAS QUICKSILVERS Las Vegas, Nevada	73,822	12	6,151	9,400
8	LOS ANGELES AZTECS Redondo Beach, California	96,606	12	8,050	9,345
9	MINNESOTA KICKS Edina, Minnesota	368,381	14	26,312	49,572
10	PORTLAND TIMBERS Portland, Oregon	241,996	12	20,166	32,247
11	ROCHESTER LANCERS Rochester, N.Y.	61,906	12	5,158	7,797
12	ST LOUIS STARS St Louis, Missouri	73,795	12	6,149	8,154
13	SAN JOSE EARTHQUAKES San Jose, California	245,753	13	18,904	25,048
14	SEATTLE SOUNDERS Seattle, Washington	316,347	13	24,334	30,406
15	TAMPA BAY ROWDIES Tampa, Florida	262,338	14	18,738	42,611
16	TORONTO METROS Toronto, Canada	68,127	12	5,677	12,123
17	VANCOUVER WHITECAPS Vancouver, Canada	103,877	12	8,656	11,352
18	WASHINGTON DIPLOMATS Washington, DC	76,692	13	5,899	11,604

[1] Figures quoted for home games only

Source: NASL Guide 1977

Exhibit 7.5: Attendance[1] at NASL Soccer Matches by Club 1976

Product Group/ Equipment	New England	Middle Atlantic	E.N. Central	W.N. Central	Region South Atlantic	E.S. Central	W.S. Central	Mountain	Pacific
1 Archery	*	15.8	19.6	10.9	26.9	12.5	2.0	4.5	7.8
2 Badminton Sets	7.9	20.4	21.8	7.5	20.9	8.4	4.8	1.3	7.0
3 Baseball and Softball	5.4	14.8	20.7	6.8	16.3	5.4	13.2	4.2	13.2
4 Basketball	4.8	16.1	20.6	6.7	16.9	7.5	10.1	3.7	13.6
5 Bicycles and Supplies	8.2	18.7	21.7	7.6	13.7	4.7	9.5	5.2	10.7
6 Billiard	3.2	21.1	22.7	9.1	11.0	4.4	7.8	6.4	14.3
7 Bowling Accessories	3.0	20.3	31.5	7.4	12.1	3.2	4.8	4.5	13.2
8 Camping	5.4	15.3	19.8	7.8	13.4	4.5	8.0	7.5	18.3
9 Exercise	4.1	20.0	21.2	7.7	14.8	5.3	7.8	6.1	13.0
10 Firearms and Hunting	6.8	14.2	14.3	8.4	19.2	10.7	13.7	3.3	9.4
11 Fishing Tackle	4.0	14.4	19.8	5.8	20.3	4.5	16.0	4.0	11.2
12 Football (American)	4.5	17.2	14.9	6.4	22.5	6.3	12.4	3.9	11.9
13 Golf	7.0	16.8	26.4	8.3	12.8	6.0	7.3	4.8	10.6
14 Ice Skates and Hockey	20.7	23.7	33.6	11.7	6.6	0.5	0.6	2.0	0.6

15 Pleasure Boats Motors and Accessories	NA	NA	NA	NA	NA	NA	NA	NA
16 Raquetball Raquets	3.2	7.7	26.2	9.6	11.2	3.7	9.4	3.9	25.1
17 Recreational Vehicles	NA	NA	NA	NA	NA	NA	NA	NA
18 Skin Diving and Scuba Gear	1.2	13.9	2.5	*	12.4	—	11.1	—	58.9
19 Snow Skiing	13.2	20.5	21.9	10.2	3.3	*	0.8	7.5	22.6
20 Snowmobiles	NA	NA	NA	NA	NA	NA	NA	NA
21 Table Tennis	3.5	17.3	19.5	7.5	17.6	2.8	10.1	3.8	17.9
22 Tennis	5.5	17.4	19.2	6.2	16.3	5.9	9.6	4.6	15.3
23 Toboggans	11.4	18.3	31.6	9.3	22.5	2.3	*	1.0	3.3
24 Water Skis	NA	NA	NA	NA	NA	NA	NA	NA

$ purchases

NA not available

* less than 0.5%

Source: National Sporting Goods Association

Exhibit 7.6: Sales of Sports Equipment by Region 1976 (% $)

Product Group/ Equipment	General Sporting Goods	Speciality/ Pro Shop	Outlet Department Store	Discount Store	Catalogue	Other	No Answer
1 Archery	23.0	17.0	16.3	14.8	9.6	14.8	4.5
2 Badminton Sets	7.3	2.7	24.9	46.6	0.9	14.0	3.6
3 Baseball and Softball	31.0	11.4	17.0	28.3	0.8	8.5	3.0
4 Basketball	25.3	10.4	22.3	23.3	2.6	12.8	3.3
5 Bicycles and Supplies	5.8	18.5	26.5	20.2	2.6	24.0	2.4
6 Billiard	6.9	29.6	33.4	5.0	9.4	15.1	0.6
7 Bowling Accessories	11.9	39.5	18.0	18.0	1.2	6.4	5.0
8 Camping	17.2	11.0	23.2	25.5	11.4	9.7	2.0
9 Exercise	12.6	10.6	42.5	18.8	6.8	5.8	3.0
10 Firearms and Hunting	14.4	1.7	23.7	40.3	6.8	12.7	*
11 Fishing Tackle	19.6	7.8	20.3	34.8	2.3	11.7	3.5
12 Football (American)	31.2	11.8	19.0	22.5	3.2	10.1	2.2
13 Golf	10.2	39.2	12.2	20.3	2.9	8.6	6.6
14 Ice Skates and Hockey	24.5	18.0	17.1	21.1	4.8	9.8	6.7
15 Pleasure Boats Motors and Accessories	NA	NA	NA	NA	NA	NA	NA
16 Raquetball Raquets	26.5	15.4	15.3	26.5	2.0	8.2	6.1
17 Recreational Vehicles	NA	NA	NA	NA	NA	NA	NA
18 Skin Diving and Scuba Gear[1]							
19 Snow Skiing	25.4	55.0	5.7	3.3	1.7	6.6	2.3
20 Snowmobiles	NA	NA	NA	NA	NA	NA	NA
21 Table Tennis	8.7	4.5	29.4	34.4	6.0	15.1	1.9
22 Tennis	14.9	14.0	23.6	31.1	1.6	10.3	4.5
23 Toboggans	13.3	3.3	19.0	31.1	2.2	26.7	4.4
24 Water Skis	NA	NA	NA	NA	NA	NA	NA

* less than 0.5%   NA not availabe

[1] Data base too small to show sales by outlet units sold

Source: National Sporting Goods Association

Exhibit 7.7: Sales of Sports Equipment by Type of Outlet 1976 (% Units)

Product Category	1975 $	1976 $	1977 $	Percent Increase 1977 vs 1976 %
Archery equipment	121.5	126.0	136.0	8
Badminton sets	15.4	21.9	24.0	9
Baseball and softball equipment	165.3	187.6	206.0	10
Basketball equipment	113.7	129.3	142.0	10
Bicycles and supplies	855.0	894.2	984.0	10
Billiard equipment	144.5	130.8	124.0	(5)
Bowling accessories	108.9*	103.9	101.0	(3)
Camping equipment	447.1*	483.2	517.0	7
Exercise equipment	191.8*	227.0	257.0	13
Firearms and hunting equipment	972.6*	985.6	926.0	(6)
Fishing tackle	469.0	475.7	444.0	(7)
Football equipment	70.1	72.5	76.0	5
Golf equipment	554.1	600.9	631.0	5
Ice skates and hockey equipment	73.6	75.9	80.0	5
Pleasure boats, motors and accessories	2,062.6	2,627.6	3,100.0	18
Racquetball racquets	11.3	14.1	18.0	25
Recreational vehicles	2,320.0	3,551.0	4,261.0	20
Skin diving and scuba gear	60.5	72.6	78.9	8
Snow skiing equipment	356.1*	404.2	441.0	9
Snowmobiles	224.0	180.0	190.0	5
Table tennis equipment	35.0	33.5	35.0	4
Tennis equipment	555.3	601.1	631.0	5
Toboggans	7.6	9.2	10.0	11
Water skis	79.8	87.0	96.0	10
Athletic goods team sales	672.6	**	**	

* *Revised*   ** *The data will be shown in a separate report*

Source: Irwin Broh and Associates

Exhibit 7.8: Projected Sales of Sporting Goods (In millions)

		£	
Sales — Cash (other products)	230		
Sporting goods and clothing	1,895	2,125	
Credit (sporting goods and clothing)		2,005	4,130
Opening stock		620	
Purchases		5,200	
		5,820	
Less Closing stock			
UK	450		
USA	3,850	4,300	1,520
Gross Profit			2,610
Expenses			
Freight		150	
Rent, rates, etc.		685	
Telephone		280	
Car		1,000	
Travel		1,895	
Brokerage and duty		720	
Postage and stationery		940	
Miscellaneous		125	5,795
Excess Expenditure			3,185
Add Depreciation (Car USA)			280
			3,465

NB: The share capital of the company is £20,000 divided into 20,000 shares of £1 each.

Exhibit 7.9: Big Ben Sports Ltd Income and Expenditure
Account 1/3/78 — 31/8/78

Appendix 7.1
The 1977 Market

by Thomas B. Doyle

The steady growth of the nation's economy out of its recent recession is reflected in the strong increase in 1976 sporting goods sales, according to the most recent statistical research released by the National Sporting Goods Association.

Actual sales of sporting goods in 1976 increased 15.2% over 1975, reaching a record $12.1 billion. Athletic goods team sales, which were projected for 1976 at slightly more than $700 million, are not included in the 1976 figure. Team sales will be reported separately.

Projected sporting goods sales for 1977 are expected to reach $13.5 billion. This would represent a 11.6% increase over 1976 actual sales.

The data, part of the copyrighted survey *The Sporting Goods Market* in 1977, is prepared for the National Sporting Goods Association by Irvin Broh and Associates, Des Plaines, Ill. The consumer survey is based on interviews with 32,000 USA families.

The survey showed the highest 1976 growth rates for recreational vehicles (53%), pleasure boats (27%), racquetball rackets (25%) and skin diving and scuba gear (20%).

It should be noted that racquetball begins with a very low base, so that dollar sales increases translate into dramatic growth percentages. But there is no evidence at present to suggest the racquetball will achieve the popularity of tennis.' Broh says.

The 1977 survey reports two product categories for the first time racquetball rackets and toboggans.

The survey projects the highest 1977 growth rates for racquetball rackets (25%), recreational vehicles (20%), pleasure boats (18%) and exercise equipment (13%).

The projections for RVs pleasure boats and snowmobiles are furnished by respective industry associations: Recreational Vehicle In??? (RVI), Boating Industry Associations (BIA) and Inernational Snowmobile Industry Association (ISIA).

If pleasure boats, recreational vehicles, snowmobiles and bicycles are excluded, the sporting goods industry is projected to show a modest 3% growth rate for 1977. The modest growth rate is projected on the basis of declines for firearms and hunting equipment (−7%) and for fishing tackle (−6%) in 1977.

Soft goods sales, in areas reported, showed stronger sales increases in 1976 versus 1975. Warm-up suits showed a 30% increase. Golf clothing showed a 10% increase, ski wear a 12% increase. Tennis clothing showed a 20% increase, versus only a 1% increase in tennis racket sales.

Reprinted from *Selling Sporting Goods*, June 1977

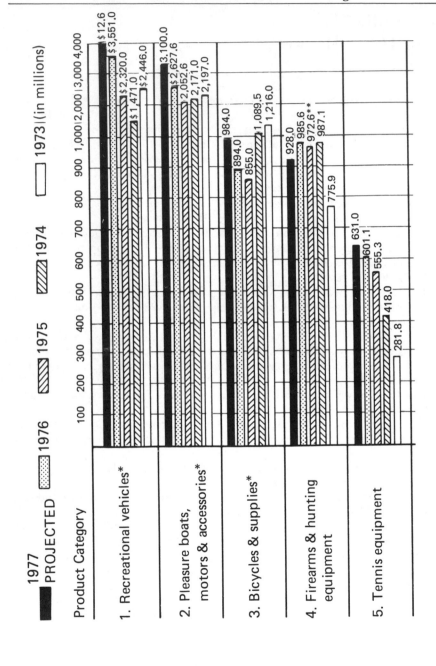

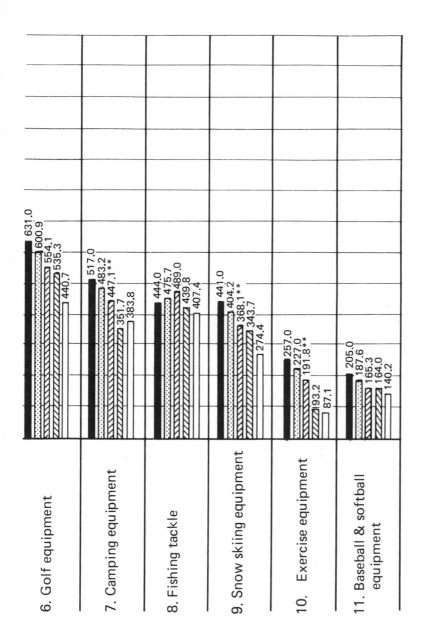

6. Golf equipment
- 631.0
- 600.9
- 554.1
- 535.3
- 440.7

7. Camping equipment
- 517.0
- 483.2
- 447.1**
- 351.7
- 383.8

8. Fishing tackle
- 444.0
- 475.7
- 489.0
- 439.8
- 407.4

9. Snow skiing equipment
- 441.0
- 404.2
- 368.1**
- 343.7
- 274.4

10. Exercise equipment
- 257.0
- 227.0
- 191.8**
- 193.2
- 87.1

11. Baseball & softball equipment
- 205.0
- 187.6
- 165.3
- 164.0
- 140.2

Sale of Sporting Goods *continued*

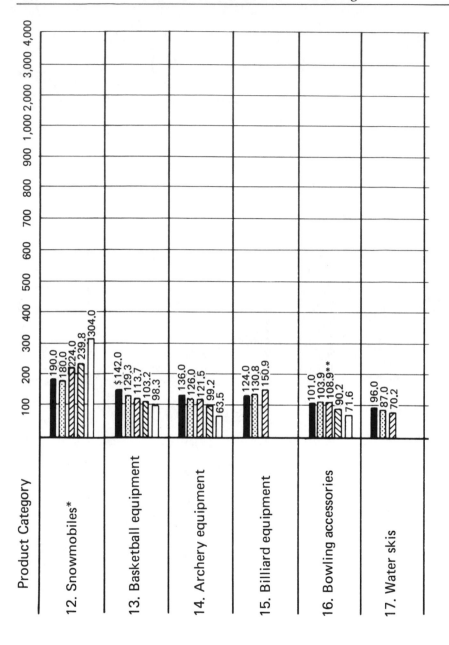

Product Category

12. Snowmobiles*
190.0
180.0
224.0
239.8
304.0

13. Basketball equipment
$142.0
129.3
113.7
103.2
98.3

14. Archery equipment
136.0
126.0
121.5
99.2
63.5

15. Billiard equipment
124.0
130.8
150.9

16. Bowling accessories
101.0
103.9
108.9**
90.2
71.6

17. Water skis
96.0
87.0
70.2

Sales of Sporting Goods

18. Ice skates & hockey equipment — 80.0, 75.9, 73.6, 107.5, 107.9

19. Skin diving & scuba gear — 78.0, 72.8, 60.5, 71.2, 65.3

20. Football equipment — 76.0, 72.5, 70.1, 68.6, 65.6

21. Table tennis equipment — 35.0, 33.5, 35.0, 38.8, 40.8

22. Badminton sets — 24.0, 21.9, 15.4, 17.1

23. Racquetball rackets — 17.6, 14.1, 11.3

*Projections are based on estimates by associations and leading manufacturers.
**Revised.

Particular Sports

Broh, who prepares the statistical survey for the National Sporting Goods Association annually, noted that 1976 showed a narrower range of increases (and decreases) in sales. Tennis, which had been 'the brightest star in the sporting goods heaven', showed an 8% growth in 1976. In 1975, tennis experienced a 30% growth.

Broh, who formed his own research company after 12 years with the Brunswick Corp., made the following observations about particular product categories.

- Archery. Unit sales for bows were down 12%, while dollar sales increased 15%. This, more than likely, reflects the dramatic shift to the compound bow.
- Basketball, baseball and football. Sales for these three sports were up at retail, both in units and dollars, perhaps indicating growing interest in these sports despite school budget problems.
- Camping. Sales increased 8%, paralleling the increase in camping nights reported by the National Park Service and private campground operators.
- Exercise equipment. The sharp rise in exercise equipment of sales (18% in 1976 versus 1975) was due primarily to the increase warn-up suit sales, which in 1976 totalled $132 million.
- Hunting and fishing tackle sales. These outdoor sports showed no increases in 1976 versus 1975. Slight declines in unit sales were offset by slight increases in average price per unit.

The 1975 retail sales of shotguns and ammunition have been revised. Shotgun sales to consumers in 1975 are now estimated at 1.7 million units with a retail value of $250.4 million. This is up from 1.4 million units with a retail value of $207.9 million shown in the 1976 report.

- Golf. The 8% increase in dollar sales in 1976 is due mainly to price increases. Unit sales remained about the same as the previous year.
- Tennis. Racket sales declined, the first time this has happened in the recent tennis boom. Even the average price of imported rackets declined in 1976, despite continued inflation.

Except for a 25% projected growth for racquetball sales and 13% for exercise equipment, Broh projects rather modest increases (4 to 10%) for most sports in 1977. He projects slight decreases in four sport areas: billard equipment (−5%), bowling accessories (−3%), firearms and hunting equipment (−6%) and fishing tackle (−7%).

Survey Methodology

For the survey, 40,000 carefully selected families representing a cross section of the USA population were sent questionnaires listing 34 sporting goods items. About 32,000 families, 80% of the samples responded.

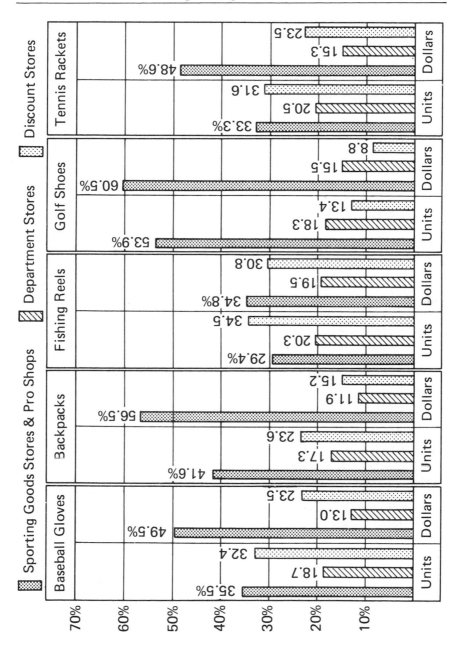

The sample of families, maintained by National Family Opinion Inc., is representative of the USA population by geographic region, annual family income, age of homemaker and population density.

Each family was asked to indicate certain information regarding products purchased in 1976. Responding families were to indicate number of items bought, total dollars spent and the type of outlet where the most recent purchase was made.

The place of purchases listed were general sporting goods stores, sports speciality and pro shop, department store, discount store, catalog purchases and other. In previous surveys, hardware stores had been reported. In the 1977 survey, they are included under 'other' in the place-of-purchase category.

'The research documents the fact that specialists sell the higher ticket items, as the previous reports had documented the fact that sporting goods stores move higher ticket items than mass merchandisers,' Broh said.

Projections for 1977 were developed by applying a research technique known as the Delphi technique. Originally developed to forecast the direction of technological growth, the Delphi technique is based on a consensus of expert opinion.

Industry experts were asked their opinion with regard to 1977 growth. A series of opinion then was developed and integrated. The industry experts are confronted with a body of opinion and asked to refine their own. Broh feels the technique is highly useful when a statistical base for current projections is not yet available.

For the 1976 market survey, Broh had projected a total market of $11.9 billion using the Delphi technique. The actual market, according to the 32,000 family panel, reached $12.1 billion — a degree of accuracy with which Broh is 'well pleased'.

The survey procedure used for the NSGA statistical report is similar to that used for 1973 though 1975. The differences are in the questionnaire design and number of products included. The 1973 survey included 60 products, but asked only the number of items bought and the dollars spent for each product. The 1974 though 1976 surveys included fewer products, but asked place of purchase.

Estimates for 1976 consumer sales are shown for several product categories not included in the consumer survey. These sales projections, based on industry estimates, include firearms and hunting equipment and water skis.

Industry estimates are also the basis for 1976 consumer projections for bicycles, pleasure boats, recreational vehicles and snowmobiles.

The Sporting Goods Market in 1977 is being sent without charge to all NSGA sustaining members. Regular and associate non-sustaining members may purchase the report for $20 per copy. The price to non-members is $35.

Companies may gather more comprehensive market data by re-surveying the purchasers identified through the 1977 NSGA report. For cost estimates, contact either Irvin Broh & Associates, Des Plaines, Ill., or Robert Goodwin at the National Sporting Goods Association, 717 N. Michigan Aven., Chicago, Ill. 60611.

The Sporting Goods Market in 1977 has been copyrighted by the National Sporting Goods Association, for permission or information on the use or reproduction of any part of the report, contact NSGA Executive Director: G. Marvin Shutt.

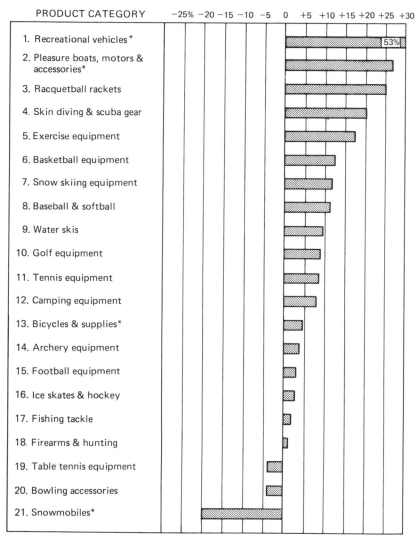

*Projections based on estimates by associations and leading manufacturers
Source: Irwin Erch & Associates

Sales of Sporting Goods
Per cent Increase (Decrease) 1976 vs 1975

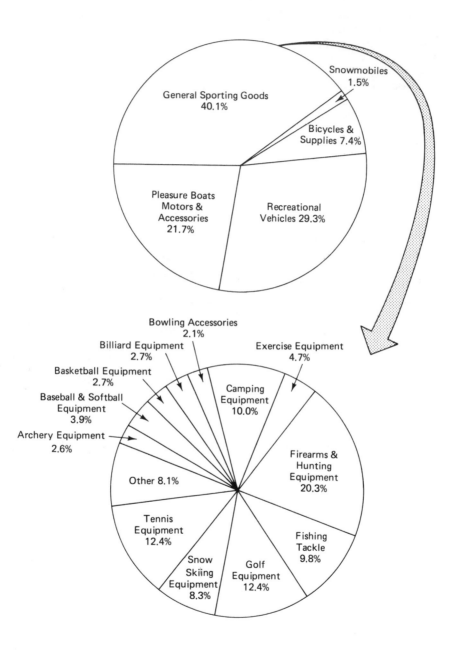

1976 Sales of Sporting Goods

VIII
'Ambush'
M. J. Baker

'In this business I sometimes think you would be better off putting your money in a building society.' For a man closely involved over the past seven years in helping to develop a new multi-million pound international market for his company this may seem a remarkable sentiment but, for Gordon Rae of Imperial Chemical Industries' Plant Protection Division, it is a realistic appraisal of the risks involved in participating in the world market for pesticides.

The 'Ambush' story really started late in 1973, at which time Gordon Rae was manager of the Plant Protection Division's Product Acquisition and Licensing Section. This section had been established in April 1972, with a remit to acquire products from organizations outside ICI which could be profitably developed and sold by the ICI Group.

In a company like ICI, with an excellent track record for in-house R & D which had led to many significant innovations, it is not surprising that the prospect of buying in new product ideas was viewed with some scepticism, and was not wholeheartedly welcomed or encouraged by all parts of the ICI Group. However, the 'not invented here' syndrome and the resistance of overseas operating units, which saw the setting up of a central activity as a threat to their independence, were only two of a number of potential obstacles which had to be overcome in bringing 'Ambush' to the market place. As of 1973, ICI had no licences to develop a product which it believed to have enormous potential as an agricultural insecticide; it had only limited experience in the agricultural insecticide market generally, and virtually none in the USA cotton insecticide market,

Prepared by Professor Michael Baker, Strathclyde University.

where the new compound was believed to have the major potential. In other words, ICI was proposing to use someone else's know-how to break into a market dominated by companies of equal size and resources, who were occupying an entrenched position.

In the following pages we describe how ICI overcame these problems, beginning with a description of the discovery of permethrin, a synthetic pyrethroid insecticide which is now known by the trade name 'Ambush'.

The Origins of 'Ambush'

The story of the discovery and development of 'Ambush' spans one and a half centuries from the first commercialization of natural pyrethrum, and has been full of fascination and its share of excitement. Natural pyrethrum is one of the oldest known botanical substances used for the control of insect pests.

The active ingredients of pyrethrum, called pyrethrins, are obtained from a species of *Chrysanthemum* which probably originated in Asia. The insecticidal properties of the dried flowers have been known for a long time, and pyrethrum has been commerically available for about 150 years.

The first production took place in Persia, now Iran, and by the mid-1800s commercial production of pyrethrum had started in Dalmatia, now Yugoslavia, and records of the first imports into the USA appeared around 1860. By 1918 imports had reached 3,000,000 lbs per year of dried flowers. In 1881 the centre of world production moved from Dalmatia to Japan, where pyrethrum had been cultivated on a small scale for several years.

Production increased so rapidly that by 1939 Japan had become the world's leading supplier. During the war, however, production of pyrethrum virtually came to a halt and has not recovered its former importance.

In the 1920s experiments on growing pyrethrum had started in Kenya, and it was soon shown that yields were higher than in Japan or Dalmatia. By the mid-1930s Kenyan production had started to encroach on Japanese markets, and by the end of the war, Kenya had become the world's biggest supplier.

Kenya has dominated world production of pyrethrum ever since. Pyrethrum is also produced in Tanzania, Ruanda and in small amounts in Ecuador and several other countries. Unfortunately supplies are subject to the vagaries of climatic conditions and shortfalls have often occurred, with the result that natural pyrethrum is also relatively expensive.

Given that natural pyrethrins, which are expensive and often in short supply, have been so widely used and for so long, it is clear that they must possess significant advantages. Amongst these may be listed the following:

wide spectrum of activity
remarkable knockdown
relatively fast, good kill
good flushing-out effects
insect repellency
very low mammalian toxicity
non-persistent in the environment.

In other words, the natural pyrethrins are near perfect insecticides, but they do have disadvantages. These are:

erratic production levels
expensive
not stable in sunlight,

and therefore:

unsuitable for agricultural outlets.

It was this combination of advantages and disadvantages which caused organic chemists to ask the questions — could the natural pyrethrins or their analogues be synthesised, and could their disadvantages be eliminated?

At this point, work on synthetic pyrethroid insecticides began. In 1947, Dr Charles Potter became Head of the Department of Insecticides and Fungicides at Rothamsted Experimental Research Station in the UK, and from 1948 onwards an organic chemist, named Dr Michael Elliott, worked under him.

At that time it was anticipated that the organochlorine, organophosphate and carbamate insecticides would solve many of the world's insect problems.

However, Dr Potter had other views and, with tremendous foresight, considered that alternative classes of insecticides, and especially those with low mammalian toxicity, would be needed in the future. He and earlier workers at Rothamsted had recognized the excellent properties of the natural pyrethrins and, particularly, their safety to man. Although Dr Potter and his colleagues considered that the instability of the natural products in sunlight might always restrict their usage to non-agricultural outlets, the natural pyrethrins were considered to be good foundation material for the study of their primary objectives, which were:

- to relate chemical structure to biological activity
- to establish principles for improved insecticides.

It should be emphasized that these objectives were set some thirty years ago, and since that time Dr Elliott and others in the USA, Japan, and elsewhere, have painstakingly progressed the understanding of chemical structural requirements needed for biological activity of insecticides by systematically synthesising and testing compounds from the lead compounds available to them at that time; namely the natural pyrethrins.

The natural pyrethrins are combinations of two acids and three alcohols, giving six compounds in total. These are:

	% of each ester
Pyrethrin I	35
Cinerin I	10
Jasmolin I	5
Pyrethrin II	32
Cinerin II	14
Jasmolin II	4

It is these six compounds which account for the rapid knockdown action and the rapid kill associated with pyrethrin extract.

Using these separate compounds, Dr Elliott showed that Pyrethrin I was the most active. Having selected Pyrethrin I, containing chrysanthemic acid and the alcohol pyrethrolone as the most promising lead compound, chemists started to change its structural features in attempts to produce novel insecticides. The first synthetic pyrethroid, called Allethrin, was discovered in the USA in 1949. It was produced by shortening the side chain of the alcohol in Pyrethrin I.

Allethrin is still used, particularly in mosquito coils where its thermostability and volatility are an advantage. Neither of these advantages are exhibited by natural pyrethrins. However, Allethrin does not show the same level or spectrum of activity as Pyrethrin I.

In 1958, in Czechoslovakia, a development in the acid moiety took place. It was suggested that the dichloro analogue of chrysanthemic acid might be effective in synthetic pyrethroids, but no advantage for this modification to the acid was revealed in combination with the early alcohols, and the importance of this acid remained unrecognized in synthetic pyrethroids for over a decade.

Meanwhile, in 1964, in Japan, a new compound called tetramethrin (Neopynamin) was reported. It contained chrysanthemic acid and an alcohol not directly related to others used in synthetic pyrethroids. Tetramethrin showed good knockdown properties but again did not exhibit either a high level or wide spectrum of activity.

In 1967, some twenty years after the first work was started at Rothamsted in the UK, the first major breakthrough was made by Dr Elliott and his colleagues. They invented the first compounds which were superior to the natural pyrethrins. Following their painstaking, systematic search of structural features essential for insecticidal activity, they discovered that the furan alcohol with chrysanthemic acid produced compounds approaching the activity of Pyrethrin I. In addition, they were even less toxic to mammals than the natural pyrethrins. These compounds were resmethrin (NRDC 104) and bioresmethrin (NRDC 107). Unfortunately neither compound was stable in sunlight and therefore they were still not suitable for agricultural markets.

However, they were very suitable for public health markets, and were licensed by the NRDC to six companies worldwide, including two in the USA.

The next significant development was reported in 1971, because chemists working independently in the UK and Japan had recognized that compounds based on 3-phenoxybenzylalcohol could reproduce some of the features of the furan alcohol and as a result Phenothrin was produced. The main advantage of this discovery was that the alcohol could be produced by a variety of routes, and was potentially cheaper than the furan alcohol. But, as with many of the developments so far, as one step was taken forward, half a step was taken back again. In this case, phenothrin was only one-half to one-third the activity of resmethrin.

Having worked so successfully on this alcohol, Dr Elliott and his colleagues began a systematic examination of modifications to the acid. After making numerous compounds (about 50) they discovered that a properly-sited chlorine was a good substituent.

This clearly re-directed attention to the neglected dichlorovinyl acid, which, when combined with the more modern alcohols, was much more effective than would have been expected, as exemplified in NRDC 134. This was a highly active compound, but still not stable in sunlight.

However, Dr Elliott was quick to realize that the components for a photostable pyrethroid were now available. In pursuance of the objectives set by Dr Potter twenty-five years previously, he combined the dichlorovinyl acid and 3-phenoxybenzylalcohol. The resulting ester was an astounding as well as an outstanding invention. The compound was coded NRDC 143 and called permethrin. The compound was more active against a wide range of insect pests than would have been predicted from the known activity of either the acid or the alcohol moieties, and it had a very low mammalian toxicity. But, above all else *it was stable in sunlight*. This was the breakthrough Dr Elliott had been working towards for a quarter of a century. A highly active compound, with low mammalian toxicity, which was stable in sunlight, had at long last been invented.

Acquiring the Licenses

The discovery of NRDC 143 was soon brought to Gordon Rae's attention. A colleague, Mr Jeff Proctor, who had heard Dr Michael Elliott present his paper (*NRDC 143 — A More Stable Pyrethroid*, Proceedings Seventh British Insecticide and Fungicide Conference, 19th–22nd November 1973), suggested that the product could have considerable potential for ICI and, within a week Mr John MacCallum-Deighton had obtained a sample for Plant Protection Division (PPD) to test in the laboratory. The preliminary laboratory tests confirmed that NRDC 143 would be a promising product to acquire. ICI's acquisition of the NRDC synthetic pyrethroids and the development of 'Ambush' had begun.

The sample of NRDC 143 was tested further at ICI's own Jealott's Hill Laboratories on flies, aphids and *Lepidoptera*, confirming the high intrinsic activity and photostability of the compound. Based on these tests, the Entomology section at Jealott's Hill approached the Products Acquisition and Licensing Section, and suggested that attempts should be made to acquire the licenses for NRDC's pyrethroid insecticides. This was to prove a far from simple task.

In describing the development of NRDC 143 it was noted that this compound was itself derived from the work on the earlier compounds resmethrin (NRDC 104) and bioresmethrin (NRDC 107), which were unstable in sunlight and so unsuited to agricultural applications. Thus, when the NRDC offered the licenses for these compounds in 1967, ICI declined to take one up, and the world rights were assigned to the following six organisation:

Wellcome Foundation ⎱
Mitchell Cotts   ⎰   UK based

S.B. Penick	}	USA based
FMC		
Sumitomo		Japan based
Roussel-Uclaf		France based

These six companies are all active directly or indirectly in public health markets, which are primarily concerned with the control of disease-carrying insects like flies and mosquitoes that are most prevalent in sub-tropical and tropical climates. Because public health applications are largely indoors and not exposed to direct sunlight, the instability of resmethrin and bioresmethrin in ultra-violet light was not considered a deterrent to adoption.

Wellcome have been active in these markets for many years, while Mitchell Cotts is a grower of natural pyrethrum and so had a direct interest in any synthetic analogues. FMC and S.B. Penick were both involved in the public health sector, and Penick had been using natural pyrethrum for many years because of its safe, non-toxic properties. In Japan, Sumitomo had a history of active research into synthetic pyrethrins, and in Europe, Roussel-Uclaf were heavily involved in the technology relevant to the development of most of the active chemicals in the new compounds.

In assigning licenses to these six companies, the NRDC gave rights 'in perpetuity', with the result that the original licensees ('head' licensees) became heir to all subsequent developments of the original compounds, including NRDC 143. Thus the NRDC found itself with a new and highly effective material, but only one of its licensees (FMC) had easy access to the cotton insecticide market in the USA, where its major potential was felt to lie. Accordingly, when approached by ICI, the NRDC had no option but to suggest that they try to negotiate a sub-license from one of the head licensees.

On 3rd February 1974, PPD approached the Wellcome Foundation, who agreed to open negotiations for the granting of a sub-license to ICI for agricultural, horticultural, and forestry outlets for all markets, with the exception of the USA and Japan, for which Wellcome did not have selling rights. The omission of the USA was particularly significant, as Rae estimated that it comprised approximately one-third of the world market for agricultural chemicals (UK = 5%). A meeting was held with S.B. Penick in May 1974 to discuss the possibility of cooperation between ICI Americas and S.B. Penick for the development and sale of the NRDC 143 series of synthetic pyrethroid insecticides in the agricultural/horticultural outlets in the USA.

At this juncture it is necessary to go back in time a few years to the setting-up of ICI's American operation, for this was to be a critical factor in the ultimate success of 'Ambush'.

In 1970, ICI decided to establish a presence in the crop protection market of the USA, where it was virtually unknown, and began to set up its research arm of the Agricultural Chemicals Division. Two years later Ronnie Hampel (now Chairman of Paints Division) went to the USA to establish a commercial operation, and set himself the objective of achieving one or more of three goals, which he considered would be essential for success, namely:

1 Acquire an established company, and/or
2 Acquire a product with significant potential, and/or
3 Make a major capital investment in production facilities.

Hampel was quick to recognize the potential of NRDC 143 in the US market, and continued the discussions with S.B. Penick during 1974. (There was little point in approaching FMC, as they were the only original licensee with agricultural interests.)

While these negotiations were taking place, further screening tests were being carried out on the compound. In May 1974 the high activity shown in the laboratory was confirmed in the first field trials in the UK, using the winter moth on apples as the target pest. Then in June, Jealott's Hill staff confirmed the activity of NRDC 143 on *Spodoptera* on cotton in Egypt. Throughout the summer, trials continued on a wide range of crops in several countries outside the USA, and on vegetable pests in the Far East and Florida. All these tests proved satisfactory, and those in Florida were subsequently to acquire a particular significance in the successful market development of 'Ambush'.

Early in 1975 a potential setback occurred when Penick rejected ICI's proposal that they act as a distributor for them in the USA, although this is hardly surprising in light of ICI's lack of a track record in the distribution of agricultural chemicals in the USA. However, this rejection was to prove to be a key turning-point in the development of the project. Hampel, appreciating the importance of the license, convinced Bob Barnett and Bill Duncan (a main Board director) that ICI should buy up Penick's license, and within a matter of days Duncan had obtained approval from the Main Board of ICI, and Hampel and his colleague Bill Hays negotiated the outright purchase of Penrick's license. The purchase of this license and the negotiation of the sub-license from Wellcome took ICI from an outsider to the biggest of NRDC's licensees with rights to sell in every country of the world, excluding Japan.

During 1975 the development of NRDC 143 proceeded apace. In general it takes between 7 and 8 years from the invention to the marketing of a new agricultural chemical in sophisticated markets such as the USA, with the main phases and their duration being as follows:

Phase	Time Scale, Years
Chemical Synthesis	Year 1
Field Screening	Year 2
Toxicological trials	Year 3
	4
Parallel development trials	Year 5
	6
Report preparation	Year 7
Government approval (e.g. USA)	Year 8

Thus, in 1975, ICI was undertaking toxicology and development trials, with a reasonable expectation of launching the new compound in 1980. In anticipation of this, ICI Americas (ICIA) was setting up a marketing organization, while back in the UK, PPD was continuing to negotiate with Wellcome for a sub-license, and developing forecasts of the market potential for the major agricultural producer countries.

Estimating Market Potential

When the potential of 'Ambush' was recognized by ICI, a Steering Committee for the global development and commercialization of pyrethroid insecticides, headed jointly by two Division directors (Ronnie Hampel of ICIA and Alan Maier of PPD) was formed, and Gordon Rae was appointed Project Manager based at PPD in September 1975. It is significant that until this time the project had been pushed forward by a very small group of people, who believed in NRDC 143's potential, without any formal recognition.

To estimate the potential for pyrethroid insecticides, the following logical analysis flow was developed:

Total acreage grown of target crop (e.g. cotton)

↓

Acreage treated with chemicals for the pest complex controlled by pyrethroids (Candidate market)

↓

Products currently used and number of applications per season

↓

Price/unit ai* applied in products currently used

↓

Price of product/unit sprayed/season

↓

Position of pyrethroid on technical grounds amongst existing products

↓

Position of pyrethroid on a commercial basis assuming that, as the market leader, synthetic pyrethroids might gain 30—40% of the potential market for pyrethroids. (Target market)

↓

A price/volume relationship for the pyrethroid

↓

ICI share of the market for the pyrethroid depending upon the number of licensees operating in each country and ICI's local strengths and weaknesses

↓

From the price/volume relationship is derived the bearable cost/ha

↓

---

* (ai = active ingredient).

Using application rates derived from field studies, bearable prices/ kg ai fob for each crop in each country is derived

↓

The bearable price for each country and all crops is determined

↓

Using best estimates of cost of production, gross margins are calculated on the fob price

↓

Using these acceptable prices and volumes, the global ICI demand in tons/yr of ai and expected fob realizations are calculated for years of maximum sales

↓

Possible sales build up by years to the maximum are then calculated

↓

The prices used in financial calculations have been reduced to take some account of a probable fall in the long term as competition from other pyrethroids and existing insecticides increase

This exercise was carried out by country and by crop, and confirmed that the largest single potential market was for cotton in the USA.

Marketing in the USA

As of March 1975, ICIA acquired the Penick license, the organization comprised eleven marketing staff — six salesmen selling seed treatments and five market research analysts. None of these staff had any previous experience of cotton, and ICIA were ill-prepared to enter the USA cotton insecticide market. In mid-1975 David Walker of PPD was appointed Marketing Director of ICIA Agricultural Chemicals Division to set up a distribution and marketing organization prior to the launch of 'Ambush'.

During the summer and autumn, market research identified the following points:

1 The cotton insecticide market had an annual value of $200 million and was confined to fourteen 'cotton states'. There is a wide variation in cultural practice, profitability, and forms of pesticide distribution between these states.
2 While there was a wide range of insecticides in common use, the market was dominated by a cheap mixture of toxaphene + methyl parathion (70% of market). There were indications of resistance to current insecticides, indicating an opening for more efficacious treatments.
3 As 'Ambush' was expected to be more effective than current treatments — probably in a ratio of two sprayings of 'Ambush' to three sprayings of alternatives — the bearable price for 'Ambush' would be above that for toxaphene + methyl parathion.
4 There was likely to be strong competition for the synthetic pyrethroid market. FMC already held a licence and sold insecticides throughout the southern states, and Shell Oil had access to another effective pyrethroid insecticide outside the NRDC patents for which they had negotiated an exclusive position for the USA from Sumitomo. Further, in the USA, Shell Oil had been selling a broad range of cotton pesticides through a large network of distributors. Their stake in the cotton insecticide market was high and their sales strength was imposing.

ICIA set an objective of a 'fair share' of the future synthetic pyrethroid market, recognizing that in view of the strength of the competition a radical approach would be necessary. Otherwise, they would be lucky to secure even a 10% share.

The radical approach selected would involve taking risks by:

1 Adopting a different form of sales/distribution.
2 Launching the product preferably before or alongside competition.
3 Having sufficient product available for sale at the earliest possible opportunity.
4 Continuing intensive field development to position 'Ambush' with the many market influencers.

Items 2 and 3 involved taking financial risks to ensure that the necessary registration data was obtained early and concurrently that production was organized prior to any registration to sell. The key to an effective form of sales and distribution was further detailed market research and its innovative interpretation.

Further market research showed that:

1 Some 12—14 distributors out of 300 held 40—50% of the business.
2 Distributors were most concerned about the disorganized state of the market, with heavy competition and minimal profit resulting from competition.
3 The main distributors had not heard of ICI, but had heard about the potential use of synthetic pyrethroids.

ICIA formulated a bold marketing policy of highly selective distribution. It was clear that if ICI could obtain a minimum of 75% of the business of key distributors, then they would obtain a sizeable share of the total market.

Market research was then used to identify exactly which companies controlled the business and the sales of each company. It also established factors which might persuade them to support ICIA. It was apparent that they would respond to a limited, selective approach to distribution if ICIA could persuade them that ICI was technically competent, commerically trustworthy and likely to stay in the US agrochemical market.

ICIA immediately appointed a handful of specialist, technically qualified, experienced cotton insecticide salesmen. Letters of intent to work together towards a long-term mutual commitment were signed with twelve major distributors in spring 1976. Joint trials work was conducted by ICIA and each prospective distributor with a view towards establishing a unique marketing position in the future, but without legal obligation by any of the parties.

The joint participative trials programme was successfully completed in 1976. All distributors then recognized the effectiveness of 'Ambush' and became convinced that ICIA were committed to a long-term business in agricultural chemicals in the USA.

In January 1977, ICIA signed contracts with eleven of the original twelve prospective distributors and added one additional distributor for a total of twelve. The contract required the distributor to sell a minimum of 75% of his future synthetic pyrethroids products in the form of 'Ambush' and that he should dedicate his promotional efforts to 'Ambush'. In return ICIA committed to each distributor:

1 To appoint no more than four other distributors in any given area of the cotton belt
2 Not to appoint any other distributors (other than replacement on default) for 5 years
3 To arrange formulation contracting if desired
4 To provide joint label identification
5 To furnish product on consignment

6 To supply a commercially competitive product
7 To provide a package of promotional aids and training support
   for distributors.

Making the Sale

While ICIA were setting up their marketing organization, development work was being co-ordinated in those countries in which
research had shown the best potential. In December 1976, PPD
signed the sub-license agreement with Wellcome so that the territorial rights of pyrethrin analogues now appear as set out in Exhibit
8.1.

A critical factor determining commercial development is the
completion of the pre-sale registration requirements of each country.
As indicated earlier, this normally takes two years (or more) in
sophisticated countries with stringent regulations, whereas it can be
little more than a formality in less advanced countries.

In the USA registration is the responsibility of the Environmental
Protection Agency (EPA), which is possibly the most rigorous screening body in the world. Environmental protection is a major issue
in the USA and EPA was created to serve this purpose. Regulation
(including registration) of pesticides is conducted with the protection
of the environment as one of the most important factors in the
decision-making process. EPA was created in 1970 and approved
numerous new pesticides between that time and 1976. However,
in 1976 registration came to a near standstill as EPA devoted almost
all of their resources to the reregistration process of evaluating all
previously registered products. It was against this background of
virtually no registrations issuing for new pesticides that ICIA sought
to get approval for 'Ambush'.

The breakthrough came in 1977 on cotton and in early 1978 on
celery when 'Ambush' was approved under emergency exemptions
and ICIA were allowed to sell 3.5 tons of the active ingredient permethrin under the residue action levels granted by the EPA. These
exemptions and accompanying action levels were granted as a result
of strong political pressure from the celery and cotton 'lobbies',
both of which argued the urgent need for a more effective form of
crop protection.

In the case of celery, there are only two significant growing areas
in the USA, in California, and Florida. In Florida the 12,000 acres
of intensively farmed celery production is controlled by a close knit

group of eleven producers, and it was these who effectively lobbied the Governor to help save the crop when threatened by pests. The Commissioner of Agriculture requested that an emergency exemption be issued and the EPA granted the use of permethrin.

Previously, the much bigger and more influential 'cotton lobby' had also applied pressure. Cotton production in the USA has always been subject to a considerable threat from pests, and failure to spray the crop can result in its total loss. The need for treatment varies considerably from nil in Texas to up to 35 sprayings in N. Carolina, and had increased significantly with the withdrawal of DDT from the market some years previously. In turn, DDT had been replaced by organic phosphorus insecticides but these had proved less effective, with the result that spraying costs had risen to a level where cotton farming was of only marginal profitability in some areas. The potential availability of synthetic pyrethroids (100 times more effective than DDT) had been made known to the cotton farmers, who exerted considerable pressure for their speedy registration.

As a result of this pressure, synthetic pyrethroid insecticides are among the few new compounds to receive clearance from the EPA since 1976, and the US market was opened up to ICIA two years earlier than forecast.

In 1978 ICIA arranged letters of intent with twenty-three additional distributors in the non-cotton areas (36 states) as a prelude to a later contract for the sale of 'Ambush' on non-cotton crops.

ICIA's twelve distributors met their contractual obligations and sold 'Ambush' as a high percentage of their synthetic pyrethroids business. In 1978 570,000 lbs ai permethrin were sold by ICIA at a value of $24.7 million. Pyrethroids achieved a 20% penetration by volume of the 43m spray acres of cotton and 45% share of the cotton insecticide market by value. ICIA achieved 50% of total pyrethroid sales in 1978.

The twelve ICI distributors had been welded together in an association — The 'Ambush Club' — from 1976 onwards. The aims of this Club were to arrange the formal meeting of the head of each distributive company at least once each year, to ensure that they all knew each other, and to allow their participation in the development of marketing plans. The distributors have an influence on ICIA thinking, and many of their suggestions have been incorporated into the forward market plans. The central theme of the 'Ambush Club' is 'Listen, Learn, and Lead'.

The 'Ambush Club' distributive system continued to provide ICIA with advantages over its competition in 1979. No major changes have been made, and the special relationship continues in 1980. It is expected to continue long-term not only for 'Ambush', but also for the introduction of other new pesticides.

Postscript

1 In 1979 the market for cotton insecticides in the USA collapsed — the pests did not come. Will they return?
2 In 1980 the price for synthetic pyrethroid insecticides plummeted, due to competitive pressures. Will it recover?

Patent Territory	British Licensees (Wellcome/ & Mitchell Cotts/ PPD Swell)	American Licensees (ICI (US) and F.M.C.)	Japanese Licensee (SUMITOMO)	European Licensees Roussel—UCLAF
UK	Non-exclusive manufacturing and selling			
Original EEC countries (6)	Non-exclusive selling			Exclusive manufacturing and non-exclusive selling
British EFTA Commonwealth	Non-exclusive selling			
Eastern Europe	Non-exclusive selling			Non-exclusive selling
USSR	Non-exclusive selling			
Middle East	Non-exclusive selling			Egypt and Israel Non-exclusive selling
Mediterranean	Non-exclusive selling			Non-exclusive selling
USA		Non-exclusive manufacturing and selling		
Canada	Non-exclusive selling	Non-exclusive selling		
Central and South America	Non-exclusive manufacturing and selling	Non-exclusive manufacturing and selling		Non-exclusive manufacturing and selling
Japan			Exclusive manufacturing and selling	
Philippines	Non-exclusive selling		Non-exclusive selling	Non-exclusive selling

(Exhibit 8.1: Pyrethrin Analogues – Summary of Territorial Rights of NRDC's Licensees)

IX
The International Marketing of Tea

R. Willsmer

In 1975, the tea-producing countries were faced with a number of marketing problems. At meetings sponsored by various international organizations (the Food and Agricultural Organisation (FAO), General Agreement on Trade and Tariffs (GATT) and the International Trade Centre (ITC)), producing countries were simultaneously considering limitations on production and generating demand by generic advertising and promotion. The background to this debate is provided in this case.

Tea in the World's Economy

Tea is not one of the great agricultural staple products, like wheat. Its importance rests on two major facts. Firstly, a very high proportion enters into world trade. Secondly, the balance of payments of the major producing countries depends to a considerable extent on the export of tea. Moreover, 95% of the tea entering into world trade originates in the developing and emergent nations. (Most of the remainder comes from China). The main source is Asia: India and Sri Lanka accounted for 56% of all tea exports in 1970–74. More than half of Sri Lanka's total earnings from exports is derived from tea. The largest African producer during the same period, Kenya, accounted for only 5%. Tea is vital to the export earnings of Kenya, Bangladesh, Malawi, Tanzania and Uganda. It is significant, as the history of tea promotion will reveal, that just over three-quarters of world trade in tea originates from present or former

Prepared by Ray Willsmer, 1981.

Commonwealth countries. Those same countries also account for more than half of the world's tea consumption. (India and the UK together account for one-third.)

One of the problems faced by the tea-producing countries has been that the area planted to tea grew steadily by just over 1% per annum between 1962 and 1974. The expansion was greatest in Africa (encouraged by land liberalization programmes), least in Sri Lanka, Iran, Turkey and the USSR and declined in Indonesia (one of the leading pre-war exporters). Over the same years, the African share of tea production rose from 6% to 10%. Latin America increased by 1% to 2% but the Asian producers experienced a fall from 93% to 88%.

A significant reason for this change has been a growing demand for cheaper, lower quality teas, especially for 'new' tea products like Tea Bags, Instant Teas and Tea Mixes.

Trends in Consumption

Trends may be summarized under five headings:

1 Large, expanding markets: USA, USSR, Pakistan, South Africa, Japan, Canada.
2 Medium, expanding: Ireland, West Germany, New Zealand, Poland.
3 Small, expanding: France, Israel, Denmark, Italy, Sweden, Switzerland.
4 Large, declining: Australia, UK.
5 Medium, declining: Netherlands.

The consumption problem is that the rate of decline in the large and medium markets has outweighed the growth rates elsewhere. The long-term trend in the UK is the real problem. The increases have been greatest among the domestic markets of India, Kenya, and Turkey.

Increases in tea consumption have, in general, been due to population growth, rather than growth in per capita consumption. Unfortunately, in the major markets, the decline in *per capita* tea consumption has more than offset the effects of population growth. The problem has been accelerated by the fact that, in these economies, young people have switched to competitive beverages (mainly Coffee and Coca Cola) with a consequent aging of the tea-consuming population.

Trends in Prices

The long-term trend in tea prices (as paid at the London auctions) has been downward since 1954. Odd periods of increase have not been sustained. The situation reflects the fact that the demand for tea is relatively inelastic, certainly in the main consuming countries. Thus, increases in the quantity of tea entering into world trade have been accompanied by more than proportionate falls in price.

Combine this situation with the economic dependence of the major producers on tea in their balance of payments and the problem is seen clearly. In years of world-wide inflation of basic commodities and capital equipment, the real value of tea exports has declined dramatically. It is also a fact of life that the tea-producing countries have, on the whole, earned smaller shares of the world's hard currencies, for which the growth of trade with the USA has been far too slow to compensate. (The newer African producers benefited greatly from the superiority of their lower grade teas in the new processes adopted by the USA and the UK in particular.)

Tea does not store well. The only variable in production terms is the intensity of plucking. The investment in land, machinery, equipment and skilled labour makes planters extremely reluctant to reduce acreage.

Tea Products

In the UK, we tend to think mainly of leaf tea in packets but, with over half the households regularly using tea bags, the old ideas are changing fast. Technically, four kinds of tea product exist:

1 Leaf tea; in packets, tins,
2 Tea bags; one-cup size or for making in pots.
3 Instant tea; made in the cup.
4 Tea mixes; as concentrates for making in the cup or pre-mixed in cans or bottles, still or carbonated.

The newer products all lead to reductions in the amount of tea consumed. Tea bags not only use lower-grade teas (as 'fillers') but the usage patterns lead to a 10—15% decline compared to the use of loose tea. Instant teas contain non-tea fillers (mainly sucrose) whilst the tea mixes contain only 2—3% tea by volume, sucrose and citric acid being the major ingredients.

Regulation of Supplies

Given the relative inelasticity of demand in the high-consumption countries, regulation of the quantity of tea entering into world trade would appear an obvious solution. It is all the more appropriate given the relatively low life of black tea.

In the early 1930s, Ceylon, India and the Netherlands East Indies entered into an International Tea Regulation Scheme to bring demand and supply into better balance. In 1933, the International Tea Committee took over the administration of the regulation scheme but, significantly, took the attitude that regulation alone would not work in the long-term unless it was also accompanied by increased promotion aimed at total market expansion. This led directly to the creation of an international body for promotion, described in the next section.

The International Tea Agreement was not renewed after 1955. Concern at the lack of an effective body led, eventually, to setting up a permanent FAO study group, the Inter-Governmental Group on Tea. Once again, the supply side was the prime concern. Concern at low prices in 1969 led to the Mauritius Agreement by which exporting countries agreed to limit their tea exports. There was some recovery in 1970 but the resolve that existed in 1969–70 gradually melted away. In 1973, the Exporters' Sub-Group of the Intergovernmental Group on Tea decided to widen its approach to cover marketing and promotion as well as regulations.

For a number of reasons, mainly natural (e.g. drought), prices in 1974 have returned to the level of 1964, a performance that can give little cause for satisfaction and does little to help the balance of payments of the producing countries.

The Sub-Group of Exporters (that part of the Intergovernmental Group on Tea primarily concerned with supply problems) put into effect an informal export quota scheme in 1970. However, the quotas have been too large to produce really significant effects on tea prices. At its last meeting (June 1974) it asked the FAO to convene a Working Party to look at the feasibility of a new form of international agreement based upon five elements:

1 Minimum price arrangements (i.e. a 'floor price' below which no exports would be allowed).
2 Regulation and co-ordination aimed at preventing build-up of stocks in importing countries.
3 Co-operation in global, generic promotion.

4 Examination of the feasibility of developing and expanding auctions in producing countries.
5 Provision of an independent source of market intelligence and research for tea exports.

History of Generic Tea Promotion

History shows that tea producers have a far more enlightened history of promotion activity than any other commodity producers. Campaigns to spread the tea-drinking habit date back to the 1870s. Most of the earliest activity was uninational and related to the major international exhibitions. From one of these, the Chicago Exhibition of 1893, came a positive step towards generic promotion. Tea interests became convinced that India and Ceylon should jointly promote 'British Grown India Types', irrespective of country of origin.

Behind this movement was the strong conceptual influence of 'The British Empire' and this was to be a recurring theme in the early years and a catalyst which is no longer relevant to the present day. Although both countries went their individual ways from time to time, the 'Empire Grown' theme united India and Ceylon either through their own joint efforts or through the medium — and assistance — of the Empire Marketing Board.

The early publicity efforts were voluntary and grower-sponsored. The increasing government awareness of the importance of creating a demand, combined with the persuasion of the contributing growers, led to the imposition of export duties and taxes which made contribution to promotional funds obligatory. The Ceylon Propaganda Cess was operative from 1893 and India followed in 1903.

Perhaps the most significant development was the formation of the International Tea Market Expansion Board (ITMEB) which arose out of the International Tea Agreement of 1933, signed by the Amsterdam Tea Association, the Indian Tea Association and the Ceylon Association. Generic promotion under ITMEB grew out of production restriction. When demand and supply are out of balance, as they were with the over-production of the 1930s, you can either restrict supply or create demand or combine the two. The regulation scheme started in 1933; ITMEB was established in July 1935.

ITMEB's work covered about a dozen countries (working through Tea Bureaux in each) until the second World War, using whatever methods seemed most appropriate to the conditions applying in each country. When ITMEB resumed its activities after the War, it was soon in the position of receiving funds from the East African producers and Pakistan. 1952 represented both the high-spot of activity and the beginning of the end. Late that year, Indonesia announced her withdrawal; Pakistan decided she could not afford full membership and, later, India withdrew on the grounds that she would derive greater benefit from employing her contribution uninationally. After the East African producers withdrew in 1954, the Board became, in effect, the overseas promotion agency of the Ceylon Tea Propaganda Board, its sole remaining sponsor.

ITMEB was a tea-grower's organization. It was virtually independent of governments. It chose to lead from strength and expand existing markets rather than develop new ones (with the conspicuous exception of the USA). To its great credit, it always believed that promotion could not be switched on and off like a tap; it had to be sustained. It set up Bureaux intended to be semi-permanent, employing local nationals and allowing ample time to understand local habits. Unfortunately, pressures developed which destroyed that principle. Of prime overall importance to any assessment of the work of ITMEB is the fact that it never had enough money to mount a full-scale campaign in any one country.

After ITMEB, responsibility for generic promotion has become a partnership operation with producers and packers jointly contributing (in proportions which vary by country) to funds administered by Tea Councils.

The Tea Councils

The US Tea Council was the first of these and actually predated the demise of the ITMEB. It arose from the inadequacy of available funds and the realization that only the matching of funds by packers and producers could produce a campaign capable of real impact. Funds of US $1 million were generated in this way. In 1953, it was formally ratified that the contribution of the producing countries ought properly to exceed those of the packers who were already making substantial contributions to the growth of the market through their brand advertising. Unfortunately, the result of the new formula was to reduce the available funds to $600,000.

The most significant of the changes in contribution rate came in 1961/2. The trade was investing heavily in the introduction of instant teas and this reduced the amount of support they felt able to give the generic campaign. A new formula was arrived at, which entailed the trade guaranteeing to produce a minimum of $150,000 a year and the producers agreeing to provide $350,000. Part of the agreement was that the Council would do those things the packers were not. Since that date, there has been no media campaign by the Tea Council; all its resources have been concentrated on educational and public relations activities of various kinds. Two things have happened over time. Firstly, the contributing countries have changed: Indonesia fell out and was replaced by contributions from African producers. Secondly, the growth of the domestic market has meant that the US trade has always exceeded the guaranteed rate. In 1974, the formula yielded a total appropriation of almost $700,000.

The United States is an iced tea market and the growth of tea has been at the expense of other beverages and notably coffee. There have been four main streams to the Campaigns: the consumer, schools and colleges, sports and entertainments. Consumer activities have been aimed at generating media comment (recipes etc.) whilst school activities have been aimed jointly at the domestic science teacher and the student. All material is supplied on request; there is no speculative mailing. The sports programme makes use of famous football coaches who carry out promotion tours and training booklets which, again, are available on request.

Although still heavily outspent (in all forms of advertising) by coffee and carbonated soft drinks, tea has shown an 87% rise in total consumption and 37% increase in per caput consumption since the Council was set up. Tea bags account for half the market with iced tea and instant tea not far behind. Although coffee consumption has fallen sharply, it still outsells tea by between four and five times.

In short, the Tea Council's budget is so small that it could not possibly account for the increase in tea sales. However, intelligently and skilfully added to the efforts of the trade (who have borne the heavy burden of product development and market launches) it has enabled the tea message to have wider coverage and considerable frequency.

Germany is the odd man out of the seven Councils in the form of its organization. It is registered as a company with each share of DM100 entitling its holder to a vote. The current ratio of contribution is 6:1 with the two producers, India and Ceylon, making the major contribution. With the limited producer participation, it is hardly surprising that a major objective is increasing awareness of the quality image of Indian and Sri Lankan tea. Since 1963, this message has been promulgated by public relations activities and, especially, through much increased participation in Fairs. There is no uni-national advertising in Germany: this is set out in the constitution of the Council and has shaped the messages used.

It is difficult to assess the value of the Council's work. Even when it did use media, it did so on an extremely small scale. The present emphasis on Fairs is one which produces a target audience at very high cost and it would take many years to achieve a high level of coverage. Perhaps because of this realization, there has been an emphasis on the number of Fairs participated in rather than their delivery of a quality audience. There are indications of a hopeful approach to the youth market which appears to justify research, at the very least, and may well offer more hopeful avenues to explore.

The Canadian Tea Council was founded in 1954 with India and Ceylon the original producer members (now joined by the East African producers). There have been many revisions to the budgetary basis, starting with a 3:1 ratio with the producers providing $75,000 and the trade Can $25,000. The latest revision, dated May 1974, still attempts to preserve the 3:1 basis with the trade paying on the basis of brand sales and the producers paying on the basis of exports to Canada averaged over the last three years. The major change in promotional emphasis came in 1969, with increased reliance upon television. Recent campaigns rely heavily on research and pre-tested commercials. The target is young housewives, nationally, and the commercials are aimed at people who have tea in the house but may not be regular drinkers.

Per capita consumption of tea in Canada shows a long-term trend to decline but, since 1969, it has first stabilized and now shows the first sign of reversal. Present trends are thus encouraging but any further progress would entail budgets well in excess of those generated in the past.

The Tea Council of Australia dates from 1963 with the original members as India, Ceylon and the Australian trade. Indonesia and Kenya came in later with small contributions. As in other Councils, the basis of contribution has changed over time. In effect, the Council is no longer operative since the withdrawal of a major packer at the end of 1972. When it had funds, the Council concentrated on the 15—20 and 20—35 age groups where the fall in consumption has been most dramatic. Consumption, both in total and *per caput*, has continued to decline. As a hot drink, tea has undoubtedly lost share to coffee. Coffee has risen by around 5% per annum while tea has fallen at a rate of 2% per annum. Total volumes are now about equal. With the company responsible for 50% of tea sales leaving the Council because it believed it ineffectual in halting the decline in tea consumption, the problems before the trade are enormous if the Tea Council is to be resuscitated.

The French Tea Council has three members: India, Sri Lanka and CEFREPIT, the trade organization. Each of the three contributes Fr.200,000, with the trade paying according to share of market. Throughout the Council's existence, the basis and the sum raised have remained unchanged. The only increase in budget came when CEDUS (the French Sugar Committee) contributed Fr.100,000 in 1965 and continued until 1972. (Cedus returned to the Council in 1974.)

Although the Council has never bought space on television, it has used the medium with free space provided by the contractors. It utilized the cinema until 1968 and radio up to the same year. Magazines were used only in 1966. Current activity dates from 1970 with the decision to halt media advertising and switch to public relations activities on a far wider scale. Media was to be left to the producing countries own campaigns and to the trade. (Trade promotion for tea seldom exceeds F.Frs.4.0m whilst that for coffee consistently runs at around F.Frs.40.0m.) Apart from the more usual contact with media which is a fundamental part of any public relations campaign, activities have been conducted with schools, sports events, lectures, demonstrations and many *ad hoc* affairs.

An assessment of the effectiveness of the campaigns is difficult. A constant budget in times of inflation does not allow much latitude. The Executive's attitude that generic media advertising has no part to play in the French market finds no support in the situations examined in many other markets. Sampling, whilst an effective effort in a country where the tea habit is so little known, is a long, slow haul. Many of the ad hoc affairs and some of the sports participations show clear signs of the Council being 'used' by the promoters — as is so frequently the case with any producer who is anxious for exposure of his product. It would appear that the budget is too small for even an effective public relations campaign, let alone media support.

The United Kingdom Tea Council was not established until 1965, despite the importance of the market in world trade. The original members were the Tea Trade Committee, India and Ceylon. East

African producers contributed from 1969–70. The Tea Trade Committee had approached the governments of India and Ceylon with the offer to match any contributions up to £500,000, thus producing a total budget of £1.0 million. In fact, the two producers offered £300,000 allowing a total budget of £600,000. This level was held for four years, the end coming when the trade announced that it could not continue to match contributions after the end of the 68–9 campaign when a major member would be withdrawing from the Council. Since that date, there have been innumerable discussions about funding until, finally, the trade withdrew from any level of campaign contribution for 1973–4. For 1974–5, the producers have contributed £150,000 with the trade paying the costs of the office and Secretariat for twelve months.

As long as the budget allowed, the campaign majored on television with the main attack launched against the younger age groups. The early, image, campaign was gradually sharpened up to make a direct attack on existing drinkers who were extolled to drink more tea. Attention was gradually switched to specific occasions. As the budget declined, media advertising was abandoned and attention switched to public relations activities. Although the target for this campaign is obviously much more limited than earlier ones, continuous research studies do show encouraging trends among the younger age groups. The only other thing that can be said with any certainty about the effects of the UK campaign (and despite several mathematical models) is that the years when the decline in tea consumption was temporarily halted were the years of high media expenditure.

The Tea Council of New Zealand was started in 1966 on the joint initiative of Ceylon and the brand leaders in the market. Current contributors are India, Sri Lanka and the tea trade. After the usual changes, contributions have settled down at NZ $24,000 from Sri Lanka and NZ $3,000 from India. The trade contribution has run at around NZ $17,000 although it has doubled in 1973/74 in the hope (not realized) that the producers would follow suit.

The Council has steadily aimed its attack at the 15–24 and 25–34 age groups with an odd and completely unsuccessful excursion at schoolchildren in 1971. The method has been variously media, public relations and a combination of the two. By their own assessments, the earlier activities were unsuccessful and the switch to total emphasis on television advertising was made in 1971–2.

The most recent figures suggest that the decline in tea consumption which has been continuous since 1965 was arrested in 1971 and that some reversal of that trend is now evident. Attitudinal research on a continuous basis confirms the validity of the Council's strategy and suggests that the specific approach adopted is having effect on the attitudes of young people towards tea.

Uninational Promotion

Sri Lanka derives its funds from a Cess on exports with a current rate of Rs 5 per 100 lbs. Promotional expenditure has risen from about 1% of export earnings in 1960—5 to 3% in 1974. The proportion of funds directed to uninational advertising (as against generic) has risen from 73% in 1968 to 85% in 1974.

Sri Lanka's uninational advertising has the virtues of continuity and consistency and a relatively greater emphasis on media than India. In recent years, Sri Lanka has tended to emphasize the non-traditional markets of the Middle East and away from her more traditional markets. This is a switch to areas where promotional means are limited and frequently subject to interference and regulation by Government agencies. The basic dilemma here is whether the need is for foreign exchange or goods. In the more developed markets, Sri Lanka has been largely competing with all the tools of the major packers but at inadequate levels of expenditure. A combination of small allocations and limited distribution of identifiable packs limits the possibilities of success severely. The present policy of running campaigns in thirty countries shows commendable zeal if little selectivity. There is no evidence of the evaluation of comparative returns from different markets.

India's promotional outlays show far more variation than Sri Lanka's. There has obviously been a substantial increase in the proportion of funds devoted to uninational promotion but the figures jump about to an extent that makes comparison almost meaningless.

India's campaigns cover twenty six countries with the emphasis very much on public relations activities (including participation in Fairs) rather than on media. As with Sri Lanka, there has been some movement away from traditional markets towards some of the restricted economies where the same comments as were made earlier are again appropriate. There have been some more recent switches between countries and the rationale behind these changes is difficult to fathom.

As in Sri Lanka, the budgets available in India produce allocations that are almost derisory in the more developed markets and some of the resultant activities may well be counter-productive. Again, the allocation of funds suggests that there can be no conscious appraisal and no assessment of relative benefits. It is a case of too little, too thinly spread.

	Average 1961—65	Average 1966—70	1970	1971	1972	1973
Bangladesh	—	10.8 *a*	10.5	4.1	—	—
India	17.0	8.3	10.8	9.8	8.7	6.5
Sri Lanka	64.7	58.7	56.1	58.7	60.1	51.0
Indonesia	2.7	1.8	1.6	2.3	1.9	—
Kenya	9.4	12.3	12.0	10.8	12.9	10.5
Malawi	34.0	22.9	22.0	20.1	19.5	16.7
Tanzania	2.6	2.6	2.3	2.5	2.4	2.2
Uganda	3.6	4.8	4.8	5.2	6.2	5.4
Mozambique	6.5	6.5	6.2	6.1	6.6	—
Argentina	0.4	0.5	0.5	0.7	0.6	—

a = Average 1967—70.

Source: Based on data in FAO Trade Yearbooks, FAO CCP TE74 EXPO 7/2 (April 1974), International Tea Committee Annual Bulletin of Statistics 1974, and IMF International Financial Statistics.

Exhibit 9.1: Relative importance of tea exports for certain countries (value of tea exports as percentage of value of all exports)

	Average 1961–65	Average 1971–73
Asia	93	87
Bangladesh	2	2
India	33	32
Sri Lanka	20	15
China *a*	16	15
Indonesia	7	5
Iran	1	2
Japan	7	6
Soviet Union	4	5
Turkey	1	2
Africa	6	11
Kenya	2	4
Malawi	1	2
Tanzania	1	1
Uganda	1	2
Mozambique	1	1
Zaire	1	—
Latin America	1	3
Argentina	1	2

a = Including Taiwan.

Source: Averages based on FAO Monthly Bulletin of Agricultural Economics and Statistics, March 1974.

Exhibit 9.2: Proportional distribution of world tea production (per cent)

	1963–65		1966–68		1967–69		1968–70		1969–71		1970–72	
	Total	per bd	Total	per bd	Total	per bd	Total	per bd	Total	per bd	Total	per bd
Irish Republic	11.20	3.96	11.63	4.01	11.65	4.00	11.81	4.04	11.41	3.88	11.95	4.02
United Kingdom	228.32	4.22	224.43	4.00	222.93	4.02	220.96	3.99	215.08	3.88	212.41	3.81
New Zealand	7.85	3.03	7.79	2.86	7.74	2.82	7.34	2.72	7.34	2.61	7.59	2.66
Australia	29.27	2.63	28.26	2.39	28.27	2.35	27.21	2.21	26.84	2.15	26.59	2.08
Canada	20.09	1.04	20.12	.98	20.55	.99	19.99	.95	20.05	.94	20.34	.94
South Africa b	16.24	.83	17.93	.85	18.54	.85	18.62	.82	18.60	.79	18.54	.76
Netherlands	9.04	.74	8.72	.69	8.15	.64	8.08	.63	8.18	.63	8.34	.63
Denmark	1.38	.29	1.53	.32	1.58	.33	1.68	.34	1.73	.35	1.86	.37
United States	58.72	.30	64.94	.32	60.01	.33	65.16	.32	68.27	.33	70.05	.34
Sweden	1.33	.17	1.68	.21	1.76	.22	1.85	.23	1.90	.24	1.97	.24
Switzerland	1.32	.23	1.30	.21	1.37	.22	1.41	.23	1.45	.23	1.51	.24
Fed.Rep. of Germany d	7.94	.14	8.00	.13	9.39	.14	8.74	.15	8.83	.14	9.10	.15
France	2.20	.04	2.72	.05	2.98	.06	3.21	.06	3.37	.07	3.66	.07
Italy	2.24	.04	2.27	.05	2.40	.05	2.55	.05	2.71	.05	2.68	.05
Soviet Union	69.00	.30	67.73	.29	70.17	.29	75.46	.31	87.13	.36	97.83	.40
Poland	5.13	.16	7.19	.23	7.43	.23	7.69	.24	8.75	.27	9.95	.30
German Dem. Rep. d	1.60	.10	1.27	.07	1.38	.08	1.54	.09	1.65	.10	—	—
Czechoslovakia	1.62	.11	1.30	.09	1.03	.07	1.25	.09	1.34	.09	1.43	.10
Iraq	18.42	2.33	19.34	2.29	18.61	2.15	20.22	2.16	20.79	2.20	20.45	2.10
Jordan	1.56	.90	2.30	1.12	2.64	1.25	2.78	1.26	2.89	1.25	2.63	1.11
Sudan	9.89	.75	11.74	.82	11.06	.74	14.25	.93	14.61	.93	17.28	1.07
Morocco	10.31	.79	12.85	.91	15.26	1.05	15.72	1.02	14.84	.96	13.15	.86
Egypt	26.09	.91	28.02	.91	26.77	.84	26.02	.80				
Syria	2.95	.57	3.39	.61	3.47	.61	3.20	.54	3.16	.51	3.17	.49
Pakistan c	25.18	.25	29.71	.28								
Sri Lanka	15.08	1.37	17.10	1.46	17.97	1.50	18.45	1.51	18.85	1.51	19.29	1.51
Iran a	19.59	.82	24.38	.94	25.08	.93	23.50	.84				
Japan	79.50	.82	88.26	.88	92.18	.91	97.64	.95	103.42	.99	107.53	1.02
Turkey	10.34	.34	18.30	.56	19.83	.59	23.96	.70	22.14	.62	23.99	.66
Kenya	3.51	.39	3.95	.40	4.24	.41	4.76	.45	5.22	.46	5.68	.49
India c	150.75	.32	183.60	.36	189.96	.36	200.73	.37	212.77	.40	222.00	.40
Tanzania	1.52	.15	1.74	.14	1.90	.15	1.70	.13	2.02	.15	2.05	.15
Uganda	1.34	.18	1.05	.13	1.17	.15	1.14	.14	1.30	.13	1.27	.13

a Year beginning 21st March.
b Including South-West Africa, Lesotho, Botswana and Swaziland.
c Year beginning 1st April.
d Including the respective sectors of Berlin.

Source: International Tea Committee: Annual Bulletin of Statistics.

Exhibit 9.3: Apparent consumption of tea in certain countries

Total: Total apparent consumption (three year moving averages, in thousand metric tons)

per bd: Apparent consumption per head of population (three year moving averages, in kg.)

	Total	*Annual*
Irish Republic	5.8	0.8
United Kingdom	−7.1	−1.0
New Zealand	−3.3	−0.5
Australia	−9.2	−1.3
Canada	1.2	0.2
South Africa *c*	14.2	2.0
Netherlands	−7.8	−1.1
Denmark	34.8	5.0
United States	19.3	2.8
Sweden	48.1	6.9
Switzerland	14.4	2.1
Fed. Rep. of Germany	14.6	2.1
France	66.4	9.5
Italy	19.6	2.8
Soviet Union	41.8	6.0
Poland	94.0	13.4
German Dem. Rep. *f*	—	—
Czechoslovakia	−11.7	−1.7
Iraq	11.0	1.6
Jordan	68.6	9.8
Sudan	74.7	10.1
Morocco	27.5	3.9
Egypt *b*	−0.3	−0.04
Syria	7.5	1.1
Pakistan *a*	18.0	2.6
Sri Lanka	27.9	4.0
Iran *e*	20.0	2.9
Japan	35.3	5.0
Turkey	132.0	18.9
Kenya	61.8	8.8
India *d*	47.3	6.8
Tanzania	34.9	5.0
Uganda	5.2	0.7

a   Period 1963−5 to 1966−8
b   Period 1963−5 to 1968−70
c   Including South-West Africa, Lesotho, Botswana and Swaziland
d   Year beginning 1st April
e   Year beginning 21st March and period 1963−5 to 1968−70
f   Period 1963−5 to 1969−71.

Source: Based on Table 9.3

Exhibit 9.4: Change in total tea consumption, average 1963−5 to
average 1970−2 (per cent)

Year	London (pence)	Calcutta (a) (Rs)	Calcutta (a) (pence)	Colombo (b) (Rs)	Colombo (b) (pence)	Kenya (Shgs)	Kenya (pence)
1962	49.0	5.26	39.5	3.86	28.9	6.81	34.1
1963	46.5	5.16	38.7	3.70	27.7	6.86	34.3
1964	47.2	4.95	37.1	3.70	27.7	6.59	33.0
1965	46.0	5.44	40.8	3.83	28.7	7.23	36.2
1966	44.8	5.74	32.2	3.47	26.0	6.53	32.6
1967	45.7	5.99	28.9	3.30	24.6	7.08	35.4
1968	43.5	5.50	30.6	3.85	27.0	5.97	34.8
1969	40.5	5.94	33.0	3.37	23.6	5.14	30.0
1970	45.7	6.53	36.3	3.60	25.2	6.34	37.0
1971	43.3	6.61	36.2	3.99	27.6	6.44	37.6
1972	42.2	6.38	33.7	4.17	27.1	5.79	32.4
1973	43.4	6.93	39.6	4.16	28.3	5.86	36.5

Source: International Tea Committee Annual Bulletin of Statistics except for sterling equivalent of prices in producing countries, for which average exchange rates for the year concerned have been used for conversion.

(a) Leaf tea for domestic consumption and export, excluding excise and export duties.
(b) Excluding excise duty.

Exhibit 9.5: Annual average auction prices of exportable teas (per kg)

	Average 1961−5	Average 1966−70	1970	1971	1972	1973 p
Asia	580.2	527.6	521.9	509.2	495.8	495.0 e
Bangladesh	1.7	43.9	56.5	18.6	5.9	11.0
India	260.4	208.1	198.3	207.0	207.8	191.2
Sri Lanka	241.6	198.8	188.1	192.1	188.0	198.0
China a	37.7	44.1	44.2	44.6	45.2	
Indonesia	19.6	14.3	18.3	28.9	29.8	30.2
Iran	0.7	0.2	0.5	0.2	0.2	
Japan	3.5	1.3	1.2	1.3	1.4	
Soviet Union b	7.9	10.8	10.1	9.7	9.8	
Turkey	0.4	1.7	1.7	3.9	3.8	
Africa	49.6	74.0	85.2	87.8	110.0	112.9
Kenya	16.4	29.3	36.9	34.1	46.2	48.4
Malawi	10.3	12.2	13.1	14.5	15.8	16.5
Tanzania	4.4	6.4	6.0	6.9	7.5	8.2
Uganda	5.9	11.2	13.3	13.4	17.6	17.4
Mozambique	6.5	8.9	8.1	9.6	11.6	11.3
Zaire	2.1	2.4	1.9	1.3	1.3	
Latin America	6.1	10.4	12.6	16.1	14.8	9.7
Argentina	4.9	7.9	9.5	11.7	11.1	5.5
Oceania		0.2	0.7	1.2	2.1	2.4
Total, all producers	636.0	612.2	620.4	614.3	622.7	620.0 e

a Estimated; including Taiwan.
b May include re-exports.
e Estimate.
p Preliminary.

Source: Average 1961−5 − FAO Trade Yearbooks; 1966−73 − for non-centrally planned economies: FAO TE74 EXPO 7/2 (April 1974) adjusted to include Bangladesh throughout; for centrally planned economies, 1966−72 − FAO Trade Yearbooks 1973, International Tea Committee Annual Bulletin of Statistics, 1974.

Exhibit 9.6: Value of tea exported from producing countries
(million US dollars)

X
The W.H. Mosse Company (A): Developing New Products

M. F. Bradley

In August 1973, Mr Jim Furlong, Marketing Director of W. H. Mosse Limited, met with his management colleagues to assess the performance of the company's soda bread mix products and to develop plans for the future. A brown bread mix had been on the Irish market since 1971 and a white bread mix had been launched one year later. Prior to the launch of Mosse's Soda Bread Mix, a competing product had established itself on the market without any extensive promotional campaign. About this time there were rumours that bread mix products in addition to the two brands already on the market were about to be launched by the larger millers; these would be likely to have significant promotional backing. In addition to the possibility of new competition the W. H. Mosse Company was facing a situation of increased production costs. Among other things it was decided at the August 1973 meeting that Jim Furlong should visit the Anuga Food Fair in Cologne during the following month to explore the possibility of exporting the bread mix. Because of the peculiar industry and market structure facing flour millers in Ireland, it was an original intention of the W. H. Mosse Company to develop new flour based products which could be exported to an enlarged EEC.

Sales Performance of the Bread Mix Products

Sales of Mosse's Brown Soda Bread Mix, which was launched during 1971, exceeded expectations. At the time of the launch the company

Prepared by Dr M. F. Bradley, University College, Dublin.

anticipated a weekly sales level of 10,000 kilogrammes. Encouraged by the performance of the brown bread mix during the first year on the market the company launched Mosse's White Soda Bread Mix at the end of 1972. Sales results for the white bread mix were, however, somewhat disappointing. All information available to the Mosse Company indicated that the trade and press appeared well disposed to both products. Nevertheless, the company was disappointed with market performance, particularly of the white bread mix.

During the twelve month period ending July 1972, the company sold 39,375 cases of the brown bread mix, equivalent to 630,000 kilogrammes at an average wholesale price of £1.79 per case. (Each case contained 16 x 1 kilo packs.) In the following year, 39,736 cases were sold at an average wholesale price of £2.03 per case. In 1971–2 the product retailed at between 13 pence and 14.5 pence per kilo pack, depending on the type and size of retail outlet. During the following year retail prices ranged from 14.5 to 16 pence per pack.

The Flour Milling Industry

Flour milling, although it is one of the oldest industries in Ireland, has been traditionally slow to adapt to new technological developments. Thus many of the smaller firms were very much concerned about the substantial rationalization programme which had been carried out within the flour milling industry during the 1960s. In 1969 there were only 17 mills as against 30 a few years earlier and 217 at the turn of the century (see Appendix 10.1).

A long-standing piece of legislation, from a period in Irish economic development when attaining self-sufficiency was a vital objective of public policy, imposed strict controls on the quantities of wheat which could be imported for milling purposes. The quota system, which still operates, became increasingly significant as Irish wheat production declined. At the same time, however, the Irish flour market had been declining and many of the surviving milling companies had begun to widen their scope of operations and to diversify into areas outside the traditional confines of flour milling.

The Company

The W. H. Mosse Company was, up to 1971, the oldest and one of the smallest companies in the Irish flour milling industry. Situated in

Bennetsbridge, Co. Kilkenny, it was located in the heart of the main Irish wheat-growing region on the banks of one of the country's largest rivers, the River Nore. Indeed some of the mill's power still comes from the river, although the main force now comes from diesel turbines. The mill contains many pieces of very old machinery, cased in magnificent wooden housing with old fashioned iron fittings. Despite its age, the mill is maintained to the highest standards. Quality control, too, is strict, with samples tested every hour and bread baked every four hours in domestic ranges simulating typical home-baking conditions. In 1968–9 the W. H. Mosse Company had a work force of eighty.

The mill had been run almost exclusively by various members of the Mosse family down through the years, and this tradition continued right up to 1968 when the executive directors were fifth generation Mosse cousins, Stanley and Pat. The senior director, Stanley, although he had not intended pursuing a business career, having served some time as a sculptor's assistant, was forced to run the business after his father's untimely death. He was nevertheless a practical business man who recognized his company's limitations, and knowing that the company needed a change in outlook if it was to continue to survive the massive rationalization which the flour milling industry was going through, he decided to bring in some marketing expertise. Thus, in 1968, Jim Furlong was recruited and appointed director of the company. Pat Mosse subsequently shifted his attentions to other Mosse family interests, so that after 1968, the W. H. Mosse Company was managed in the main by Stanley Mosse, now Production Director, and Jim Furlong, the new Marketing Director.

Jim Furlong introduced a dynamic combination of youth and experience into the W. H. Mosse Company. Unlike Stanley Mosse, he had gained a wide range of valuable experience first in management consultancy and later in the bakery industry. Although, also unlike Stanley, he was still in his early thirties, Furlong was well grounded in general management, financial and marketing techniques.

Selection of Development Strategies

Faced with a peculiar industry structure and a less than buoyant flour market, Mosse's management considered that the options open to the company fell into two groupings. There existed a number of opportunities in the retail flour end of the firm's activities and there were a number of possibilities in the animal feeds side of the business. Mosse might attempt any one or a combination of the following development programmes:

1 Break into the bulk bakers' flour business,
2 Intensify efforts in the retail flour market to capitalize on an existing distribution system,
3 Launch a baker's product along the lines of the Hovis development (a refrigerated part-baked loaf) in the United Kingdom,
4 Introduce cake and bread mix type products to the domestic bakery and retail trades,
5 Follow a similar new product development programme designed specifically for the export market, and/or
6 Expand the animal feeds business to exploit EEC developments in the agricultural sector.

After considerable discussion and some degree of persuasion it was agreed to proceed in a limited fashion by developing the bulk flour business, since the company would be taking on a logical extension of the existing business. It was recognized, however, that the pursuit of the bulk bakers' flour market would mean considerable competition and low profit margins. Furthermore, the firm in developing this market would be doing nothing very different from the existing operation; hence the need to consider other possibilities.

In 1970 the Mosse Company entered the animal feeds market by forming Mixrite (I) Limited through a linkup with Crosfields and Calthrop, the UK animal feed compounders, subsequently taken over by Dalgety. The Mosse Company was able to take advantage of the research facilities of Crosfields and Calthrop and their expertise in producing concentrates and pre-mixes. This enabled Mixrite to produce for approximately one quarter of the Irish animal feeds market which relies on buying in supplements. The new company produced concentrates of high protein value for sale to feed compounders and farmers. Increasing industrial costs on the one hand and the anticipated trend towards larger production units in the farming community, particularly in the dairy sector in anticipation of Ireland's entry to the EEC, gave rise to the possibility that farmers would grow an increasing quantity of feed requirements and buy-in vitamin supplements for mixing on the farm. A market for feed supplements was also expected to exist among the small off-farm compounders.

In addition to pursuing these possibilities, the company explored the potential of the market for proprietary type breads such as Hovis. While each of the above showed distinct possibilities from both a production and marketing point of view, the development of new consumer products for the domestic and export markets held the greatest promise for the marketing team. There were, however, a number of considerations which could influence the fortunes of the company. If it decided to export, the W. H. Mosse Company could expand its production beyond the quota limitations imposed by the industry-wide marketing regulations. This was possible as long as the new venture did not interfere with the domestic flour marketing arrangements. Possibilities under this heading were highly regarded by the expansion-minded management in the company. Furthermore, the company realized that, should it become involved in export marketing, it could draw upon outside help. Coras Trachtala (CTT), the Irish Exports Promotions Board, was established to help Irish companies exploit overseas marketing opportunities. At this time, however, the company believed that it did not have much to offer on an export market. Consequently, the W. H. Mosse Company felt that there was a need to develop new products which would be acceptable on both the domestic and export markets. A flour-based product was especially attractive to the company since a significant amount (20—30% of the wheat volume) of residue grain shells were left after the extraction process and these could be used in the making of animal feeds. The company was at the same time looking for a product which not only boosted turnover but which would have a high value added, since its existing line items were almost all of a low contribution value.

Development of Soda Bread Mix Product

By 1971 it appeared obvious to Jim Furlong and his management team that a bread mix produced by W. H. Mosse and sold to retailers and bakeries would not only increase the utilization of the company's salesforce but it would also introduce a high margin item to the Mosse product line which consisted almost exclusively of low contribution products and commodities. (A bread mix is a product which requires the addition of liquid, mixing, kneading, and baking to produce a loaf of bread.) A bread mix product, introduced by Howards of Crookstown, Co. Cork, another small family firm, had been on the market since early 1971 and was performing well without much promotional back-up. The W. H. Mosse Company felt that a bread mix was the ideal and obvious target for its production and marketing efforts for the coming years.

The Quota Problem

There was however one important drawback to this line of thinking, which was clear to Moss management from the outset. Since a soda bread mix would consist of approximately 80% flour or wheatmeal the production of this product would reduce the quantity of ordinary flour the company could produce under the quota system established in the industry. After some deliberation Mr Furlong surmounted the problem by employing a procedure successfully adopted in 1969 in the case of Mosse's Abbey Home Ground Flour. To circumvent the restrictions on flour output imposed by the quota, the company had earlier located a mill which had not until then utilized its quota to the full. By supplying the mill, owned by the Cistercian Monks of Mount St Joseph near Roscrea, with wheat to be ground on traditional stone grinders, the Mosse Company at once capitalized on the image imparted by the association with the monastery and also expanded total flour sales without infringing quota regulations. The procedure adopted in the case of Abbey Stone Ground Flour was also followed in the case of the wholemeal flour required for the new bread-mix products.

Bread Mix Production Costs

Additional costs involved in setting up the bread-mix programme included the extra transportation cost of carrying wheat to Roscrea and wholemeal on the return journey, an additional blending-mixing machine, product development and packaging development costs. The blending-mixing machine cost £8,000 while the cost of developing the packaging amounted to £200 which represented the fee paid to a design consultant. (Industrial Development Authority Machinery Grant Schemes and CTT packaging cost schemes were in operation at this time.) Total mill product development costs, based on estimates of staff time, amounted to £1,500 approximately.

During 1972—3 the firm installed an ultra-modern packaging machine which was used for the bread mix products but was also used for the ordinary retail flour products. The capital cost of this machine plus ancillary equipment amounted to £45,000. The cost of the actual ingredients varied with movements in raw material prices. Flour, being about 80% by volume of the final bread mix product, represented 65% of ingredient cost approximately. Other ingredients used include whey powder, dried full cream milk, soya flour, acid calcium phosphate, bicarbonate of soda and salt.

However, fluctuations in raw material prices shifted these proportions from time to time.

New Product Concept

The bread mix consisted of materials which would produce a typical brown bread dough on the addition of a quantity of water. Consequently, the need for buying a wide range of ingredients, measuring them out, mixing them and kneading them would be eliminated. Furthermore, since the raising agent was included, the problem of measuring and spreading the right amount and the right dispersion of baking soda or powder would be removed. The mix could also be used to make scones. A standard one kilo pack would make two average sized brown loaves, or an amount of scones depending on size desired — approximately 24 average-size scones would be possible.

Product and Market Tests

Before attempting to launch the bread mix, Mosse management observed the sales trends of the Howard bread mix products which were launched on the Irish market one year earlier. While the evidence supported the claim that a market existed for their particular product, it was decided to test the acceptability of the product on the Irish market. This was done by supplying people in the immediate vicinity of Bennettsbridge with samples of the product during the Spring and Summer of 1971 and then analysing user reactions. In addition, a number of bakeries were asked to co-operate by producing bread from the bread mix. Jim Furlong recognized at the time that while this approach was not very thorough it did nevertheless indicate to the company the kind of response which was to be anticipated from a nationwide launch. The Mosse Company produced one bread mix which they called Mosse's brown soda bread mix. The company wished to produce a mix which would produce a bread acceptable to a very wide range of preferences.

In addition to testing the product locally, the company availed itself of an opportunity to test the bread mix on the UK market. It was felt by the company that tastes and preferences for this type of product would be reasonably similar in both countries. A number of cases of the brown bread mix were distributed through a contact the company had in the north of England. As a result of this

experiment, the UK consumer reaction to the product was considered favourable. It was at this stage that the company's activities
in the UK became known to the London office of Coras Trachtala
(CTT) in July 1971. Furlong accepted an invitation from CTT's
Mr Bernard Rogan to present the Mosse bread mix to the press
and trade representatives at a reception in Ireland House in London.
A number of loaves were baked during the reception and representatives were able to sample the product. The presentation arranged
by the CTT office was considered by the company to have been
highly successful. The bread mix was picked up and promoted by
the press as an interesting product which would be highly acceptable in the UK market. Trade representatives present wanted to
place orders for the bread mix; however, the Mosse Company was
not yet in a position to launch in the United Kingdom. Encouraged
by the favourable reception in the UK, Furlong decided to press
ahead with the bread mix marketing programme in Ireland.

Home Baking

A cookery expert writing in one of the national newspapers calculated that there was no great difference between the cost of
making an ordinary loaf of home baked brown bread and loaf using
brown bread mix. However, costing varied depending on the recipe
used. While Mosse's Mix was composed of two parts brown flour
to one of white along with milk, powder, salt and leavening agent
additives, a common recipe used by Irish housewives consists of
8 oz plain flour, 8 oz wholemeal, ½ pint milk plus a 'pinch' of
raising agent, to make an average sized loaf. Wholemeal cost 11 p
per kilo in 1971. One ounce (oz) = 28 grammes and one pint = 0.57
litres.

   According to the same expert, the housewife does not typically
measure out quantities of ingredient nor does she go to the trouble
of sieving these ingredients to get her baking soda or powder evenly
distributed. Consequently, there is a 'surprise' element in brown
bread baking, the negative element of which is almost totally removed when using the brown bread mix. However, the fact that
little time is taken measuring and sifting implies that there would
be little difference in the time element of brown bread making using
either method.

   As regards the availability of ingredients for bread making, the
most important factor, in the case of the urban housewife at least,
is the availability of milk. Using the water-based brown bread mix

eliminates the need to re-budget milk orders on baking days. Brown bread is generally baked on its own, since it requires a very high oven temperature. However, the advent of home freezers was seen as method of economizing, since it would allow 'mass-baking' of bread — a week or a month's supply at one time. A survey of 685 housewives in Ireland, indicated that Irish housewives invariably make soda bread and do not use yeast in baking.

National Launch of Mosse's Soda Bread Mix

During the Winter and Spring of 1971–2, the company continued to test the product on a limited scale in the south-east of the country. At the same time, plans for a national launch were being developed. A brown soda bread mix was presented at a press conference held in the Shelbourne Hotel in Dublin on November 4, 1971. The bread mix was promoted as an interesting product, which would receive the fullest company commitment possible. The public relations agency engaged for the occasion stressed the small company image and the associations with the monks of Mount St Josephs in Roscrea. The entire cost of this aspect of the programme cost the company in the region of £300.

Distribution Decisions

By July 1972, Jim Furlong and his sales manager, Dan Kennedy, together with five salesmen, organized the distribution of the new product. Before launching nationally, Kennedy realized that while the company was very strong in the south-east, it had virtually no distribution elsewhere. A distribution link-up arrangement with Shakeltons, another small family miller situated at Lucan on the outskirts of Dublin (and with whom W. H. Mosse eventually merged) had alleviated that situation somewhat. However, the W. H. Mosse Company was still virtually unknown among the large Dublin-based multiples, and since these controlled over 40% of Irish retail grocery trade, they represented a vital link in the distribution chain. The company had arranged with a small Dublin advertising agency to plan an autumn launch for the product. To ensure that adequate supplies would be on the store shelves at the time of the launch, Dan Kennedy and his sales team spent much of the Summer meeting store managers in an effort to convince them of the benefits of stocking-up early. At the end of July there was virtually no penetration in the Dublin area.

A week before the launch, however, the product was available almost in every store of consequence. Mosse's had organized 90% of total distribution in time for the launch and Dan Kennedy was successful in gaining access with the product to all the multiples in the country. To help convince store managers that the Mosse bread mix programme was in earnest, the company had an insert prepared for the August-September issues of 'Retail News' and Checkout. This exhibit featured a well-known personality who at this time was playing a leading role in a TV 'soap opera' set in rural Ireland (Exhibit 10.1).

Because of the new concept involved, the company and the advertising agency both felt that point of sale material would prove invaluable in supporting the launch. The principal ingredient was a two-page leaflet which emphasized the wholesomeness and ease of preparation of the bread-mix (Exhibit 10.2). In addition to the 150,000 point of sale brochures used, the company also arranged for a number of in-store demonstrations and displays.

Packaging and Pack Size Decisions

Packaging posed a number of problems for the company. It was felt that to capture the benefits of the stoneground image the package would have to reflect an old-world feeling of traditional goodness. In addition, it was necessary that the pack should promote the idea that the bread mix was as good as any natural product since it was based almost entirely on natural ingredients. The company settled for an old style wrap over paper bag as used in the retail flour trade. The pack design was subdued to reflect the traditional image. Furthermore, such a pack would stand out among the brighter presentations then becoming popular on supermarket shelves. There was some disagreement about the size of the retail pack to produce. It was recognized that the half-kilogramme pack would be the optimum size from the consumers' viewpoint. However, the initial sales volume would be higher if a larger pack were used. Jim Furlong believed that by producing the bread mix in a kilogramme pack size, there would be less chance of the company losing customers if the housewife failed to produce an acceptable bread from the first trial. By having the equivalent of two loaves in the pack, purchasers would be encouraged to try a second time whereas repeat purchases of a half kilogramme pack would be negligible if the first mix resulted in unacceptable bread.

Advertising Campaign

The actual advertising programme began at the end of September 1972. The campaign lasted two months and consisted mainly of 15-second TV slots with a number of 7-second slots as back-up. The total launch budget was £5,000 for the year September 1972 to the end of August 1973. Both Furlong and Padbury's, the advertising agency, realized the risk of placing 'all their eggs in one basket'. If the campaign failed they both realized that the bread mix was finished as far as the domestic market was concerned. Jim Furlong commented that a restricted budget situation placed many a small firm in a risky situation: 'a product may be excellent but unless the resources are available to communicate with the market the entire effort will be in vain'. Towards the end of 1972 the company and Padbury began to develop a second advertising campaign. This time the campaign was to be confined to TV only. In addition to promoting the bread mix products, Mosse's wished to use the campaign to promote an institutional package covering a range of the firm's flour products. The agency at this stage wanted to incorporate the association with the monks of Mount St Jospeh while at the same time everyone was concerned not to offend the monks in any way and after much discussion the 'Mosse the Miller' campaign was underway (Exhibit 10.3). As part of the campaign programme, the agency produced a 30-second film which went on the air just after Christmas 1972, when bonus transmissions were available on Radio Telefis Eireann. In the week following Christmas the commercial appeared fourteen times on TV for which the company paid for seven transmissions. The campaign ended in April 1973.

Bread Mix Launch Costs

The actual costs of the national launch of the bread mix products came to £10,000, a large part of which was attributable to the TV campaign (Exhibit 10.4).

A Market Re-Appraisal

During the Spring of 1973, as the advertising campaign was in full swing, a number of issues arose which required a more detailed assessment of the entire marketing programme for the bread mix products. Apart from the disappointing sales figures for the white bread mix, which were continuing despite the advertising campaign, there were a number of more fundamental issues involved. It was not clear to the company whether its products should be placed in competition with flour-based products or with bread products. A number of retail outlets favoured a merchandising programme which associated the bread mix products with flour while other stores shelved the products alongside the bread counter. In addition very little was known about the people who bought the bread mixes, nor was much known about the people who might buy these products. It was not until this stage that Furlong realized that very little was known about the bread and bread mix markets in Ireland in terms of hard factual data. While it was recognized that the historical decline in the consumption of bread would continue it was nevertheless accepted that a number of shifts in consumption patterns had occurred and such shifts would be repeated in the future. To decide how these changes would affect the bread mix products the Mosse Company decided to investigate the bread and bread mix markets in greater detail. Such information was considered by the Mosse Company to be vital to any decisions about the future of the bread mix products on the Irish market. Furthermore, such information would also prove extremely valuable were the company seriously to consider the export market. To develop an overall picture of the domestic bread market the company could rely on a number of published sources, many of which contained information on the more important aspects of the market.

Bread and Flour Market in Ireland

As in most western countries, the consumption of bread in Ireland was on the decline. Per capita consumption of bread declined by 10% in the nine-year period 1963–72. In addition, household flour used primarily to make bread in the home declined by almost 41% during the same period. With that rate of decline in bread consumption the total population would have to grow at a much higher rate to offset the decline in total bread consumption. In the early 1970s the average annual consumption of bread per capita was approximately 131 pounds. (For details of bread types produced by Irish bakeries, distribution channels used, and bakery production costs see Appendix 10.1.) Annual per capita consumption of household flour was estimated to be 48 pounds approximately. (Exhibit 10.5.)

While the consumption of all bread was on the decline, the production of standard bread was on the increase. In 1972 63.8 million batch loaves were produced which was significantly higher than batch bread production in previous years. On a quarterly basis there was also some indication that batch production was increasing. During the same period the production of fancy bread also increased (Exhibit 10.6).

In a sample survey of the main Irish bakers, it was found that the average bakery would turn out about 65% of its total bread output wrapped and sliced. (National Prices Commission, Occasional Paper No. 20.) Of this figure by far the largest proportions would be in the form of large pan loaves (48% of total bread production as against 17% for batch bread). Up to 88% of a bakery's production would be in the form of standard loaves, i.e. pan and batch loaves, with 2% slimming loaves and the rest in miscellaneous bread forms (e.g. Vienna rolls, turnovers, baskets). The 2 lb or 800 g size represented 73% of a typical bakery's total bread sales.

Between mid-February 1972 and mid-May 1973 the prices of white bread increased only slightly while the Food Price Index increased by 23%. During the same period flour prices increased only marginally (Exhibit 10.7).

Irish Market for Bread Mixes

At the beginning of July 1973, 685 Irish housewives were interviewed to provide factual information on the market for home-baked bread and scones and to ascertain the penetration, current awareness, and usage of bread mixes in general and more specifically to examine those factors with respect to the two Mosse products. The more pertinent features of the Irish market for bread mix products as found by the researchers are presented in Exhibit 10.8.

MOSSE'S BROWN BREAD MIX…

Proven Success in South East Ireland and in the U.K. ~ and now available in your AREA!

and NOW a great NEW

TV

and RADIO CAMPAIGN will make SALES rise even FASTER

30 SPOTS AT PEAK VIEWING TIMES

Radio 45 SPOTS AT PEAK LISTENING TIMES

so stock up NOW!

Since Mosse's Brown Bread Mix was first test-marketed in the South-East region of Ireland, it's been going from strength to strength, from success to success! Because housewives have tried it, liked it — and bought it again and again!

Mosse's Brown Bread Mix is a boon to the busy housewife of today because it enables her to give her family all the goodness of traditional home-made bread — without the fuss and bother. There's no need to add Buttermilk or sour milk, soda or salt because all the ingredients are already in the mix. All that's required is to add water, knead the dough and pop in the oven. And in an hour — perfect home-made brown bread everytime!

Mosse's Brown Bread Mix is based on Abbey Stoneground Wholemeal — ground between millstones in the traditional manner by the Cistercian Monks in Roscrea. It has a rich nutty flavour, no germ is removed — so the whole wheat goodness comes right through. Small wonder it's been so well received! And now a major national advertising campaign will bring the message home forcibly to *your customers* —

Exhibit 10.1

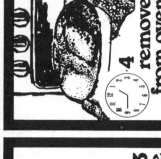

Just add water and it's oven~ready!

Mosse of Bennettsbridge—the people who have been milling quality flour since 1820—have come up with the answer to the busy housewife's prayer—with Mosse's Brown Bread Mix. Now it is possible to give your family all the delicious goodness and nourishment of your own baking—without the time-consuming fuss and trouble—and perfect results are certain! There's no need to go chasing around for a multitude of ingredients any more—all the ingredients are already in the mix! All you have to do is add water to the mix, make into a dough—then pop it into the oven.

Mosse's Brown Bread Mix is based on Abbey Stoneground Wholemeal—ground between millstones in the traditional manner by the Cistercian Monks in Roscrea. It has a rich nutty flavour, no germ is removed—so the whole wheat goodness comes through to you. That's what makes Mosse's Brown Bread Mix the finest you can buy! All the ingredients are already in the pack so you need

✱ NO BUTTERMILK or SOUR MILK
✱ NO SODA ✱ NO SALT

It's fast and easy—and ensures perfect results! Mosse of Bennettsbridge are famed for their quality flours:

Mosse Sunlight Flour, Mosse Wheatmeal, Abbey Stoneground Wholemeal, and now, there's new Mosse's Brown Bread Mix—so choose a Mosse Flour for all your baking requirements!

Here are some of the enthusiastic comments from leading newspaper gourmets about Mosse's Brown Bread Mix.

"Makes two very delicious loaves in no time at all." *Irish Press*
"You get heavenly brown bread for little effort and not too much cost." *Evening Standard*
"Make a delicious looking and tasty loaf in about an hour." *Observer*
Guardian
"Delicious."

Mosse's Brown Bread Mix~ Home Baking Made Easy!

Exhibit 10.2

Exhibit 10.3

Category	Cost
	£
Television	6,300
Point of Sale Material	2,000
Store Displays	1,700
Total	10,000

Exhibit 10.4: Bread Mix Product Launch Costs

Year	Bread	Flour
	Pounds Per Capita	
1963	144	81
1968	137	64
1969	134	59
1970	131	56
1971	131	51
1972	130	48

Source: Central Statistics Office

Exhibit 10.5: Bread and Flour Consumption, 1963–72

Period	Category	Bread Type (millions)		Total
		Batch	Fancy	
1971	2 lb loaf	66.8	121.6	188.4
1972	2 lb loaf	63.8	121.3	185.1
1973	2 lb loaf	55.5	93.2	148.7
	800 g loaf	17.8	29.5	47.3
	Total	73.3	122.7	196.0

Source: Central Statistics Office

Exhibit 10.6: Bread Production in Ireland 1971–3

Exhibit 10.7: Food Price Index and Retail Prices for Bread and Flour

Period	All Food Price Index	White Bread a		Flour b	
		Sliced	Unsliced	Plain	Self-Raising
	(Mid-Aug. 1968=100)		Retail Prices (Pence)		
1972					
mid-Feb	131.6	13.4	13.0	22.8	23.5
mid-May	134.6	13.4	13.0	23.0	23.7
mid-Aug	140.9	13.5	13.1	23.0	23.7
mid-Nov	141.4	13.4	13.0	22.9	23.6
1973					
mid-Feb	153.4	13.4	13.1	23.2	23.7
mid-May c	161.4	13.5	13.1	23.4	23.9

a Prices refer to a 2 lb loaf (1 lb = 0.454 kilos).
b Prices refer to 2 kilo bags of flour.
c Estimated.
Source: Central Statistics Office

Exhibit 10.8: Home Baking and Use of Bread Mixes Among Irish
Housewives, 1973 Research Findings

A. Frequency of Home Bread Baking

	Age Group			
	16—34	35—44	45—54	55 or older
	Percentages			
Weekly	36	62	63	51
At least once a month	54	70	74	64
At least once during previous year	61	77	78	69
Never	29	15	15	21

Note: Farmwives not included.

B. Type of Bread Baked

	Social Group				
	ABCI	C2	DE	F	All Groups
	Percentages				
Always/Mostly White	16	25	43	37	32
White/Brown Equally	44	54	42	36	43
Always/Mostly Brown	40	21	15	27	25

Continued

C. *Brand Shares and Type of Bread Mix Used*

	Bread Shares		Bread Mix Type	
	Normal Use	*Last Occasion*	*Brown*	*White*
		Percentages		
Mosse's	49	51	38	13
Odlums	28	27	16	11
Others	23	22	17	5

D. *Profiles of Bread Mix Users and Mosse Buyers*

	In Previous Month	*Bread Mix Users In Previous Year*	*Normally Use Mosse's*
		Percentages	
Geographic			
Dublin	36	32	37
Other Urban	27	25	27
Rural	37	43	36
Social			
ABCI	34	37	46
C2DE	50	45	40
F	16	18	14
Age			
16–34	20	22	29
35–54	50	43	47
55 or older	30	34	24
Household Size			
1–2	30	25	19
2–5	44	48	54
6+	26	27	27
NUMBER OF INTERVIEWS	65	179	84
			TOTAL = 328

Continued

E. Summary of Conclusions by Research Firm

1   The bread mix market was 70:30 in favour of brown.
2   Urban middle class housewives were more likely to bake brown bread than white bread.
3   Brown bread mixes were more successful than white bread mixes and the Mosse product had successfully exploited this segment of the market.
4   Slower progress was expected with a white bread mix since the major market for this product was among farmers' wives and the rural community.
5   However, Mosse White Soda Bread Mix was on a par with Odlum's White and
6   On a more general level the future market for white bread mixes would have to be based on acceptance among rural bread makers.

Appendix 10.1
The W.H. Mosse Company (A):
Industry Notes and Statistics

The Irish Flour Milling Industry

Although flour milling is one of the oldest industries in Ireland it was only during the 1870s that technological developments gave rise to the present type of mill based on the roller system. The use of roller mills in place of the older stone grinders required a high capital but low labour content. The new system facilitated the production of flour on a larger scale and the production of a variety of flours concurrently. The principal effect of the new technology was fewer and larger mills.. By 1900 there were 217 mills in the country primarily concerned with wheat milling but by 1973 this number had fallen to 17 (Table 10A.1).

During the 1890s the use of artificial methods of bleaching flour was prohibited in America. As a consequence, American flour, which was being imported into Ireland in large quantities, was replaced by British, artificially-bleached flour. British millers were thus in a position to capture practically the entire Irish market for imported flour. To combat the new competition from Britain, the Irish millers attempted to ensure for themselves a definite share of the domestic market. One of the results of these endeavours was the introduction of quotas.

Table 10A.1. The Irish Flour Milling Industry, 1900–73

| Milling Group | Year | | | | | |
	1900	1917	1927	1957	1962	1973
			Number of Mills			
Odlum					8	7
Ranks					5	3
Independents					17	7
Total	217	80	32	35	30	17

Source: Department of Agriculture and Fisheries: *Flour Milling Industry*, 1965 and National Prices Commission: Occasional Paper No. 16.

The Quota System

The Agricultural Product (Cereals) Act of 1933 introduced a licensing system for flour millers which placed an embargo on flour imports except under licence and it also placed a statutory limitation on the volume of flour each mill could produce. This quota for each mill was calculated on the basis of the capacity of an individual mill expressed as a percentage of total national capacity. These quotas provided for excess milling capacity of 10% over normal consumption, with the object of introducing and maintaining a competitive element in the industry. The Acts provided that penalties may be imposed when less than 90% or more than 100% of the licensed quotas are milled in any year.

A Rationalization Programme

In 1967 there was still thirty five flour mills operating in Ireland: by 1962 five mills had closed, for economic and other reasons, leaving thirty mills in operation. It was very clear to the industry that the available milling capacity still considerably exceeded the demand for flour. The statutory limitations placed on mills under the licensing system exceeded the amount of flour in total then being used in the country and several of the smaller independent mills were in severe financial difficulties. To preserve a viable industry in the face of imminent, forced closures a rationalization policy was accepted. Under the rationalization scheme accepted by the industry was a new system of voluntary limitations on flour output. The 'quota limitations' were calculated on the same basis as the still extant statutory limitations except that the percentage for each mill was applied to the current actual demand for flour, monitored on a weekly basis. For this purpose the industry was divided into three groups, Odlums, Ranks and the Independents. Odlums were allowed a quota of 39.88% of total flour production divided among their 8 mills as they chose. Similarly,

Ranks were allowed 32.67% of their five mills while the remaining 27.45% was allocated among the seventeen independents. A central fund was established to help solve redundancy and closure problems. The biggest problem existed among the independents and after discussions six mills agreed to close and take compensation from the fund. These mills all ceased to operate at the end of 1962 and their quotas were divided among the eleven remaining Independents who contributed proportionately to the fund.

By 1965 a further four Independents had closed under the scheme leaving seven still operating. In addition, Ranks closed one mill in 1963 and another in 1971 while Odlums closed one mill in 1966. The voluntary rationalization scheme, with its central fund for compensatory payments, ceased to apply after 1965 although voluntary limitation on output quotas was still effective in the late 1960s.

Diversification in Flour Milling Industry

To combat the effects of a declining flour market in Ireland many of the existing milling companies have extended their business interests to areas outside the traditional line of endeavour. Some of these outside interests are related to flour milling while a number are only remotely related to milling. The Ranks group controls three mills, each of which has a provender mill alongside. This group also controls grain handling and storage facilities and bakeries. The Odlum group on the other hand has many outside interests but the milling companies within the group are all concerned only with milling, including provender milling, or with the grain trade in some way. Of the five Independents, four also engage in provender milling and three have baking interests. Three have grain drying and storage interests and two have farming interests. A variety of non-agricultural activities are also carried out through subsidiary companies.

Market for Flour in Ireland

A feature of the flour industry common throughout the western world is the steadily declining level of consumption. As people become more affluent their consumption of flour decreases on a *per capita* basis. Thus, unless the population of a country is increasing at an equivalent rate total flour consumption decreases. As might be expected from this, *per capita* consumption of flour was lower in the United States than it was in the United Kingdom. In turn, *per capita* consumption of flour in the United Kingdom was lower than it was in Ireland. (Table 10A.2.) The volume of flour used had decreased from 269,000 tonnes in 1960–1 to 210,000 tonnes in 1972–3. The decrease over the period had been substantial and retail flour, that is flour sold to the consumer through retail outlets, had declined at a faster rate than bakers' flour or flour sold by the mills to the bakeries. (Table 10A.3.)

Table 10A.2. Consumption of Flour in Selected Countries, 1945–73

Year	United States	United Kingdom	Ireland
		Kilos per capita	
1945	68	100	125
1950	61	92	120
1955	55	83	112
1960	54	77	95
1965	50	70	82
1970	50	67	72
1973 *a*	48	63	70

a Estimated

Source: National Prices Commission, Occasional Paper No. 16.

Table 10A.3. Consumption of Bakers' and Retail Flour in Ireland, 1960–73

Year	Bakers' Flour (Industrial Consumption)		Retail Flour (Private Consumption)	
	Output	Per Capita	Output	Per Capita
	('000 tonnes)	(Kilos)	('000 tonnes)	(Kilos)
1960/61	167	59.3	102	36.4
1965/66	154	53.5	84	29.2
1966/67	152	52.9	82	28.3
1967/68	151	52.5	78	27.0
1968/69	150	52.1	74	25.5
1969/70	150	51.9	70	24.2
1970/71	148	49.7	66	22.4
1971/72	149	50.1	63	21.5
1972/73	150	50.3	60	20.1

Source: Irish Flour Millers Association. The per capita data for 1972–3 are based on the population level estimated for 1971.

Flour Production

Estimates by the Agricultural Institute would indicate a 70% extraction factor for wheat going into flour production. In other words 1 tonne of wheat will, on average, result in 0.7 tonnes of flour after milling. The balance of the grain after the milling process is completed is normally turned into wheatfeed, bran or pollard, all of which can be used as animal feeds.

Table 10A.4. Irish Wheat Consumption/Intake 1970–3

('000 tons)

	1970	1971	1972	1973
Domestic Production	375	380	277	229
Imports	117	125	204	361
Total Supplies	492	505	581	590

Source: Central Statistics Office

Market Shares

Because of the peculiar industry marketing arrangements already described, it is not possible to refer to market shares in the normal sense of that term. Ever since 1933 flour mills have been rationed in their output, first by the licensed quota and more recently by the voluntary limitations agreement. The output quotas for the various milling companies still in production in 1973 are presented in Table 10A.5.

Table 10A.5. Market Shares — Quotas, Flour Milling Companies

Milling Group	*Market Share/Quota*
	%
Odlums	39.88
Ranks (Ireland)	32.67
Independents:	
Dock Milling Co. Ltd	4.60
Bolands Limited	9.86
Barrow Milling Company	1.97
Milford Bakery and Flour Mills	3.29
S.A.G. Davis and W.H. Mosse Ltd	5.25
G. Shackleton Ltd	2.48
Total	100.00

Source: National Prices Commission, Occasional Paper No. 16, and Discussions with the trade.

To increase their market strength in face of the artificial limitations imposed upon them, a number of milling concerns have attempted to secure tied-outlets for their output such as a bakery chain. In the four years 1970–73, sales of flour to tied outlets rose from 45,000 tonnes to 50,000 tonnes or from 21.2% to 24.5% of total output. Two of the concerns had tied outlets taking over 60% of their own production in 1973 while two others had no tied outlets at all. The remaining concerns all had tied outlets taking between 16% and 34% of their output. It is evident that with respect to tying up their outlets, the flour mills have been much more successful in coming to an arrangement with the bakeries than with retail establishments. (Table 10A.6.)

Table 10A.6 Flour Sales by Type of Outlet, 1972–3

Type of Outlet	Product	
	Bakers' Flour	Retail Flour
	Percent of Product	
Tied Outlet	33.0	2.1
Non-Tied Outlet	63.0	97.1
Other Mill	3.2	0.8
Total	100.0	100.0

Source: National Prices Commission: Occasional Paper No. 16.

Table 10A.7. Market Segments for Flour 1972–3

Segment	% Total Production
Bakers' Bread making	72
Catering and Baking Trade	14
Retail market	14

Source: National Prices Commission Report No. 27.

Marketing Communications

In a contracting market such as flour, combined with output quotas, normal commercial practices do not apply. If the marketing efforts of one company gain sales at the expense of other millers and result in a sales volume exceeding the output quota, then that concern has to buy the additional flour from other millers; it cannot increase its own output. Each of the existing milling companies continually seek new ways of promoting flour sales, albeit with little success. Apart from sales to tied outlets there was little brand loyalty for bakers' flour which accounts for approximately 72% of all flour sales. Bakers can and do change their source of supply. Because of this it is necessary for millers to maintain a constant physical presence in the form of a sales force in order to preserve their existing share of sales. Advertising has been an important marketing weapon of firms in the flour milling industry. (Table 10A.8.)

Table 10A.8. Advertising Expenditures Five Firms, 1970–2

Year	T.V.	Press	Types of Advertising Radio	Promotion	Total
	£	£	£	£	£
1970	37,074	7,020	12,662	23,342	80,098
1971	23,386	9,873	14,017	20,342	70,008
1972	24,737	3,173	14,057	20,681	62,649

Source: National Prices Commission, Occasional Paper No. 16.

Profitability in Flour Milling

During the recent past there had been considerable improvement in the profitability of the flour milling industry. Two reasons were given: the first was due to the price increase granted in bakers' flour by the National Prices Commission in early 1972 and on retail flour in March of that year. The second reason for improved profits was the industry's ability to control production and other costs. Low profit situations and losses were, however, quite frequent in the industry due to the cyclical nature of market factors. The average revenue, costs and profit of the industry for the period 1970–2 are presented in Table 10A.9.

Table 10A.9. Revenue, Costs and Profits in Irish Flour Milling Industry 1971–3 (Year to 31st August)

Revenue/Costs/Profits	1971	1972	1973
		£ per tonne	
Sales	73.05	79.37	80.07
Costs			
Net Grist	48.39	48.13	45.12
Wages	3.97	4.03	4.23
Power	0.71	0.74	0.87
Sacks & Handling	2.33	2.36	1.94
Selling Costs	0.99	1.00	1.09
General Admin. Expenses	5.77	6.05	6.77
Repairs and Renewals	1.30	1.27	1.20
Discounts and Allowances	1.32	1.27	1.26
Freight	2.61	2.72	3.09
Depreciation	1.37	1.45	1.59
Interest	2.86	2.52	4.52
Total	71.62	71.54	71.68
Profit	1.43	7.83	8.39

Source: Compiled from National Price Commission, Occasional Paper No. 16.

The Bakery Industry in Ireland

The Irish bakery industry in common with the bakery industries of many Western countries is typified by a number of large firms which dominate the market and numerous smaller firms scattered throughout the country. Because of the nature of the bakery business it is difficult to quantify the number and size of firms involved in baking. Many firms are engaged in the specialized baking of fancy breads, cakes and confectionery products which are not strictly comparable with the ordinary loaf. It has been estimated that in early 1973 there were approximately 280 bakeries in Ireland in total. Nearly half of these were located in the eastern part of the country with about 15 bakeries located in the Dublin area. The Dublin firms accounted for more than half the total industry output.

Bread Production Costs

Bread output is normally measured in units based on sacks; one sack is equivalent to 280 pounds weight. It has been estimated that for 1972 the average industry cost of producing bread from one sack of flour was £35. In 1972 flour represented about half the total production cost, labour accounted for a further 10% and distribution costs were estimated to be in the region of 20% of total costs. Other ingredient costs amounted to about three percent of the total while overheads were typically of the order of 10%. Considerable cost variations occurred between bakeries in the industry. The cost of labour in the bakery industry has been a source of concern to many firms. Average weekly earnings for male workers in the bakery industry were £35.70 per week in mid-1973 while the average number of hours worked was 47. Women worked fewer hours on average per week (36) and received a weekly wage packet of £19.50.

Bread Types Produced and Yields

In 1973 there were two principal types of bread being produced by Irish bakeries, pan bread and batch bread. Both bread types are referred to as standard bread to distinguish each from fancy and special breads. In 1973 standard bread was produced in two sizes; a 2 lb loaf and a 1 lb loaf. In mid-1973 metrication was introduced into the bakery industry with the result that loaves of 800 grammes and 400 grammes began to be produced. Bread yields in early 1973 were estimated to be as follows: 227 800-gramme loaves or 446 400-gramme loaves from one sack of flour. Production costs also differed to take account of the difference in wrapping and slicing costs.

Channels of Distribution

By 1973 shops and supermarkets had become the most important outlets for the bakeries. About 75% of total industry output was sold through these outlets. Medium-size bakeries tended to rely much more on shops and super-markets than did their larger or smaller counterparts. This reflected the higher degree of private label production among medium-size firms at the time. Small firms distributed approximately 25% of their output through retail shops controlled by the bakeries. Door-to-door sales accounted for about 15% of total industry sales in 1973.

Irish Households

In the late 1960s Irish households were estimated to fall into the social and locational categories shown in Table 10A.10.

Table 10A.10. Social Grade Categories by Location of Irish Households

		Location		
Social Grade	*Greater Dublin*	*Urban*	*Rural*	*Total*
AB	10	9	5	6
C1	20	19	10	12
C2	27	25	15	17
DE	42	45	30	34
F	2	1	41	30
Total	100	100	100	100
(Sample Size	186	357	330	687)

Definitions of social grades used:

Social Grade	*Social Status*	*Occupation of Head of Household*
A	Upper middle class	Higher managerial, administrative or professional
B	Middle class	Intermediate managerial, administrative or professional
C_1	Lower middle class	Supervisory, clerical and junior management
C_2	Skilled working class	Skilled manual workers
D	Working class	Semi or unskilled workers
E	Those at lowest subsistence level, pensioners, casual workers	
F_1	Owning or working 30 acres of land or more	
F_2	Owning or working less than 30 acres of land.	

Part C
Developing the International Marketing Programme

In domestic markets, the marketing plan is based upon selecting the target market segment, appraising the actual and potential wants of buyers in the segment and developing a marketing mix which offers a competitive advantage. In international marketing, however, there are two additional steps which precede such analysis. Firstly, the business has to decide which markets it should enter and how many it should develop. Secondly, it has to choose a method of penetrating each foreign market — direct or indirect exporting, joint venture, or establishing an overseas subsidiary.

The decision to market overseas is a corporate strategy choice. A business can choose among alternative growth directions: expanding its market share at home, developing new products, expanding overseas or diversification. The correct strategic emphasis depends upon the balance of opportunities and the company's own capability profile. One of the mistakes new international marketers make is attempting to operate in too many overseas markets. This diffusion of effort makes it difficult to acquire the detailed market knowledge and expertise to plan effectively and risks spreading limited resources too thinly. Choosing a country in which to operate should be considered as an investment decision: management should choose those countries which have the market potential to offer a high return on investment and which match the company's knowledge and skills.

In deciding how to enter a foreign market there is a wide variety of alternatives: indirect export through home-based export companies, direct export through the company's own sales force, setting up overseas subsidiaries to market or even produce the product, licensing, and joint ventures. The right choice depends upon the company's goals regarding the volume of business desired, its resources that can be committed to developing overseas operations, and its knowledge and skills. There is invariably a trade-off; while indirect exporting is easy to establish and requires only a small commitment of the company's management and resources, its payoff is rarely high because the company has little control over the marketing programme adopted overseas and because it can count on only a limited commitment from its export agent, who will normally be selling the products of a number of other companies.

After the method of entry is chosen, the marketing mix has to be designed in such a way that it is geared to the appropriate target market segment and exploits the differential advantage of the company. A key issue in designing the marketing mix for foreign markets is to what extent management should look for standardization across markets. Standardization of product, advertising, price, and method of distribution makes for much easier head office planning and control and often offers significant economies of scale. However, with the great variations between markets and overseas environments, such standardization can be extremely costly if it prevents the company matching its offer with the wants of buyers in the local market. Successful international marketing planning looks for a balance between the local pulls for heterogeneity in marketing and the advantages that can be gained from looking for common elements which have general application in a number of markets.

XI
Comshare Ltd
Making Computers Make Sense
J. Saunders

Comshare Ltd was formed in February 1971. November saw the first customers assessing the company's single Xerox SDS 940 computer using the sophisticated Commander I operating system. By the end of 1973, with over two hundred customers, Comshare had become one of the most successful and fast growing time-sharing and remote processing computer bureaux in the UK.

Comshare Ltd in the UK and Comshare Inc. in the USA were trading as general purpose problem-solution bureaux. Although they were growing rapidly and were able to maintain a lead in terms of low storage costs and service, it was realized that the market was becoming crowded and highly competitive. A large number of bureaux were able to supply a similar range of programmes, languages and facilities at reasonable cost. The service provided was becoming a commodity with price competition likely to squeeze future profits unless action were taken.

Comshare, Inc.

IBM introduced the first commercially viable computer in the early 1960s. Until that time computers were rarely used by other than highly trained technologists solving mathematical problems. The IBM 1400 series was designed to take advantage of the more commercially valuable information-handling capacity of computers. It was purchased and operated by a large number of enterprises but still demanded a host of specialist staff to operate it.

This case was prepared by John Saunders, Bradford University, and was financed by the Foundation for Management Education.

Comshare Inc. was founded by six people in 1966 to take advantage of the fruits of two projects undertaken at American universities:

PROJECT-MAC at MIT developed a way of connecting a relatively large number of terminals to a single computer. Until that time computers had operated in a batch mode with single jobs being input on specially prepared punch cards or paper tape, processed and output by line printer or other media. Such an arrangement demanded centralization of computer access and specialized staff. The newly developed time-sharing facility allowed a large number of teletype or video terminals to be simultaneously linked to a single computer. The computer shared its time between the terminals, giving each operator the impression that they had the whole machine at their disposal. General Electric continued the development of the time sharing concept.

At Ann Arbor a second research group were developing a 'user oriented' computer service — an operating system that non-specialist staff could operate. The Commander I system suitable for Xerox SDS 940 computers was completed in 1966. The system was acquired by two companies, Tymshare and Comshare.

The development of 'time sharing' and a 'user oriented' operating system allowed the decentralization of computing. Time sharing removed the need for centralized input and output by coupling a number of terminals to a computer. The terminals could be remote, (for example, in the users office) as there was no need for them to be near the computer. The 'user-oriented' operating system made it easy for non-specialists to use the remote terminals, thus reducing their dependance on centralized specialist staff. In 1966 Comshare Inc. became one of the first companies to link the new computer technology to that of long distance data-transmission via telephone lines. This enabled the company's customers throughout the USA to access Comshare's computers at Ann Arbor by making a local telephone call into one of Comshare's nearby offices.

Operating as a 'general-purpose, problem solving bureau' Comshare Inc. grew rapidly, earning a revenue of $3,827,000 in 1969. In that year a marketing agreement was made with the Polysar Corporation to form Comshare Ltd of Canada. Comshare Inc. had a minor shareholding in the new company that was to market the products of Comshare Inc. in Canada. The Polysar Corporation, the world's largest producer of synthetic rubber, is a wholly-owned subsidiary of the Canadian Development Corporation, an agency of the Canadian

Government. The agreement emanated from Polysar's two-fold plan to expand its interests in technology-oriented fields and to enter the fast-growing world market for information processing.

Comshare Ltd

In 1970 a group of young managers from General Electric in the UK had decided to leave the company and set up their own computer bureau. They estimated that they would need £1m to start the venture and went to North America in search of funds. One of the companies approached was Polysar who decided to back them. After buying the world-wide licence outside the USA for the Commander I operating system, Polysar, in a joint venture with Comshare Inc., established a European subsidiary in the Netherlands, Comshare International BV. This was to be the holding company used to fund the venture by the young team of British managers. In February 1971 Comshare Ltd was formed in the UK. Kevin Eades, ex-Sales Director of General Electric, famous sportsman and TV personality, was made Managing Director of Comshare Ltd. Bryan Cray, the twenty-nine year old President and Chief Executive Officer of Comshare Inc. became President and Managing Director of Comshare International BV.

Growth and Development

Between initiating their service, using Commander I on a single SDS 940 computer in November 1971, and December 1973 Comshare Ltd grew rapidly. Initially the company had forty staff, a head office in London and two area offices: a midlands office in Birmingham and a northern office in Wakefield, Yorkshire. These were linked to the computer in Chelsea by private telephone lines enabling customers near the area office to use the service by means of a local call. By the end of 1972 the company had over one hundred customers and had earned a revenue for the year of £121,000. In the following year, two more area offices were opened, the number of customers topped 200 and revenue exceeded £500,000.

Simultaneously Comshare Inc. was developing new products. Experience had led to the identification of shortcomings in Commander I itself so the Commander II operating system was developed.

This was based on the newer and more powerful RXDS Sigma 9 computer. In addition a sophisticated yet user-oriented Data Management System was added to the line of basic packages and languages available on Commander II. The first Commander II system was installed in the UK in November 1972. Demand grew and in August 1973 a second Sigma 9 was ordered for Comshare Ltd.

The Best is Not Enough?

Comshare Inc. and Comshare Ltd had grown hand-in-hand by providing what they considered to be a first-class, general purpose, time-sharing service. The chief vitrues were:

> very cheap on-line storage,.
> good program development support staff,
> a good communications network,
> excellent diagnostics (especially on FORTRAN the leading scientific language),
> COMPOSIT 77 (Commander II's powerful data management system),
> the user-oriented Commander II operating system.

By the end of 1973 it was becoming evident, particularly in America, that the provision of an excellent, general purpose, time-sharing service was not enough to guarantee profitable growth. Although the service given had improved over the years, the majority of usage was still by technologists using fairly basic facilities. Since the introduction of COMPOSIT 77 other application packages had been added to provide facilities other than basic computing.

Competitive 'third party services' were being actively sought. These were systems developed by organizations (the third party) but offered to customers as part of the Comshare service. Despite this, most of the facilities could be provided by almost any bureau and increasingly by the user's in-house time-sharing computer. In addition, as users became expert their dependance upon the facilities provided by particular sources declined. This made switching between supplier easy. The computer time-sharing market was showing signs of entering a period of commodity trading.

To compete, bureaux were being forced to offer a widening range of products to potential customers. Supplying and supporting these pushed costs up, while competition and technological advances were forcing prices down. The likely profitability of a small company like Comshare in such a market was poor. Unless some way could be found to avoid the trap, the prospects were gloomy.

Comshare ... The Consultants

From 1974 the key to the new strategy of Comshare Ltd was the provision of a 'value-added service'. According to 1975 sales literature:

> The development of a system to suit individual needs, coupled with training businessmen to use them efficiently, is the cornerstone of the Comshare philosophy.'

The service had been evolved to combat low sales and as a result of customer demand. By working with customers to develop a purpose-made, computer-based solution to problems, Comshare Ltd was able to add value to the basic time-sharing service. The value added was in the form of help given to customers in the development and implementation of purpose-made systems, customer training and support. Appendix 11.1 is a case history that illustrates the type of work being undertaken.

The provision of such a service demanded that Comshare Ltd employ numerous highly qualified sales and support staff. Each area sales office contained three major groups.

1 Sales Executives. Likely to make first contact with clients, they were trained to identify customer problems and suggest ways that Comshare services would be able to assist.
2 Customer Support Executives were responsible for defining technical solutions to customers' problems and working with customers on a day-to-day basis. They were also responsible for ensuring the service levels were maintained and that advice was always readily available.
3 Commercial Services who carried out complete projects for clients. Their responsibility would include the design and implementation of a solution, documentation and the training of the customer's staff to a standard necessary to ensure successful operation of the system.

There was also a Technical Support group responsible for identifying and developing new applications. Sales executives were often recruited from competitors while customer support executives and commercial services staff came from a variety of backgrounds but were generally young graduates trained in management science or mathematics. Many were recruited after they had become familiar with the service while working for one of Comshare's customers.

In addition to providing purpose made systems Comshare Ltd were also selling an increasingly wide range of general purpose packages. FCS and PLANMASTER were offered to the rapidly growing market for financial planning tools. SDRC provided a sophisticated range of packages to help civil engineers. There were many others. Most were 'third party packages' designed by outside bodies who received royalties whenever a customer used the package on the Comshare system.

While supplying an increasingly wide customer base Comshare was also expanding into Europe. The original SDS 940 computer with which Comshare Ltd had began trading was sold to Telesystemes, Paris. A subsidiary of the French Post Office, Telesystemes provided the Commander I service under licence in parallel with its own time-sharing service. Comshare BV in The Hague and Comshare SA in Brussels were established, one under each of Comshare Ltd's Sales Managers for the North and South of the UK. The location of both offices was guided by multi-national customers requesting that the Comshare network be extended to areas of interest to them. As the multi-nationals were potentially heavy users of the service in Europe, the two European offices were thought to be low-risk ventures.

By providing a 'value-added service' Comshare Ltd was able to maintain a high growth rate (Exhibit 11.1). The company was successful but the provision of a highly customer-oriented service was causing strain. Customers were being 'bought' by providing expensive, resource-hungry system development. True, the 'value-added service' did result in a customer who was highly committed to Comshare but much of the development work undertaken was so customer-specific as to be unuseable elsewhere. Each new customer thus necessitated a prodigious programming effort. The problem was compounded by Comshare Ltd rarely saying 'no' to a prospective customer so being forced to try to provide in-depth support over an increasing range of services. Additionally, since Comshare's staff wrote systems for customers the users had little understanding of the systems they were using. This resulted in Comshare offices being forced to provide an increasing burden of support as customer specific systems were installed. The support requirements of the customer-oriented service were beginning to swamp the company. It was becoming obvious that an alternative form of 'value-added service' was needed.

A Revolution in Evolution

From their early days Comshare had realized that the company could not be the best across the whole computer services market. Competing against the industries massive market leaders in the USA had been avoided.   However it was not until the late 1970s that Comshare moved from moderate specialization to a strategy of aggressive specialization unique in the industry.   For the first time business was turned away.   Bryan Cray, President and Chief Executive Officer of Comshare Inc. explains the rationale behind specialization:

'To be the leader in our markets requires not only considerable investment, but considerable knowledge of both computer technology and the marketplace as well.

'For example, in order to develop solutions for the Certified Public Accounting (CPA) profession, we have to be familiar with all the intricacies of accounting.   That way, we can not only meet, but anticipate the needs of the CPA profession. And, indeed, our CPA clients have come to expect that kind of responsiveness from us.   They expect us to monitor what's going on in their profession, and help them solve their problems by providing three things: One, computer technology.   Two, people who are knowledgeable in the accounting discipline and in computer solutions for that discipline.   And three, specialized problem-solving software.

'That kind of expertise is beyond the capabilities of general purpose computer services vendors ... and it's that kind of expertise which is the difference between them and us.   Basically, that's what the specialization strategy of Comshare is all about.

'In implementing this strategy, we provide what we call value-added service, which are very big buzzwords in the computer services industry currently.   What value-added service means, at least to Comshare, is specialized expertise and thoroughness — special people trained to solve problems in the client's discipline, in the client's language and in the way the client wants.

To do that, our people must know as much, if not more, about the problem being solved than the client does; there is a value in our people, in addition to the value of the sophisticated software and all the computer power we bring to bear in creating a solution. And finally, the ultimate value of Comshare's service is this: our service tangibly increases the productivity of the user — that is, it improves either the user's profits or output.'

To guide future growth and development of Comshare by the major strategy of specialization, a set of corporate objectives and strategies were formulated (Appendix 11.2). One consequence of specialization was the rationalization of products actively marketed. Although products were not removed from the system, commercial effort of Comshare Ltd was concentrated on four 'speciality product lines' (Exhibit 11.2):

COUNSELA (local government)
MONITA (banking)
PARSEC (financial management)
VISOR (discrete manufacturing materials management).

Comshare Inc. had five 'speciality product lines':

PROFILE (human resources management)
COMPASS (certified public accounting)
PARSEC (financial management)
4.1.1 Systems (telephone company traffic administration)
Trust Management Systems.

To provide the level of expertise and service inherent in 'speciality marketing' the recruitment policy was changed significantly. New marketing, sales, customer support and account executives were selected for their familiarity with the 'speciality markets'. A major source of staff was clients who used Comshare products. This change in policy necessitated a shift in the training needs of new staff. In mid-career, accountants and bankers etc. were being retrained as sales or marketing executives. Induction training and staff development were seen as so critical to 'speciality marketing' that they were the responsibility of the marketing director.

The evolution of Comshare's style of marketing did not stop with the introduction of 'speciality marketing'. The 'speciality product lines' such as PARSEC were originally seen as groupings of products likely to be of use to a 'speciality market'. By 1979 the individual products of the 'speciality product line', such as FCS, PLAN-MASTER and QUESTOR within PARSEC, were being made inconspicuous to the client. For PARSEC the initial interest of prospective clients was drawn by the problem solving benefits of the brand (Exhibit 11.2). Attention would then be brought to a particular 'brand capability' of direct interest to the manager, an 'application guide' (Exhibit 11.3) being used to illustrate the capability. A client's interest would be further increased using an 'installation guide' — a simplified mini-manual for an idealized application available on the system. After a short training course based upon the particular 'brand capability' the customers would be able to construct their own tailor-made system. Comshare felt that there was no need, at any stage, to tell the customer that the capability was actually an application of a sophisticated data management system like QUESTOR, backed by a Commander II operating system installed on a SIGMA 9 computer. However, if a client desired a general facility like QUESTOR he would be familiarized with PARSEC's data management capability.

Comshare growth during the 1970s had been accommodated by relatively minor changes to the organization. However, by mid 1979 it was becoming obvious that organic development had created an organizational structure inappropriate for the company's size and future business. A major re-organization ensued to give a more centralized structure (Exhibit 11.4). During the reorganization Keith Lucking, the director who had previously been responsible for marketing in Comshare Ltd became group vice-president for sales and marketing of Comshare Inc. Ray Ostell, who had previously been sales director for Central UK, was promoted to become European marketing director. He was the first director to be solely responsible for marketing.

During the late 70s Comshare's growth (Exhibit 11.1) and distinctive marketing style made them the recognized market leader in the UK. Having taken the initiative the company intended to stay ahead. As the new marketing director, Ray Ostell would have to spearhead Comshare's thrust into the 80s. The company had been highly successful but in the process of determining the way ahead, several issues had to be borne in mind.

1 The company's European operations had not been as successful as their performance in the UK and America had lead them to expect. By 1979 the company had five European offices with one other close to opening. They had proved expensive to establish and operate. An attempt had been made to employ entrepreneurial managers to head the national concerns. Although the policy had been largely successful, the company was concerned that their 'lack of understanding of national characteristics' made the task very difficult. In 1979 the revenue for the European offices was expected to contribute well below 10% of the revenue of Comshare International BV and be barely profitable.

   According to Ian Lynch, the strategic planning manager of Comshare Ltd, the European operation had been starved of resources.   Little effort had been made to Europeanize the service. At one time it had been hoped that FCS would be transferred to Europe as successfully as it had been to America.   Although attractive to a few multi-nationals it had not been adopted on a large scale.   The European offices survived on VANILLA — Comshare's term for low value-added general purpose systems. There were barriers to success in Europe.   The Benelux countries were thought to be four years behind the UK in the adoption of sophisticated management techniques.   In Germany — known as the graveyard of bureau services — managers were aware of techniques but unable to purchase outside their own organizations. Additionally, General Electric dominated the German market. So established were they that links to General Electric services were often built into buildings along with other utilities.   Revenue from Commander I, marketed by Telesystemes, France, were regarded as unsatisfactory.   Although national policies made it difficult for a non-domestic company to start operations in France it was hoped to offer Commander II service there in the future.

Comshare Inc. had recently exercised an option to buy a larger share of Comshare International BV from Polysar.   The result was the parent company's heightened interest in the management of the European operations by Comshare Ltd.   The European orientation of Comshare Inc. had to be further increased by the move of Keith Lucking to America.

2 Much of the growth of Comshare Ltd had followed the rapid adoption of corporate planning models by companies.   Comshare Ltd had two such systems — FCS and PLANMASTER, both part of PARSEC since 1978.   In a recent comparative evaluation of systems by an independent researcher, Real Decisions Corporation, FSC was highly praised as being in a class of its own in ease of use and cost effectiveness.   EPS Consultants, the authors of FCS, had asked Comshare to market the product in the early 70s.   Only after considerable effort by 'the third party' did Comshare realize the potential of the product and back it. The symptoms were not yet showing but many in Comshare expected that the FCS and PARSEC market would soon be reaching maturity.

3 Although feverish marketing activity had been associated with the launch into 'speciality marketing', it was not easy to see that it had been effective.   The markets ascribed to the speciality market Business Managers, had grown, but no more quickly than

'opportunistic sales' outside the specialities. In addition VAN-ILLA sales as a proportion of total sales tended to be holding steady.

4 It had not proved easy to recruit business specialists of the right quality to be trained as speciality sales personnel. Some within Comshare were now suggesting that it would be easier to give professional salesmen in-depth accounting skills.

5 Industry pundits were forecasting the decline of computer bureaux as mini-computers grew in popularity.

Financial	1972 £'000s	1973 £'000s	1974 £'000s	1975 £'000s	1976 £'000s	1977 £'000s	1978 £'000s
Revenue	121	511	1,433	2,468	3,641	5,550	8,521
Operating Profit	(308)	(234)	224	216	524	1,393	2,286
Net Profit Before Tax	(383)	(386)	80	102	377	1,151	1,520
Fixed Assets	141	129	207	376	364	2,041	3,717
Total Capital Employed	185	159	300	387	754	1,842	3,336

Operating	1972	1973	1974	1975	1976	1977	1978	1979 (Projected)
Employees	43	91	122	158	180	196	310	
Field Sales Staff	6	11	12	23	36	40	65	100
% of Accountants in the Field Sales Force					7%	19%	19%	29%
Number of Area Offices	3	5	8	10	11	12	14	
Machine Storage (Mega bytes)	100	200	500	1200	3100	4200	6000	

Exhibit 11.1: Comshare Ltd Summary Statistics

APPLICATIONS

Comshare offers four product ranges: PARSEC (financial management), VISOR (materials management), MONITA (banking), and COUNSELA (local government).

PARSEC
In 1978, PARSEC accounted for more than 50% of Comshare UK revenue. PARSEC products include:
PLANMASTER – financial planning.
FCS – financial and corporate modelling – a product developed by EPS Consultants and bought by Comshare. EPS is still responsible for FCS.
QUESTOR – a database manager which interfaces with other Comshare systems.
TACTICS – statistical analysis.
COMPOSIT 77 – database management.
SITE – proprietary database for demographic analysis.

VISOR
VISOR is designed particularly for engineering companies who assemble from identifiable piece parts. It comprises:
VMM – materials management system for handling stock control and order processing.
VPS – production scheduling.
VRL – a reporting language designed to be used within VPS and VMM to produce specific reports.

MONITA
The MONITA range is aimed at a very specific market – banks active in the international money market, except the UK clearing banks. Comshare intends to develop MONITA over the next five years into a range of products to meet every dp need of this market.

Comshare has been working with foreign banks for the last five years and MONITA has been developed through that experience. There is one principal product – FEAMIS (Foreign Exchange Accounting and Management Information System). A FEAMIS user has a microprocessor terminal linked to the central computer. That arrangement permits deals to be recorded as soon as they are transmitted; the user can also have timely reports on currency positions, for example.
Comshare will be adding to the MONITA range, by packaging applications such as credit analysis and portfolio management. With the emphasis on distributed processing, there will be more foreign exchange applications, and proprietary databases will be introduced.

COUNSELA
For the last four years, Comshare has been a major supplier of computer services to Government. In 1978, the services accounted for nearly 20% of revenue. The service to local authorities has evolved into a range of products called COUNSELA, which includes:
PREMIS – a system which monitors expenditure of council house maintenance for building managers.
Financial planning for treasurers. Time-sheet analysis – a system to help a technical service director schedule resources.
Vehicle maintenance is still under development.
COUNSELA has been marketed only as a coherent range of products since the beginning of the year and Comshare intends to concentrate on these products to establish the range.

Source: Which Computer August 1979

Exhibit 11.2

GRAPHICS — a facility which can be used with any specialist system to represent any data in graphic form.

TERMINALS

Comshare does not supply terminals but it has a department which does nothing but advise clients on the right kind of terminal for the service they require. 'This is a totally impartial, free service — and it is necessary.'

OTHER SERVICES

Conventional time-sharing is still available.

LANGUAGES

Pascal
Coral
Fortran
Basic
Cobol
APL

and data managers such as QUESTOR and TACTICS.

STAFF

Comshare employs 330 staff, divided into sales and marketing, technical, product development administration and strategic planning.

USERS

Comshare has more than 1,100 users in the UK.

HARDWARE

There are six systems, configured as follows:

2 x Sigma 9 CPU
512K memory
2 x mag tape (9-track)
1 x mag tape (7-track)
12 x 86MB discs

2 x Sigma 9 CPU
512K memory
2 x mag tape (9-track)
12 x 86MB discs

1 x Sigma 9 CPU
256K memory
2 x mag tape (9-track)
7 x 86MB discs
6 x 200MB discs

1 x Sigma 9 CPU
192K memory
2 x mag tape (9-track)
10 x 86MV discs

1 x Sigma 9 CPU
256K memory
2 x mag tape (9-track)
14 x 86MB discs
8 x 200MB discs

Comshare is continually upgrading its hardware. By this month both the single-processor configurations will have been made dual processors and the 86MB discs will have been complemented with 200MB discs.

As part of the Comshare communication network, there are two Interdata 8/16E municomputer as lead front-end processors in Chelsea and 19 Interdata 50s as remote multiplexors in the sales offices.

This network links the London computer centre to Comshare computers in Ann Arbor, Michigan, and Toronto. It also allows a customer to dial any of the 17 UK sales offices or the European offices in Paris, Brussels, the Hague and Cologne.

Parsec
THE CHALLENGE OF CHANGE

To cite the fact that today's business environment is becoming increasingly more complex is to state the obvious. But stating the 'obvious' does not lessen the truth of the statement, or the impact of the fact.

Budgets, Energy Crises, Currency Fluctuations, Inflation, Material Shortages, Legislation, Taxes, Strikes – the pressure of external influences and rapid changes is making it progressively more difficult for the modern business to react effectively to them, let alone anticipate them.

Whatever occurs in the short term, you want your business to survive and succeed in the long term. Staying alive may be acceptable, but staying ahead must be the real objective.

Staying ahead means making the right decisions at the right time. It means being able to anticipate as well as react to events and business needs. It means possessing the ability to turn the shock of change into the impetus of advantage.

PARSEC is the financial management service that helps you to stay ahead. It is a specialised, dedicated service that offers you the means to analyse, plan and effectively control your business. PARSEC does not make your decisions for you, but it does make it possible for the right decisions to be made at the right time.

PARSEC is the positive answer to the challenge of change.

Exhibit 11.3

Continued

Parsec
THE NEEDS OF BUSINESS

BUDGETS AND CASHFLOW
Budgetary planning and control, and cashflow forecasting are necessities of all businesses – but necessities that are repetitive and time-consuming. PARSEC offers specialised computer-based systems that overcome repetition and drastically reduce the time expended. PARSEC releases effort, so that it can be more profitably used to examine plans and budgets in-depth; to compare activities, to report variances and to evaluate the effects of inflation and other changes.

COSTING AND PERFORMANCE CONTROL
Pricing decisions, variance analysis, resource allocation, inventory evaluation are the outcome of an effective Costing and Performance Control system. PARSEC has the facilities to undertake the complex and arduous computation essential to achieve these results.

STRATEGIC PLANNING
Longer-term planning and analyses are important if the best use is to be made of a company's assets, capabilities and opportunities. Risk and Sensitivity analyses are just two of the many useful modelling facilities available within PARSEC and examples of how informed judgements can be made.

PROJECT EVALUATION
Projects such as an acquisition or merger, diversification or rationalisation, or investment in new plant and premises require the careful examination of all feasible alternatives before the right decisions can be made. PARSEC undoubtedly offers this capability.

CONSOLIDATION AND CURRENCY CONVERSION
Multi-location companies are faced with particular problems of co-ordination and consolidation. In addition, multinational companies are concerned with currency conversion. PARSEC is the convenient and economic answer to these concerns.

Exhibit 11.3   *Continued*

The Parsec Service

Comshare's European Computer Centre is located in London. It contains a massive custom-designed computer installation that is engineered, maintained and continually developed by some of the most experienced time-sharing professionals in the business.

COMPUTERS

Comshare's communications network covers the whole of the United Kingdom, and links to our 14 local offices and to our French, German, Dutch and Belgian operations. This facility extends to the American and Canadian networks. Customers access the network and computer centre via a normal telephone connection to their local Comshare office.

NETWORK

SYSTEMS

PARSEC embodies the philosophy of making the computer make sense which means the systems are easy to use, flexible and responsive to customer needs. They encompass three areas: planning and control; the collection and manipulation of data; general financial analysis and reporting. All PARSEC systems utilise simple English commands.

PARSEC enjoys the enhancement of a wide range of additional facilites. For example, we have the most advanced off-line printing system in Europe which offers considerably improved quality, efficiency and economy over conventional computer printout. Other services include a Customer Enquiry Desk ('Helpline'), a number of proprietary databases, and bulk data input from a variety of media.

Powerful Computers, Sophisticated Network, Specialised Systems,
Dedicated People, Comprehensive Training, Complete Documentation,
and valuable additional facilities together form the PARSEC SERVICE. Each of them
is a vital part of the whole and offers an extraordinarily professional financial planning
and control capability. But it is also more than just the sum of its parts. It is unique.

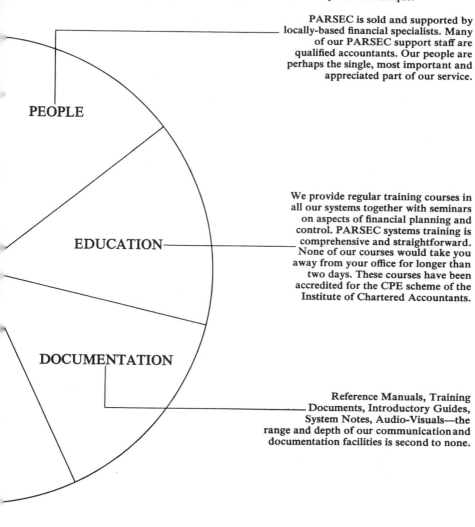

PARSEC is sold and supported by
locally-based financial specialists. Many
of our PARSEC support staff are
qualified accountants. Our people are
perhaps the single, most important and
appreciated part of our service.

We provide regular training courses in
all our systems together with seminars
on aspects of financial planning and
control. PARSEC systems training is
comprehensive and straightforward.
None of our courses would take you
away from your office for longer than
two days. These courses have been
accredited for the CPE scheme of the
Institute of Chartered Accountants.

Reference Manuals, Training
Documents, Introductory Guides,
System Notes, Audio-Visuals—the
range and depth of our communication and
documentation facilities is second to none.

PEOPLE

EDUCATION

DOCUMENTATION

Continued

Parsec
THE BENEFITS OF SERVICE

The fundamental benefit of the PARSEC service as a whole lies in its unique capability for problem-solving and analysis, for planning and control.

PARSEC is an interactive, computer-based service which means that information, analyses and reports are available quickly, easily and when they are needed.

PARSEC offers the benefit of its communications network, an invaluable facility for multi-location and multinational companies. However, the basic benefit of the network is the same for all our customers, irrespective of location or size – immediate access to powerful computer systems at the lowest price possible.

PARSEC systems meet the needs of modern business – from monthly budgeting to corporate modelling. They successfully balance the requirements of financial specialisation with the necessities of flexibility, ease of use, and responsiveness.

PARSEC people are financial specialists. We talk your language, about your needs, in your office. Our emphasis upon dedicated experienced people is absolute – as is their value.

PARSEC offers a complete approach to successful training. We are proud of our record.

PARSEC provides comprehensive documentation. The benefit of simple, well-designed and extensive material is that it enables users confidently to develop and extend their own applications.

PARSEC can justifiably claim to have a greater body of expertise in understanding and meeting financial planning and control needs than any other computer services bureau. We speak the same language, have sympathy and experience of the problems, and can advise and help effectively.

The benefits of the service are like the features of the service – greater than just a sum of the parts. PARSEC is the positive answer to your needs.

Exhibit 11.3   *Continued*

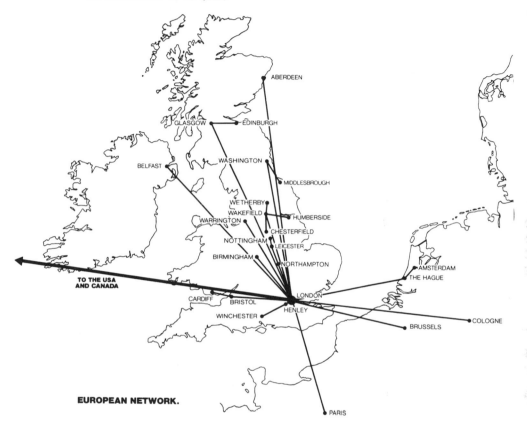

Exhibit 11.3

ASSET REGISTER

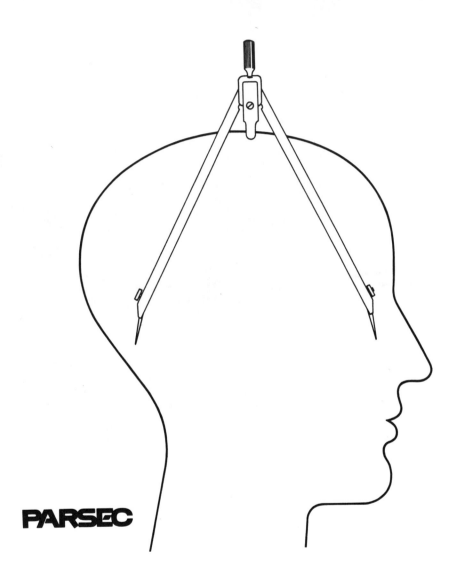

PARSEC

Exhibit 11.4   *Continued*

Introduction

The demands placed on a company's fixed asset reporting system are increasing.

Companies already require a system which can monitor the location of assets and their value, allowing effective physical auditing.

Managers need a method for calculating the historical depreciation charges on different classes of assets, a method which can allocate these charges to cost centres or other categories.

Such requirements already impose a substantial administrative burden.

Soon this workload will increase. It seems inevitable that companies will have to adopt current cost accounting methods for calculating depreciation charges and this will increase the burden on conventional systems to intolerable levels.

To meet this challenge managers are demanding comprehensive yet flexible asset register systems. Systems which reduce their administrative workload and equip them for the future. Systems they can understand and control.

The PARSEC service can provide a solution. PARSEC is a complete service consisting of a range of specialised products for data management, analysis and planning together with training, continuing support and advice.

This booklet describes how PARSEC can provide an Asset Register system which will drastically reduce the work involved in maintaining the system, cope with diverse accounting and charging requirements, and which provides the facility to produce reports instantly. Above all the PARSEC asset register system can adapt quickly to meet changes in accounting conventions and company reporting requirements.

Exhibit 11.4   *Continued*

The Asset Register

The asset register is one of the basic records of a business. It provides a basis for the calculation of depreciation, the physical verification of a company's assets and is often extended to include records of maintenance history.

As such the register contains a large amount of information about each asset: its original cost, net book value, depreciation charges, cost centre, physical location and other details.

This mass of data has to be updated to record acquisitions, disposals and other movements. All changes to the asset register should be recorded to provide a full audit trail.

Details of movements often have to be summarised, for example by asset type for posting to the general ledger.

The system has to calculate and record depreciation charges using the appropriate historical depreciation method and be flexible enough to accommodate current cost accounting methods, including the appropriate indices.

It should be capable of accommodating any additional requirements the company may have, such as the maintenance history of assets or machine performance records. Transport departments may require dates for licensing and vehicle testing to be automatically reported.

Physical audits will run more smoothly if they are based on a well organised and up-to-date asset register.

Finally, the asset register system has to be able to produce reports such as detailed plant registers, depreciation charges by cost centre and maintenance histories by asset.

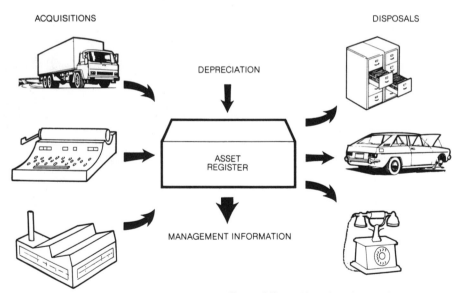

These activities must be performed accurately and can consume large amounts of the valuable time of accounts staff. Particularly at the year-end when it can least be afforded.

To reduce this burden and provide a reliable and efficient asset register, financial managers require a system which can handle large amounts of data quickly and easily, and provide reports with the minimum of effort.

Exhibit 11.4   *Continued*

The PARSEC Asset Register

The PARSEC service to financial managers can provide a solution.

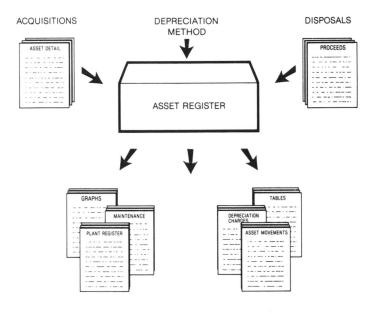

PARSEC uses a database management reporting system to handle the large volumes of data required to maintain an Asset Register.

It is a computer based system which is used from your office. A terminal connects you to COMSHARE's computer system via a telephone.

Exhibit 11.4   *Continued*

How it works

The PARSEC Asset Register has a highly efficient method of storage and is easy to use. The data is held as a simple list of Asset details.

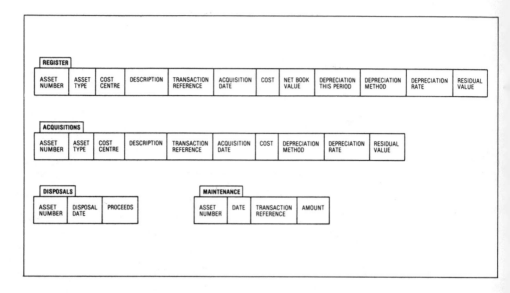

This method of storage allows access to any item of data. Once installed the structure of the Asset Register can be altered to take account of changes in information requirements or accounting conventions.

Exhibit 11.4

Continued

Entering Data

The PARSEC Asset Register adapts to fit your way of working, it
will accept data in a wide variety of forms. Data may be entered
directly into the system from a terminal or taken from source
documents via punched cards or magnetic tape. This is
particularly useful when the system is first set up.

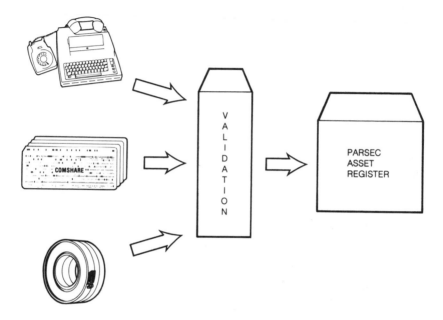

The system must be accurate and so the PARSEC Asset Register
allows you to specify validation rules. These are only entered once
and are then applied automatically to additions or modifications to
the register.

Exhibit 11.4   *Continued*

Reporting

Because the PARSEC system relieves the finance department of all the tedious figure work and calculations, managers can get the reports they need rather than settle for those which can be produced in the time available.

Standard reports like this Historical Depreciation report can be produced quickly by issuing a few simple commands.

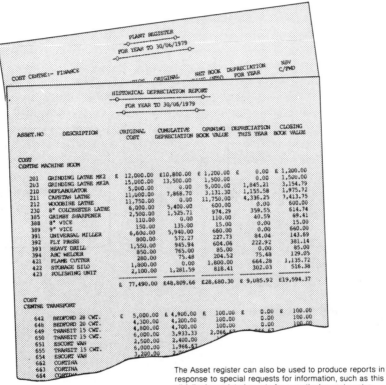

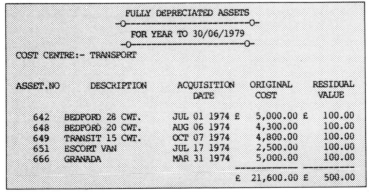

The Asset register can also be used to produce reports in response to special requests for information, such as this listing of all fully depreciated assets for a particular cost centre.

ASSET.NO	DESCRIPTION	ACQUISITION DATE	ORIGINAL COST	RESIDUAL VALUE
642	BEDFORD 28 CWT.	JUL 01 1974	£ 5,000.00	£ 100.00
648	BEDFORD 20 CWT.	AUG 06 1974	4,300.00	100.00
649	TRANSIT 15 CWT.	OCT 07 1974	4,800.00	100.00
651	ESCORT VAN	JUL 17 1974	2,500.00	100.00
666	GRANADA	MAR 31 1974	5,000.00	100.00
			£ 21,600.00	£ 500.00

FULLY DEPRECIATED ASSETS
FOR YEAR TO 30/06/1979
COST CENTRE:- TRANSPORT

Exhibit 11.4   *Continued*

The PARSEC Asset Register system can produce clearly laid out tables such as these breakdowns of depreciation charges by cost centre and asset type.

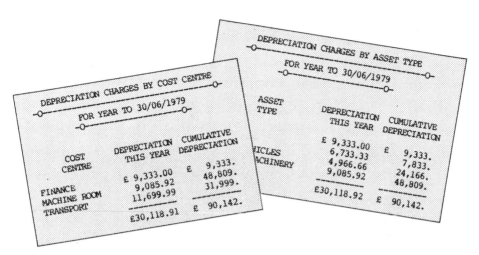

DEPRECIATION CHARGES BY COST CENTRE
FOR YEAR TO 30/06/1979

COST CENTRE	DEPRECIATION THIS YEAR	CUMULATIVE DEPRECIATION
FINANCE	£ 9,333.00	£ 9,333.
MACHINE ROOM	9,085.92	48,809.
TRANSPORT	11,699.99	31,999.
	£30,118.91	£ 90,142.

DEPRECIATION CHARGES BY ASSET TYPE
FOR YEAR TO 30/06/1979

ASSET TYPE	DEPRECIATION THIS YEAR	CUMULATIVE DEPRECIATION
...ICLES	£ 9,333.00	£ 9,333.
...ACHINERY	6,733.33	7,833.
	4,966.66	24,166.
	9,085.92	48,809.
	£30,118.92	£ 90,142.

MAINTENANCE HISTORY BY COST CENTRE
FOR YEAR TO 30/06/1979

ASSET.NO	DESCRIPTION	Q1	Q2	Q3	Q4	TOTYEAR	CUMULATIVE MAINTENANCE	BOOK VALUE THIS YEAR	AQUISITION DATE
COST CENTRE TRANSPORT									
ASSET TYPE CARS									
662	CORTINA	£ 25.65	£ 20.25	£ 32.40	£ 24.03	£ 102.33	£ 156.33	£ 1,066.67	MAR 14 1977
663	CORTINA	26.50	20.92	33.48	24.83	105.74	133.64	2,100.00	AUG 19 1977
664	CORTINA	30.78	24.30	38.88	28.84	122.80	122.80	3,600.00	MAY 11 1978
665	CORTINA	34.20	27.00	43.20	32.04	136.44	136.44	4,000.00	MAR 01 1979
666	GRANADA	42.75	33.75	54.00	40.05	170.55	395.55	100.00	MAR 31 1974
671	GRANADA	59.85	47.25	75.60	56.07	238.77	238.77	7,000.00	OCT 22 1978
ASSET TYPE GOODS VEHICLES									
642	BEDFORD 28 CWT.	£ 42.75	£ 33.75	£ 54.00	£ 40.05	£ 170.55	£ 350.55	£ 100.00	JUL 01 1974
648	BEDFORD 20 CWT.	36.76	29.02	46.44	34.44	146.67	301.47	100.00	AUG 06 1974
649	TRANSIT 15 CWT.	41.04	32.40	51.84	38.73	163.73	336.53	100.00	OCT 07 1974
650	TRANSIT 15 CWT.	51.30	40.50	64.80	48.06	204.66	312.66	2,066.67	APR 21 1977
651	ESCORT VAN	21.37	16.87	27.00	20.02	85.27	175.27	100.00	JUL 17 1974
655	TRANSIT 15 CWT.	51.30	40.50	64.80	48.06	204.66	258.66	4,033.33	JUN 26 1977
654	ESCORT VAN	27.36	21.60	34.56	25.63	109.15	166.75	1,133.33	SEP 03 1976

If maintenance records are included on the asset register the system can provide detailed reports for monitoring the costs incurred.

Exhibit 11.4   *Continued*

PARSEC — the service to financial managers

The PARSEC service can provide a comprehensive yet flexible Asset Register system which will reduce the burden of administration and equip the company to meet the impending change to current cost accounting.

Like all COMSHARE services PARSEC is fully supported by documentation, training and a full range of customer support facilities.

Exhibit 11.4   *Continued*

UNITED KINGDOM, COMSHARE LTD., LONDON.

HEAD OFFICE.	32-34 GREAT PETER STREET, LONDON SW1P 2DB. 01-222 5665/TELEX: 851 918750.
	10 GROSVENOR GARDENS, LONDON SW1W 0DH. 01-730 9991.
ABERDEEN.	5 HADDEN STREET, ABERDEEN AB1 2NU. 0224-574203
BIRMINGHAM.	MARLBOROUGH HOUSE. 679 WARWICK ROAD, SOLIHULL, WEST MIDLANDS B91 3DA 021-704 4151.
BELFAST.	WINDSOR HOUSE, BEDFORD STREET, BELFAST BT2 7EG 0232-40060
BRISTOL.	KENHAM HOUSE, WILDER STREET, BRISTOL BS2 8PD. 0272-425701.
CARDIFF.	24 PARK PLACE, CARDIFF, CF1 3BA 0222-371033
EDINBURGH.	20 COATES CRESCENT, EDINBURGH EH3 7AS. 031-225 6034
GLASGOW.	12 NEWTON PLACE, GLASGOW G3 7PR. 041-331 1536
LEICESTER.	JAMES HOUSE, 55 WELFORD ROAD, LEICESTER LE2 7AE. 0533-545242.
WAKEFIELD.	RAINES HOUSE, DENBY DALE ROAD, WAKEFIELD, YORKSHIRE WF1 1HR. 0924-77132.
WARRINGTON.	BLADEN HOUSE, HAYDOCK STREET, WARRINGTON, CHESHIRE WA2 7UW. 0925-37342.
WASHINGTON.	THE GALLERIES, WASHINGTON CENTRE, WASHINGTON, TYNE & WEAR NE38 7SD. 0632-464771.
WINCHESTER.	33 SOUTHGATE STREET, WINCHESTER, HAMPSHIRE SO23 9EH. 0962-64467.

BELGIUM, N.V. COMSHARE SA, BRUSSELS.

BRUSSELS.	TWEEKERKENSTRAAT, 7 RUE DES DEUX EGLISES, BRUSSEL 1040, BRUXELLES. (02) 230 85 45

THE NETHERLANDS, COMSHARE BV, THE HAGUE.

HEAD OFFICE.	KONINGINNEGRACHT 56, 2514 AE, DEN HAAG. 070-46-93-57.
AMSTERDAM.	AMSTELDIJK 166, GEBOUW RIVIERSTAETE, 7E VERD, 1079 LH AMSTERDAM. 020-42-77-91.

FRANCE, TELESYSTEMES, PARIS.

PARIS.	10 RUE DE VERDUN, 92100 BOULOGNE. (1) 604 65 65

GERMANY, COMSHARE GMBH, COLOGNE.

COLOGNE.	QUATERMARKT 5, 5000 KOLN 1, 0221 210897.

EUROPEAN COMPUTER CENTRE.

	P.O. BOX 197, LONDON SW3 5RL. 01-351 4399

UNITED STATES, COMSHARE, INC., ANN ARBOR, MICHIGAN.

CORPORATE HEADQUARTERS.	WOLVERINE TOWER, P.O. BOX 1588, ANN ARBOR, MICHIGAN 48106. (313) 994 4800/TWX: 810-223-6014.
ATLANTA.	3355 LENOR ROAD, ATLANTA, GEORGIA 30326. (404) 252-8911.
BOSTON.	20 WILLIAM STREET, WELLESLEY OFFICE PARK, WELLESLEY, MASSACHUSETTS 02181. (617) 235-3650.
CHICAGO. (DISTRICT).	6300 RIVER ROAD, ROSEMONT, ILLINOIS 60018. (312) 696-4200.
CHICAGO. (AREA).	222 SOUTH RIVERSIDE PLAZA, SUITE 830, CHICAGO, ILLINOIS 60606. (312) 648-0910

CINCINNATI.	FIFTH AND RACE TOWER, SUITE 703, CINCINNATI, OHIO 45202. (513) 421-5020.
CLEVELAND.	ORANGEWOOD PLACE BLDG., 3690 ORANGE PLACE, BEACHWOOD, OHIO 44122. (216) 464-9053.
DALLAS.	8585 NORTH STEMMONS FREEWAY, SUITE 607, DALLAS, TEXAS 75247. (214) 630-8811.
DETROIT.	17117 WEST NINE MILE, SUITE 1025, SOUTHFIELD, MICHIGAN 48075. (313) 559-1400
HOUSTON.	7505 FANNIN, SUITE 301, HOUSTON, TEXAS 77054. (713) 795-4451.
LOS ANGELES (AIRPORT).	6151 WEST CENTURY BLVD., SUITE 906, LOS ANGELES, CALIFORNIA 90045. (213) 649-4520.
LOS ANGELES (DOWNTOWN).	700 FLOWER STREET, SUITE 1218, LOS ANGELES, CALIFORNIA 90017. (213) 629-5551.
MINNEAPOLIS.	SHELARD TOWER, SUITE 840, ST. LOUIS PARK, MINNESOTA 55426. (612) 546-3556.
NEW YORK.	1114 AVENUE OF THE AMERICAS, 28th FLOOR, NEW YORK, NEW YORK 10036. (212) 398-6600.
PHILADELPHIA.	111 PRESIDENTIAL BLVD., SUITE 219. BALA-CYNWYD PENNSYLVANIA 19004. (215) 835-6644.
PHILADELPHIA (TRILOG DIVISION).	1700 MARKET STREET, PHILADELPHIA, PENNSYLVANIA 19103. (215) 564-3404.
PITTSBURGH.	1306 GRANT BUILDING, PITTSBURGH, PENNSYLVANIA 15219. (412) 355-0540.
SAN FRANCISCO.	690 MARKET STREET, SUITE 900, SAN FRANCISCO, CALIFORNIA 94104. (415) 956-6676
ST. LOUIS.	7777 BONHOMME, SUITE 1304, CLAYTON, MISSOURI 63105. (314) 862-7212.
WASHINGTON D.C.	1745 JEFFERSON DAVIS HIGHWAY, SUITE 502, ARLINGTON, VIRGINIA 22202. (703) 524-1405.

CANADA, COMSHARE LTD., TORONTO, ONTARIO.

CORPORATE HEADQUARTERS.	230 GALAXY BOULEVARD, REXDALE, ONTARIO M9W 5R8. (416) 675 6363.
CALGARY.	700 SECOND STREET SW, SUITE 3400, CALGARY, ALBERTA T2P 2W2. (403) 269-7635.
CAMBRIDGE.	1497 QUEENS BOULEVARD, KITCHENER, ONTARIO N2M 1E3. (519) 744-4484.
HAMILTON.	42 JAMES STREET SOUTH, SUITE 33, HAMILTON, ONTARIO L8P 2Y4. (416) 523-0700.
LONDON.	747 HYDE PARK ROAD, LONDON, ONTARIO N6H 3S3. (519) 472-1570.
MONTREAL.	1130 SHERBROOKE STREET WEST, SUITE 500, MONTREAL, QUEBEC H3A 2T1. (514) 282-8011.
OTTAWA.	99 BANK STREET, SUITE 606, OTTAWA, ONTARIO K1P 6B9. (613) 236-9651.
QUEBEC CITY.	125 RUE SAINT PIERRE, QUEBEC CITY G1K 4A8. (418) 694-0552.
SARNIA.	724 KEMSLEY DRIVE, SARNIA, ONTARIO N7V 2M2. (519) 337-7368.
TORONTO. (CENTRAL)	11 ADELAIDE ST. WEST, SUITE 703, TORONTO, ONTARIO M5H 1M2. (416) 366-8111.
TORONTO. (WEST)	41 VOYAGER COURT NORTH, REXDALE, ONTARIO, M9W 4T2. (416) 675-6363.
VANCOUVER.	740 NICOLA ST. SUITE 200, VANCOUVER, B.C. V6G 2C2. (604) 687-3244.

JAPAN, JAIS-COMSHARE, TOKYO.

HEAD OFFICE.	SUMITOMO TSUKIJI BUILDING, 5-4-14 TSUKIJI CHUO-KU, TOKYO. 03-542-8681/TWX: 72-0252-2377.
OSAKA.	DAISAN FUJI BUILDING, 1-90 ITACHIBORIKITADORI, NISHIA-KU, OSAKA. 06-531-6374.

MAKING THE COMPUTER MAKE SENSE.

Exhibit 11.4

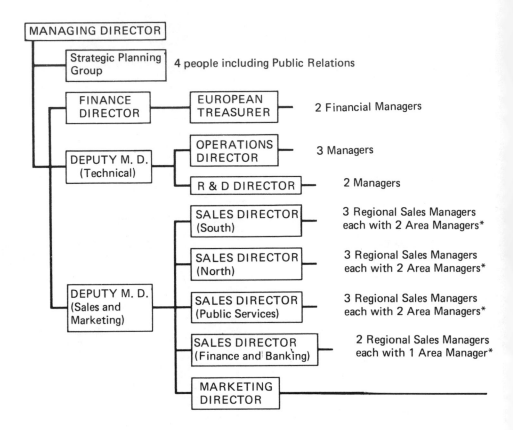

MANAGING DIRECTOR

Strategic Planning Group — 4 people including Public Relations

FINANCE DIRECTOR → EUROPEAN TREASURER — 2 Financial Managers

DEPUTY M. D. (Technical) → OPERATIONS DIRECTOR — 3 Managers

R & D DIRECTOR — 2 Managers

DEPUTY M. D. (Sales and Marketing)

SALES DIRECTOR (South) — 3 Regional Sales Managers each with 2 Area Managers*

SALES DIRECTOR (North) — 3 Regional Sales Managers each with 2 Area Managers*

SALES DIRECTOR (Public Services) — 3 Regional Sales Managers each with 2 Area Managers*

SALES DIRECTOR (Finance and Banking) — 2 Regional Sales Managers each with 1 Area Manager*

MARKETING DIRECTOR

* On average each Sales Area Manager has the following working for him:

1 Sales Executive, 1 Account Executive,
2 Customer Support Executives.

Exhibit 11.5

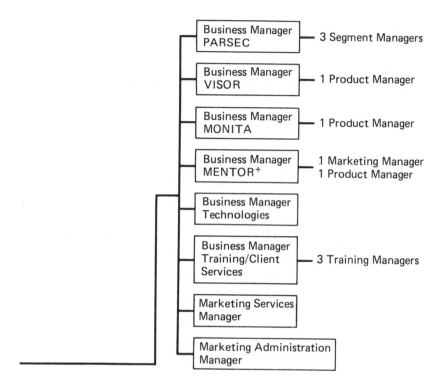

+ New Product under development.

Exhibit 11.5

Appendix 11.1

Case History

Company X had a problem estimating what the cost would be to manufacture cartons to a customer's specification. Each carton had differing amounts of printing, were of different sizes and of different shapes which required multi-coloured printing, specialized box-cutting and glueing. For any one carton there was an enormous number of combinations of machines; for example if a job required five-colour printing should it be printed twice on a four-colour machine or three times on a two-colour? Should the boxcutting be done on a large, fast machine requiring a high set up time or should it be done on a slower-running machine with a lower set up cost, and how fast would the gumming machine operate on differing quantities?

A program has been written by Comshare which asks a series of questions so that the estimators can specify what type, size and colour of carton they wish to make. The program then tries all the possible methods of manufacture until it finds the least expensive method. It then prints out which machines have been selected, how many hours each will take and what the costs of each operation will be. Finally, the total costs are printed including the packing costs dependent on the type of packaging to be used.

Using the Comshare facilities the estimators can now produce an estimate in five minutes whereas previously an estimate could take between thirty minutes and two hours.

Changes in production speeds or cost centre rates can be quickly included in the program so that all new estimates take account of the new data available, thus removing the possibility of an estimate working on old data and producing the wrong estimate.

The tedious part of the estimator's task, i.e. doing all the arithmetic for the different machine costs and speeds, is removed and therefore allows the estimator more time to apply his experience to areas where it is much more use, such as selection of materials and method of manufacture.

Finally, the estimates that are produced are much more accurate than was previously possible as the program always picks the best combination of machines and there is no chance of clerical error in the arithmetic.

Appendix 11.2

Corporate Objectives

1 To achieve profitable growth from stable revenues.
2 To assure long-term corporate survival.
3 To be the best in chosen markets.
4 To be an Ethical Organization.
5 To sustain a professional and exciting work environment to attract, motivate and retain good people.

Long-Term Strategies

1 To be the leader in a few 'speciality markets' by providing a 'speciality product line'.

   A 'speciality market' is a set of enterprises or individuals with identifiable needs that can be met with a computer-based solution, and that can be grouped by industry, discipline, need or geography.
   (Acceptable 'speciality markets' needed to fulfil a comprehensive list of detailed requirements too commercially sensitive to be disclosed here.)
   A 'speciality product line' is a set of interrelated products which serve all the needs of a single speciality market.

2 To maximize 'value-added' — the work added by Comshare to the raw material.

   Achieved by:
   (a)   Offering speciality product lines.
   (b)   Staffing with top quality people.
   (c)   Using the most up-to-date technology.

3 To maximise 'multiplier effects' by seeking commonality between services provided.
4 To operate within a preplanned environment with an open mind towards creativity and opportunism.

XII
Stewart Wales, Somerville Ltd
D. Cook

Company Activities

The principal activities of Stewart Wales, Somerville, are those of 'manufacturing and marketing specialist surface coatings'. In particular the products, which are not to be confused with conventional paints, are specifically designed to fill two specific market needs:

1 The long term preservation and decoration of exterior and interior building surfaces and industrial building components, i.e. walls, roofs, floors.
2 The protection of metallic surfaces from corrosion, chemical attack and atmospheric pollution, and for finishing manufactured parts and pressings.

Consequently the company finds itself operating in three main fields:

(a) **The New Buildings Market** embraces specifications raised through architects, Government ministries and local authorities from design to construction stages.

   The objects are to provide durable protection, add decorative feature, reduce recurring maintenance costs and overcome inherent shortcomings of materials used in construction, e.g. dusting concrete and friable asbestos, etc.

(b) **The Maintenance Market** covers protection and decoration of plant and buildings of all types. This market embraces virtually every industrial establishment in both developed and

---

Prepared by David Cook, Bradford University, 1981.

developing countries, including government armed forces, local authorities, and agricultural outlets.

(c) **The Production Market** refers manufacturers of industrialized building components including those involving metals where, in addition to high quality finish, protection is required against rough usage, corrosion or chemical attack.

Company Formation

Arthur Wales left school at 14 and four years later, in his own words, 'discovered a lack of practical education'. As a result he persuaded a number of local colleges and institutions to allow him to follow parts of several courses in the broad 'commercial area'. Later, at 23, he joined Dexion Ltd in Glasgow as a salesman and soon after enrolled on a three-year part-time (evenings) management studies course at Glasgow University. Soon after completing the course he joined the Sunbeam Electric Corporation of Chicago as their UK general sales manager designate. After he had spent the first six months in the field to get to know the customer and the product range, in his own words:

'the idea of starting my own business really began to crystallise. I thought that if I could sell other companies' goods, succeed and make profits for others there was no reason why I could not succeed in a business of my own.'

While thinking of the possibility of starting his own business Arthur Wales drew up a personal balance sheet. He had had extensive experience of industrial selling but possessed no capital and would therefore require a business that was the opposite of capital intensive. He needed a product that would sell quickly and generate a good volume of repeat business. He wished to keep his overheads to a minimum. At this stage in the mid 1950s, as a result of his reading and selling experience, he became interested in the development of plastics and was

'aware that no product existed that could suitably prevent the dusting (dusting is the tendency of concrete floors gradually to disintegrate and produce an unpleasant dust) of concrete, a problem which costs industry vast sums of money every year. I felt if I could marry the properties and advantages of modern plastics to produce a surface coating that could be easily applied like conventional paint, yet prevented dusting, then I would in fact have something very worthwhile, in fact, a liquid plastic.'

Consequently he conducted a search in the Commercial Library in Glasgow of German patents, which under war reparations agreements were made available to British businessmen. In fact the breakthrough came not with German work but with published American research into synthetic rubber and plastic resin. Having found what he thought he was after, he approached a company in the West of Scotland. Wales' proposition was that if the company was given his plastic resin information and the performance specification of the liquid plastic required, and did the development work, he would create a market, sell the product and license the company to manufacture the product on his behalf. In October 1958, after a successful development and testing programme, Wales formed Stewart Wales, Somerville (the latter being his wife's maiden name), operating from his home in Cambuslang on the outskirts of Glasgow.

Developments

At its inception the company possessed £312.50 capital. Obviously, it was not economically possible to recruit any full-time paid staff and consequently fifteen agents were appointed on a commission only basis. The commission paid was 20% of sales. It was not until two years later that the first staff-salaried salesman was appointed and in 1962 the company moved to its present site at East Kilbride. A 99-year lease was signed with the East Kilbride Development Corporation, leasing 1 acre of ground upon which was built a small office and 3000 square feet of warehouse. By October 1964 the business had expanded to such an extent that the office was extended and a single storey factory and laboratory was built. With an eye to the future these buildings were designed to allow expansion both upwards and outwards. At this point, the agreement was ended with the licensed manufacturer because technical resources were required to enable SWS to conduct product R & D.

Experience of surface preparation prior to surface coatings treatments for steelwork led SWS to the development of a product which showed commercial possibilities in other areas. This represented a market opportunity and in 1966 Glenvil Products Ltd, a fully-owned subsidiary of SWS was formed. The company offered a deliberately restricted range of specialist cleaning materials, initially intended to remove industrial grease and baked-on carbonaceous deposits. As this side of the business expanded, the product range was extended, so that now Glenvil cleaning and hygiene products are in daily use in hotels, restaurants, canteens, hospitals, food processing factories, abattoirs etc.

In the Managing Director's view the two most intractable problems the company has faced since its formation are those of finance and marketing.

Management Team

SWS's management team comprises of three people and is as follows:

Stewart Wales — Founder and Managing Director with particular responsibilities for sales and marketing both at home and abroad. Mr Wales also oversees all promotional activities (e.g. publications, special literature, technical manuals etc.), liaison with customers and the recruitment, training, and evaluation of the sales force. Spends a good deal of time in the field, particularly on overseas trips.

Andrew Condie — Technical Manager in charge of the laboratory including quality control and product development. Responsibilities also include production, raw material supply and storage, finished good storage, plant and general maintenance, and distribution.

Donald McInnes — Commercial Manager. Trained as an accountant and is responsible for all of the company's administrative functions including purchasing, personnel, finance, legal affairs, employment, pensions and insurance etc.

Currently, thirty two people are employed.

Managerial Philosophy

In his own words Stewart Wales regards SWS as being essentially a sales and marketing organization with manufacture being a necessary evil. Having said that, however, he points out the vital role played by chemists and technologists in the R & D process searching for new products and applications. In fact during the late 1970s there were twice as many R & D as production staff.

Because of the emphasis on sales and marketing, great stress is placed on the sales force itself and on communications in general.

Role of The Sales Force

Consistent with the analysis that the organization is essentially a sales and marketing operation, a key role is allocated to the salesmen. SWS and Glenvil employ seven and ten salesmen respectively and one field manager each, the latter reporting direct to the Managing Director. The job of the SWS salesman is entirely different to his counterpart in Glenvil. The former is regarded as a problem-solver whereas the latter is considered to be more of a trained order taker.

The SWS salesman, rather than selling the physical product of liquid plastic, offer the buyer the benefits of protection, durability, reduced maintenance costs etc. His task is really an educational exercise of justifying a series of trade-offs, whereby a product that is about 30% more expensive than industrial paint can offer medium- to long-term savings. The key people in this buying process are thought to be architects and specifiers both in local authorities and private practice as well as chief engineers and maintenance personnel in industrial enterprises. It is not feasible nor economic for there to be any flexibility or job switching between the salesman of SWS and Glenvil respectively.

The role of the Glenvil salesmen is initially to introduce the products to new customers and then to ensure that they place regular repeat orders for increased value and range. This is achieved through service calls at pre-determined intervals to check that the customer is maintaining minimum stock levels and to advise on replenishment orders. Glenvil employs a Contracts Manager whose function is to negotiate with groups, such as hotel and restaurant chains, hospitals, industrial catering contractors, and local authority education departments with the object of getting Glenvil appointed as approved suppliers to all the establishments that these groups control.

As a policy, initiated by Stewart Wales, the company 'grows its own timber'. Hence all recruits to the sales force undergo a carefully controlled programme of training. The ideal candidate for the

Glenvil sales force is about 30 years old, preferably with some kindred selling experience, who is a hard-working self-starter and is expected to break even in three to six months. Because of the different nature of the job the SWS candidate often working with a long lead time (one to two years) is younger, say 22–25, with a good education (A level plus; possibly someone who has left university prior to graduating) offering a high selling ability and able to influence people. Previous selling experience is not required but the company will not recruit an ex-paint salesman, as he will have been selling on price alone. The SWS salesman is expected to break even after one year. His training consists of a one week full-time company induction programme followed by on-the-job supervision and training to acquire product knowledge and skill in the industrial selling situation unique to liquid plastics. After twelve to eighteen months the trainee salesman's progress is formally reviewed and if it is satisfactory he is appointed a territory representative. After training a salesman's salary increases by £1,000 to £4,000 plus bonus. During training the embryo salesman is given a company car, expenses, etc.

Personal selling is by far the most important element in the company's marketing mix. On price no discount is offered. The company does not advertise per se, the only sales promotion being the sales literature itself, plus press releases on product development and occasionally space taken at exhibitions.

Entry to The Export Market

The turning point for SWS in the export market was the Yom Kippur war of 1973, the conflict between the Arabs and Israelis which directly led to oil being used as a political weapon by OPEC (Organization for Petroleum Exporting Countries) and a consequent quadrupling of the crude oil price. At that time the UK market was depressed, SWS anticipated a decline in business with a consequent cash flow crisis, and Stewart Wales was beginning to think about the possibility of selling into other markets. It was a centre page spread of the magazine Trade and Industry, pointing out the new opportunities for businessmen in the Middle East as a result of the latter's newly found wealth, that acted as the catalyst. On the criteria of oil wealth and population, two countries — Iran and Nigeria — stood out to Stewart Wales as being prime market targets. Being short of both money and time, he did not consider formal market research and decided Nigeria was probably the more attractive prospect, because it did possess some British connections and there would be no language problem as would be the case in Iran.

Promptly, it was decided to appoint exclusive distributors for Nigeria. Advice and help was sought from both the Department of Trade and Industry Export Services and the Nigerian High Commission but neither were able to offer a great deal of immediate assistance. Mr Wales therefore decided to visit Nigeria, wrote to warn the British High Commission in Lagos of his impending arrival and within eight weeks of the Yom Kippur War was in Lagos.

The objective of the trip was not to assess market potential but to appoint a stockist/distributor. The services of the Commercial Officer of the British High Commission were used and a French company was quickly appointed as sole agent. The price for any product to the agent was UK price minus 40% + CIF charges. (NB This large discount was intended to fund local promotional activity but it was never used for this purpose.) On his return home, Mr Wales waited for the orders to flow in but very little happened. To establish what was happening Mr Wales visited the agent, staying for about eight weeks to offer training and general assistance. It was quickly noticed that when he was present at any negotiations the sale was made but that overall the agent was not prepared to spend any of his own time and money pushing a new product, especially when he had already established a profitable business carrying a number of other lines. There was 'too much cash chasing too few goods'.

As a result SWS and the French company parted and a Dutch company was appointed as a replacement agent. On this occasion the terms agreed were UK price minus 25% + CIF charges. The 'saved' 15% was to be used to finance trips to Nigeria by UK sales personnel three times per year, 28 days per visit. The new arrangement proved satisfactory and £150,000 worth of business was generated within eighteen months. Nearly all of the business was being generated on prestige contracts concentrated in Lagos. In April 1975 the Nigerian government subjected the product to import controls, the implication for SWS being a £100,000 budget deficit in that financial year.

Fortunately, immediately after the toehold in Nigeria had been established, an agency had been started using similar principles in the Arabian Gulf. Two salesmen, Bob Hughes and B. Fancourt, were therefore sent to the Middle East concentrating on Saudi Arabia,

Egypt, Bahrain, and Dubai, to fill the gap. They managed to return home with orders for £70,000 and the promise of a further £100,000 of business in the next six months. Not all of this business actually materialized.

In the next three years the export side of the business increased by some 42% from £198,369 in 1975–6 to £282,701 in 1977–8.

Export Organization

As a policy SWS has no Export Manager or department. Rather than have a formal export salesman, three senior salesmen are deployed in 'joint overseas/UK home-based operations'. The individual is assigned both a home sales area and an overseas territory and he has to generate sufficient sales both at home and overseas.

Problem

In July 1978 Mr Wales was evaluating how the company could increase its level of performance in export markets and was considering in particular the potential that must exist in the EEC, especially Germany.

Products	Description
CO SEAL	liquid plastic dressing
HEAVY DUTY CO SEAL	liquid plastic dressing
ECONOTEX	textured plastic finish
ECONOCOAT	decorative plastic emulsion
GALVALLOY	rustproofing liquid metal alloy
ECONOPLAS	liquid plastic finish
MEP	metal primer/conditioner
SWS FUNGICIDE	moss lichen and algae killer

Exhibit 12.1: SWS Product Range

CO SEAL	5 litre tins
	25 litre open top drums
HEAVY DUTY CO-SEAL	5 litre two compartment tins
ECONOTEX	5 litre tins
	10 litre polypails
	25 litre open top drums
ECONOCOAT	5 litre tins
	10 litre polypails
	25 litre open top drums
GALVALLOY	10 Kilo tins
ECONOPLAS	5 litre tins
	25 litre open top drums
MEP	5 litre tins
SWS FUNGICIDE	25 litre drums

Exhibit 12.2: Pack Size Availability

	%
CO SEAL Liquid Plastic Dressing	49
ECONOTEX Textured Plastic Finish	7
ECONOCOAT Decorative Plastic Emulsion	3
HEAVY DUTY CO SEAL Liquid Plastic Dressing	9
GALVALLOY Rustproofing Liquid Metal Alloy	8
ECONOPLAS Liquid Plastic Finish	12
MEP METAL CONDITIONAL Metal Primer	2
THINNER	10
	100

Source: Company Records

Exhibit 12.3: Analysis of UK Sales, % Cash Value 1978

	1975–6		1976–7		1977–8	
	£	%	£	%	£	%
Europe	33,077	16.7	45,401	17.3	57,659	20.4
Nigeria	116,454	58.7	162,148	61.6	55,617	19.7
Middle East	46,343	23.3	54,015	20.5	165,011	58.4
Other	1,495	1.3	1,457	0.6	4,414	1.5
	198,369	100.0	263,021	100.0	282,701	100.0

Source: Company Records

Note:
During these years the UK Construction Industry continued the decline which set-in subsequent to the 1973 'Yom Kippur' Arab-israeli War.

The contraction of home sales had to be offset by the newly developed export markets, as a matter of survival.

Exhibit 12.4: SWS Overseas Sales

	1977	1976	1975
	£	£	£
Turnover	711,471	637,531	600,479
Profit before Taxation	67,518	57,992	65,992
After charging:			
Depreciation	24,661	14,989	9,337
Directors Emoluments	17,704	14,181	12,279
Auditors Remuneration	4,582	4,059	3,749
Loan Interest	7,941	5,995	4,830
Plant Hire Charges	2,729	2,680	1,247
Contract Hire Motor Vehicles	–	4,840	8,185
	57,617	46,744	39,627
Exceptional Items	8,187	–	8,500
	75,705	57,992	57,492
Taxation	25,083	27,234	34,051
Profit after Taxation	50,622	30,758	23,441
Extraordinary Item	–	–	(15,860)
	50,622	30,758	7,581
Less: Minority Interests	1,351	347	1,012
Profit attributable to Parent Company	49,271	30,411	6,569
Balance brought forward	83,757	53,346	43,889
Balance carried forward	133,028	83,757	50,449

Exhibit 12.5: Stewart Wales, Somerville Ltd
Consolidated Profit and Loss Account (Y/e 8th October)

	1977	1976	1975
	£	£	£
Fixed Assets	191,185	130,294	69,773
Patents and Trademarks	302	164	84
Preliminary Expenses	83	83	83
Investment			
Current Asset			
Stock	95,506	65,471	51,410
Debtors and Prepayment	188,759	147,348	144,015
Short Term Deposit	80,703	58,991	46,054
Cash and Bank	2,022	4,276	5,207
	366,990	272,086	246,686
Current Liabilities			
Creditors and Accruals	183,776	123,220	97,316
Bank Overdraft	27,558	830	494
Taxation	21,560	31,457	31,010
Hire Purchase Creditors	41,075	21,089	9,988
Directors' Current Accounts	8,000	6,000	5,900
Foreign Taxation	1,640	1,270	185
Provision for Damages Claim	2,539	25,000	25,000
	286,148	208,866	169,893
Net Current Assets	80,842	67,220	76,793
	272,412	197,761	146,733
Share Capital	33,900	33,900	33,900
Reserves			
Capital	1,724	1,724	1,724
Retained Profit	133,028	83,757	50,449
	134,752	85,481	52,173
Deferred Taxation	70,290	43,813	24,120
Long-term Loans	25,349	27,798	30,118
Minority Interests	8,121	6,769	6,422
	272,412	197,761	146,733

Exhibit 12.6: Stewart Wales, Somerville Ltd
Consolidated Balance Sheet (Y/e 8th October)

	Turnover	*Exports*	%
1975	600,479	166,844	27.8
1976	637,531	249,393	39.1
1977	711,471	283,227	39.8

Exhibit 12.7

Product	Description/Use	Treatment	Examples
CO SEAL RANGE	Transparent co-polymer-based liquid plastic possessing properties of tough durability and chemical resistance. Specifically designed for sealing concrete, asbestos, brick, plaster, stonework, cement render, etc.	Brush Spray gun Roller Touch dry 30 mins Recoatable 12 hours	Hotel complex – Indian Ocean Derby Ring Road Chimney treatment Irish Electricity Supply Board High rise flats, East Kilbride Development Corporation Tafawa Balewa Stadium, Lagos, Nigeria Nene Valley roads and bridges, Northampton
HEAVY DUTY CO SEAL	Two-pack polyurethane reinforced liquid plastic with excellent adhesion to concrete, cement rendering, brick, unglazed tile, stone, roughcast, plaster and asbestos cement. Interior and exterior application particularly where aggressive conditions. Not suitable for bitumous surfaces.	Brush Spray gun Roller Touch dry 2–3 hours Recoatable 6–8 hours	Methane drainage house NCB Slaughter house, Castleford Asbestos building panels, East Kilbride Development Corpn Withington Swimming Baths, Manchester Malting house, Oakwell Brewery Barnsley Brewery Co. Ltd
ECONOTEX	One coat textured composition gives durable and decorative finish to sound and suitably primed brick, stonework, masonry, pebble dash, hardboard, plaster board, asbestos, cement and other non metallic interior and exterior building surfaces.	Brush Roller Touch dry 30–45 mins Hard dry 4–6 hours	Northgate Leisure Centre, Chester Preston Bus Station Federal Government Secretarial Lagos, Nigeria NCB – miners houses, Rotherham Dun Laoghaire Car Ferry Terminal, Dublin

Product	Description	Application	Drying Times	Uses
ECONOCOAT	Decorative thixotropic liquid based coating. Designed for all interior non metallic building surfaces, e.g. plaster, wood, building board.	Brush unthinned Roller Add 5–7% water Spray Add 10% water	Touch dry 30 mins Hard dry 2–3 hours	
GALVALLOY	Anodic metal coating designed to prevent rusting of ferrous metal. Can be applied at any stage of fabrication of iron and steel plate or section or as a temporary barrier coating for immediate application to shotblasted surfaces.	Brush Roller Spray	Touch dry 15–20 mins Recoatable: Brush 4 hours Spray 2 hours Hard dry 12 hours	Tinsley Viaduct Pipeline Rotherham Football Stadium Leyland Lorry/Car Bodies
ECONOPLAS	General purpose thixotropic liquid plastic coating. Formulated on a special polyurethane plastic base it is designed to protect and decorate previously primed or painted ferrous metal surfaces, flame sprayed zinc, cadmium and pre-etched aluminium, particularly from atmospheric pollution and chemical attack.	Brush Spray gun Roller	Touch dry 2 hours Hard dry 48 hours Recoatable 8 hours	BISF steel houses, Borough of Castleford Pylons Electricity Boards Filter tanks, Whitbread Brewery

Exhibit 12.8: Product Range Analysis

XIII
The International Development of the Access Credit Card

C. McIver

How a Credit Card Works

Credit cards, as most people know them, were born in the United States in the early 1960s. The first successful cards were Diners Club and American Express. Nowadays these two cards, and others like them, are known to credit card technicians as T & E (travel and entertainment) cards. They provide a means of identification for the affluent and enable them to pay later for their purchases rather than on the spot. But they provide no credit facility for the user, over and above his or her monthly purchases; they are elitest in their distribution, being confined mainly to the AB classes (American Express claims to reject nearly 50% of those applying for cards); and cardholders are required to pay an annual subscription to the 'club'.

For the organizers of T & E cards the main operational problems are:

1 the selective recruitment of cardholders, together with credit control within the limits of the transactions for which the cards are used
2 the selective recruitment of retailers willing to honour the card, concentrating particularly on the hotels, restaurants, airlines, car hire companies and retailers likely to be frequented by the AB classes
3 the mechanical process of collating and analysing the monthly transactions between cardholders and retailers, billing the former and crediting the latter

---

Prepared by Colin McIver.

4 the prevention of fraud, resulting from theft, counterfeiting or improper use of cards.

Coincidentally with the invention of T & E cards, the 1960s saw a dramatic acceleration in the public's use of credit in the advanced world, as the savings habit gave way to the borrowing habit. It was a natural development that the credit card concept should be extended to give cardholders a revolving line of credit over and above the value of their monthly purchases; and that the banks should start to make the running on the development of credit cards. The Bank of America, with its Americard, was a pioneer in making this transition.

In operational terms, the additional credit facility and the involvement of large banks added several new dimensions to the credit card. It became a mass market, rather than an exclusive 'product', becoming available to any individual with a bank account who would qualify for a bank loan or overdraft. It required the recruitment of a much wider spread both of cardholders and of co-operating retailers; it increased the scale and complications of the transaction processing, accountancy and credit control activity very substantially; and it made the prevention of fraud a potentially more formidable problem.

The dimensions of the credit card revolution at this point should not be exaggerated. By 1979 some 21% of UK adults possessed one or more credit cards of one kind or another (including store credit cards). But the use of credit cards was still heavily concentrated in the ABC1 social groups and they still covered only a very small minority of financial transactions as the following figures from a 1979 market survey indicate:

Individuals' method of payment by value *(all transactions over £3)*	*% of all adults*
Cash	58
Cheques	27
Standing orders/other methods	13
Credit cards	2
	100

(Needless to say almost all transactions under £3 are handled in cash.)

But the future of credit cards is incalculable, as technology advances and the habit of using them grows. It is improbable that cash will ever disappear as a convenient and understandable method of payment, despite the risks and expense involved in its transportation. But already the technology is available in the form of magnetic tape and microchips, to record financial transactions and other day-to-day data on the credit card, making it potentially the equivalent of a portable bank account. The full implications of such developments — and the problems they will bring in their train — have still to be worked out.

The Benefits of Credit Cards for those involved

The bank-issued credit card represents in effect a three-way partnership between the cardholders, the retailers and others who accept the card and the issuing bank or banks (either administering the operation direct or through an intermediary like the Joint Credit Card Company described below).

For the cardholders the benefits are fairly obvious:

1 They can reduce the risks involved in carrying cash.
2 They have a useful means of identification with what should be (if the issuing company has done an effective selling job with retailers) a large number of suppliers, ranging from normal retailers through hotels and restaurants, airlines, railways and hire car companies to public utilities and eventually perhaps local taxation authorities.
3 For the careful user it provides up to 7 weeks free credit, since payment for transactions at the beginning of one month is not required until the 25th of the following month.
4 In addition it offers a revolving credit facility, related to the cardholders credit standing.

There are also quite specific advantages for co-operating retailers, to justify the commission they are charged:

1 the opportunity to offer their customers an extended credit facility at minimal cost and at no risk
2 immediate payment as 'cleared funds' of sales vouchers when paid into a bank account
3 a reduction in cash handling, providing improved security
4 guaranteed payment on credit card purchases
5 the opportunity to attract additional customers by displaying the credit card symbol.

For the issuing banks the benefits are rather more complex and longterm. The main advantages can be summarized as follows:

1 It represents an additional customer service, helping the banks in their competitive task of attracting more customers not only from other financial institutions but from the cash society.
2 If efficiently administered, a credit card can be a more economical method of handling customers' transactions and lending them money than the more familiar procedures of cashing and clearing cheques, or negotiating loans and overdrafts.

But these benefits will only accrue if the banks keep their administrative arrangements in step with the build-up of their cardholder and retailer base. It is not a simple case of the more the merrier.

The History of Access in the UK

The first bank-sponsored credit card to be issued in the UK was the Barclaycard. This was launched by Barclays Bank Ltd in 1966, as an autonomous member of the Bank Americard system. For the remainder of the 1960s, the other three large UK clearing banks monitored the Barclaycard's progress, while preparing to launch their own credit cards in the event of its success.

But as its success became increasingly obvious, the other banks research revealed that the retail market (if not the public) would be reluctant to accept another three credit card schemes. They also recognized that there could be distinct economies of scale in a joint venture, rather than three or more competing cards each with its own administrative base.

So in 1971 Lloyds, Midland and National Westminster Banks came together and formed the joint Credit Company Limited as a jointly-owned service company with the responsibility for promoting and administering what was to be known as the Access Credit Card. Shortly before the card was launched in October 1972 the three founder members were joined by Williams & Glyn's Bank and the Royal Bank of Scotland. Since the total deposits of the co-operating banks exceed $100,000mn and they have a total of some 10,000 branches spread throughout the country, the new company was launched from a pretty substantial launching pad.

From the outset each of the participating banks set up its own Access department, and the division of responsibility between these departments and the Joint Credit Card Company was clearly defined.

The banks' Access departments are responsible for:

— the recruitment of new cardholders from amongst their personal customers
— the setting of credit limits
— credit control of cardholder accounts
— funding the use of the cards.

The Joint Credit Card Company is responsible for:

— providing complete computer facilities for processing cardholder and retailer accounts
— providing an authorization facility for retailers and banks
— establishing and maintaining the retailer base.   For this purpose the company maintains a national sales force with 100 representatives, covering the whole of the UK
— the general marketing of the scheme, including national advertising and promotional activities.

The development of the Access business between 1972 and 1979 was not without its ups and downs, largely because of the constant fluctuations in government credit policies over this period; the facilities which cardholders were offered and the force of the sales appeal had to be modified from year to year in line with these fluctuations.   But by 1979 the organization could boast some 4.5 million cardholders and 161,000 co-operating retailers.   Its total turnover had risen from £150mn in 1974 to £910mn in 1979.   And the Joint Credit Company's computer establishment in Southend was processing over 2 million vouchers a week.

Why 'Export'?

In the early 1970s the managements of the Joint Credit Card Company and the co-operating banks' Access departments were heavily engaged in building up their UK network of cardholders and retailers, and in organizing the computer systems and communications procedures needed to cope with the rapidly expanding workload.   The idea of overseas development must have seemed both wearisome and likely to invite collapse of the new administrative structure.

Moreover the potential profit return on overseas operations was not particularly inviting.   Now that bank credit cards have come to stay, it is clear that no large bank can be fully competitive without offering this facility to its current account customers. But the profit and loss account of a credit card operation would show only two sources of income — the interest paid by those cardholders who elect to take advantage of the loan facility on their outstanding debit balance and the commissions paid by retailers on their credit card transactions. On the expenditure side of the ledger there is the heavy cost of the central computer operation, the cost of communications between the member banks and the Joint Credit Card Company as well as with the cardholders and co-operating retailers, the marketing costs of building up and securing the cardholder and retailer bases, together with management and administrative overheads. A hostile accountant might add that there should be some allowance for financing the 'float' (the money paid over to retailers but not yet recovered from cardholders); and that it may not be entirely legitimate to take full credit for the interest earned on loans to cardholders, since much of it might have been borrowed from the banks through overdrafts or other methods. Printing a plastic credit card may be equivalent to printing money in relation to the national money supply; but it is by no means a 'licence to print money', so far as the banks' profits are concerned.

But in the broader context of the banks' business development strategy, the arguments for overseas expansion were very strong:

1 In an epoch when travel was the number one growth industry, a credit instrument that was usable only within our own small island would not be permanently acceptable to customers.
2 With London fighting to maintain its primacy as the western world's leading financial services capital, it would be inconceivable for the leading London banks to be left behind in the general movement towards internationalization of banking facilities.
3 The main competitor, Barclaycard, had already made its first moves towards internationalization by joining the VISA organization.
4 The impending development of 'intelligent' credit cards, capable of recording transactions through a magnetic stripe or microchip, already on the horizon, suggested that the importance of credit cards could grow exponentially as technology advanced.

There was no question in management's mind that sooner or later international development would be obligatory. And the first steps in this direction were taken as early as 1973.

How to 'Export'?

It was easy enough to make the decision in principle that the facilities offered to Access cardholders should be extended overseas, and that the participating banks should involve themselves in the international as well as the national development of credit card systems; but just how to do it was not so easy.

The most obvious problem in 1973 was the stringency of exchange control in the UK (now of course greatly relaxed) whereby the government limited the funds which British residents could spend or transfer abroad. A credit card which could be used at will, within the limits of the user's own credit rating, either at home or abroad, would clearly cut across the credit control system.

A second problem was that the development of Electronic Fund Transfer systems in North America and in the main European countries with which an international credit card would be concerned was uneven; the system in one country was (and still is) not fully compatible with the system in others. Since a credit card system of any size cannot be operated economically without an efficient and mutually compatible EFT network, it seemed clear that at that stage and for some time to come any international operation would have to be in effect an alliance of national operations rather than a global system.

A third problem, already touched on, was the likely economics of any kind of centralized international system. It was difficult enough to balance the books in the UK, where there was a solid base to build on. With their 10,000 branches to act as issuing houses and credit controllers for the Access cards, together with an efficient automated clearing system, the UK banks had a solid infrastructure to build on and could legitimately think in terms of marginal costing in certain areas. To start from scratch in a foreign country would be another story.

A fourth factor, which put paid to any thought of going it alone, was the same consideration that prompted the foundation of the Joint Credit Card Company in the first place — the proliferation of credit cards and the unwillingness of retailers, as well as cardholders, to take on yet another card.

In the United States, where credit cards have become a way of life, a 1978 Nielsen report indicated that there were then some 579 million credit cards in use, with 75% of American households possessing an average of 5 cards apiece. The majority of these cards were issued by oil companies, department stores and other large retailers and were not directly competitive with bank credit cards; but they took business away from the bank credit cards, as well as taking up space in the cardholder's wallet. The breakdown of the 579 million cards was as follows: 77% issued by large retail concerns, 20% issued by banks or bank related organizations, 3% issued by non-banking groups specializing in T & E cards.

In Western Europe the credit card habit had bitten much less deeply than in the US — and considerably less deeply than in the UK — but most of the major American cards, as well as sone European-originated cards, were already available for those members of the public who were interested.

Who to Join?

Having made the inevitable decision 'if you can't beat 'em, join 'em', the Access Management had to decide what organization to link up with on the somewhat attenuated basis enforced by foreign exchange control. At that time the organizations most likely to succeed appeared to be:

VISA
Interbank
American Express
Diners Club
Eurocard
Carte Blanche

Of these systems VISA had and has the largest number of card-holders, the great majority of them in the US. By 1979 it could claim 78 million cardholders worldwide (a 300% increase over 1975) total sales of $33bn (700% over 1975) 3 million merchant outlets worldwide and more than 11,500 affiliated banks. Of its 78 million cardholders 9 million were in Europe — half of them in the UK through the Barclaycard association. Interbank was and is the other major international scheme, based on an association of affili-ated banks; it administered the Master Charge scheme, now known as MasterCard. Like VISA its cardholders are heavily concentrated in the United States (according to the last available figures it had 58,700,000 cardholders there, compared with VISA's 61,300,000) and runs only slightly behind VISA in its worldwide cardholder count.

The other four cards are all T & E cards, lacking the revolving or extended credit facility. The most widely-distributed is the American Express card, with 10.5 million card members worldwide and about 350,000 merchants recognizing it. It has a consciously upmarket bias, claiming for example that the average British card-holder has an income of £12,500 a year, which is reflected in the characteristics of its co-operating merchants. It is of course an integral part of the American Express International Travel and Banking Organization.

Diners Club is an equally upmarket T & E card. It has approxi-mately 750,000 cardholders in Western Europe − approximately the same number as the American Express card − but is much weaker than American Express in the US. Its worldwide cardholder count is 3.5 million. One of the UK clearing banks co-operating in the Access scheme (National Westminster) is a substantial share-holder in Diners Club. The other two cards were and are consider-ably smaller in terms of worldwide cardholder count; Carte Blanche now has approximately 800,000 cardholders worldwide and Euro-card approximately 400,000. But all of Eurocard's 400,000 card-holders are in Europe, whereas Carte Blanche has a relatively low European cardholder penetration.

Despite its relatively small number of cardholders, largely due to the selectivity required when virtually unlimited credit is offered, Eurocard has had an interesting history. Eurocard International S.A. was formed in 1965 by a Swedish company AB Finans Vendor, a company closely connected with a leading Stockholm bank, which had a successful experience in marketing an early credit card called the Rikskort. It was launched as a low capital venture (the initial capital was $200,000) for the cautious exploitation of four principal assets:

1 the credit card operational experience already gained in Sweden
2 a network of member establishments and a body of cardholders formed from the merger of the Scandinavian Nordkort and the British Hotels and Restaurants Association's BHR credit card
3 the involvement of several of Vendor's partners in the Amstel Club, a group of European finance companies, prepared to co-operate by providing a base of operations for Eurocard in most European countries
4 an exclusive recommendation for Eurocard by the International Hotel Association.

Eurocard International now has a central office in Brussels, owned by 17 participating Eurocard companies, and a European clearing system. But all cardholder relations are maintained by the local Eurocard company, including card issuance, cardholder billing, merchant recruitment and payment, sales, advertising and marketing. 30 out of the leading 50 European banks now participate either directly or indirectly in the Eurocard system; and plans have been laid for expanding the present European base of 400,000 cardholders to 2 million cardholders by 1985.

For the Access organization, Eurocard was interesting as a way of infiltrating the developing European credit card market at a time when any major involvement was precluded by exchange control regulations and other inhibiting factors. But in the long run it was a selective, upmarket credit instrument; and it was confined to the under-developed European market. These apparent disadvantages were resolved by the fact that in 1969 Eurocard had become a member of the Interbank Card Association, one of the two international market leaders already described. Since VISA was already associated with Barclaycard, it had to be a long-term policy for Access to join the Interbank system if it was to have a wide international potential; and a link with Eurocard would be compatible with this longer-term intention. So in June 1973 the Joint Credit Card Company signed an agreement with Eurocard International, forming an association which was cemented in 1978 when JCC purchased a 20% stake in Eurocard. Then in 1975 Access joined the Interbank Card Association. Access, Eurocard and MasterCard credit cards are now mutually accepted in the combined total of 3 million outlets throughout the world; and the Access clearing centre in the UK is linked with the Interbank clearing centre in the US and the Eurocard clearing centre in Brussels.

What is Happening Now?

In the early 1970s the Access Management could not do much more about international development than stake its claim through the Eurocard and Interbank tie-ups. It was necessary to concentrate on building up an efficient and flexible infrastructure in the UK in order to service foreign cardholders visiting this country; and the service which could be offered to British cardholders travelling overseas was severely restricted by exchange control regulations.

By the late 1970s, however, the central computer and the communications system were working satisfactorily and the relaxation of foreign exchange regulations had removed at least some of the problems of internationalization. In September 1978 the agreement between Interbank and Access was extended to allow visiting card-holders of Interbank, Eurocard and Standard Bank of South Africa (which had joined the Interbank Association) not only to use their cards for purchases at Access outlets, but to withdraw cash from any of the UK banks co-operating in Access to the extent of £60 per day. (This was subject to an authorization call being made to the Joint Credit Card's head office at Southend and identification being produced by the cardholder.) On a reciprocal basis, Access cardholders can now purchase goods and services at Interbank outlets worldwide; and can draw up to £100 in local currency equivalent in any one day at member banks of the Interbank chain which display the Access logo.

It has always been a major marketing problem with all credit card schemes to educate and persuade cardholders into making full use of their cards and the facilities they represent. Habit is strong and new cardholders tend to revert to their habitual methods of payment (cash or cheques) unless constantly prodded.

One method of prodding is through media advertising. This is the responsibility of the Interbank or Eurocard company in each of the individual countries where the credit card facility is offered; and mentions of the international facility will be phased into the domestic advertising in each country, to the extent that they are justified by the local companies' development plans. In addition advertising has already been started in the focal points for inter-national travellers. Access has placed posters on board the cross channel ferries, featuring the co-ordinated international facility offered by the three (now four) cards and picking up the theme of the domestic advertising, which emphasizes the convenience of using Access, 'your flexible friend' for a wide variety of transactions. Access also has large illuminated posters at both Gatwick and Heathrow, advising visiting cardholders of the links between the three main groups. Eurocard currently has airport posters at Brussels, again showing the various logos within the joint inter-national scheme; and Interbank is currently advertising in in-flight magazines with the theme 'we circle the world' linking the various cards within the group.

Point-of-sale display in co-operating retail outlets is another form of selective and cost-effective reminder, in the early stages of the international build-up. In the UK the Access retail sales force is actively engaged in supplementing the Access logo in as many retail outlets as possible with a card proclaiming that international card-holders are welcome and featuring the four cards.

Once again, however, the Access Management would emphasize that international market development cannot be allowed to outstrip the build-up of the administrative and electronic infra-structure. During the 1970s the low-key working relationship with Eurocard and Interbank brought about markedly increased efficiency in handling payment authorizations, particularly with America, and also settlement of transactions. Both authorization and settlement have been transferred to electronic systems, allowing authorization within two minutes and settlement on a daily basis, with a world-wide arrangement and a net settlement figure at a designated account. European authorizations, however, are still handled by telex and settlement is made individually between countries; there is obviously room for considerable improvement here, as and when the actual and potential size of the business justifies the investment cost.

What Next?

Life would be quite comfortable for the Access Management, if it were possible to think in terms of a systematic development of the business, co-ordinating the planned build-up in the number of cardholders, the usage by cardholders of their cards, increased co-operation from the existing member banks and new banks to be brought into the fold, and from associated merchants — all of this timed to keep step with the development and harmonization of the administrative infra-structure.

Unhappily for their peace of mind, the rapid advance of technology — in relation both to the credit card operation and to other forms of fund transfer by the international banks — makes straight line growth improbable.

The credit card revolution has already run through three phases. The first was pre-war, when department store and retail chain credit cards identified credit-worthy customers with charge accounts and facilitated the process of charging their purchases to their own or company accounts. This, of course, involved no electronic gadgetry or major risk of fraud or administrative breakdown. After the war came the T & E cards with their wider application as purchase instruments, but still no great need for continuous credit control or electronic funds transfer after the cardholder had passed the initial credit screening.

The bank-related credit cards like Access, Barclaycard, VISA and Master Charge (now MasterCard) added a totally new dimension, with the extended or revolving credit facility. This has necessitated both a tighter control system and a much speedier system for validation and transfer of funds. Lifting the cards from a national to an international dimension will introduce yet further complications.

But this is not the end of the story. Credit cardholders who take a look at the back of their cards will observe that as well as the strip which carries their signatures there is a strip of electronic tape. In the case of the UK cards, this at present serves no useful purpose. But it is there (complete with a 'watermark' device to discourage fraud) in the confident expectation that the credit card will eventually become 'intelligent' — that is, that it will be capable of recording whatever credit balance the cardholder wishes (and his bank will permit him) to carry; and of deducting from it the value of the various purchases he makes until the time comes to reload the card with another credit infusion. To activate the strip (or possibly a microchip, if technology outstrips marketing and administration) will require a new generation of 'card-reading equipment' in the associated banks and merchants. But this will come. The question is when — and how the pace of market development can keep up with the investment cost.

XIV
W. H. Mosse Company (B)
Developing International Markets
M. F. Bradley

In October 1974 Mr Jim Furlong, Marketing Director of Davis-Mosse, was planning a visit to the S.I.A.L. International Food Fair in Paris which was due to take place during the following month. His company had arranged to make a presentation there of their breadmix product range. Knowing that he would meet many food buyers from all over Europe, Mr Furlong hoped to explore further the possibility of expanding the company's exporting activities. Already they had successfully exported the product range to the United Kingdom but the company was less successful in the Netherlands where they introduced the bread mixes on a trial basis after the previous Anuga Food Fair during 1973. Most of the present exporting activity had its origins in a series of meetings held during April and May of 1969 when the Mosse Company, as it was then, sat down to formulate a development plan and marketing strategy for the company. (See the W. H. Mosse Company, A.) The bread mix products had now been on the Irish market for almost four years and had achieved a satisfactory level of acceptance. The company was, however, facing a number of difficulties on the domestic market. An indifferent future potential for the bread mix product range forced the company to consider whether it should become more involved in exporting and if so, there was the decision of selecting new markets which would yield the highest promise of success. Alternatively, the company could choose to concentrate on the Irish and UK markets where it had already gained considerable experience. The decisions taken with respect to these issues would to a large extent determine the future of the

Prepared by Dr M. F. Bradley, University College, Dublin.

breadmix programme and to a lesser extent they would determine the overall development of the company.

Historical Background

In 1973 the Mosse Company merged with the company of S. and A. G. Davis Ltd, Enniscorthy, Co. Wexford. This arrangement was entered into, both parties having considered the continued rationalization in the Flour Milling Industry and Ireland's entry into the EEC (1st January 1973) with its considerable competitive and other ramifications for the small Irish miller. Davis was somewhat the larger of the two firms and had been concentrating on feed compounding and flour milling. The merger resulted in a number of benefits to both parties. The overlap of Davis and Mosse operations in the south east was eliminated. The new group could now buy their foreign wheat requirements in bulk without having to rely on intermediary handlers. In addition, the merger resulted in production being centralized in Enniscorthy where there was sufficient capacity to mill the total requirements for a declining total market. The merger also gave the new group a greater share of the quantity of flour marketed under the quota system on the domestic market. Finally, the merger provided additional support both in terms of financial back-up and personnel to the growing exporting operation of the Mosse Company.

Sales Performance of Bread Mixes in the Domestic Market

Since their launch in 1971 sales of Mosse's Bread Mixes have exceeded 150,000 cases on the Irish market. Total revenue for this period was estimated at just under £330,000. Before launching the product the Marketing Director stated that he would be happy if sales reached 10,000 in kilos of bread mix per week. The actual sales record was 39,375 cases in 1971–2 rising to 39,736 cases in the following year but falling off to 34,487 cases in 1974. Average wholesale prices were £1.79 per case in 1971–2 rising to £3.00 in 1974. During 1973–4 the company did not promote the product at all, due to severe price control measures imposed on the industry by the National Prices Commission. The company believed that this was the main reason why sales in these latter two years were not as favourable as the earlier experience. As with retail flour sales, a pronounced seasonal pattern also occurs in the sales of bread mix products. Approximately 60 to 65% of sales occurred in the six-month period October to March each year. This had an effect on promotional campaigns and to a lesser extent on distribution. In terms of market share the Mosse product had 85% of the Irish market in 1971—2. The balance was held by Howards. Odlums entered the market with a bread mix product during 1972—3 and Ranks introduced a competitive product in 1974. The Davis-Mosse company believed that these trends combined with the absence of promotional expenditure in recent years accounted for the decline in market share for their products (Exhibit 14.1).

The United Kingdom Market

For any Irish company and especially any small Irish Company, the UK tends to become the market in which any export aspirations are first tested. The ease of access due to geographical proximity and the lack of any complexity — as regards tariffs, quotas, import licences and health regulations — which tends to typify international marketing activities, makes the UK market a particularly attractive one for Irish companies. As a CTT adviser pointed out, trade is simplified by the common language and currency, and these, along with other similarities, often lure Irish companies into viewing the UK as a larger version of the Irish market. Consequently, the tendency is often to merely extend marketing strategy to cope with size.

In the case of Mosse's the UK market offered a further attraction in that Irish food exporters had established wide acceptance among UK consumers since the Kerrygold butter and the Irish beef, extensive marketing efforts had begun in the early 1960s. The company's management were of the opinion that Irish and UK eating habits were not too different and the main problems it would have in establishing a substantial export trade would be with distribution and supply. At the same time, however, Mosse's were aware that there were some significant regional variations in dietary content and tastes which would have to be investigated.

During the Spring and Summer of 1971, as the new bread mix product was being tested in the south-east of Ireland, the Mosse Company availed itself of an opportunity to distribute a number of cases of the bread mix through a contact a company director had in the north of England. It was felt at the time that tastes and preferences for this type of product would be reasonably similar in both countries. As a result of the experiment UK consumer reaction to the product was considered favourable. (See The W. H. Mosse Company, A.)

In addition to the initial favourable acceptance of Mosse's Brown Bread Mix on the UK market, the company also had considerable data on the UK bread market in general which indicated that exporting in a serious capacity to the UK could result in an attractive pay-off. A number of recent trends in the UK bread market which held some promise for Mosse's management included the shift in consumption towards brown and speciality breads and the increasing emphasis on traditional methods of preparing foods.

Thus Stanley Mosse and Jim Furlong, although they had little or no experience in international marketing or involvement with the UK market, were quite confident about the future of the Mosse brown soda bread mixes in this very attractive potential export market.

United Kingdom Market for Bread

The UK market for bread in 1973 has been estimated to be in the region of 2.64 million tons. In 1956, with a population of some four millions less, consumption was in the order of 3.77 million tons per year. In terms of retail value the market has grown due to inflation and the added value such as the convenience provided by the sliced loaf and the growth of the more expensive speciality products such as slimming breads. While the bread market in 1973 was worth £446m at retail prices, which was effectively double the 1956 value, the percentage of food expenditure on bread during the past number of years had remained rather constant until 1973 when the share dropped somewhat.

The consumption of brown bread had remained steady for a considerable number of years in the British market. The 'other' category tended to decline somewhat during the early 1960s but more recently the interests in products to assist slimmers had given this section a renewed lease of life. The effect had been a recent downturn in the consumption of ordinary white bread. (Exhibit 14.2.)

The UK Bakery Industry

The UK bakery industry is highly competitive, as indicated by its innovative marketing. The industry is dominated by three very large firms which follow a policy of matching competitive actions.

The big three of the bakery trade control two-thirds of all production through their 200 plants. A further 100 or so large bakeries have most of the remainder. However, some 5,000 family bakers still existed and shared approximately 5% of the market. The three major companies were Ranks Hovis McDougall, Associated British Foods and Spillers French. As in Ireland, rationalization also occurred in Britain taking the form of a complex series of integrations involving flour milling, baking, retail outlets and the animal feeds products which result from the milling process.

A recent innovation in the bread market has been the arrival of the part-baked loaf. The housewife buys a semi-finished refrigerated product then bakes it in an oven for twenty minutes. The idea behind the development was to combine the freshness of newly baked bread with the convenience of buying a mass product brand. Ranks' 'Take and Bake' was first in the field followed very quickly by Spillers 'Homebake'. After an initial enthusiastic response, sales of these products fell to much less than 1% of the wrapped bread market. At the time it was judged that the products were relatively expensive and not very convenient.

In the market for bread, slimming breads were a special case. The aim of the producers of slimming bread was to provide bread which gives less calories on a slice-for-slice basis. This was done by reducing the starch content, adding protein, or simply by making the slices lighter. The forerunners of modern slimming breads were the Energen starch-reduced rolls. Since then the market had expanded considerably. Total sales of slimming breads in 1972 were £16 million, in 1973 sales reached £21 million and it was estimated that in 1974 sales were approximately £23 million.

Total advertising expenditure on bread increased from £2.5 million in 1969 to £3.5 million in 1973. This compared with £238,000 spent by the industry in advertising in 1955 when most of the expenditure was by Hovis Limited. In 1968 the bulk of the advertising was through the medium of television, which then accounted for over 90% of the total. Before 1968 most advertising concentrated on the standard loaf of each of the major companies in the market. The leading bakeries engaged in the promotion of branded bread products primarily to maintain their bargaining position with retailers, especially the larger food chains. In addition, by continued reminders to consumers of existing known brand names, brand advertising was designed to discourage the larger supermarket chains from integrating into baking. Few of the bakeries believed in competitive advertising as a means of increasing sales.   Nevertheless, with the specialist type breads considerable sums were being successfully spent on advertising.

Approximately one-third of press and television advertising went on slimming bread. Nimble regularly spent more than £500,000 annually on advertising followed closely by Slimcea. However, the ratio of advertising to sales was low at approximately 0.77%. This compared with a ratio of 2% for 1935.

The Big Three in the baking industry in the United Kingdom had one or more interests in the principal forms of bread distribution. Spillers French supplied their co-op partners and the Lyons outlets, Ranks controlled distribution companies, such as Marchi Żeller, and ABF had bakers' shops such as Tip Top as well as Fine Fare supermarket chain.

In May 1974, the British Market Research Bureau interviewed 964 housewives to investigate where bread was being bought and the type of bread purchased. It was evident that the introduction of the wrapped loaf and the element of convenience combined with improved keeping qualities had strengthened the hand of the grocer over the traditional bread roundsman. The grocer/supermarket was dominant in the retail selling of bread and this was particularly true in the northern part of the country. Bread was frequently sold in the supermarkets in this part of the country as a cut-price item to attract people into stores. Class and age differences were not, however, as pronounced.

There were a number of pronounced differences among the types of bread purchased by the British housewife. In the survey, housewives were asked the type of bread purchased by them in the previous week. As the data referred to buying occasions and not to quantities bought, the data somewhat overstate the picture with respect to brown and speciality breads which are normally sold in small loaves.   Families with children are the heavy purchasers of the wrapped white loaf. Brown bread is purchased more frequently by housewives without children than those with children.

United Kingdom Market for Mosse's Bread Mix

Supported by the reaction of the press and trade at the reception in CTT's London office during the summer of 1971, the Mosse Company decided in November 1972 to commission more detailed research of the United Kingdom market. The information already available on the bread market was of a general nature and the company felt that it should have some reaction to its bread mix from the market place.

Having identified the urban consumer as their primary target — just as they had done in the Irish market — Jim Furlong and Stanley Mosse were naturally most interested in the North of England where they had had most involvement so far, and of course in the massive marketplace of urban England, the city of London. (It was estimated at this time that 70% of grocery buying power was concentrated in the Greater London area.) Manchester was identified as the most important representative of the company's involvement in the former area and so London and Manchester were identified as the two areas which should be investigated at this stage.

A marketing research firm was commissioned to examine the London and Manchester markets. With respect to the London research, a two-stage programme was adopted. Discussion groups were held with three groups of 10 housewives each, to investigate attitudes towards the Brown Bread Mix in terms of preparation, taste, appearance and overall acceptability as a product. Secondary objectives included those of examining, in depth, the reactions to packaging, mixing instruction, name, pricing and promotional concepts. Each of the three London groups belonged to the ABCI social classes. At the time the housewives were recruited to take part in the discussion groups, each was given a half-kilo pack of the product in a plain bag with no identification of the firm and asked to prepare it according to supplied instructions before coming to the session.

In addition to the discussion groups a number of placement tests were carried out on the product. From the London suburbs 50 housewives were invited to try a 'blind' half-kilo pack of Mosse's Brown Bread Mix. These housewives were asked to complete a questionnaire after they tried the product. As an incentive to complete the questionnaires the housewives were offered either 25p in cash or 25p worth of the product. Of the 50 housewives selected, 40 had returned completed questionnaires by the deadline set by the research company. The principal results of this research as reported by the research company are set out in Exhibit 14.3.

UK Market Launch of Mosse's Bread Mix

At this stage Jim Furlong considered that his company had enough information to continue marketing in the United Kingdom. Consumer and trade reaction to both the brown and the recently introduced white bread mix had been proving favourable. The Mosse Management faced the decision of how it should operationalize a full-scale marketing programme in the United Kingdom.

Advertising Campaign

Since so much of UK grocery purchasing power was concentrated within the London region, a launch in that area in the Autumn of 1973 was preferred by the company as an alternative to the originally planned north of England launch. It was suggested to Mosse that a viable TV campaign in the London area would generate consumer demand and facilitate a valuable merchandising function. A London-based advertising agency made a number of recommendations for a London TV campaign which might be carried out during September—October 1973 (Exhibit 14.4).

Distribution

The selection of an appropriate channel of distribution provided Mosse's with one of the most important and most difficult problems in developing this, their first export market. Having decided on aiming their market efforts at the potentially huge London market, they identified a number of alternative arrangements from which they could select their eventual channel of distribution. The main alternatives open to Mosse's were to channel the soda bread mix products through a food broker, *or* secondly through an ordinary distributor *or* thirdly, direct to speciality stores.

As food brokers are specialists they would offer a service to both buyers and sellers of food items which involves basically bringing together parties to arrange a trading relationship, but they can and do offer much more as 'specialists' in this particular field. In return for a commission, a food broker would offer Mosse's the time-saving facility of introducing them to a number of interested buyers and, as an executive pointed out to Jim Furlong, the broker would have as great an interest in encouraging actual trade between the parties, since commissions are normally paid only on the occurrence of a transaction. The broker could also offer specialized market advice and customer profiles. As the soda bread mix products did not comprise that great a proportion of the overall Davis-Mosse production operation, the time-saving possibility was very attractive to Jim Furlong who had overall marketing responsibility for the company.

Finding a suitable distributor in the London area proved a formidable task. With the help of CTT an extensive search was undertaken to identify suitable candidates. Eventually Jim Furlong, in liaison with the London office of CTT, was able to single out (after a process of preliminary search and interviews of interested distributors) one particularly attractive candidate. Waissel's Limited of London distributed to most of the food stores large and small in the South-East of England. In addition to this essential feature, Jim Furlong admired the outlook and approach of the company. He said at the time 'what we want is a distributor who aggressively goes after the food store business, and Waissel's, in the person of Sidney Waissel, the managing director, offer just that'. Furthermore, Waissels was an established food distributor and Sidney Waissel had developed a wide range of important contacts in the retailing end of the industry over the years. Since Mosse's were most interested in establishing maximum volume in turnover terms, such contacts were particularly attractive (Sidney Waissel had mentioned Woolworths and Safeways among other outlets to Jim Furlong as being on his list of close contacts).

The other main alternative opening to Mosse's was the speciality store. Howards of Crookstown, Cork, who had preceeded Mosse's into the Irish bread mix market, had already begun to market their soda bread mix products through the speciality store chain of Fortnum and Mason. The products were offered in attractive 'high-class' box packs, obviously aimed at a rather up-market range of consumer. As Mosse's were designing a new pack for the UK market, the notion of matching Howard's strategy did not particularly concern Jim Furlong. Although in the long term volume prospects were perhaps limited, the speciality stores did offer the prospect of higher margins. Under the speciality heading could also be included the possibility of supplying delicatessens, health food stores and the like which were at this time becoming very significant in terms of food retailing in cosmopolitan London.

Before Mosse's had made their final decision as to distribution channel, Waissels came up with the idea of running an introductory programme for Mosse's. As a preliminary offering, Sidney Waissel arranged for a week long in-store demonstration/market test of the brown soda bread mix in each of ten Woolworth stores located throughout England. The in-store promotion was held during the week commencing 22nd May 1973. Sidney Waissel considered the demonstration to have been very successful and in a follow-up letter to Mosse's stated that 'store managers were well pleased and considering that we were introducing from cold the brown soda bread mix only, the results, in our opinion were more than satisfactory. The average of all ten branches was 23 cases'. Jim Furlong was favourably impressed.

Costs and Pricing

While recognizing that costs would vary depending on the distribution channel selected, Mosse's estimated that, for 1973—4 at least, the average ex-mill price f.o.b. Enniscorthy would be in the region of £2.01 per case. They also estimated that for a wholesaler or distributor who provided a transport and storage service and who bought full container loads of the soda bread mix products, the average margin expected would be 50% on the ex-mill cost. The retailer, in turn, would be expecting to add a margin of about 33% on this wholesale price. On this basis, the estimated retail price of bread mix was in the region of 12.5p per lb.

As they continued to explore the United Kingdom market, Mosse's came to realize that while there were strong similarities between that market and the Irish market for its soda bread mix products, there were also considerable differences between the two markets. In particular, it was clear from the research that the company had commissioned, that tastes were definitely different. Jim Furlong and Stanley Mosse believed that the UK consumer was more willing to try new products than was a typical Irish consumer. However, Mosse's did recognize that the UK consumer would have to be educated in the use of the soda bread mix products since they were relatively new to the market. Point-of-sale material to be distributed at retail store level was prepared as a consumer aid (Exhibit 14.5).

Other differences which were realized by the company, included the more stringent food labelling regulations in the United Kingdom (Exhibit 14.6).

Nevertheless, despite these problems, Stanley Mosse and Jim Furlong were still confident that with the right marketing they could achieve their objective of developing an export market which would in the long run provide maximum returns in terms of revenue and profits. As Stanley Mosse said to the press: 'being a small company has its advantages in that we, for example, because of our size, can cope with any problems which arise, quickly and effectively'. A further incentive to develop the UK market in the short term in order to reap longer-term benefits, were the wide range of aids that Coras Trachtala (CTT), the Irish Exports Promotions Board and the Industrial Development Authority (IDA) were offering to Irish firms. (See Appendix 14.1.)

With the aid of such incentives, Jim Furlong believed that, depending on wholesale and retail margins for the soda bread mix products, the company could expect to break even, or perhaps make a small profit on its first year's trade in an international market.

Sales/Prices/Shares	1971—2	1972—3	1973—4
Unit Sales (Cases)			
October—March	25,594	23,842	23,659
April—September	13,781	15,894	12,739
Year	39,375	39,736	36,398
Wholesale Prices			
£ per case*	1.79	2.03	2.07
Retail Prices			
Pence per Kilo pack	13—14	14.5—15.5	15—16
Market Shares			
Mosse (%)	85	50	48

* Case contained 16 x 1 kilo packs.

Exhibit 14.1: Bread Mix Sales, Prices and Market Shares, Ireland 1971—4

Year	Weekly Bread consumption in home (oz/per capita)	Weekly Bread expenditure in home (pence per capita)	Share in food expenditure (Percent)	Bread prices* (Pence per lb)	Value of consumption by bread types		
					White %	Brown %	Other %
1960	45	9	6.2	2.9	73	8	19
1964	42	11	6.4	3.5	78	9	13
1968	38	12	6.5	4.5	77	9	14
1971	36	14	6.2	5.4	75	9	16
1972	34	15	6.2	5.8	74	9	17
1973	33	16	5.7	6.2	73	9	18

* Large Wrapped White Loaf.

Source: National Food Survey (UK)

Exhibit 14.2: Bread Consumption, Prices and Expenditure, United Kingdom 1960–1973

The Product:

1 This type of brown bread was unfamiliar to the majority of London house-wives who took part in the groups or placement tests.
2 About two-thirds of the participating housewives found the end product acceptable including one-third who were enthusiastic.
3 Flavour and texture of the bread were the major determinants of product acceptance. The enthusiasts described it as 'nutty', 'wholesome', 'tasty', and 'chunky'. The critics reported it as 'stodgy', 'tasteless', and 'did not rise properly'.
4 Whether they liked the bread or not, most housewives found it easy and quick to prepare although a number did not follow the instructions on the pack.
5 The bread mix was perceived as a flour-type product and was not seen as a cake mix. Housewives in the groups and placement test would expect to find the product in their grocer stores alongside either the flour or bread.

Presentation and Labelling:

1 The ordinary flour type pack was very favourably received. Housewives were adamant that a cake-mix type pack would be most unsuitable.
2 Considerable difficulty arose over the name 'Brown Bread Mix'. For United Kingdom housewives this title was misleading. The researchers suggested titles such as 'traditional', 'Old Fashioned', 'Country' or 'Home-Make'.
3 The necessity to use the term 'soda bread' also gave rise to difficulties. Many housewives, especially the younger ones associated 'soda' more with washing than baking.

Price and Pack Size:

1 Most of the housewives tended to price the product low. The average price estimated by the housewives in the product test who were most favourably disposed towards the bread-mix was 8p to 9p for the half-kilo size. The ideas or price were partly based on the price of flour and more particularly on the known level of 10½p for the standard loaf.
2 The enthusiastic housewives rejected the idea of paying 23p to 25p for a kilo pack. There was little interest in the kilo pack anyway since the product was viewed as a speciality bread rather than an everyday product.

Exhibit 14.3: UK Product and Placement Test of
Mosse's Brown Soda Bread Mix: Research Findings

Continued

Differences between London and Manchester:

1 The Manchester group, unlike the London groups, was more inclined to identify the product as a health food on the one hand and to position it with cake mixes in the local grocery store, because they viewed it more as a convenience food.
2 While a flour type pack was preferred to a carton there was a strong suggestion that the relatively subtle colouring and style of the existing Mosse pack would be less effective in the Northern part of the country.
3 Because of price many of the Manchester housewives viewed the product as an occasional purchase only, as a treat or a standby product.

Conclusions of Research Firm:

1 Since there was very little consumer interest in any easy-to-prepare bread mix, the success of Mosse Brown Bread Mix would depend almost entirely upon the acceptability of the end product.
2 In a promotional programme there was a need to concentrate on projecting the desirable taste and texture of the product. The fact that it was easy and quick to make was an ancillary benefit.
3 The proposed retail price would inhibit both trial and subsequent frequency of purchase. Hence it would be necessary to convince potential buyers of the inherent quality of the product.

Exhibit 14.3: UK Product and Placement Test of
Mosse's Brown Soda Bread Mix: Research Findings

Relative Effectiveness

	Schedule I	Schedule II	Schedule III
Airtime Cost	£10,500	£10,500	£13,500
Number of Spots	23	21	25
Housewife T.V.R.	260	333	418
Estimated Coverage	72%	79%	83%
Average Frequency	3.6	4.2	5.0

The basic difference between Schedule I and Schedule II was that the former would use 30-second exposures concentrating on daytime coverage while the latter would use a core of 20-second exposures across the board, coverage backed up by high frequency 15-second messages within 'dealer support spots'. The additional expenditure indicated in the third schedule would secure an additional 30-second peak spot and at least one more prime off-peak and two more 'dealer support spots'.

Exhibit 14.4: Proposal for London Region TV Campaign

Just add water and it's oven~ready!

Here's the real old-fashioned taste of wholemeal goodness you can bake yourself for the whole family to love. Mosse's Soda Bread Mix–in Brown and White–gives you a baking success that's fast and easy.

You just add water–that's all–mix it into a dough. It takes about five minutes, then you just pop it into the oven, bake for forty minutes, and you've got the most delicious wholesome treat you can give your family–*and* you make it yourself!

Mosse's Brown Soda Bread Mix is based on Abbey Stoneground Wholemeal which gives a rich nutty flavour unlike anything you've tasted before.

White or Brown, it's unlike bread you buy–with Mosse's you share the secrets that keep alive the traditional pride in home-baked bread ... so wholesomely unique that when you've tasted it we think you'll agree....

It's the magical taste of bread from time gone by

Mosse's Traditional Bread Mixes

Exhibit 14.5

Continued

Baking Magic, in Brown & White

Exhibit 14.5

Labelling regulations are very detailed and strict observance is maintained. Since bread in the UK is typically a yeast type product, all breads not based on yeast must carry this information on the pack. Hence a soda bread would have to contain the word 'soda' in the product name. A summary of the labelling regulations in operation at the time follow:

1 The product name must be approved by the appropriate authorities.
2 The product weight, country of origin, name of manufacturer must be specified on the package.
3 Product ingredients must be specified on the pack in a separate box. Ingredients must be listed in a descending order by weight.

Exhibit 14.6: United Kingdom Food Labelling Regulations

Appendix 14.1
Aids to Irish Exporters

There are a number of aids available to Irish firms involved in export marketing. Among the more important are the tax relief obtainable on earnings accruing to the firm from overseas sales and the various government grants which are in the main channelled through CTT, the Irish Exports Promotion Board. A brief outline of the support given under these headings is presented below.

Export Tax Relief

The following is a summary of the relief from taxation on profits made on the export operations of Irish companies, taken from Leaflet No.4 published by the Revenue Commissioners.

This relief is granted to companies (whether or not registered or managed or controlled in the State). The relief is, broadly speaking, confined to profits arising from the sale of goods which have been manufactured in the State and exported by the company claiming the relief. Where the company is not the manufacturer of the goods exported, relief may be claimed by it only where the goods exported are sold by wholesalers. Relief may also be claimed, subject to conditions, in respect of profits arising from the rendering to non-residents of certain services such as design and planning services in connection with foreign engineering projects and the processing of materials belonging to a non-resident.

The profits which are attributable to exports are wholly relieved of income tax and corporation profits tax for a continuous period not exceeding fifteen years and are relieved at gradually reducing rates for the succeeding period of not more than four consecutive years. The reducing rates are 80% for the first of these four years and 85%, 50%, and 35%, for the second, third and fourth years respectively. In no case may relief be given for any year or period ending after April 5, 1990.

A measure of unilateral relief from double taxation is granted to a company which derives dividends or interest from the investment in a foreign subsidiary of profits which have been relieved from tax under the exports relief provisions. Unilateral relief is confined to dividends or interest arising in countries with which comprehensive double taxation agreements are not in force.

Incentive Grants Scheme

In discharging its function as a promoter of Irish exports, Coras Trachtala, the Irish Exports Promotions Board, provides a range of incentive grants to be availed of by exporters. The principal grants include Demonstrations, support for Advertising and Promotion, Fairs, Exhibitions, Design and Consultancy, Marketing Research.

Advertising and Promotion

Grants may be made to exporting firms in the context of total export marketing plans towards the cost of new advertising/promotional campaigns in overseas market areas. For North America the maximum grant payable was £16,000. Elsewhere the maximum grant payable was £8,000 per product per market.

Fairs, Exhibitions and Demonstrations

Grants may be made to exporting companies towards the cost of undertaking approved fair or exhibition participation, or demonstration, subject to a number of conditions. The maximum grant allowed is 50% of approved direct costs incurred. Entertainment costs may not be included. The maximum grant was £1,000 for any one project in Europe and £1,500 elsewhere. The maximum grant for each company was £5,000· in Europe or £7,500 elsewhere.

Design and Consultancy

Grants may be made to manufacturing companies towards the cost of engaging designers to survey their design needs and recommend future design policy or to design an individual product or range of products. The maximum grant payable was 50% of the designer's or consultant's fees and expenses but the grant did not exceed £2,000.

Marketing Research

In the context of a marketing plan, grants may be made to exporting firms towards the cost of undertaking formalized professional marketing research and consultancy in overseas market areas. Grants may be for 50% of direct costs subject to a maximum of £5,000.

Production Grants

Various Industrial Development Authority new machinery grants were in operation at this time.

Appendix 14.2
Continental European Markets

In close liaison with CTT executives, Jim Furlong was able to identify the major potential export markets outside the UK. Although one contact with a Dallas, Texas mail order firm later proved that there was an opening in the US market (cases of soda bread mix were exported unmodified and the Dallas firm placed Mosse's on its Christmas catalogue) and although there was a possibility of manufacturing under licence in Australia, it was to the Continental European markets that Mosse's looked upon with most interest. Eventually having attended various trade fairs — both the larger ones such as ANUGA (Cologne) and SIAL (Paris) and some smaller local ones — and having analysed each of the potential markets with the help of CTT, Jim Furlong was able to short-list his target markets. Germany, France, Netherlands and Belgium comprised this list.

Fresh from their experiences in the UK market, the Mosse management saw clearly that widely different distribution systems obtained in each of the Continental European markets of interest to the company, and that all such differences would have to be identified and closely studied before actual marketing could begin. With the geographic situation of Ireland *vis-à-vis* the Continent of Europe, Mosse's were aware too that in examining such markets there was a relatively high investment in terms of both costs and management time.

Jim Furlong proceeded with this examination of the selected markets by arranging visits to each. The fact that CTT had an office in all of the relevant countries was of great benefit to him. Furlong later recalled that the visits had 'proved invaluable in assessing the practical potential of these markets'. He discovered that not only did the relative importance of retail outlets from bread and flour products vary throughout continental Europe but also purchasing habits of consumers varied considerably. In taking such differences into account in practical terms, Mosse's again called on the services of CTT. With their help, Jim Furlong was able to identify viable segments of the markets and also to develop profiles on distribution networks in each market.

From his experience in the UK market, Jim Furlong had come to the conclusion that in export marketing the personality of a company's distributor or agent was of utmost importance. He had made a mental note to look for, on the positive side, signs of friendliness, interest and determination and, on the negative side, any signs of apathy or feintness of interest in assessing potential distributors or agents for Mosse's products.

Having made several visits to the Continent and having obtained data from a number of sources, particularly the individual CTT offices in the respective countries on his short-list, Jim Furlong was able to set out summary analyses of all he had learned on the potential markets. For each country his approach was to develop a 'country profile', summarizing the relevant factual data on the particular country and then set out the specific market details available to him. (Comparative data on European countries is included in Appendix 14.3.)

Germany

Furlong's 'country profile' was as follows: 'The country's climate provides colder winters and hotter summers than are common to Ireland. It becomes more continental as one travels southwards. While German is spoken throughout the country there are quite varying regional dialects. CTT recommended that although many German businessmen speak English, trade literature and all correspondence should be in German. The country's standard of living is considerably higher than in Ireland, and as in all six EEC countries, the metric system has been in operation for years. Although agriculture is shadowed somewhat by the performance of industry, Germany produced significant amounts of cereals, the main categories being rye and wheat. At the same time, however, food imports are high and Ireland exported a considerable amount of meat to Germany. The currency used, the Deutschmark was relatively strong compared to sterling. There are three cities in Germany with populations in excess of one million (West Berlin, Hamburg and Munich) and five approaching one million (Cologne, Dortmund, Dusseldorf, Essen and Frankfurt).'

A major potential problem, which occupied much of the Mosse Management's consideration of the German market, concerned food regulations. These regulations were very intricate and varied according to region; and Mosse's realized that this would make it necessary for the company to prepare to meet with a whole range of restrictions on their exports to that market. This problem was compounded by the fact that the wrap-over style pack in use on the Irish and UK markets would not be acceptable in Germany. With these problems in mind, Mosse's proceeded to examine the German market in more detail.

Bread Production

It has been estimated that approximately 200 varieties of bread are produced in Germany. Retail sales of bread have been placed at an annual value of DM8,000 million, of which 75% was accounted for by artisan output and the remainder by industrial bread. The number of artisan bakers in 1974 was estimated by EIU to be about 35,000 and that of industrial producers at below 300. Bread production had increased substantially in Germany during the period 1971—4 (Table 14A.1).

Table 14A.1. Production of Bakery Products, Germany 1971—4

Product		1971	1972	1973	1974(est.)
Bread	(000's tons)	889	929	932	978
	(DM million)	1,144	1,241	1,328	1,467
Rolls	(000's tons)	92	90	99	98
	(DM million)	150	149	165	174
Pastry	(000's tons)	91	106	102	105
	(DM million)	322	374	379	399

Source: EIU: Marketing in Europe, No.152

Bread in Germany is noted for its regional varieties. Very few German bread manufacturers have been able to achieve more than a regional penetration. However, mergers and take-overs had been taking place recently thereby reducing the number of independent suppliers. By the end of 1971, 94 companies, representing approximately 30% of the total number and employing about 70% of total bakery workers, accounted for more than 70% of the total output of bread and related products.

Bread Consumption

As with other western countries the consumption of bread in Germany during the past number of years had shown a pronounced downward trend. Annual *per capita* consumption of bread and related products is estimated to have contracted from 96 kilogrammes in 1950 to 65 kilogrammes approximately in 1971. At present 82% of all bread sold is accounted for by whole loaves and the remaining 18% is sold as sliced bread.

Bread Distribution

Bread and related products had been estimated to make up about 6% of total supermarket food sales and 4.5% of turnover in general food outlets. The main channel for the consumer market, which distributed about 80% of industrially baked bread, was the direct delivery from producers to retailers (95%) whereas wholesalers who concentrate on special type breads handled only 5% of sales. It was estimated that between 1970 and 1974 the share of all bread sold through bakeries and pastry shops fell from 64.5% of the total to 59% while the share being sold through general food stores increased accordingly (Table 14A.2).

Table 14A.2. Distribution Outlet for Retail Sales of Bread, Germany 1970–4

Retail Outlet	1970	1974 (est.)
	Percent	
Bakeries and Pastry Shops	64.5	59.0
General Food Stores	35.5	41.0
Voluntary Chains	16.4	17.0
Retailers Buying Association	6.7	7.0
Food Multiples	5.7	8.0
Others	6.7	9.3

Bread Imports

There had been little foreign trade in German produced bread. During 1971 approximately 1.1% of total German bread sales were sold abroad. However, German imports of bread have been increasing. In 1971 bread imports were valued at DM28.4 million of which two thirds represented imports of crispbread from Sweden. The switch in German consumption patterns towards more sophisticated and more health-oriented eating habits favoured the production of special bread varieties. Crispbread has benefited from this trend.

According to Jim Furlong, the typical German housewife was not unlike her Irish counterpart. Rural connections were strong and country goodness was held in high regard. The younger generation were regarded as being very willing to try something new and something different.

As the analysis of the German market proceeded, a number of unexpected opportunities came to Jim Furlong's attention. Furlong learned of a German food chain which was seeking a private label operation to compete with an established and successful national branded soda bread mix product. In this context he did not foresee any difficulty in producing for the private label market while at the same time marketing the company's branded products in Germany. This view was supported by the fact that yeast bread mix under the 'Dr Oetkar' brand name was being produced at this time on the German market, and it was rumoured that two more companies, Kraft and Diamonte, were also considering entering the market. The yeast bread mix was produced on the same principle as the soda bread mix but much more time was involved, since strenuous kneading was required and the dough mix had to be allowed to 'set' for a while before baking. The resulting bread corresponded to the yeast bread produced by bakers. Furthermore, Furlong had also come into contact with a very friendly and interested food distributor in the Munich area who appeared to have extensive contacts in the retail trade.

Belgium

Belgium has a temperate climate, quite similar to that of Ireland. The official languages are Flemish and French and, since language is a contentious matter in Belgium, diplomacy is always required. English is widely understood at a business level and is generally more acceptable than French in the north of the country (Flemish-speaking area). It is better, although not essential, according to CTT sources, to use French rather than English in Brussels and in the south of Belgium. The standard of living is approximate to that in Germany. Agricultural production is extensive and the country is self-sufficient in sugar, eggs, butter and meat. The chief crops are oats and wheat. Despite the self-sufficiency in meat, Irish exports are well represented by meat produce. About 36% of the population is situated in urban areas, the most important of which are Brussels (1 million) and Antwerp (926,000).

Jim Furlong learned from CTT that distribution methods varied with the product, but that generally speaking, manufacturers had found it best to sell consumer goods through a distributor carrying stocks. Furthermore, the services of wholesalers and manufacturers agents were extensively used in the distribution of consumer goods, although at the same time a number of important retailers, in addition to department and chain stores, buy direct from manufacturers and importers. Many importers employed travellers to visit retailers regularly.

Bread Production and Consumption

No statistics on the production of bread in Belgium existed but it was estimated that in 1974 annual bread consumption was running at approximately 680,000 tons per year. However, bread consumption was reported to be falling at an annual rate of between 2% and 3%. The varieties of bread which may be sold in Belgium, the weight, and price, were defined by law. In recent years there had been a growing preference for improved varieties of bread (pain ameliore) which in 1974 was expected to account for about half of bread sales. It was expected that bread consumption in Belgium would continue to decline by about 2% per year. However, industrial bakers were expected to expand their operations at the expense of the artisan bakers.

Bread Distribution

Bread was usually sold wrapped. It was estimated in 1974 that 90% of bread sold was in sliced form. There was a tendency for purchasers to prefer smaller loaves, as younger consumers preferred fresh bread, in contrast to older generations who liked bread to be a day old before eating.

Approximately 60% of all bread was retailed through some 7,000 retail bakeries. Some retail bakers also distributed door-to-door. A survey of distribution patterns carried out in 1973 had shown that 38% of purchases were made at a bakery, 39% of purchases were made from a door-to-door service, 12% of purchases were made from general grocery stores, 7% from supermarkets and 4% from department stores. The market was highly competitive and the larger retail outlets tended to rely on a number of suppliers, switching their custom to the baker offering the best margins. For these reasons they supplied and sought to avoid being dependent on one retailer for more than 15% of sales.

Bread Prices

Retail bread prices in mid-1974 ranged from BFll for a 500 gram household loaf to BF18.5 for a 400 gram loaf of browń bread (Table 14A.3).

Table 14A.3. Retail Bread Prices (Sliced), Belgium, May 1974

Bread Type	Size	Price
	(gram)	(BF)
Household Bread	500	11.00
Improved Bread	450	11.00
Wholemeal Bread	600	17.00
Brown/mixed Bread		18.50

Source: EIU store checks

Bread Imports

Imports of bread into Belgium are of minor importance. German varieties are the most popular among imported breads. The principal varieties include crispbread and unleavened bread.

France

Jim Furlong 'country profile' was as follows: 'The climate is not unlike that of Germany and the same approach to language should be adopted. A very high standard of living is enjoyed and the proportion of income being spent on food and clothing is declining. Agricultural output is very significant with a rapidly increasing cereal production concentrated on wheat. Irish exports to France consist mainly of agricultural products, however, with beef, veal and skim milk heading the list. The French franc is not quite as strong against sterling as the deutschmark. A third of the population (some 50 million) is aged 20 or less, and the main centres are Paris (9 million), Lyon (1 million), Lille-Roubaux-Tourcoing (1.3 million) and Marseilles (1 million). Paris is the principal marketing and distribution centre and about half the nation's business is done there.'

Furlong was also aware that a considerable amount of cereals were imported into Ireland from France and that his contacts in the Irish Milling Industry would in turn have many contacts in that industry in France.

As in the case of Belgium there were no official figures for bread production in France. However, estimates of 3 million tons per year had been made. Bread consumption continued to decline, having fallen by three kilogrammes *per capita* to 196 kilogrammes between 1970 and 1971.

The market for pre-sliced and packed bread in the early 1970s was expanding at about 25% per year. Turnover in this type of bread was estimated to have reached FF100 million in 1972, representing 1.5% of the overall bread market which was assessed to be worth FF6,800 million in that year. About 70% of pre-sliced loaves were bought in self-service outlets as against 20% in grocery stores and 10% in bakeries.

France was a net importer of bread and the position in 1973 showed imports exceeding exports by FF82 million in value and by 25,000 tons in volume. The UK bakeries had been attempting to gain a substantial foothold in this market. In the autumn of 1973 Rank-Hovis McDougall acquired 80% of the capital of a leading French bakery group with an annual turnover of FF45 million approximately, and this enabled them to achieve penetration through the so-called 'boulangerie ring' which was behind most anti-competition moves in the French bakery industry.

As in Germany, food regulations posed a difficult obstacle for Irish exporters. In France, however the problem was of a rather different nature. The French regulations contained clauses which made it difficult to sell a soda-based product on the market. This brought a different problem to light for the Mosse Management as regards French culture in terms of bread-baking traditions; bread produced in France normally uses yeast as the raising agent. Beside this, Mosse's were aware that the French operated a number of non-tariff barriers to imports which could be applied on the smallest of technicalities and which, as many Irish exporters had discovered, could delay access into the French market for months or even years.

Netherlands

The Netherlands has a marine climate with cool summers and mild winters similar to those in Ireland. While Dutch is the national language, English is widely spoken and at most business meetings the services of an interpreter are unnecessary. As in France, a high standard of living is enjoyed. Dutch agriculture is highly productive, but cereal production is minimal. Irish exports were mainly agricultural, however, concentrated on beef and dairy produce. The currency, the Guilder was relatively strong against Sterling. The population, in an area half the size of Ireland, was approaching 14 million. The largest cities are Amsterdam, Rotterdam (both 1 million) and The Hague (700,000). Amsterdam is the principal financial, commercial and cultural centre.

The CTT executive adivising Furlong on the Dutch market pointed out that while substantial business is done directly with importers, it was nevertheless advisable to appoint an agent. Given the small area of the country and the excellent transport system which existed there, it was obvious that nationwide distribution of any product could be handled with ease. Having made a number of preliminary visits to The Netherlands, Jim Furlong began to believe that there was a significant market potential for both the brown and the white soda bread mix products.

Consumption

Per capita consumption of bread in The Netherlands contracted from 61.5 kilogrammes in 1960 to 46.9 kilogrammes in 1971. However, there was evidence that this downward trend had levelled off in recent years. Expenditure on bakery products in current money terms had risen substantially during the period 1969—73 (Table 14A.4).

Table 14A.4. Consumer Expenditure on Bakery Products —
The Netherlands 1969—73

Bakery Product	1969	1970	1971	1972	1973
			Fl. million		
Bread	894	923	994	1,095	1,194
Cake	36	37	39	N.A.	N.A.
Biscuits	59	59	63	N.A.	N.A.
Industrial Pastry	415	464	500	N.A.	N.A.

N.A. = Not available

Source: EIU. *Marketing in Europe* No.149

Dutch Home Baking

A feature of The Netherlands market which appeared of particular relevance to the marketing of food to be prepared in the home was the type of baking facilities available in the home. Traditionally, the Dutch have used cooking facilities which required the preparation of bread type products on the top of the cooker as opposed to in an oven. However, the younger generation was beginning to buy cookers with ovens as opposed to their older counterparts who preferred the cooker without the oven included (Table 14A.5).

Table 14A.5. Sales of Gas Gookers (000's) — The Netherlands 1971—4

Gas Cookers	1971	1972	1973	1974(est.)
With Ovens	102	106	113	150
Without Ovens	189	206	204	225

Source: EIU *Marketing in Europe*, No.151

Retailing

The major food retailers in The Netherlands were the large multiples: Albert Heijn Supermart N.V. (Ahold Group) had 637 branches and operate 403 super- markets; Simon de Wit were associated with Albert Heijn and had 182 super- markets while De Gruyter had over 500 stores, 386 of which were self-service shops and 60 were supermarkets; Edah N.V. had 300 branches, including 50 supermarkets.   Consequently, it was clear to Jim Furlong that Mosse's needed an agent or distributor who had extensive contacts among these major retailer organizations.

Mosse's had met a large Dutch food distributor at the 1973 Anuga Fair, and sometime after they decided to contact him. A number of meetings were held to discuss marketing details, and through these Jim Furlong had been impressed by the size of the distributor's operation as well as the personality of its managing director. Mosse's agreed to appoint the distributor to market the soda bread mix products in The Netherlands for an initial period of six months. However, it soon became apparent to Jim Furlong that the venture was not as promising as had appeared to be the case earlier, in that the Dutch distributor displayed a marked lack of interest in the Mosse products. The agreements had now expired and the relationship was not renewed.

Appendix 14.3
General Market Data

Table 14A.6. Population in Selected Markets, 1971

Market	Age			
	Under 15	From 15 to 64	65 and Over	Total
	%	%	%	(000's)
Ireland	31.2	57.8	11.0	2,950
United Kingdom	24.0	63.2	12.8	55,811
Germany (FR)	22.4	63.7	13.9	60,651
France	24.8	62.3	12.9	51,005
Italy	24.4	64.6	11.0	53,748
Netherlands	27.2	62.6	10.2	13,120
Belgium	22.8	63.6	13.6	9,745
Luxembourg	20.9	66.5	12.6	331
Denmark	23.2	64.5	12.3	4,950

Source: Eurostat *Basic Statistics of the Community* 1971

Table 14A.7. Selected Measures of Living Standards

Market	Grain[a] as flour	Meat[a]	Passenger[b] Cars	Television[c] Sets	Telephones[c]
	kg/capita/year		Per 1,000 population		
Ireland	90.5	83.6	139	170	103
United Kingdom	71.5	72.3	222	293	269
Germany (FR)	66.0	87.2	253	272	226
France	76.2	96.0	256	214	171
Italy	129.0	57.3	210	180	174
Netherlands	63.4	65.7	212	233	259
Belgium	78.4	82.7	223	209	210
Luxembourg			289	207	324
Denmark	70.1	62.5	231	277	342

a 1970–1
b 1 January 1972
c 1 January 1971

Source: Eurostat *Basic Statistics of the Community* 1972

Table 14A.8. Selected Grocery Statistics, 1971

Country	Average Number of People per Grocer	Average Annual per Capita Grocery Expenditure	Average Annual Turnover per Grocer
		£	£
Ireland	227	38	9,000
Britain	488	67	33,000
Germany (FR)	341	99	34,000
France	367	82	30,000
Italy	276	21	6,000
Netherlands	741	61	45,000
Belgium Luxembourg	273	72	19,000

Source: Nielsen *Marketing in Europe* 1972

Part D
Organization and Control of the Marketing Effort

Given a decision to make a strategic push into overseas markets, a company needs to establish the organizational structure capable of implementing the strategy. It also requires a planning and control system that will integrate each element of the marketing mix and make the business responsive to expected opportunities and threats in the international marketing environment.

Planning is an important vehicle for stimulating management to evaluate the implications of the changing marketing environment, to set clear objectives and strategies and to seek performance improvement. Planning in the international firm is necessary at both the national level and at the headquarters level. A comprehensive planning system will cover: an assessment of the national marketing environment, an evaluation of the performance of the business in the market, clear long- and short-term objectives, a strategy statement, an outline of the marketing mix, and a programme for implementing the chosen direction.

In developing its planning system the international firm should look towards integrating national, regional and international plans into an overall company plan that best utilizes organizational resources to exploit global opportunities. This does not mean that each country will have the same objectives; on the contrary, radically different strategies and priorities will often be required in different markets. But the company should aim at a common format so that comparisons can be seen and lessons learned from progress in the various markets.

A well-structured plan should form an important part of the international company's control system. Control consists of measuring actual performance in the market and comparing it with planned performance. If the variance against budget is un-favourable, this is a red flag that should attract the attention of managers at regional and international headquarters who will investi-gate and attempt to determine the causes of the unfavourable variance and what might be done to improve performance.

One of the most complex and controversial problems in inter-national businesses is developing an organizational structure to implement the strategy. Any organizational design has to attempt to reconcile a host of desirable but partly conflicting objectives: clarity in the assignment of tasks, easy to coordinate, maximizing the company's product and technical knowledge, functional ex-pertise in marketing, finance, personnel, etc., and area or country knowledge. Some companies are structured on product lines, others on geographical lines, but more and more are having to develop complex matrix structures which attempt to coordinate along several of these dimensions.

XV
Metskin Ltd
M. Baker

In January 1979, William Evans, Managing Director of Metskin Ltd, was reviewing the progress which he had made in developing overseas markets for the company's unique casting alloy and process 'Metskin' as the basis for planning future strategy for the company. In particular Mr Evans was concerned with three broad issues:

1 Which markets to develop next
2 Which segments within those markets should receive primary emphasis
3 What marketing approach should be followed in establishing a presence in the new markets.

Developing the Product

Metskin Ltd is the wholly owned subsidiary of a large diversified multinational company whose turnover in 1978 topped the £1,000 million mark derived from 12 Divisions controlling nearly 250 companies. There are very few countries in the world in which the Group is not represented. Metskin was set up in 1973 specifically to exploit the properties of a new material developed in the group's R & D laboratories.

The behaviour of any alloy is of fundamental importance in determining what methods will have to be used in fabricating components, parts and assemblies. In very simple terms, metals may be shaped in either the hot or cold state, depending upon the relative plasticity

This case was made possible by the co-operation of a firm which remains anonymous. It was prepared by Professor M. J. Baker, University of Strathclyde.

of the material in the two conditions and the cost factors involved. In general the more complex the shape required, the greater the amount of work needed to achieve that shape and the higher the costs involved. For example, very complex shapes may require the use of extremely expensive multi-stage dies and tools and successive phases of treatment in both the hot and cold condition in order to accomplish the desired end results.

Over the years a variety of approaches to the fabrication of metals has been developed, including hammering and forging, rolling, extrusion, piercing, drawing, pressing, spinning and powder metal-lurgy. Concurrently with the development of improved methods of fabrication there has been a continuing search for ways and means of improving the properties of the more common metals — iron, aluminium, copper, zinc and lead — and their alloys, as well as the development of alternative materials and methods of fabrication. Of particular significance in the latter category are the development of plastics and, to a lesser degree, rubber.

As a result of these developments the design engineer has a wide range of alternatives to consider when drawing up the specification of a new product. Clearly, in order to be able to select between these alternatives it is essential that he be very explicit about the desired properties of the finished product. It is also of considerable importance that he have some feeling for the likely volume of demand, together with an indication of the relative importance of the part, component etc. which he is designing. The importance of these considerations is fairly obvious.

Firstly, the nature of the product will dictate the performance characteristics required in terms of weight, strength, hardness, conductivity, fatigue and creep properties etc. These performance characteristics are critical and must be present in a material if it is to merit consideration.

Secondly, the volume of likely demand is important because this will dictate which manufacturing methods are most appropriate. For example, the dies to manufacture steel pressings for a new model of car would cost of the order of £1.5 to £2 million and could only be justified if very large sales were anticipated. It is for this reason that specialist car manufacturers make far greater use of hand labour in fabricating car bodies. However, the nature of the labour and the material used will vary according to our third factor — the relative importance of the part. Thus, in the case of Rolls Royce's metal is used which requires highly skilled panel beaters while in most other small volume producers the preferred material is GRP (glass reinforced plastic) which can be hand-laid in moulds by semi-skilled workers. However, the relative importance of a part or component more often depends upon its function within a much larger assembly, so that parts for aeroplanes, turbines, nuclear generators, safety equipment etc. are usually selected on technical criteria rather than on price considerations.

Other things being equal, however, it would be irrational to select a higher-priced solution solely because it is higher priced, and materials technology has been very much preoccupied with developing equivalent solutions at a lower price. Metskin falls firmly into this category, in that it offers the advantages of a metal with a high strength to weight ratio which can be cast to give extremely complex shapes, thinner and lighter than is possible with any other alloy or process without the cost of expensive dies and tools. Hence it possesses performance characteristics which differentiate it significantly from orthodox castings or pressings, yet it can use comparatively low cost tooling.

Defining the Market

The development of Metskin itself followed two distinct phases. From 1966 to 1972 members of the group's research laboratories worked closely with the primary material producer in developing an alloy with special properties for which a provisional patent was awarded. From 1972 to the end of 1973 the emphasis switched from research to development with the production of the materials under factory conditions and the commencement of extensive casting trials. (At present, Metskin only sells fabricated parts, although it is possible it may sell the material itself and licence the process to other fabricators at some future time.)

By the end of 1973 the parent company was sufficiently satisfied with progress to establish Metskin Ltd as an independent subsidiary and appointed Bill Evans, an engineer who had worked on the development of the material and process, as managing director. The most pressing problem facing Bill Evans was which market to develop first, for the versatility of Metskin made it attractive for a multiplicity of end use applications. In common with most new ventures, initial operations were on a modest scale, and the primary responsibility for selling the product into the market rested with Evans himself and one assistant.

Bill Evans' basic dilemma of where to start was compounded by the knowledge that the main Board had set certain sales targets for the early years of operation and performance related to those targets would be critical to continuation of their support. In common with many managements, the main Board's sales projections were essentially linear in nature, whereas most past experience suggests that successful new products exhibit exponential growth in sales volume implicit in the shape of the product life cycle curve. One factor which underlies the basic shape of the product life cycle curve is the tendency of people to try new products, on a limited basis, before committing themselves to adoption and large scale use. Thus, in the early stages of market development, Bill Evans expected that he would have to do a great deal of missionary selling in return for small, trial orders.

Based upon his evaluation of the product profile, Evans felt that Metskin offered significant benefits in the manufacture of complex shapes in quantities below 10,000 where high tool costs would render multiple pressing, conventional casting, or deep drawing of conventional metals/alloys uneconomic.

In addition, the high temperature capability of Metskin gave it a strong competitive edge over plastics which enjoyed a price advantage. Given these advantages and its basic performance criteria, Evans selected seven specific end use markets for attention:

1 Aerospace
2 Architectural use — cladding, fixings, etc.
3 Case shells for portable instruments
4 Commercial vehicles
5 Gaming and vending machine cases
6 Instrument housings
7 Specialist vehicles.

Because of its versatility, considerable difficulty was experienced in developing realistic forecasts and budgets for the new material. For example, the value added in fabricating components for the aerospace industry was significantly greater than for architectural use, where volume rather than complexity tended to dominate. Similarly, case shells for portable instruments command a superior margin to trim for commercial vehicles and so on. To allow for these variations it was decided that in the early years of market development the best approach would be to impute a value per ton sold, and to use this as a basis for setting company sales targets.

By 1973 it was estimated that £250,000 had been invested in

research and development, and it was decided to amortise this over ten years. In order to cope with the anticipated diversity of applications, several different casting machines had to be acquired, and an installed capacity capable of a theoretical maximum output of 5,000 tons per annum was considered the minimum initial investment at a cost of £3 million. This also was to be amortised over ten years with other fixed costs estimated at £175,000 per annum. Variable costs were estimated at £450 per ton against an average selling price per ton of £1,000.

Precise forecasts of market size were considered unnecessary, as the market potential of any of the segments was far in excess of Metskin's theoretical output. In common with other innovations which are direct substitutes, the problem is not one of market size but the potential for, and speed of replacement of, existing materials. Assessment of Metskin's particular advantages led Evans to believe that Architectural Panels etc. offered the best immediate opportunity and were expected to count for 25% of sales in early years. Vehicle applications were looked for to provide a further 25%, with shells for instruments and vending machines 19%, and Aerospace 6%. All other applications were expected to provide the remaining 25%.

Based upon the assessment of market potential and the initial capital investment required, the main board directors set Evans a target of £2,500,000 sales per annum in five years, using a straightforward linear extrapolation for years 1 − 5, after which the project would be reassessed in its entirety. However, it was made clear to Evans that performance would be monitored on a three-monthly basis, with a major review every year, at which he would be required to account for any significant departure from planned performance.

Selling-in began in 1974 and, as expected, generated a great deal of interest. However, many design engineers did not have an immediate application for Metskin as they were committed to other materials and suppliers. Also, while the new material offered great potential, most prospective users wished to try it for themselves and so only placed small trial orders to test the company's ability to live up to its claims. As a consequence, production orders were received from only a limited number of customers who had had a previous production problem for which Metskin had seemed to offer the only solution.

The basic dilemma of finding sufficient short-term requirements necessary to generate a satisfactory sales volume to keep the main Board happy, versus the longer-term potential of joint development with customers with the latent promise of wide-scale use, was compounded for Evans by the deepening economic recession of 1975. In an interview with the case writer Evans described his dilemma and his subsequent efforts to expand into foreign markets as follows.

Metskin goes International

'Originally we had decided that we would set up a profitable UK operation to prevent dissipating what management resources we had. However, in 1975 the recession really began to bite and it became apparent that if we were to stick to our original policy, it was going to take us years to build up enough business in the UK. At that point we decided that we must spread into Western Europe as we felt this was the market we could manage most effectively.

'The first thing I did was take advice from someone elsewhere in the group who worked essentially in Western Europe. He was in an allied industry and what I did was define to him what we had to do to get a sale because we had a very peculiar product. It had a very high technical content and the only way that one could possibly make a sale was first of all to meet the potential customer, explain to him precisely what we had, because he did not know otherwise what you did have, discuss its relevance to his requirements and then begin talking about sales. There was no way that anyone would ever approach you first. So we had to find people who were prepared to get up and go out. When we set up the company we had approaches from several existing group agents or representatives or associates in Europe. Essentially we had simply parried these but when we decided to open up then each of them was seen. Only in two cases did a person who approached us end up by being a contact.

'We started off first of all in Sweden. Now in Sweden I had a contact already who had been a customer of mine for many years and I knew that he was a very good salesman. I also knew he had very good contacts throughout Sweden. The existing group agents, or one of them, had also approached me so I saw both of them but I appointed the one who had been my old customer as Agent. I explained to him very clearly the amount of effort that would have to go in to get anything out. So we started off with a fairly clear understanding as to what the end programme would have to be. After that I spoke to some other people in Belgium and in Holland. None of the existing group contacts were of any use because essentially they were people who were responding to enquiries for bulk materials made by the group. However, I met one in Belgium who had a subsidiary company in Holland so I was attracted by the prospect of being able to work in two countries, with one outfit working under two different names, so that in Belgium it was the Belgian company and in Holland it was the Dutch company but the same person or people. The input that there should be from the agent had been thought about very carefully and it was made a condition of the Agency that the agent would employ, at his expense, a man full-time on our work. We reached agreement on that and it was a straight commission payment. The man was appointed and he started work towards the end of 1976.

'In France, again at about the same time, I met one of our own stockists and having explained to him the amount of work involved he said yes, he was very interested and he was interested in long-term return rather than short-term gain, which seemed ideal, and we appointed him in France. He was based in Paris. In Germany we set up one of our own companies as agent. In Ireland we set up one of our own stockists as agent, that is in Eire. Then the last one really is Denmark. What we did there was rather different. We went through the British Overseas Trade Board. We explained to them what our requirements were and I had already been approached by some of our own people whom I obviously had to see. We then worked through the Embassy who introduced us to two companies and we did in fact appoint one of these companies as our agent. That was in 1977 and that is the last one that we set up. In every case we tried to explain clearly and carefully the amount of input that was required because obviously it was not in their interests nor was it ours that we should get the wrong people.'

What actually happened?

'Well, starting from the top in Sweden, the agent tried to work from his desk. We gave him support from here but virtually nothing came of it. We explained to him why and he started doing more calls, we visited and supported. He then began picking the odd order up. He got one for an on-going job which was really very useful. It was worth about £60,000 a year turnover to us. We got him into some of the more important companies, SAAB for example, and he began to respond by putting more effort in and after a very slow start, that one is beginning to go along really quite nicely.

'I think the next one was Benelux. That was a fairly traumatic experience because we got one tiny order in the first year and the man was working full-time. It then began to build up very, very quickly so that in the second year his order intake was somewhere around £80,000 and he now has one or two contacts where the work is coming in in chunks of about £30,000 a time. His orders this year should be somewhere over £150,000. So after a really disappointing start, that one has now worked very well.

'In France our experience was very similar to Sweden. There the man did some more visiting than in Sweden but we established fairly early on that he did not have a sufficient understanding of our product. We gave him additional training to remedy that but we found he was coming back to us with enquiries where very obviously the company had a major problem and was lashing around desperately for a solution. We did not get the sort of enquiries we were looking for. We gave a lot of support, we gave press conferences and we did support visits but it really was not working out. I then visited the agent and we decided that we would let it run for a further six months with direction from us to see if it really was worthwhile following up, because he and I both felt that if it was successful in Holland, there was really no reason at all why it should not be successful in France.

'What we decided was that we would see what happened in Denmark which I might as well deal with next because in Denmark we got a very low level of enquiry. We visited and supported the agent there; we must have had four or five visits to him. We visited customers and we had done quite a bit of publicity but it was getting nowhere. So we decided that what we would do as one last fling was give a seminar in Jutland to an invited audience and we had, I think, a total of 80 potential users attend two separate sessions where we produced components and talked about what we had and who the users were and what the benefits were. That was three months ago. We have yet to have a follow-up enquiry so we are now in the situation where we are going to write Denmark off.

'In France we had said if the Danish approach works then we will consider using it in France. I think we will now almost certainly write France off too because there are other areas where we can identify a better return for the same amount of effort. In Germany we had a very slow start because the person involved could only give a little of his time to it and it worked out at about a day a week. However, he did pick up business, he picked up business worth about £60,000 a year and on top of that about £60,000 a year in his second year of operation. But it was completely insignificant compared with the German economy as a whole and we decided that we should change our approach completely there, so what we did was ask our agent, who as I said earlier was an associate company. We asked him instead to seek a potential partner for us in Germany and that partner should have a very good knowledge and very good customer contacts of the type that we were looking for and be able to absorb the technical content of what we were doing.

'Well we did ultimately find such a company and we reached an agreement with them whereby we would give them sole distribution rights for the German speaking areas, they would pass all their enquiries to us, we would quote them and they would then mark up and sell them to their customers. The agreement said that when sales reached a certain level, and we are talking about around three quarters of a million pounds per annum, we would at that point set up a joint operation to fabricate within or near the German-speaking area and we would then supply raw material from here to that joint operation. It was thought that we should probably be ordering machines for that within two years. That started six months ago, we have had some exceptionally good enquiries and we have had four orders to date. The business we already had we of course passed on to the new company.

'Ireland was interesting. Two years after we set Ireland up we got our first communication from them and that was to wish us a Merry Christmas. Having told them that I intended to terminate the agreement we then chased it up with them. They were a company that were really trying to find a new approach. They had been stockists for years and they were now looking for other avenues to explore which would be a little more rewarding than the ones they had been in and they were very keen on getting a new product which we could by now demonstrate as having a wide range of application and being potentially profitable to a successful agent. So we decided that we would give that another go. What we arranged was that our sales director would spend a week there doing visits and presentations to select groups of companies and that is taking place next week. The beauty of Eire of course is that it is very close, I suppose it is no closer than Western Europe but getting materials through to them is very straightforward. So we have had quite a mixture of success.

'Sweden, I think, is going to pay off both for the agent and for us. Germany I am now very happy about. I think that is well under control and going along nicely, and Holland really has been extremely successful but we had that terrible, nerve-racking first year; Ireland we shall wait and see. Denmark, not terribly sure of the reasons for failure there but I cannot afford to find out. France, I am sure of the reasons. It is that we simply have not done enough leg work.'

Agency Support

Having reviewed the broad sequence of events leading to the establishment of agents, Bill Evans then elaborated on the support given them.

'The first thing we would do of course is train whoever was going to be dealing with the product over there and what we normally said was that we expected that man to come here for at least two weeks and probably two lots of two weeks so that we can completely familiarize him with the detail of the process and the product. We then said that we would send technical people over, preferably for two or three day visits, fairly frequently in the first instance. Now I would expect to do that every four to six weeks in the first instance to get in to the potential customers. We also emphasized very strongly that if there were ever a clash of interests between an order for the UK and one for Europe that we would always give preference to the European one, and we emphasized this in every country.

'The other thing we said was that whenever they asked for technical support we would provide it and we made it as open as that. We said that if you want someone to come, ask and we will send someone immediately and we did that realizing that it could be abused but that if it was abused it was very easy to correct, in fact it was never abused by any of the agents and it was used. In Holland where they had such an input and where we saw the potential we set up a permanent exhibition in Eindhoven which is close of course to a major customer, or potential customer, and we took that for a period of nine months so that we then had somewhere where not only the Dutch but the Germans could take customers or potential users along and show them the hardware, which of course makes such a difference. It is very difficult to talk abstractly about this. That we felt really did pay off. We ended up with having, I think, about fifty people from Phillips in total visit our exhibition and of course we gave seminars there too. People attended by invitation only and I think virtually all of their senior designers have now been to these seminars so this we felt was a very useful approach and of course it was a slight modification to that which we tried in Denmark with no success. In Sweden we decided that to try to get additional support we would exhibit at the Stockholm Fair, which we did in October of 1978. We got really quite a good response at that fair and would probably exhibit again.

'We do a lot of PR work in this country and with each of the agents we send them copies of any PR work we do here, in some instances for them to pass on and have released. Normally for them to select and for us to use our contacts to have them released in their areas. Now that could be either through Embassies or it could be through PR Agencies where the group has contacts.'

When asked if there was any significance in the fact that the Danish agency had failed and was the only one initiated through the BOTB, Evans stated:

'I think it failed because of the agent, but the support that we got from the Embassy was unbelieveable, it was really quite excellent. The reason we didn't use Embassies elsewhere under BOTB was that we were already set up, but even then in Sweden where we had already appointed the agent, having got in touch with the Embassy there, through the BOTB in the first instance, in dealing with the press, mainly in dealing in the press and for that matter in getting contacts, the Embassy really could not have been more helpful. In so far as Denmark is concerned, having been introduced to the Embassy there they listened to our requirements, they put up two candidates of which we selected one, both of them were of very high calibre, certainly both of them were better than any we had been in touch with. Having then selected one of them, they supported us in our PR work. We explained what we did in this sort of situation was to have a PR news conference to launch it. They offered us the use of their premises and we used one of their rooms for that reception and they laid on the buffet for us and everything else. The ambassador came and introduced us and I think for that reason we had a much better turnout at the news conference than one would normally expect. With press releases both in Sweden and in Denmark, press releases supplied to the Embassy they put out on their paper to their contacts and it's picked up, and the support we got there was really admirable.'

Looking back on his experience of the past three years, Evans expressed the view that while he had no previous experience of setting up an export operation, he considered his approach a sound one.

'I think it was a fairly sound approach and I still don't see a better one given the limitations that one had at the time. Of course, if you had someone with very much more experience it may well be that one would go through the BOTB earlier, I don't know. But, if one has contacts and can spot one or two to start off then that is probably the most effective way to do it. Particularly, when you consider that appointing agents must take up a very limited part of the time because you are in a total development with a new product and a new company.

'I felt it was so important that I had to get involved. I did involve other people, I had assistance from various sources, but it was so key to our entire operation that I felt it was something I had to be involved in. It probably took 15% of my time the first year and nearer 20% in 1977 and 1978.

'In retrospect I find it difficult to draw morals from the whole thing because I think even if I were starting afresh I would still be looking for the man to whom you are important, who can absorb the technology and whom you can really depend on to go out and fight for the work. The most successful cases without a doubt were where we made it a condition of the agency that a man be employed full-time on our business. Then there was no question about commitment, it was there.

'When I first started I felt 7½% commission was a sufficient incentive but, when it became obvious that it was a much longer haul than we had thought at the beginning, and we had evidence of this in the UK operation, I changed that in that I offered 10% on a one year basis. Then, putting pressure on the various agents it seemed that even that was inadequate so we then put it on a sliding scale where it is 15% up to a certain sales level, then 10% then 7½%. I think the last one is right. Mind you, I thought the other two were right at the time as well.'

What Next?

Since 1976 sales have quadrupled and are now running at a rate of over £1 million per annum. In 1976 exports accounted for 7% of sales; in 1978 they had risen to 42%. Clearly the international market has contributed significantly to the company's overall growth and Evans has further plans for expansion.

'I think we understand the market now and certainly what we would say now to a potential agent is no different from what we would say when we set them up, because it does need a tremendous effort. What we can demonstrate to an agent now is success in various areas, which we could not do then and I think they simply were not prepared to invest the time and obviously the money but if we were to try to set up another agent, in France for example, that would take a good six months before we probably set foot over the first customer's doorstep. It requires a very great deal of support from us. It needs a great deal of effort from me personally in selection and I really think that there are places where we could get a much better return more quickly.

'It might be interesting to look at what we intend to do from here. The next major thing — we have some specialist interests in Italy and we would propose to move in there and either set up a man to deal with that particular sector which is the specialist motor car field or we would simply deal with it direct from here. The other area that we would propose moving into in the short term is North America and our feelings at the moment are that we should adopt the approach that we did in Germany. What we will do is find someone who is strong in the market and sell through them, manufacturing here in the first instance with a view to setting up manufacturing in the USA or Canada on a joint venture when sales are at the right level. And this of course is very attractive to both partners because it eliminates the risk, certainly reduces it very considerably.

'When I talk about someone who is strong in the market I mean someone who has a deep knowledge and good contacts with the people who use the material that we use and also are almost certainly supplying the sectors of the market that we are trying to break into so we are talking about things like aerospace, which would be slightly specialist, or electronics. We want partners who really know the market place, the technology we have, and who can grasp it all.

'We are talking about three very special cases when we are talking Germany, Italy, and the United States, for three very different reasons. One option obviously was to try to sell into Germany, as Germany was the single potentially biggest market that we could see in Western Europe but when we looked around the group, and indeed elsewhere, we could find no single success story where someone had set up a marketing operation from the UK in Germany and we could see no reason at all why we should succeed where the others had failed and obviously it would be a very expensive operation to mount. It would also be a very difficult one to manage and really it was for that reason and because of the vast market that was there that we thought that the most sensible thing was to find someone who really did know their way around the market place and who had the contacts which we had and I am sure was the right thing to do in that country. In Italy we at this point are really interested in one very limited market, which is specialist motor vehicles so you probably only want to talk to certainly not more than four companies and possibly not more than about eight individuals. Possibly we can deal with that here, or there may be someone on the spot who has the necessary contacts and intelligence to deal with it for us. In so far as the United States is concerned, given you are talking about a very big market, there is the problem of geography and of course there is the problem of cash, however big the group is. At this point it seems to us that probably the best way to get in is to find a partner, again with all the marketing strengths and skills. Now that partner of course could be either small or large and we could expand there once we had established the market, with his participation at from anything from zero to in practice 50%.

'We are in a situation where we have a product that is completely new internationally and we want to get into the international team as quickly as possible and it always comes back to the question of what you can manage and what gives you the best return at any point in time for the end product you can make. Our next move after that is into the Far East and there we have various choices open to us. We could do a similar thing to what we are now considering doing in the States or we could offer licenses. Again because of geography even the partnership one does not look terribly attractive, it probably looks relevant to America on a joint operation, the way America with a joint operation looks to a direct operation in Western Europe, and I think we would almost certainly offer licenses there. But the return on that is not sufficiently great for us to put it in before the more direct operations in North America and Western Europe and we have other decisions to make. There is the chance of putting in a turnkey operation in Eastern Europe and we have to decide at what point it would be appropriate to follow that one up.

'Well, what would you suggest we do?'

XVI
SIRA Institute Ltd
J. Wilmshurst

Thirty-three year old David Berry sat in the 'den' of his large family house, hearing the laughter of his three young children as his wife took them off to bed. He wondered what time *he* would get to bed, with the rough draft of his report to the Board still to be completed. Four months ago, in August 1973, he had been appointed Marketing Director of SIRA Institute Ltd and the thought still gave him a feeling of excitement and achievement. But now was the crunch. How was he to handle the situation that confronted him?

David's memory took him back to his first visits to SIRA. The pleasant offices in a big, old house in spacious grounds in commuter-belt Chislehurst, Kent, just outside London. The well-equipped laboratories and workshops set around these grounds.

His appointment underlined the Board's intention to take SIRA into a fully commercial, competitive posture, after more than half a century as a quasi-government body.

The Background

SIRA had been founded in 1918, as the British Scientific Research Association. It was funded originally from membership subscriptions and more recently from a combination of these subscriptions and a government grant. Its prime task (as expressed in the 1970 amended Articles of Association) was 'To undertake and promote research, development and other scientific and technological work in order to

Prepared by John Wilmshurst, 1980.

advance the UK capability in scientific and industrial measurement control ...'

During the three interviews leading to his appointment, Managing Director Sam Carlisle and his colleagues had explained to David the later developments of the organization. During the 1960s a gradual change in the method of funding had taken place and more and more of SIRA's income was now derived from projects undertaken directly for industrial companies and paid for by them. During this transition period the government added grants of from £1 to £5 for every £1 obtained from industry. Ultimately, in 1973, the final step was taken and SIRA became entirely responsible for its own finance. (In 1970 the name had been changed to SIRA Institute Ltd).

Sam Carlisle had gone on to elaborate:

From 1963 to 1973 SIRA's income had remained static at £500,000 per annum. Of this sum, 35%–50% came from government funds, the remainder from UK industry. The main current contract, SIRA's biggest ever, was work on a major telescope project for the Greenwich Observatory. Value of the contract to SIRA was £150,000. (Company accounts are shown as Exhibit 16.1.) The approaching end of this contract would coincide with the final withdrawal of government grants.

The Board had therefore decided that aggressive action had to be taken to generate more business and the appointment of a Marketing Director was an important step towards it. David Berry's experience had seemed interesting to SIRA because he was a technical man with considerable and relevant marketing experience. After an Honours Degree (followed by postgraduate research) in Metallurgy at Sheffield University he had joined Yorkshire Imperial Metals as Development Metallurgist. His work led to a number of patents in techniques concerned with explosive welding, high pressure extrusion, etc.

When explosive welding took off commercially, David moved into marketing to help exploit it. Then he went to Metals Research Ltd, at Cambridge, where he pioneered the marketing of semi-conductor materials for light-emitting diodes. Eventually he moved to the United States to market there for Metals Research these materials and the equipment to produce them. Three years later he came back to the UK as Group Marketing Manager, responsible for marketing electronic analytical equipment to universities and major research establishments. The SIRA Board saw this as the right kind of background for the colleague they needed to help them adopt a more positive marketing stance.

David agreed with them, but now that discussion on a sunny June afternoon was four months away and the night was cold outside. SIRA was an interesting, outstandingly competent and very friendly organization, but could he persuade it to take the steps he believed to be necessary?

The Problem

For SIRA would have to change direction radically, he felt, if the decline in its fortunes was to be halted and reversed. Technically, SIRA was in good shape. 60% of its entire staff of around 150 were technically qualified, most of them graduates or equivalent. Their competence in technical matters in their chosen fields was without question. But commercially they seemed to operate on a much lower plane and David found the word 'naive' coming into his mind. After fifty years of operating under varying levels of government protection and with the Treasury ultimately 'picking up the tab', could the organization change its approach fast enough?

Age and outlook could be problems too. At thirty-three, David was by far the youngest member of the Board whose average age he guessed was near sixty. All brilliant technically and first-class at dealing with customers on a professional level, would they be able to see it his way if he proposed radical changes?

And then the biggest headache of all. How radical should the changes be anyway?

Board discussions had produced the following set of objectives:

1 To conduct a profitable business as a contract engineering, technical service and technical training organization.
2 To maintain a high degree of technical skill in all aspects of our work and to ensure that technological leadership is maintained in our principal areas of expertise.
3 To provide opportunity for staff development and continuity.
4 To maintain a position of independence.

Further discussion decided the following basic strategies:

1 Concentrate attention upon areas of business/products that are profitable and achieve growth so that overheads can be spread.
2 Ensure that we maintain a substantial level of R & D in our work and ensure that specialist skills can be bought in.
3 Maintain technical/commercial challenge in our work and recruit principally at the lower end of the scale.

4 Ensure that our activities are seen to be free from outside influence by maintaining a balanced spread of customers and by
actively publishing our independent status.

David felt he could support these policy statements, but they still
left some important questions open. For instance:

1 To what extent should UK government departments still be seen
as a major source of business?
2 Should the present total reliance on UK industry continue, or
should business be sought from overseas?
3 Which overseas countries represented the most fruitful sources
of business?
4 Which of SIRA's wide range of activities offered the best competitive advantages? (See Exhibit 16.2.)

There was no doubt in anyone's mind (and David was thankful
that this much was clear) that some action *had* to be taken, for at
least three reasons. Firstly, the static turnover over the past ten
years (which in fact represented a decline in real terms) at a time
of considerable market expansion. Second, the final termination of
direct government support, and third, the imminent completion of
the Greenwich Observatory contract.

There was no dissension at all in the company about this, but did
they all realize the implications? Until recently, David's intention
had been to take things slowly, step by step, but this no longer
seemed possible, because as these deliberations were going on the
Middle East oil crisis came. Governments and industry alike slashed
their expenditure, slashed staff, cut back on investment programmes
and development programmes or extended them over much longer
time scales.

SIRA now had to face battling for the extra business it needed
within a much more constricted market situation.

The Options

A study of the potential market was judged to be essential but
quantitative research of market size was deemed unnecessary in the
light of the small market share that SIRA needed. However the
collective experience of SIRA executives provided substantial
qualitative information that can be summarised as follows:

1 In the UK, government and industry alike were imposing severe

cut-backs in response to the oil crisis. Competitors would be fighting at least as hard as SIRA (and perhaps with better marketing competence) to win a major share of the rapidly dwindling business.

2 The situation in continental Europe and in North America was very similar, with the additional problems of being less familiar to SIRA which had little previous involvement in overseas contracts.

3 The Middle-Eastern countries would be looking for ways to spend their increased oil revenues. However SIRA's expertise was probably in the wrong fields for them to be able to benefit.

4 This left the multi-government organizations (the 'supranationals'). These were in a better state because they were funded by individual governments who had made long-term commitments. The fact that they were essentially in the business of sub-contracting had considerable appeal.

5 Desk research into the main relevant multi-government agencies suggested the following as the most likely sources of business and David had already sounded out the rest of the Board on the idea of launching a campaign to get business from them:

(a) EURATOM
(b) The European Space Agency
(c) CERN
(d) The Micro-biology unit at Heidelberg
(See Exhibit 16.3 for brief details of these organizations.)

The Board's reaction was immediate horror. One reason given was that SIRA had no experience of overseas markets and indeed there was a strong feeling that SIRA ought not to sell overseas technology developed for UK industry with UK capital. Another reason was that it had no experience of operating as a normal commercial subcontractor, as opposed to a quasi-government agency. There seemed a distinct likelihood that it would find itself competing strongly with its customers. Besides which, all its management systems (including pricing procedures) were geared to UK government contract work.

It was undoubtedly true that taking the line David was proposing would put severe strain on SIRA's limited financial resources and could well lead to total collapse. There was a strong feeling in favour of 'battening down the hatches' and 'riding out the storm' with whatever government work could still be secured. When the immediate crisis was over, spending by government and industry would gradually increase again and *that* would be the time for SIRA to launch out into uncharted waters.

The Products

In an attempt to determine what products SIRA really had, David had examined the various sections of the business one by one and his findings can be summarized as follows:

Industrial Instrumentation

This accounted for approximately 40% of total business. Historical sales performance adjusted to current prices showed a steady growth of sales at the rate of about 4% per annum in real terms. Also profitability had been improved by the more efficient working practices made possible by greater sales volume and the introduction of new facilities had been the major contributor to growth and profitability.

Business in this area was fairly well assured since two major customers with long-term contracts accounted for about 50% of the sales volume (hence also the more limited expansion in these areas). Investment in new facilities had clearly paid off and had enabled a more comprehensive service to be offered and better margins to be generated. Future business prospects should be enhanced by the increasing volume of Government legislation which would be likely to force up demand for these types of service. Similarly the oil crisis (which was the cause of difficulty at the present time) had stimulated much interest in energy conservation and the organization was well placed to secure business in this area.

Industrial Optics

This also accounted for approximately 40% of total business. Sales performance showed a substantial improvement (part of which could be argued to have been offset by the decline in Engineering business). Sales had increased at the rate of about 5% p.a. in real terms and profits had been maintained at a satisfactory level.

However, not everything was satisfactory. The traditional market, the UK optical industry was, like its European counterpart, suffering substantially at the hands of the Japanese. Accordingly much of the design work done for this industry was in danger of drying up. This had been anticipated to some extent and the Industrial Optics and Engineering departments had invested in the emerging electro-optical technologies so that they would be able to serve the more buoyant market segments. Similarly these two departments had built up precision mechanical engineering skills to add to the services they could offer to the market.

It was clear that to continue to build up the necessary facilities would depress profits. However, in order to justify this action it would be necessary to demonstrate that there would be a ready market and that SIRA were able to serve it. David Berry believed that despite certain shortcomings this represented an area of potential uniqueness.

Engineering

Business had been declining and virtually nothing had been done to arrest this. However, a new, young manager (appointed at the same time as David Berry) was now in charge and very aware of the problems. It appeared clear that the Department relied upon Industrial Optics to provide the design input for its work. Rarely was simple manufacturing sold (since small jobbing shops would be more competitive). The combination of advanced technical design and high grade construction seemed to offer the sort of profitable business that SIRA needed. Thus markets needed to be found in high technology areas where the blend of design and manufacture that SIRA could offer could demand high prices.

The historical separation of this department was thought to be counter-productive to this aim.

Marketing

This, only really formed since David's arrival, was a resource-consuming department and, as such, viewed with caution by the management, even though it employed only six people. But it seemed possible that its value to the company could be enhanced by creating more obvious links between its promotional activities and contracts gained, and by developing work which produced added value and was contribution-earning in its own right.

Under the latter category David saw distinct possibilities in two areas in which the department was already engaged to some extent. First market research assignments in SIRA's specialist fields — on a fee basis for clients — and second, seminars in SIRA's areas of specialist knowledge — open to all-comers on a fee basis.

As a result of his analysis of the company's background, achievements and resources, David came to the conclusion that there were really two main products where SIRA had a real advantage. One was electro-optical engineering and the other, general technical service. The second of these was of much wider application and hence had a much bigger market potential. In the first, SIRA had a greater degree of uniqueness. On the other hand it called for a higher level of capital investment and involved working in a much more restricted market.

The Task

David ran over again in his mind the way SIRA appeared to him. Its history and present state presented peculiar problems, but also it had some important strengths. SIRA owed its present form largely to Jim Franses, a Council member and now Deputy Chairman under the new set-up — which would not formally come into being until January 1st, 1974.

The Council had directed the affairs of SIRA since its inception. It was appointed by member companies of SIRA and thus, inevitably, Council members tended to identify with the interests of their own company rather than with SIRA as a separate entity. Jim Franses ran his own small company producing control systems. During discussions on the future of SIRA he had strongly expressed the view that SIRA had 'got to have something more pointed and sharp-ended' than its existing methods of conducting business. He then steered the development of the new management structure which stemmed from the discussions in due course.

Sam Carlisle, the existing Director of SIRA under its old constitution, was appointed Managing Director of the new Executive Board. Sam, aged 55, had been with the Admiralty, then with the British Iron and Steel Research Authority. Two of the other executive directors were Terry Flanagan, 50, and Lionel Baker, 42. Both were physicists, both had been with SIRA virtually all their working lives. David Berry would become the third executive director. Existing members of Council continued as non-executive directors and would still have considerable responsibility for long-term policy.

Terry was head of the Industrial Instrumentation section of SIRA and Lionel headed up Industrial Optics. Both were outstandingly competent technically and both had good contacts throughout the industries from which their business came. Indeed, much of SIRA's business in recent years had come in through these contacts (who in any case mainly worked for companies who were subscribers to SIRA). However, Terry's and Lionel's main task had been to develop the technical excellence of their departments and the work they carried out. Because of a high level of success in this, morale in SIRA was very strong — although (or perhaps because) most people were blissfully unaware of the commercial realities. However Flanagan and Baker were not alone in viewing with some unease the necessity actively to seek business which SIRA's new financial base and management approach would bring about.

Thus they had welcomed the appointment of David Berry to head up the newly activated commercial 'sharp end' of the business. Inevitably though, their enthusiasm was modified to some degree by thoughts of 'what do I stand to lose?'. So David had complete confidence in the technical competence and performance of his senior colleagues and the teams they led. However, the lack of a strong commercial viewpoint and of any planned marketing activity gave him plenty to work on.

Competition was not lacking. Many other developed countries had government backed or fully-commercial research associations similar to SIRA. Notable in the latter category was *Battelle* of Columbus, Ohio, operating also in Frankfurt and Geneva and with an office in London. Battelle is a fully commercial organization. Also the Max Planck Institutes in Germany and TNO in Holland who were funded primarily by the respective governments. Unlike SIRA however they had for some time had a strong commercial wing.

This brought David's thoughts full circle back to what might be the best way to tackle the market, bearing in mind the need to secure the cooperation and support of Lionel Baker and Terry Flanagan and the approval of the Board as a whole. Up to now they had run their individual sections (each about 40 strong) as virtually separate entities. The Engineering Department had provided a service to the other two (but David could see that it would need to develop considerably to provide the necessary back-up for the kind of business he was going for). He formed in his mind a mental picture of the organization he envisaged for the future — a combination of what Sam Carlisle had outlined to him and the way he himself pictured it (projected organization chart Exhibit 16.4).

David reckoned that, fortunately, his colleagues were aware of SIRA's dangerous over-dependence on technical expertise and lack of commercial direction. However, he very much doubted if even Sam Carlisle was fully aware of the dangerous implications of the stagnation, in real terms, of SIRA's income.

Something had to be done, something immediate and effective.

But it was no good setting his heart on a particular approach unless he could carry his colleagues with him. His report had to be not just sound but utterly convincing — and if his secretary didn't have the rough draft before he went off to Bristol in the morning, the finished report would never be ready in time for the next Board meeting.

Looking at the clock and taking a sip from the half-cold cup of coffee at his elbow, David picked up his pen.

Profit and Loss Account for the year ended 31st March 1974

	Notes	1974 £	1974 £	1973 £	1973 £
Turnover	(1)		643,894		497,494
Profit for the year	(2)	83,679		5,971	
Investment income	(3)	14,463		12,768	
Profit on sale of capital equipment		5,629		598	
Profit on sale of quoted investments		149		—	
		103,920		19,337	
Adjustments for previous years	(4)	4,299		(49)	
			108,219		19,288
Transfers to reserves	(5)	(81,425)		(3,282)	
Balance transferred to accumulated profit	(5)	(26,794)		(16,006)	
			(108,219)		(19,288)

Balance Sheet as at 31st March 1974

	Notes	1974 £	1974 £	1973 £	1973 £
Current Assets					
Debtors	(6)	169,514		133,362	
Retentions and work-in-progress	(7)	46,926		32,313	
Short term loans	(8)	85,000		42,081	
Cash at bank and in hand		6,088		3,564	
			307,528		211,320
Less **Current Liabilities**					
Creditors		71,448		41,973	
Receipts in advance	(9)	103,754		75,446	
			175,202		117,419
Net Current Assets			132,326		93,901
Investments	(10)		244,232		174,861
Fixed Assets	(11)		219,507		219,084
			£596,065		£487,846
Represented by					
Reserve Funds	(5)		445,846		364,421
Accumulated Profit	(5)		150,219		123,425
			£596,065		£487,846

The notes on pages 7 and 8 form part
of these accounts.

On behalf of Sira Institute Limited

(signed)   (signed)
Chairman   Managing Director

Exhibit 16.1: SIRA Financial Accounts 1974

The following extracts from a SIRA brochure indicate the range of services it offers:—

SIRA Services

As an advanced technological centre, the Institute:

- undertakes R & D and applied development in instrument technology and industrial optics
- provides facilities for precision equipment design and manufacture, and for precision mechanical, electronic, and electrical engineering
- provides technical and commercial information on instruments and associated equipment
- carries out market research and business evaluations.

SIRA is an independent organization which is structured to allow companies to derive the full benefits of contract R & D, engineering, and technical and business services. As a SIRA customer, you derive benefit from:

Cost-effectiveness
The promptness with which work can be completed, together with your control of total expenditure, ensures you a quick financial return on development work placed with SIRA.

Control
Your interests are safeguarded at all stages, confidentiality is assured, and progress and performance are monitored to suit your requirements.

Multi-disciplinary approach
A wide range of expertise is drawn on to co-ordinate all skills required for your work, and can often provide rapid solutions to your problems.

Access to advanced technology
You gain access to experienced staff, familiar with the latest technical advances, backed by well-equipped laboratories.

Back-up
R & D projects can be costly to initiate, especially if you take recruitment and training into account. SIRA can 'switch over' to you additional skills and resources to meet demand.

Objectivity
As an independent organization, SIRA provides objective consultancy and project results.

Technical innovation
Where known techniques are unable to resolve a client's problem, SIRA develops new techniques and equipment to meet the need.

Exhibit 16.2: SIRA Activities and Services   *Continued*

Areas of Technology

While SIRA provides consultancy in all aspects of measurement and control, its R & D contract facility and technical services are concentrated in four basic areas of technology. By adopting a multi-disciplinary approach, SIRA combines the expertise within each of these areas to provide an effective, practical, comprehensive, problem-solving and development capability. In its activities, which range from evaluation of technology trends and market prospects through conceptual and detailed design to manufacture, SIRA brings clarity and objectivity to bear on product and process development.

Industrial instrumentation
    automatic inspection of surfaces and discrete components,
    chemical composition analysis,
    moisture measurement and control,
    evaluation of process instruments.

Industrial optics
    objective measurement of optical materials and components,
    design and technology of optical systems,
    design and manufacture of advanced electro-optical systems.

Engineering
    development, design, manufacture, supply of:

        instrument mechanisms and fine mechanics; high performance servo and drive systems; wide dynamic range analogue systems; real-time digital processing systems,

    materials research, bonding techniques, and chemical processes,
    electron microscopy for surface studies and microanalysis.

Marketing
    technical and commercial information,
    business evaluation,
    market research,
    seminars and symposia.

Instrument Design, Development and Manufacture

SIRA supplies and maintains special-purpose equipment for scientific and industrial research, and undertakes new product development. Development and design teams, working to national and military standards and procedures, are geared to respond quickly and accurately to requirement specifications.

    SIRA's engineering capability centres on fine and precision mechanisms, servosystems, motor drives, and analogue and digital systems. This capability

Exhibit 16.2   *Continued*

is backed by facilities for industrial and ergonomic design, and the resource is structured to combine flexibility with total project planning and control.

Examples: — precision instruments for defence use, such as navigation or weapon sighting
— image-quantity assessment gauge for the optical industry.

Optical Engineering

There is a demand in many industries for measurement systems that are more accurate, faster and automatic. SIRA undertakes the design, manufacture and quality assessment of the advanced electro-optical and optical systems now widely used in industrial, research, and military applications.

Examples: — electro-optical gauges for width and diameter measurement in industries such as plastics and steel
— manufacturing aids for the optical industry, e.g. for lens centring and mounting.

Quality Assurance

SIRA undertakes the design, manufacture, installation and commissioning of advanced instruments and systems for automatic inspection of strip and sheet materials (metals, paper, plastics, textiles, glass), for discrete components, for fibres (e.g. wires, glass filaments), and for printed materials. Application of these developments brings down industrial costs, overcomes scarcity of skilled labour, meets new quality control requirements, and improves productivity, and makes for a more consistent product.

Examples: — equipment for the detection of printing faults
— surface inspection systems for strip products such as steel, paper, textiles, plastics.

Process Measurement and Control

Measurement and control play a vital role in most industrial processes. SIRA has extensive experience in studies and applications of process control. Such applications can improve the efficiency of energy utilization, increase yield and throughout, raise productivity, and improve product quality.

Continuous chemical composition analysis confers these benefits in many industrial processes. SIRA is engaged in research on the properties of ion-selective electrodes and their application to industrial process materials and effluents, and in work on sampling systems for on-line analysers.

In industrial process control, an important variable to be measured is moisture content. SIRA has already developed and installed moisture measurement and control systems in such industries as ceramics, food, fertilizers, bricks,

Exhibit 16.2

Continued

pharmaceuticals and minerals. Existing measurement techniques (e.g. infrared, microwave) are used wherever possible, while new methods are developed when required.

Examples: — water quality control analysis
— moisture measurement in the pharmaceutical industry.

Instrument Evaluation

Impartial information on the performance of commercially available equipment is a prerequisite for making the right decision when a company is purchasing numerous instruments or instruments for control of critical processes. Performance evaluation can provide much of the independent, detailed information that the instrument user needs to match an instrument to his application. The same evaluation data can provide the instrument manufacturer with the means to improve the design of his equipment.

SIRA undertakes comprehensive assessment of the performance of all industrial instrumentation, irrespective of country of manufacture. The evaluations are carried out by experienced staff in well-equipped laboratories backed by extensive environmental testing and approved calibration facilities. Products evaluated include electronic components, and pneumatic process instrumentation, control components, chemical process analysers, non-destructive testing equipment and laboratory instruments.

Examples: cement industry, oil industry.

Commercial Services

SIRA has a high reputation for commercial/industrial consultancy in the instrumentation industry. The unique combination of technical, marketing and business expertise that SIRA can offer is employed by instrument manufacturers and users throughout the world. Services available include:

Business studies
Business studies are undertaken by professional staff for individual clients on a confidential basis. In-depth experience in business consultancy, and a wide knowledge of the factors affecting industry enable SIRA to put forward practical corporate plans to satisfy commercial objectives.

Information
The Siraid information services satisfies a large demand for information on commercially-available equipment (scientific and industrial) and answers some 7,000 enquiries a year. Besides being available to instrument users, Siraid passes some 15,000 sales opportunities each year to instrument manufacturers.

Exhibit 16.2 *Continued*

Consultancy
SIRA's consultancy service covers all aspects of instrumentation from industrial market research through to engineering design. Although many of the assignments are confidential, open sale reports (which have been recognized by the highest professional award) are prepared on subjects such as water pollution control, instrument markets, and safety instrumentation.

Technology transfer
This important function is effected via seminars, symposia and training courses for engineers and managers. Subjects cover many facets of SIRA's technical and commercial expertise. Events are held at venues from London to San Diego, Tokyo to Delft.

Some SIRA Clients

Admiralty Surface Weapons Establishment
Anglo-Australian Telescope Board
Beckman-RHC Ltd
Borax Consolidated Ltd
British Gas Corporation
British Petroleum Co. Ltd
British Steel Corporation
Burroughs Machine Tools Ltd
Central Electricity Generating Board
Creusot-Loire (France)
CSR Australia Ltd
Donnelly Minors Ltd (Eire)
Dynamit Nobel AG (W. Germany)
Eurotherm Ltd
Fisons Ltd
Fischer & Porter Ltd
GEC-Elliott Process Instruments Ltd
Greater London Council
GTE Sylvania (USA)
Gulde-Regelarmaturen BV (Netherlands)
Home Office Central Research Establishment
Honeywell Europe SA (Belgium)
Imperial Chemical Industries Ltd
Independent Television Companies, Association Ltd
Institut de Recherches de la Sidérurgie Française
Johnson Matthey & Co. Ltd
KDG Instruments Ltd
Kodak Ltd

Exhibit 16.2   *Continued*

Mars Ltd
MEL Equipment Co. Ltd
SA Metallurgie Hoboken-Overpelt (Belgium)
Ministry of Defence
Mullard Ltd
Wm Nash Ltd
National Research Development Corporation
Ottico Meccanica Italiana
NV Philips Gloeilampentabrieken (Netherlands)
Portals Ltd
Post Office
Premaberg (UK) Ltd
Rank Xerox Ltd
Redifon Flight Simulation Ltd
Redland Tiles Ltd
Royal Armament Research & Development Establishment
Saab-Scania (Nordarmatur Division) (Sweden)
Scienta SA (Belgium)
Shell Internationale Petroleum Maatschappij NV (Netherlands)
Shell Research Ltd
Smiths Industries Ltd
SNIA Viscosa (Italy)
Stahlwerke Bochum AG (W. Germany)
Standard Telephones & Cables Ltd
Stanford Research Institute (USA)
WF Stanley & Co. Ltd
UK Wiseman Ltd
Unilever Ltd
Verein Deutscher Eisenhüttenleute (W. Germany)
Vickers Ltd
WIB (Netherlands)
Wiggins Teape Ltd

Exhibit 16.2: SIRA Activities and Services

EURATOM

Set up with a view to co-operation in the development of atomic and sub-atomic processes — for 'peaceful' use. In the event each member country went its own way and continued with separate development of commercial projects. Controlled from Brussels, with centres in Varese (Italy), Northern Holland, Northern Belgium and Karlsruhe.

European Space Agency

Headquarters in Paris, technical set-up at Noordvik near Leiden.

Responsible for extra-terrestrial research. This involved the design and building, on a sub-contract basis, of research and communications satellites (but *not* launching vehicles and equipment).

Funded by levy on member countries and administered by the EEC.

CERN (Centre Européan de Recherche Nucléaire)

Very long term 'peaceful' nuclear research. Centrally funded, based in Geneva. The work is planned by CERN staff and is then implemented through sub-contracts for example particle accelerators, cryogenic chambers, together with the necessary computers, instrumentation and civil engineering work.

Microbiology Unit (at Heidelberg)

Recently established, modelled on CERN, said to be under-staffed.

Exhibit 16.3: Note on the main European Community
'supranational' research and development bodies

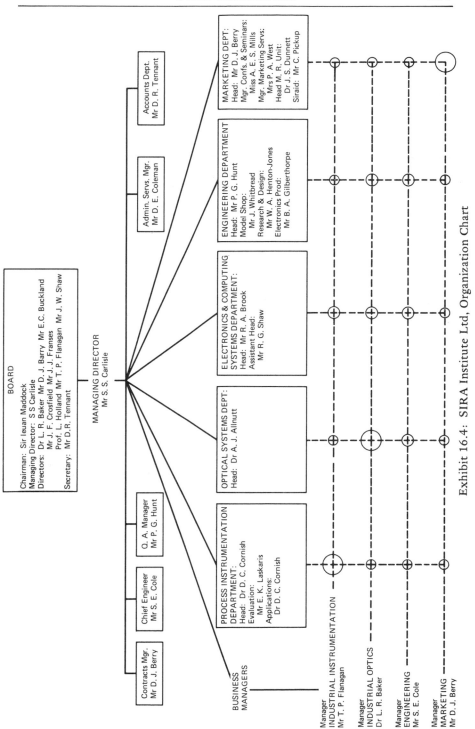

Exhibit 16.4: SIRA Institute Ltd, Organization Chart

BOARD
Chairman: Sir Ieuan Maddock
Managing Director: S S Carlisle
Directors: Dr L. R. Baker Mr D. J. Barry Mr E.C. Buckland
Mr J. F. Crosfield Mr J. J. Franses
Prof. L. Holland Mr T. P. Flanagan Mr J. W. Shaw
Secretary: Mr D. R. Tennant

MANAGING DIRECTOR
Mr S. S. Carlisle

Accounts Dept.
Mr D. R. Tennant

Admin. Servs. Mgr.
Mr D. E. Coleman

Contracts Mgr.
Mr D. J. Berry

Chief Engineer
Mr S. E. Cole

Q. A. Manager
Mr P. G. Hunt

MARKETING DEPT:
Head: Mr D. J. Berry
Mgr. Confs. & Seminars:
Miss A. E. S. Mills
Mgr. Marketing Servs:
Mrs P. A. West
Head M. R. Unit:
Dr J. S. Dunnett
Siraid: Mr C. Pickup

ENGINEERING DEPARTMENT
Head: Mr P. G. Hunt
Model Shop:
Mr J. Whitbread
Research & Design:
Mr W. A. Henton-Jones
Electronics Prod:
Mr B. A. Gilberthorpe

ELECTRONICS & COMPUTING
SYSTEMS DEPARTMENT:
Head: Mr R. A. Brook
Assistant Head:
Mr R. G. Shaw

OPTICAL SYSTEMS DEPT:
Head: Dr A. J. Allnutt

PROCESS INSTRUMENTATION
DEPARTMENT:
Head: Dr D. C. Cornish
Evaluation:
Mr E. K. Laskaris
Applications:
Dr D. C. Cornish

BUSINESS
MANAGERS

Manager
INDUSTRIAL INSTRUMENTATION
Mr T. P. Flanagan

Manager
INDUSTRIAL OPTICS
Dr L. R. Baker

Manager
ENGINEERING
Mr S. E. Cole

Manager
MARKETING
Mr D. J. Berry

XVII
ABM Chemicals Ltd
J. E. Lynch

ABM Chemicals Ltd, of Woodley near Stockport, is a medium-sized company engaged in the manufacture and marketing of a wide range of chemical products. The company operates seven factories throughout the UK and employs upwards of 600 people. Sales turnover in the 1978–9 financial year was just over £17 million. Since 1972, ABM Chemicals (and its original parent company Associated British Maltsters Ltd) have been wholly-owned subsidiaries of the multinational Dalgety Organization.

In July 1978, Fred Lidster, the Managing Director of ABM Chemicals (ABMC) decided to initiate a review of the company's marketing effectiveness with particular emphasis upon the export operation. The Dalgety Organization had recently purchased two other chemical concerns and was currently reorganizing all its chemical interests into a separate chemical division. Mr Lidster was anxious to ensure that ABM Chemicals did well in any inter-divisional comparisons. In this regard, he felt that export performance could be a key source of competitive advantage for ABMC. There had been significant changes in ABMC's export policy and organization in recent years and Mr Lidster wanted to obtain an objective assessment of the impact and effectiveness of these changes prior to finalising his plans for the 1980s.

This case was prepared by Dr James Lynch, University of Bradford, and was financed by the Foundation for Management Education.

Company History

ABM Chemicals Ltd had its origins as a subsidiary of Associated British Maltsters — the leading UK supplier of malt and related products to the brewing and distilling industries. Over time Associated British Maltsters had developed a small but increasing interest in the chemical industry. This diversification policy had brought about the acquisition of several small chemical producers which ABM amalgamated into a separate operating unit called ABM Industrial Products Ltd. ABM's chemical subsidiary was particularly skilled in the development of EDTA (Ethylene Diamine Tetracetic Acid) products for the detergent and cleansing markets.

As part of their continuing diversification into chemicals, Associated British Maltsters purchased, in 1972, Glovers (Chemicals) Ltd of Leeds. This was a small but profitable firm which specialized in chemical compounds called surfactants. Also purchased was a Glover Subsidiary — Chemicals Compounds of Darlington — whose expertise was in the provision of speciality organic chemicals. This collection of chemical interests inside ABM, including the new acquisitions, was given the title of ABM Chemicals Ltd.

The next major change came in November 1972, when Associated British Maltsters (and all its subsidiaries) were purchased by the Dalgety Organization. Dalgety is a broadly based international group of agricultural, food and associated businesses with a world-wide turnover approaching £800 million. In recent years Dalgety has pursued an active policy of diversification from its original base in wool-broking. The ABM purchase reflected this policy as did the subsequent purchase of two other chemical companies — Federated Chemical Holdings Ltd (a major international trader in fine and industrial chemicals) and Murphy Chemical Ltd (specialists in agrochemicals for the farm and garden). Dalgety has now re-organized its chemical interests into a separate Chemical Division, although the constituent companies, including ABM Chemicals, continue to trade independently.

The ABM Chemicals Product Range

The total range of products produced by ABM Chemicals is very extensive. The technologies of its constituent companies have been merged in such a way as to ensure that ABMC is a leading supplier of chemicals to an unusually wide range of industries. There are four major product groups which are the basis of the company's marketing effort:

General Chemicals (roughly 45% of turnover)
Food   (roughly 25% of turnover)
Surfactants   (roughly 15% of turnover)
Brewing   (roughly 15% of turnover).

A brief description of these product areas and their major applications is listed below.

General Chemicals

The General Chemicals Group encompasses a wide range of EDTA (Ethylene Diamine Tetracetic Acid) sequestering agents, inorganic and organic chemicals which have an equally wide range of applications.

Sequestrants are used to bind or complex metal ions in solution to prevent them from reacting adversely with other substances in the solution. Thus they have important applications in the cleaning of boilers and processing plant in dairies and breweries; in bottle washing; and in the manufacture of cosmetics and detergents. Additionally, metal salts of EDTA, chelates, are widely used in the agricultural industry.

The inorganic chemicals produced by ABM comprise metal acetates, sulphites and chlorides. The metal acetates are used for applications such as floor polish manufacture, crisp flavourings and the purification of Penicillin. Sodium and potassium sulphites are used in photographic processing. They are also used as preservatives for cooked meats, sausages, jams and marmalades. Ammonium chloride is supplied for use as an expectorant in cough mixture while potassium chloride is used in many pharmaceutical preparations.

Amongst the fine organic chemicals are a number of important pharmaceutical intermediates used in the manufacture of Penicillin and other anti-biotics. They are also used in sedatives, cough suppressants and skin creams. In addition, the fine organics section provides brighteners for the electroplating industries, fluxes for car radiator suppliers, latex coagulants to rubber manufacturers and hormone regulators to tomato growers.

Also within the General Chemicals heading is a range of photo-sensitive chemical products known as diazo compounds. These are

used in the production of light sensitive paper, microfilm and litho-
graphic plates.

Food

The products of the Food Group of ABM Chemicals consist of a
large number of enzyme preparations, malt products and syrups,
which serve numerous food industries. These include sugar processing, ice-cream manufacture and the milling and baking industries.

In addition to the enzyme preparations there is a range of malt
products, both extracts and flours. These products are used extensively in the food industries to add colour and flavour to a number
of foods including malt bread, white bread, breakfast cereal, confectionery, biscuits and 'night-cap' drinks.

Surfactants

Surfactants are compounds which lower the surface tension of a
liquid or the interfacial tension between two liquids. There are three
main types — Anionics (negatively charged), non-ionics (no charge)
and cationics (positively charged). ABMC manufacture all three
types together with a number of blended surfactants.

Anionic Surfactants. ABMC's range of anionic surfactants include
sulphates, phosphates and sulphosuccinates. They are efficient
wetting, foaming and dispersing agents and find application in a
large number of industries. Anionics are used in shampoo, cosmetic
and surgical scrub formulations. They are effective detergents for
textile scouring, metal cleaning and other cleansing operations. They
are also efficient dispersants for solid particles particularly in the
manufacture of paints, pigments and inks. Antistatic agents for
plastics and textiles and conductivity additives for electrostatic
spray paints are also applications for this type of surfactant.

Non-ionic surfactants are particularly suitable for the preparation
of ointments and creams for the pharmaceutical or cosmetic industries since they are non-toxic, and non-reactive. Their emulsifying
and wetting properties find use in many other industries including
the leather trade, metallurgy, and horticulture.

Cationic surfactants are used as adhesion aids for road making;
corrosion inhibitors; textile softeners and conditioners; additives
for electrostatic spray paints and as antistatic agents. Many of the
cationic surfactants have bactericidal properties and thus have important applications in the prevention of microbial spoilage and

contamination in animal husbandry, food processing, water treatment, pharmaceuticals and toiletries.

Blended Surfacants are used as emulsifiers for weedkillers, as dispersants for pigments in paint and as emulsifiers and dispersants for the pharmaceutical and cosmetic industries.

Brewing

A range of enzyme preparations is produced for the brewing industry. These assist in protein degradation, foam control, stability and sterilization during the brewing process.

Products for Export Markets

ABM Chemicals do not produce a separate range of export products. The product mix does, however, vary between home and export sales reflecting the differing needs of the two markets as shown in Table 17.1.

Table 17.1. Product Mix

% Annual Sales Turnover: Average Last 4 Years

	Home	*Export*
General Chemicals	47	41
Food	26	30
Surfactants	16	12
Brewing	11	17
	100	100

Further variations can be seen in the types of product areas which are exported to particular important markets:

Western Europe Products are supplied from across the whole range.
America Brewing Auxiliaries; Enzymes; Dyeline Chemicals; Pharmaceutical Intermediates; Surfactants.
Africa Sequestrants; Enzymes; Malt Extracts and Flours; Brewing Auxiliaries.
Australasia Sequestrants; Pharmaceutical Intermediates; Inorganic Chemicals; Brewing Auxiliaries; Enzymes; Malt Extracts.

Sales and Profit Performance

There have been major changes in recent years in the scale of the ABM Chemical operation both at home and abroad. A summary of key statistics is outlined in Table 17.2. (More comprehensive financial information — 5 year P/L Accounts and Balance Sheets — are shown in Exhibit 17.1. Comparative Dalgety parent company financial information is shown in Exhibit 17.2.)

Table 17.2. ABM Chemicals Ltd: Key Sales Statistics

Year	73—4	74—5	75—6	76—7	77—8	Est 78—9
Total Sales (£ million)	7.7	9.6	10.6	15.0	16.9	17.3
Export Sales (£ million)	1.5	3.5	4.1	6.4	6.2	6.3
(% Total Sales)	(19)	(36)	(39)	(43)	(37)	(36)
Pre-Tax Profit (£ million)	0.7	0.5	0.5	1.2	1.0	N/A

* Company Financial Year Ends 30th June

The ABM Chemicals Export Operation

Organization Structure

The various external organizational changes at ABM in recent years — the Glover take-over, the Dalgety development etc. — have been reflected in several changes in the internal organization. These can be seen as falling into four key phases:

1 'Pre-Glover' (ABM Industrial Products Ltd)

During this period, within an overall functionally divided organisation structure, the marketing set-up at ABM followed the traditional lines of a simple home/export split. There were separate Home and Export Sales Managers each reporting independently to the Marketing Manager, as shown in Figure 17.1.

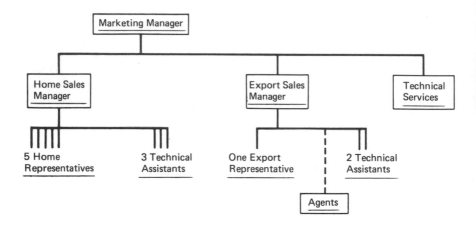

Figure 17.1

This simple structure worked adequately since the level of export involvement at ABM Industrial Products was small and sporadic, with only limited conflicts of interest between home and export priorities.   Additionally, the product range was clearly focussed round the company's EDTA expertise.   This meant the sales managers could handle the relevant technical aspects of their role relatively easily.   This structure was to prove unsuitable, however, when the organization expanded to include Glovers (Chemicals) Ltd and Chemical Compounds.   The increasing diversity and complexity of the product range led to problems which precipitated changes in the marketing organization structure.

2 'Post Glover' (ABM Chemicals Ltd) 1972–3

In essence the new structure was designed to inject a necessary measure of additional technical expertise relating to the new products now marketed by the company.   Three new product managers were appointed who reported directly to the Marketing Manager. Their brief was to maximize the profit contribution of their specific product group.   The new structure was therefore as shown in Figure 17.2.

In theory, the new set-up should have brought increased effectiveness to both the home and export marketing operations.   In practice, this did not work out.   The change in structure coincided with a period of massive domestic demand.   Raw materials generally were in short supply, prices obtainable were escalating and it was very much a seller's market in the UK. Thus the company's Home Sales team found they could sell the total available production at excellent prices. Export sales, which had never been a dominant force in the organization, predictably suffered. This external trend was compounded by the fact that the new product management team had all been recruited from a home sales background. Their natural inclination was to favour home sales requirements at the expense of export needs. Since market conditions meant that they could now meet their basic brief by concentrating on the domestic market, this is exactly what happened. Additionally, the new organization structure gave the product managers equal seniority with the sales managers, so the Export Sales Manager was placed in a most awkward position. He had to do the best he could for his markets against all the prevailing internal trends. Inevitably ABM Chemicals' export performance suffered. Important export orders could not be honoured, delivery dates were delayed, overseas agents became discouraged and the company's export reputation was tarnished.

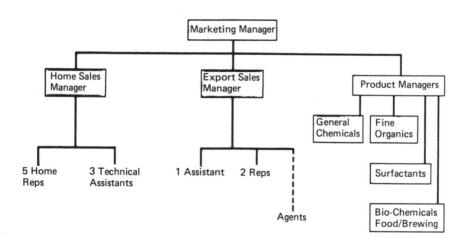

Figure 17.2

This was clearly a most unsatisfactory state of affairs, albeit an understandable outcome of prevailing circumstances. At this point, ABMC top management realized that positive remedial action must be taken. It was generally recognized that the favourable home market position was artifical and unlikely to last much longer.

Exports would inevitably, over time, be the key to future growth in volume and profits. It was particularly important, in the light of the Dalgety takeover, to demonstrate clearly ABM Chemical's operational effectiveness and future profit potential. It was therefore decided that the company must make a more positive commitment to export growth. Mr Lidster, the then Marketing Director, felt that such a commitment could only be made an operational reality by a revised marketing organization structure.

3 The New 'Export-Oriented' Structure (1973)

The major change the company decided upon was to abolish completely the traditional idea of a separate 'Home' and 'Export' operation. It was agreed that each product group, under a marketing manager, should be assigned responsibility for the profitable marketing of their products *worldwide*. The new structure was thus as shown in Figure 17.3.

Figure 17.3

4 Export Marketing Initiatives

The move to a new organization structure was accompanied by several other important export marketing initiatives. The most significant move was the development of a strategy of export market concentration. Priority markets were carefully selected for special marketing attention — in particular the European Common Market Countries and North America. America was a potentially vast market with no language barriers. The EEC too was a major market with the added advantage of being virtually 'on the doorstep' in travel terms. Additionally, most scientifically-trained Europeans (i.e. most ABMC customers) were able to speak and/or understand English.   Because of these positive factors it was decided that Western Europe should be considered as effectively a 'home' market area.   Traditionally, overseas travel plans had had to be individually cleared at board level.   It was now decided that once the yearly travel budget was agreed, the approval of specific individual EEC trips should be within the authority of the relevant Product Group Marketing Manager.   In the other major priority export markets such as Australasia and Africa, authority to travel was assigned to nominated senior executives although additional personnel could visit those markets if a special need arose.   The travel budget itself was substantially increased and the whole climate of managerial opinion inside the company became one of positive encouragement towards export market travel.   Many more export sales visits were made and a far wider range of personnel, including technical support staff, went out to export markets to meet agents and customers.

This new positive approach to exports was particularly marked in the liaison between ABM Chemicals and its agents.   The Company had agents in over fifty overseas countries.   A conscious effort was made to strengthen the links between ABMC and these agents.   More liaison visits were made and the level of technical back-up was increased.   Marketing support literature was sharply upgraded in quality and presentation as a result of increase in the relevant budget allocation.   Significantly more of the technical literature supplied to agents was in the appropriate foreign language.   More priority was given to training ABMC export marketing personnel in foreign language proficiency.   Agents meetings were held both in the UK and overseas to build morale and increase commitment.   The advertising budget was increased and more European and other foreign journals were used.   A determined effort was made to upgrade the service provided by the overseas Shipping Department and to give extra priority to the general area of customer liaison.   The company was determined to take every step necessary to become a major chemical exporter.

Export Sales Performance

The impact of the more positive commitment to exporting at ABMC was soon reflected in improved export sales as shown in Table 17.3.

Table 17.3. ABMC Export Sales (£ million)

	74–5	75–6	76–7	77–8
Western Europe	1.6	1.5	2.5	3.5
North America	0.6	0.9	1.8	1.7
Rest of World	1.3	1.7	2.1	1.0
Total	3.5	4.1	6.4	6.2

A Further Organizational Development

ABM Chemical's management felt that the new approach to export marketing and the new organization structure had been moves in the right direction. However, several internal personnel changes have necessitated further recent adjustments to the marketing structure.

Mr Lidster, the Marketing Director, has been promoted to the post of Managing Director. No new Marketing Director has been appointed but the Marketing Manager General Chemicals has been promoted to a new post of General Marketing Manager.

The Marketing Manager Surfactants has been promoted to the post of General Sales Manager. In this position he has line responsibility for both the Surfactants and General Chemicals Groups, along with certain other important responsibilities for Sales Representatives, Technical Services, and Advertising.

The post of Marketing Manager Organics has been eliminated, with responsibilities being shared out between the General Chemical and Surfactant Groups. The new (and current) marketing organization is thus as shown in Figure 17.4.

Next Steps

All these changes and developments were in Mr Lidster's mind as he reviewed ABMC's export performance. Clearly much progress had been made and the Company now had a far better export track record than had seemed likely only a few years before. The general progress in exports had been made despite world over-capacity in chemicals and the unpleasant pressures of inflation and a fluctuating pound.

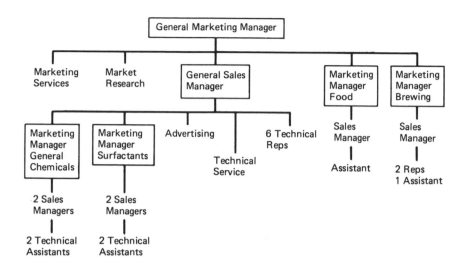

Figure 17.4

Nonetheless Mr Lidster felt the Company had no grounds for complacency. The last year (ending 30th June, 1979) had been specifically designated 'Export Year'. A whole range of special activities and incentives had been devised to hammer home this theme, e.g. staff competitions, regular export bulletins, special internal posters, Union Jack case stickers etc. However, latest information suggested that 1978—9 export sales would be only broadly in line with the level of the previous two years. While there were many mitigating factors (e.g. a major UK lorry drivers' strike and a rapidly strengthening pound which reduced price competitiveness) Mr Lidster wanted to be sure that all the lessons of the previous few years had been fully understood. He therefore asked his marketing team to provide answers to the following two key questions:

1 What is your assessment of the major strengths and weaknesses of the current export operation?
2 In the light of that answer, what changes, if any, should now be made to ABM Chemicals' Export Marketing operation to ensure maximum effectiveness?

PROFIT AND LOSS ACCOUNT — YEAR TO 30th JUNE					
1974	1975	1976	1977	VALUE IN £000's	1978
7699	9574	10550	14950	Total goods sold:	16920
6785	8887	9836	13487	From this we must deduct Materials, wages, admin., selling & distribution expenses amounting to:	15567
914	687	714	1463	This left a trading profit before provision for wear and tear	1353
203	237	255	288	Deduct wear and tear provision (Depreciation)	392
711	450	459	1175	Leaving a profit before taxation of:	961
401	(178)	532	69	Our Corporation Tax amounted to:	385
310	628	(73)	1106	Leaving us with a profit after tax of:	576
BALANCE SHEET **What we owned (assets) and what we owed (liabilities) on 30th June**					
1974	1975	1976	1977	VALUE IN £000's	1978
ASSETS					
576	595	1434	1465	Land and Buildings at valuation	1618
1320	1403	1396	1667	Plant, machinery and equipment at cost less depreciation:	2121
1896	1998	2830	3132		3739
1200	1575	1927	2309	Stocks and Work in Progress:	3042
(59)	(80)	(85)	334	Amounts owed by/(to) other Group Companies:	(570)
2176	1873	2239	3116	Amounts owed by customers	2862
3	3	3	3	Cash	4
5216	5369	6914	8894	TOTAL ASSETS	9077
LIABILITIES					
243	524	470	827	Short Term borrowings	941
884	707	1500	557	Owed to Government in Tax	975
1618	1559	2397	2773	Owed to Suppliers:	2607
2745	2790	4367	4157	Total Liabilities:	4523
2471	2579	2547	4737	Book value of capital employed:	4554

Exhibit 17.1: ABM Chemicals Ltd

£ Million

Analysis of Results for 1978 by Activity Within each Area	Australia	New Zealand	UK	USA	Canada	Total	1977 Total
Turnover	139	105	383	86	74	787	725
Profits							
Agriculture	(0.5)	2.7	4.2	0.3	—	6.7	7.8
Chemicals	—	0.1	1.7	—	—	1.8	1.2
Food Processing and Distribution	(0.6)	1.4	0.7	1.9	—	3.4	(0.7)
Lumber	—	—	—	—	7.4	7.4	4.4
Malting	—	—	4.0	—	—	4.0	2.2
Other	0.5	0.7	0.2	0.4	0.8	2.6	3.4
	(0.6)	4.9	10.8	2.6	8.2	25.9	
1977	(0.2)	6.9	8.2	(1.4)	4.8		18.3
Central Income and Expenses						0.1	(0.2)
Interest on Euro Currency Loans						(1.6)	(1.0)
						24.4	17.1

Analysis of Turnover by Activity	1978	1977
Agriculture	299	283
Chemicals	40	15
Food Processing and Distribution	147	114
Lumber	34	24
Malting	41	43
Other	226	246
	787	725

Group Profit and Loss Account for the Year Ended 30th June 1978	Australia	New Zealand	UK	USA	Canada	Group Head Office	Total
Group Profit before Interest	5.1	7.1	12.3	3.5	8.3	0.6	36.9
Interest on Short-term Borrowings	(4.0)	(1.0)	(1.3)	(0.8)	(0.1)	(0.1)	(7.3)
Interest on Long-term Borrowings	(1.7)	(1.2)	(0.2)	(0.1)	—	(2.0)	(5.2)
Group Profit before Tax	(0.6)	4.9	10.8	2.6	8.2	(1.5)	24.4
Taxation	(0.9)	(1.6)	(2.3)	(0.1)	(4.0)	(0.4)	(9.3)
Effective Tax Rate	—	33%	21%	4%	49%	—	38%
Group Profit after Tax	(1.5)	3.3	8.5	2.5	4.2	(1.9)	15.1
Minority Interests	(0.2)	(1.3)	—	—	—	—	(1.5)
	(1.7)	2.0	8.5	2.5	4.2	(1.9)	13.6
Extraordinary Items	(1.8)	0.2	(0.3)	(0.1)	(0.1)	1.0	(1.1)
Group Profits available for Distribution	(3.5)	2.2	8.2	2.4	4.1	(0.9)	12.5
Contribution to Earnings per Share	(4.9)	5.7	24.4	7.2	12.1	(6.0)	38.5

Exhibit 17.2: Analyses of Results and Balance Sheet (Dalgety Ltd) *Continued*

£ Million

Group Balance Sheet at 30th June 1978	Australia	New Zealand	UK	USA	Canada	Group Head Office	Total
Group Funds	37.9	25.1	66.4	19.1	14.7	(2.0)*	161.2
Minority Shareholders' Interests	0.4	17.8	0.1	—	—	0.2	18.5
Local Loan Capital	18.6	16.4	19.9	1.1	0.6	9.0	65.6
Deferred Taxation	0.5	0.8	4.4	—	—	(2.6)	3.1
Capital Employed	57.4	60.1	90.8	20.2	15.3	4.6	248.4
Bank Balances and Deposits	2.4	3.3	0.7	0.9	—	14.7	22.0
Debtors	35.3	32.9	39.9	13.0	7.9	3.2	132.2
Inventories	33.1	31.3	47.0	18.9	7.7	0.4	138.4
Current Assets	70.8	67.5	87.6	32.8	15.6	18.3	292.6
Short-term Borrowing	32.2	15.8	22.7	10.6	0.5	3.4	85.2
Creditors	20.5	21.3	35.1	12.2	9.1	3.7	101.9
Taxation	0.5	0.3	1.1	0.1	2.6	2.0	6.6
Dividends Proposed and Declared	—	—	—	—	—	5.0	5.0
Current Liabilities	53.2	37.4	58.9	22.9	12.2	14.1	198.7
Net Current Assets	17.6	30.1	28.7	9.9	3.4	4.2	93.9
Associated Companies and Investments	15.4	3.7	2.1	1.2	—	0.3	22.7
Fixed Assets	22.2	26.1	59.5	8.4	11.2	0.1	127.5
Goodwill	2.2	0.2	0.5	0.7	0.7	—	4.3
Net Assets	57.4	60.1	90.8	20.2	15.3	4.6	248.4

* This represents investment in overseas subsidiaries financed by the Parent Company's loan capital.

Exhibit 17.2: Analyses of Results and Balance Sheet (Dalgety Ltd)

XVIII
Anderson International: Lenta Toothpaste

G. K. Randall

In March 1979 Brian Hargreaves, the Corporate Marketing Director, Personal Products, of Anderson International Ltd headquarters in London, England, was chairing a meeting to discuss pricing of Lenta Toothpaste; present were the Marketing Directors of the UK and German companies Anderson Company Ltd and Anderson GmbH, and their Product Group Managers (Toothpaste). An organization chart is shown in Exhibit 18.1.

After discussion had continued for an hour without any obvious conclusion, Hargreaves called for summaries. Gunter Schmidt, Marketing Director in Germany, began:

'The UK price of Lenta to the trade *must* be increased on 1st April when we put our price up. We have proved that when there is a price difference of more than DM 0.32 per pack between UK and Germany, the UK product is imported into Germany and undercuts our own. This parallel trade not only harms our sales but has a serious impact on our relationship with the retailers. Banded packs make it even worse, and should be kept right out of Germany.' (A banded pack is one in which two or more units of the brand are banded together by the manufacturer and sold at a discounted price, for example 'Two for the price of one'.)

Carol Jones, Product Group Manager (Toothpaste) in the UK, replied:

'The German proposal means that instead of our planned retail

Prepared by G. K. Randall, Thames Polytechnic 1981. Information on the company and on competitive brands have been disguised.

selling price of 32p, we would be selling at 36p. Even at 32p we
are above the main competition at 30p; the market average will
also be around 30p. At the higher price we would be bound to
lose share, and I reckon our profit shortfall for the year would
be up to half a million pounds. We are selling banded packs only
to major multiples, and we've got to preserve freedom of action
in the market place.'

Background

Anderson International is fifty years old in its present form but its
component parts have a longer history. William Anderson started
working in his father's retail chemist's shop in the North of England
in the last decade of the 19th Century. William expanded the
business into a chain of shops, and began to look for ways of increasing sales and profits still further. Branding — the production and
distribution of a product under a single brand name rather than
individual retailers' names — was in its infancy, but William was
quick to see its potential. He developed a way of manufacturing
toothpaste of consistent quality in large volumes, and named it
Lenta (later to become known all over the world, this was in fact
William's private pet name for his wife).

Lenta was sold to other retail chemists as well as in Anderson's
own shops. Sales grew rapidly, helped by Anderson's adoption of
mass advertising of the brand name in a pattern later recognized as
the classic development of a pull strategy (advertising to consumers
creates demand for a national brand, and this demand 'pulls' the
product through the distribution channels).

The success of Lenta led to the development of other brands;
the retail side continued to expand, but was soon dwarfed by the
manufacturing and sales of branded goods. William, and his sons
and nephews who followed him in the business, took Anderson's
into the many countries of what was then the British Empire, both
to establish secure supplies of raw materials and to open new
markets. The company also grew at home by acquisition of competitive and complementary businesses, particularly after Anderson's
went public because of problems caused by death duties. A decisive
step came in the early 1930s when firms in France and Germany
were acquired, and the name Anderson International adopted.

By 1980 Anderson International was a British-based multi-national
of more than 200 companies operating in almost every country in

the free world, with manufacturing facilities in over 60.   Because of the way it grew, it contained a great diversity of products and services, though over half of its business was in consumer products; retailing accounted for less than 10%, and other products or services included shipping, chemicals, pharmaceuticals, travel agencies and insurance.

Research and development has always been a major concern, both with the established businesses and in new areas.   Around 10% of the total R & D budget is allocated to 'blue-sky' projects; the group is currently examining applications of micro-electronics, particularly in distribution and retailing.

Organization

Although the growth has sometimes appeared haphazard, Anderson's has periodically re-shaped its structure and grouped businesses together.   Its basic organizational philosophy is claimed to be decentralization, expressed by one director in these terms:

> 'The managers of the local operating companies are the ones closest to the market place, they know best what their consumers want, so as far as possible they must make the decisions. This will also help to encourage initiative and maintain an entrepreneurial drive which can easily be smothered in a large corporation.'

On the other hand, the Group's top management had long recognized that unfettered autonomy could lead to anarchy.   In searching for economies of scale and for control, they tried to take a global view of sourcing and, increasingly, of branding and distribution. There was therefore a system of regional management, and of divisional control.   For each Division, which contained a set of cognate products and/or services, there was a Corporate Director with a seat on the main board.   He acted as general manager of the Division (though not so titled) and had a staff of functional directors including a Corporate Marketing Director.   This corporate group was responsible for the overall strategy of the Division.   The Board had deliberately not codified the exact limits of the authority for specific decisions of local operating managers as against the corporate group, preferring, as one senior manager put it, 'To rely on the good sense and feelings of group solidarity of our managers to sort out any conflicts'.

Lenta Toothpaste

Lenta toothpaste is a major world brand with a long history. It is sold in over fifty countries around the world, with heavy advertising support in many of them. In Western Europe the market is highly competitive, with the major multi-nationals dominating but with local manufacturers active in most countries.

The two major benefits of toothpaste are protection against decay and a cosmetic/beauty effect; the latter may be further sub-divided into breath freshness and whiteness/brightness of teeth. Lenta is positioned in most markets in the cosmetic-whiteness segment.

Pricing is felt to be a key element in the mix by most marketing people in the business. Relative prices paid by consumers are shown in Exhibit 18.2. Lenta, Span and Dentrif are all Anderson brands; Protect and Dazzle are from the major multi-national competitors.

Sales and brand shares for UK and Germany are shown in Exhibits 18.3 and 18.4.

Lenta in Germany

Lenta is one of the major brands in the Anderson GmbH portfolio, contributing 15% of its operating profit in fiscal 1979. Manufactured locally, its production costs are high, relative to the UK, because of higher labour costs and lower actual volume. It was the sharp increases foreseen in both raw material and labour costs that had forced the proposed price increase in April 1979.

As Hans Mueller, Product Group Manager (Toothpaste) explained:

'The Managing Director is insisting on the price increase, but I am worried, for several reasons.

First, the market is price-sensitive. In the past we have acted as price leader, and the other brands have always followed our lead. Now, they might hang on at a lower price for a while to gain share. Second, Grossmans (a major US-based multinational) are launching Dazzle; if we give them some leeway in pricing, we might allow them to establish the brand there. Thirdly, one of the major multiples has baulked at the posted price increase and has said it simply won't carry Lenta any more; as they took 15% of volume last year this is a serious blow.

All these are local market problems and we will have to live with them; after all our competitors have similar cost structures to ours. What really worries me is the parallel trade risk: I'll try to explain why.

'We know that UK manufacturing costs are lower than ours, and we can't do much about that in the short term. We reckon that if the difference between best prices to the trade in UK and Germany is more than DM 0.32 per pack, imports into Germany increase (for relative prices see Exhibits 18.5 and 18.6). We keep our ear to the ground and pick up most instances of importing, and in October/November, when the price difference had increased to DM 0.42, we got to know of ten instances in which importers were selling to the trade at around DM 1.00 against our price of DM 1.13. The point is that if *some* retailers are promoting imported Lenta at very low prices, all the others will stop promoting it at *our* price.

There is a further problem caused by banded packs. I know Carol Jones (Product Group Manager, Toothpastes, Anderson UK) has claimed that UK banded packs can't possibly get into Germany, but we know that they do. Some are on sale now, either still banded or cut and sold separately, at prices between DM 0.98 and DM 1.38 per tube. This compares with a major multiple selling at DM 1.50 and a department store at DM 1.96.

Taking all this together, Lenta's brand position and profitability could be ruined.'

As a result of his analysis, Mueller asked the Corporate Marketing Director to take action to bring UK and German prices closer together. As the German company had already told its sales force about its planned increase, the trade were being informed. Mueller was worried that some retailers would immediately turn to importers and seek long-term contracts for UK supplies: he therefore asked that the UK price be increased by at least DM 0.12 per tube as quickly as possible, but at any rate by February 1980. He also requested that Anderson UK be dissuaded from offering banded packs, arguing that it was a relatively unimportant activity for the UK company but potentially very damaging to the German.

Lenta in UK

Although formerly a brand leader, and still a major brand, Lenta is the second string in Anderson's UK stable — Span, positioned slightly more in the breath freshness/hygiene segment, took overall brand leadership in 1976.   Nevertheless, the strategy is still to promote Lenta strongly and maintain its share.

Carol Jones, commenting earlier on the German proposal, had said.   'We are operating in a price-sensitive market, and we can't just jump up as they seem to expect.   We know from experience that our share depends heavily on our price relative to the rest of the market.   Selling at 36p would give us a price index of 122%, which would be bound to drive our share well below 5%: in July 1978 we had an index of 115% and only achieved a 4.8% share.

'I did some calculations on the sort of price differential we would have to live with, and it would mean at least 3% drop in market share against plan.   Volume is the key to profit in this business, and our loss of tonnage would take over £400,000 off our target profit contribution for the year.   To move our price as fast as Germany wants would be commercially disastrous.

'Naturally we are sympathetic to their parallel trade problems, and have tried to help.   We set up a system of controls so that in the areas likely to export (London & Midlands) wholesalers could buy only a limited amount per promotion.   For most other brands, wholesalers account for about 28% of total volume; for Lenta since the controls, the figure is only 23%, and in the areas I mentioned the fall has been dramatic.

As to banded packs these are not offered to wholesalers any more, and we just don't see how they could be getting through to Germany.'

Dennis Butler, Marketing Director, added that the plan for Lenta was not haphazard, but used a carefully planned, consistent mix targeted to the known market.   'We have evaluated non-money-off promotions for Lenta', he pointed out, 'but frankly the likelihood of their playing a significant part in a viable marketing mix for the brand is slim'.

Mr Butler confirmed his belief that the export controls were working, and expressed the view that the supplies of Lenta reaching Germany were not just from the UK, but also and perhaps mainly from France and Holland; there were even rumours that some US packs had been seen!

Parallel Trade

Parallel trade is a phenomenon which occurs when a brand is sold in several countries: if the price at which the manufacturer sells differs between countries, entrepreneurial agents import from a low-cost to a high-cost country, and under-cut the domestic product. Differences in costs to the manufacturer (raw materials, labour, indirects), in efficiency, and in strategy may all account for differences in selling price. Variations in exchange rates will also affect relative price.

A manufacturer may want to control parallel trade in his brands, either because he wishes to pursue different pricing strategies in different markets or because his costs cannot be brought into line in the short term. There are a number of considerations which affect such control.

EEC Actions

The Competition Directorate of the European Economic Community ('Common Market') has been particularly energetic in trying to prevent any activities which reduce free competition within the Community. In this context, parallel trade is seen to increase competition and therefore to be of potential benefit to consumers by lowering prices. Any actions by companies to limit parallel trade are therefore liable to be regarded with suspicion and may be subject to intervention: for example, the system of exclusive distributorships of Scotch whisky in other EEC countries prevented parallel trade, was deemed to keep prices artifically high, and was therefore declared illegal. Similarly, Trade Mark rights are not allowed to prevent parallel trade within the EEC. Use of different brand names in different countries would clearly limit parallel trade; the decision of the European Court in such a case is summarized in Appendix 18.1.

Promotions

There is considerable variation in what is permitted by law in the field of promotions. For instance, promotions requiring proof-of-purchase are quite legal in the UK but are banned in Germany. The effect of this may be that if such a promotion were prominent on a label or pack, then imports would have to be re-packaged or re-labelled.

In many promotions, the offer is limited to the home country, and would therefore be of no value if the product were exported.

Language

Legislation varies from country to country about what, if anything, must be in the local language. In France, for example, all text must be in French; in others, certain things such as warnings or ingredients must be in the local language. The greater such demands, then clearly the greater is the expense of re-labelling.

For some products, such as calculators or washing machines, all instructions and advice must be translated; this may also apply to consumable products where instructions are important. If a third party re-labels and translates literally, this would often be construed as breach of copyright and could therefore be prevented. However, a literal translation may not be necessary.

Product Formulation

Many countries now have legislation which bears directly on what products may contain. Such legislation, which is usually concerned with health and safety or pollution prevention, may prohibit certain ingredients. In extreme cases a positive list may be issued, i.e. a list detailing exactly those ingredients that may be used in a given product. Where legislation differs between countries it may form a barrier to parallel trade.

In some countries there are detailed regulations about the registration of product formulation. Where the requirements are so rigorous that only the manufacturer can meet them, parallel trade will be limited.

Other Legislation

Many countries now have legislation designed to protect consumers in various ways. Since there is considerable variation in what is prohibited this may limit parallel trade in particular products: for example, a UK washing-up liquid whose pack showed a lemon would be illegal in Germany.

Weight labelling regulations exist in most countries, and may be important if, for example, unit price must be shown. In these and other areas, detailed examination of the laws and regulations of the countries concerned will be necessary.

Production Planning and Rationing

If parallel trade is completely unrestricted, then a low-cost manufacturing country will be liable to demand for exports. When the company makes a low-price offer to the trade in its own country, that could lead to a huge increase in export demand, which production simply cannot meet. If rationing is then imposed, it must be done in a way which is clearly non-discriminatory.

Trends in Distribution Channels

Changes in the retailing of most fast-moving consumer goods have been sweeping since the 1960s. The self-service revolution in food retailing started in the USA, and spread to Europe; initially Great Britain led the European field, but in the 1970s was caught up and overtaken by other countries, notably France and Germany.

The effect of the change to self-service was to give a great impetus to the growth of multiples. The accent on low prices and low overheads led to bulk buying and still lower prices relative to small independent counter-service stores. This trend led to multiples gaining an ever-increasing share of the grocery market — by 1977 they had more than 50% of the UK market.

In maintaining their hectic growth rate, supermarket chains developed larger and larger stores, and increased the range of goods stocked, both to fill the increasing space and to compensate for the flat market experienced in pure food lines. Products like toothpaste, which had formerly been sold in specialist outlets such as chemists and pharmacies, began to be stocked by supermarkets, whose great buying power and superior efficiency allowed them to offer lower prices for identical products. Now the bulk of sales of toiletries is through supermarkets.

A major effect of the growth of multiples has been a change in the balance of power as between manufacturer and retailer. Previously the large manufacturers were dominant: led by the multinationals, they were huge relative to the independent store or small chain; they were sophisticated in marketing and management; and they were spending heavily on advertising to create consumer demand which would 'pull' brands through the distribution channels.

The position by 1980 was very different. The sheer size of the major chains in each country allowed them to talk to manufacturers as at least equal partners, and increasingly in some markets as reluctant and demanding ones. In particular, a multiple could now buy and offer his own private-label brands in competition with branded products, a development which in itself caused considerable bitterness amongst some manufacturers, who saw them as parasites on their expensively-nurtured markets.

The increasing pressure on shelf space from new products and brands has also given added leverage to multiples' bargaining power. In many product fields a chain will stock only the brand leader, its own label, and one or two others. Although a heavy advertising campaign is still seen as valuable support for a brand, multiples have increasingly been interested only in price, and negotiations centre round discounts, bonus rates and advertising allowances to the retailer.

By 1980 the growth of multiples was slowing down, and they began increasingly to compete against each other for further growth rather than merely taking share from other types of outlet. The latter had themselves fought back by organizing voluntary chains to increase their buying power.

As good levels of distribution are crucial to brands' success, manufacturers have become increasingly aware of the necessity of good relationships with the trade, and will go to some lengths to protect those relationships.

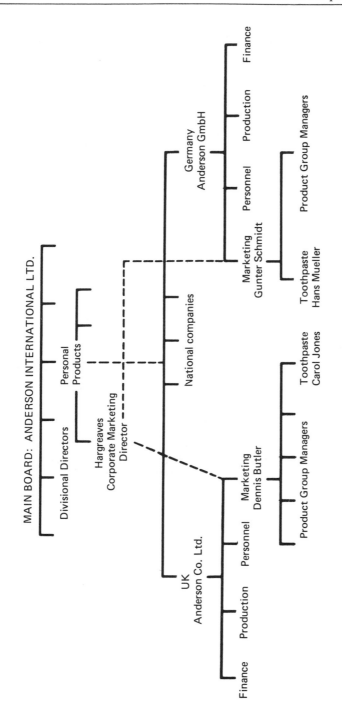

Exhibit 18.1: Organization Chart

Average prices paid (p) *50 ml size 4 weeks* *ending:*		*Lenta*	*Span*	*Dentrif*	*Protect*	*Dazzle*
1978	7 Jan.	31.8	30.8	31.6	28.6	32.0
	4 Feb.	32.6	31.4	31.0	28.8	31.6
	4 Mar.	33.0	31.2	31.0	30.8	31.2
	1 Apr.	33.6	31.0	31.4	30.0	31.8
	29 Apr.	33.2	30.6	31.6	30.6	32.4
	27 May	31.8	31.0	32.0	30.8	31.8
	24 June	33.4	31.2	33.0	30.0	30.8
	22 July	32.8	31.0	33.0	30.8	31.2
	19 Aug.	32.4	29.8	31.8	29.8	32.0
	16 Sept.	32.8	28.6	32.2	30.0	32.0
	14 Oct.	31.6	27.8	30.4	28.8	32.2
	11 Nov.	30.4	27.4	29.6	28.0	31.6
	9 Dec.	28.8	27.4	29.0	27.6	30.8
1979	6 Jan.	29.8	27.2	29.4	27.4	31.4
	3 Feb.	29.2	27.2	29.6	26.8	30.4

Source: Anderson UK

Exhibit 18.2: Anderson International Ltd: Lenta Toothpaste
(Prices paid by consumers 1978–9 UK)

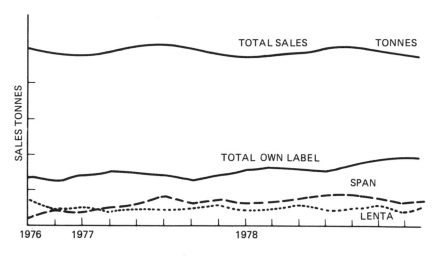

Exhibit 18.3: SALES : UK 1976—8. June 1976 = 100

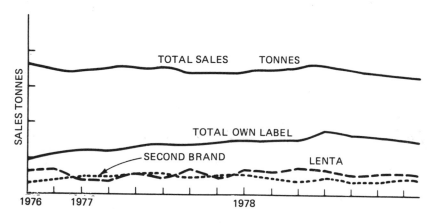

Exhibit 18.4: SALES : GERMANY 1976—8. Scale: same as UK

Year	1976				1977						1978					
Month	6/7	8/9	10/11	12/1	2/3	4/5	6	7/8	9/10	11/12	1/2	3/4	5/6	7/8	9	10
50 ml pack: in UK (p) (1)	17.7	19.5	17.6	19.3	18.6	19.8	23.9	26.4	24.6	26.4	25.7	23.9	23.9	22.7	23.2	23.2
exchange rate (2)	4.57	4.41	3.97	4.05	4.11	4.08	4.05	3.98	4.05	4.05	4.03	3.82	3.84	3.84	3.86	3.68
in Germany (DM)	0.81	0.86	0.70	0.78	0.76	0.81	0.97	1.05	1.00	1.07	1.04	0.91	0.92	0.87	0.90	0.85
50 ml pack: in Germany (DM)	1.32	1.32	1.22	1.22	1.22	1.22	1.22	1.22	1.22	1.22	1.22	1.22	1.22	1.22	1.22	1.22
Price difference UK – Germany	0.51	0.46	0.52	0.44	0.46	0.41	0.25	0.17	0.22	0.15	0.18	0.31	0.30	0.35	0.32	0.37
Market share for UK – Lenta in Germany (%) (3)	1.8	1.7	3.4	4.1	2.3	2.2	1.1	1.9	0.5	0.4	0.2	0.2	0.3	0.5	0.1	0.6

Source: Anderson GmbH

Notes: (1) These represent the German company's best estimate of best prices to the UK trade.
(2) Average exchange rate for the period.
(3) Based on syndicated panel data; one major chain excluded because it has long-term buying contracts.

Exhibit 18.5: Anderson International Ltd: Lenta Toothpaste. *Critical Price Difference*

Year	1978		1979					
Month	11	12	1	2	3	4	5	6
50 ml pack:								
in UK (p)	22.7	22.7	22.7	22.7	24.1	24.1	24.1	24.1
exchange rate	3.71	3.74	(3.74)	(3.74)	(3.74)	(3.74)	(3.74)	(3.74)
in Germany (DM)	0.84	0.85	0.85	0.85	0.90	0.90	0.90	0.90
50 ml pack:								
in Germany (DM)	1.23	1.23	1.23	1.23	1.23	1.33	1.33	1.33
Price difference UK – Germany (DM)	0.39	0.38	0.38	0.38	0.33	0.43	0.43	0.43

Source: Anderson GmbH

Notes: (1) These represent the German company's best estimate of best prices to the UK trade.
(2) Average exchange rate for the period.
(3) Based on syndicated panel data; one major chain excluded because it has long-term buying contracts.
(4) 1979 exchange rate = estimates (figures in brackets).

Exhibit 18.6: Anderson International Ltd: Lenta Toothpaste. *Price Difference: Future Estimates*

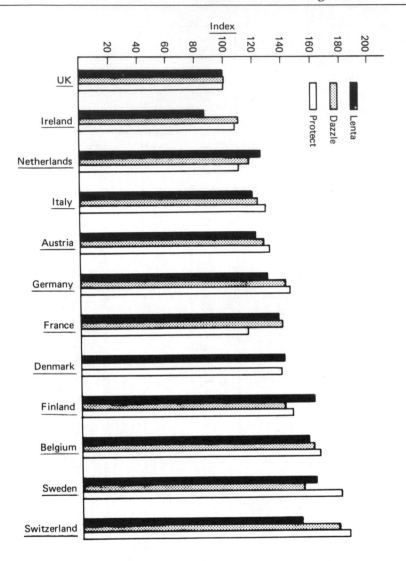

Exhibit 18.7: Anderson International: Lenta Toothpaste
Competitive Price Comparisons

Appendix 18.1
Centrafarm B.V. Rotterdam

American Home Products Corporation, N. York (AHP)

AHP uses different trade marks for the same medical preparation in the UK and Holland, since the trade mark used in the UK was not available for use in Holland (UK trade mark SERENID, trade mark in Holland SERESTA).

Centrafarm imported SERENID from the UK to Holland and put the trade mark SERESTA on the UK pack together with the words 'Centrafarm B.V., Rotterdam, Telephone 010–151411'.

AHP attacked Centrafarm on the basis of infringement of its Dutch SERESTA trade mark, as Centrafarm had used this mark without consent from AHP.

The European Court decided that the action by AHP was justified in principle unless it could be shown that AHP had used the system of applying different trade marks in different Member States to the same product for the purpose of artificially dividing the Common Market, thus making it unattractive for traders to sell the products under the same trade mark from one EEC country in the other. It was left to the National Court to decide whether or not a system of deliberately dividing the Common Market was sought by the Trade Mark owner.

It is still uncertain who will have the onus of proof but in future, it will not be possible to prevent importers from tampering with trade marks on products for the purpose of facilitating their importations in other EEC countries unless it can be shown why different trade marks are used for the same product in different EEC countries. It will be important to be able to prove that there were very good reasons to select a different mark and that it was not done merely to divide the Common Market for commercial purposes.

XIX
The Hygeia Company

J. J. Ward

In August 1977, Mr Charles Roberts, director of Hyag Chemicals Ltd, met Mr John Moore and Mr Brian Hanley, the Managing Director and General Manager respectively of Hygeia Ltd, to review developments in the UK market for a range of agricultural chemical products and to plan for the future development of that market. The previous two years had seen the company's sales to the UK achieve rapid growth. One product, Hyquat, now had a significant share in the growing UK market in the face of competition from the world's largest agrochemical groups. This fact in particular posed certain dangers for the future of Hygeia in the UK. Success had been achieved without much publicity or heavy promotional expenditure. It resulted from the discovery of a niche in the market to which the larger companies had not reacted as quickly as Hygeia. However, Hygeia management felt that competitors were unlikely to neglect this market segment in the coming years.

The Development of Hygeia and Associated Companies

Hygeia Ltd was founded in 1939 and was located in Galway, Ireland. The company initially formulated sheep dips and disinfectants, and with the advent of the war years, formulated and manufactured a number of chemicals which otherwise would not have been available

Prepared by Dr James J. Ward, University College, Galway, Ireland. © Dr James Ward and IMEDE (Institut pour l'Etude des Méthodes de Direction de l'Entreprise), Lausanne, Switzerland, 1980.

to the farming community in Ireland. The most important of these products were Mercurial Seed Dressings, and the Insecticide DDT. Hygeia Limited was the first company outside of Switzerland to manufacture this insecticide, which was a very important breakthrough for the company and its customers. About mid-1950 the company manufactured MCPA and 24D, the first selective herbicides. About that time also Hygeia Ltd introduced anti-coagulant rat baits to the Irish market. The company continued to expand its line of sheep dips, insecticides, fungicides, seed dressings and rodenticides. In 1962, Hygeia Ltd was appointed agent for Bayer of Germany.

About 1966, Maxan Ltd, a subsidiary of Hygeia Ltd, commissioned a new plant near Galway City to produce agrochemical powders for export. Export sales were achieved in many countries, including the UK, Germany, Canada, Sudan and Australia. A new company, Agrichem Limited, was formed in 1974, to continue development in the export field, particularly in the UK.

The formation of another new company, Hyag, followed, with the objective of faster UK market development. Managing Director John Moore felt that further progress in the UK depended upon active involvement in distribution to the end user. Consequently Hygeia branded products to the UK and developed a family brand concept with the aid of its advertising agency.

Hyag Chemicals, a company jointly formed by Hygeia and the UK firm of Roberts and Hewett, had in the previous two years become the main marketing arm in the UK for Hygeia. Prior to the formation of Hyag, the marketing of Hygeia products had been handled by Agrichem Ltd which was then Hygeia's export company (see Exhibit 19.1). Agrichem was an Irish registered company and this led to certain problems when its tax free concessions from the Irish government expired. To overcome these, Hyag had been registered in the UK. The marketing system used in the UK by Hygeia and its associated companies bore little resemblance to that used for the same products in Ireland. In 1976, approximately 30% of the company's sales were to export markets.

Marketing of Hygeia Products in Ireland

Hygeia products (see Exhibit 19.2) were sold under both the company's own brand and to other companies for private branding in the domestic Irish market. Overall the company had up to 60% of the market in the main product categories, 25—30% of this being with Hygeia brands. Further expansion it was felt, would take customers from companies already being supplied with products for private branding.

Distribution of Hygeia brands in Ireland was direct to retailers as there were no wholesalers in this sector. In effect this meant supplying 1,500 different retailers on whom a company representative called every 8—10 weeks to take orders. Delivery by the company's own delivery fleet accounted for 80% of the total. Hygeia had little control over retailers except for weedkiller products. There was no recommended retail price and no merchandising of products by the company. For weedkillers, Hygeia appointed agents in the domestic market. Once agents were selected, they were given the franchise for an area of which there were over twenty in the Republic. The company also provided promotional back-up for these agents.

Promotion of Hygeia Products

The promotion budget increased five-fold in the period 1975—7 from £5,000 to £25,000 per year. This expenditure was allocated mostly to advertising and public relations with a very limited amount going to point-of-sale material. An advertising agency and a PR firm were used by the company to assist on promotion.

The company generally followed a policy of using institutional advertising (see Exhibits 19.3 — 19.5). It was considered important to promote the name of Hygeia but the company also used brand advertising when promoting its own labels. A limited amount of promotion in the form of bonuses to customers was also undertaken.

Hygeia Product Development Strategy

With many years' experience in the formulation of chemicals, Hygeia had built up a large internal body of knowledge and expertise in the field. It had thus been in a position to develop formulations itself in addition to manufacturing under licence from other companies. Hygeia sourced raw materials from a world-wide market that included Eastern Europe, Italy, Germany, Israel, Japan. In the development of new products for its various lines Hygeia used two approaches: (1) basic research to develop products which the company itself could patent; (2) continuous search for products which were already being produced elsewhere and which were coming off patent or for which the patent had certain weaknesses which Hygeia could exploit. An example was DDT, one of the company's major products and the one on which the initial Hygeia growth was based. It came into the Hygeia product line because the vigilant Hygeia founder took advantage of an oversight in the original patent.

Hygeia, through the British directors of its UK subsidiary Hyag, and in particular Mr A. M. Thoms, kept a systematic watch on product developments in the field, including scrutinizing the patents of competitor's existing products. In this way Hygeia tracked competitor's activities, and market needs and trends. Company representatives and agents were also used to identify market needs. In addition the company subscribed to a continuous veterinary market survey, compiled by the Pharmaceutical and Allied Industries Association, which provided market trends and market share data for the company on an on-going basis.

Hygeia's Export Performance

Hygeia's principal export market was the UK, representing over 30% of total sales. The relative importance of Hygeia's export sales to total sales had grown rapidly since 1976 as can be seen in Table 19.1.

Table 19.1. Hygeia Export Sales as a Percent of Total Sales (1974–8)

	1974	1975	1976	1977	1978
Percent of total	14%	14%	14%	30%	35% (estimated)

The relative growth rates in domestic and export sales are illustrated in Table 19.2.

Table 19.2. Index of Domestic and Export Sales Growth (1974–8)

	1974	1975	1976	1977	1978
Domestic Sales	100	106	117	168	221
Export Sales	100	100	114	433	741

The UK Agrochemical Market

The Financial Times (June 20, 1977) characterized the situation in the UK agrochemical market of recent years as follows:

'Held down by the price restraint, restricted by the encroachment of international legislation and scorched by freak weather conditions, the agrochemicals industry now appears to be heading for a period of comparative stability. For an industry that had become accustomed to a traditional pattern of fairly settled growth, agrochemicals has been confronted over the last four years with serious challenges as it has gone through a complete cycle from steady expansion to shortage and now back again to surplus.'

In 1976, industry turnover increased by less than 2% in real terms. In herbicides, where UK industry has a tradition of successful innovation, the unusually dry summer had led to widespread pest attacks throughout Europe and to a sharp increase in sales. Domestic sales increased 42% in real terms and export sales by 74%. Herbicides account for 66.5% of total sales with domestic UK sales of £60.1 million.

The Financial Times went on to quote industry spokesmen in the UK who argued that the increasing burden of standards legislation was slowing entry of new products on to the market:

'During the last five years it is estimated that the time taken to get a new product from the point of discovery and the issuing of a patent, through its trial clearance, provisional clearance and finally full commercial clearance and thence on to the market has been lengthened by some two years.

To bring a product on to the market from scratch is now taking a research and development programme stretching over seven to ten years, whereas as little as five years ago the process was estimated to last five to seven years. Equally, the research costs have escalated to the point where the industry is reckoning on an expenditure of £4 million to £6 million per successful product. Whether or not it is yet the case that costs alone are holding up product development is still to be proved, but it is certainly the case in the US that the number of new products registered in the last two years has dropped as a result of problems with the federal regulatory authority, the Environmental Protection Agency.'

R & D steadily required companies to take greater and greater risks and over longer timescales, resulting in transfer of interest to other, more profitable areas. Mr J. A. Smith, the agrochemicals manager of Shell, had been quoted as saying that product innovation was now conducted by only a handful of companies. A reason for this was the growth and complexity of the information required by various authorities before a product could be registered for commercial use. Dow for example, in 1976, estimated that 34% of its pesticide R & D expenditure went on discovery research while 66% went on product registration and development. This compared with a ratio of 53% to 47% in 1970.

As to the future, the Financial Times concluded:

'But as the demands of agriculture for greater productivity grow, much of the industry's opportunities for growth will come in the more intensive use of agrochemicals. As much as 95% of all cereal crops in the UK, for instance, are already sprayed at least once, but opportunities are opening up as farmers become increasingly aware of how the multiple use of pesticides can help safeguard the profitability of their crops.'

UK Market Segments

The UK market, which accounted for less than 5% of the world total, was broken down by segments according to product. The major segments were for insecticides, fungicides and herbicides. Other minor segments include preparations for plant control such as growth regulators. Table 19.3 shows the trends in the various segments.

Table 19.3. UK Agrochemical Sales 1971–6 (£ million)

	1971	1972	1973	1974	1975	1976
Herbicides	26.1	21.7	31.5	40.2	50.8	60.1
Fungicides	3.0	3.3	5.7	8.0	8.1	9.8
Insecticides	7.4	12.2	12.7	9.4	10.4	16.0
Total (including some additional to above)	38.7	42.9	55.0	64.5	72.2	96.6

Sources: Business Monitor (1971–3) and British Agrochemical Association (1974–6)

The major consumer of agrochemicals in the UK was the cereal farmer who in the 1970's had record returns on his crops. Chemicals had become very significant in increasing both the quality and quantity of yield. An estimate for market growth in 1975 predicted an annual rise of 10% in the UK demand for agrochemicals and 12—15% in the world generally. (The appendices to this case provide data on trends in UK agriculture.)

UK Distribution Structure

The channel structure for agrochemicals marketing in the UK underwent significant changes in the 1960s and 1970s, reflecting changes in the farming structure itself and in new methods for crop growing.

The traditional outlets for farm chemicals were the retail merchants and cooperative stores who were served by wholesalers in the normal manner. More recently, however, the wholesalers had become much more significant in the channel system and a new form of wholesaler-farm consultant assumed major importance. Such a firm was Roberts and Hewett, the Hygeia distributor. Roberts & Hewett estimated that the UK in 1977 had 300 such wholesalers covering the country, about 150 of whom were large and accounted for up to 80% of the total market. Hygeia had a network of 20 distributors whom they had established to cover the UK through Roberts & Hewett. These distributors generally marketed direct to farmers. Charles Roberts' comment on the traditional merchants and coops was that 'they tended to sell, while the new type of distributor marketed his products'.

The Roberts & Hewett approach to marketing was based on building up a personal relationship with the farmer-customer. The firm offered him a complete advisory service on what to sow, when, and how, and followed this up with advice on how to look after the crop as it grows. Their approach was summarized in The West Midland Plan which was part of their promotional literature outlining their service (see Exhibit 19.6). The plan portrayed Roberts & Hewett as crop management specialists and not just suppliers of agrochemicals.

Charles Roberts estimated that to justify R & H involvement with an individual customer an expenditure of £40 per acre per year was required.

R & H felt that in the West Midland Region of England, their home base, they had about 20—25% of total market.

Hygeia UK Market Entry and Development Strategy

Hygeia had for a number of years exported to the UK by selling unbranded products to other manufacturers. During this phase in their development, the approach to exports was somewhat passive. They filled orders which came from other producers who then did the marketing to the end user. During this phase Hygeia was little more than a production operation, filling job lots for the major companies. In the mid-1970s the company examined its position in the UK and identified three possible strategies for market expansion. These were:

1 Expand the previously successful operation.
2 Set up a distribution network tailor-made for Hygeia.
3 Team up with an established UK distributor.

These alternatives were evaluated by Hygeia as follows:

1 Expand the previously successful operation of selling unbranded products to larger manufacturers orders: While in many ways this would have suited a small company competing with the giants of the industry, it had disadvantages in terms of control and in terms of developing the Hygeia brands which were available in Ireland.
2 Set up a distribution network tailor-made for Hygeia: This approach would have given the company increased control of the marketing function in the UK but it would have meant investing in market development almost from an unknown position. Heavy costs would have had to be incurred in promotion and in hiring a marketing team. In addition, while the company had a number of products which dominated the Irish market and had a well developed distribution network, the experience gained there would not be of great value in the UK where agrochemical marketing was more sophisticated.
3 Team-up with an established distributor in the UK: This approach was chosen. The distributor selected was Roberts & Hewett Ltd (R & H), a firm based in the West Midlands of England. R & H was a young company with an aggressive growth outlook on the market, run by two former sales representatives, John Hewett and

Charles Roberts, who had previously worked with major agro-chemical marketers. Hygeia had already experience of doing business with R & H through its export marketing arm, Agrichem Ltd. At the same time as Hygeia had decided to sell through a distributor in the UK Roberts & Hewett were searching for exclusive rights to products which would compete with the majors in the industry and also offer them attractive margins. This apparently fortuitous coincidence of 'search and discover' on the part of both companies resulted in the formation of a new UK based marketing company for Hygeia products jointly owned by R & H and Hygeia.

Roberts and Hewett were selected as distributors on the basis of Hygeia's previous acquaintance with them and without consideration of alternative distributors. In the words of Mr Moore 'It seemed like a natural combination'. Mr Moore also believed strongly in motivating his distributors by providing attractive margins and, in the case of Roberts and Hewett, giving the further incentive of equity participation in their marketing company.

The new marketing company was named Hyag and was a UK registered company.

The UK Distribution Structure for Hygeia Products

With the formation of Hyag the distribution of Hygeia's products in the UK followed the pattern shown in Figure 19.1.

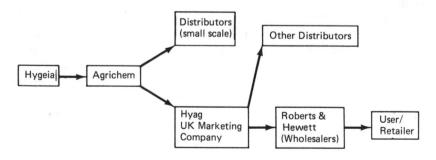

Figure 19.1

As Figure 19.1 shows, distribution of Hygeia products reflected a hybrid structure combining the system used prior to Hyag's formation with the more recently developed approach including Hyag.

The strategy was now for Agrichem to sell unbranded products and Hyag to deal in branded sales in the UK.

Roberts and Hewett had been expanding their own distribution network from a regional base in the West Midlands. They now had a distributor network of 50 covering a major portion of the UK and were searching for more agressive growth' companies as distributors.

Roberts & Hewett did not sell exclusively for Hygeia. As wholesalers they were distributors for some of the major companies as well. For example, they were the fifth largest UK distributors for BASF. This involvement with other producers who were competing directly with Hygeia posed certain problems and conflicts and appeared likely to limit, potentially, the growth of Hygeia's UK sales. R & H acknowledged that they could not allow sales of Hygeia products to get too large in market share terms or they could lose the major companies. However, the large companies also needed R & H because they were important UK distributors. Thus, there was a question of a balance to be maintained by R & H.

Marketing Mix Strategy

As a small company competing in the UK with major multinationals, Hygeia was constrained in its freedom to make decisions on some elements of the marketing mix. This applied particularly to pricing. Hygeia's maximum prices according to Mr Moore were determined by the large companies. Considerable leeway existed, however, for pricing below maximum prices and this was used to make dealer margins attractive and still produce reasonable returns. Hyag used a 'push strategy' in which dealer relations were emphasized and fostered by high margins. This contrasted with the policy of the larger companies, such as ICI, Bayer, BASF, etc., who invested heavily in advertising. Hygeia's policy had been to rely on building up strong channel relationships with little advertising. Advertising however, was being considered for future use when the company had additional high volume products. An important question was, when would advertising become a feasible or worthwhile investment for the company?

One aspect of Hygeia's product strategy had been to take advantage of patents which had expired or which were weak, and to exploit them. Hygeia's growth in the UK had been chiefly due to one such product, cloromequat, marketed in the UK under the brand name Hyquat, which had in two years captured over 20% of the UK market.

The principal products in the Hygeia range apart from Hyquat were Hyban, a cereal herbicide, Dymethoate, an insect control for most agricultural crops and Hystore. Other products were also exported from the Hygeia home product range but only to round out the line.

The company had no product patented in the UK. Hygeia's major success, Hyquat, had its main use in cereals, acting as an agent to stiffen and shorten straw and thereby prevent lodging as well as certain diseases. This segment of the agrochemical market was still small but becoming increasingly interesting to the industry. The total market worldwide was estimated to be $300 million in 1976 with the European market assuming major importance. However, the major successes in this market sector were isolated and to date only two products, one of which was cloromequat, were regarded as important products in the overall agrochemical group.

Most of the major companies in the industry appeared to have research projects in this area and several international groups such as Roche, which had not to date been active in the traditional areas of agrochemicals, were now devoting considerable attention to developing plant growth regulators like Hyquat. Thus, the plant growth regulator sector of the industry could become much more significant if major applications were developed for some of the products then in research. Competition in this sector could increase with the entry of new firms. The major outlet in Europe for cloromequat was in wheat, but applications for growth regulators existed in other crops including tobacco, sugarcane and rubber.

Three manufacturers apart from Hygeia supplied cloromequat. These were BASF, Cynamid and Makhteshim, an Israeli group. Hygeia's success in this sector was attributed to the company's small size relative to competition, resulting in its encroachment being regarded with little concern. However, Hygeia could not now be ignored by larger competitors and expected increased competition in what was a highly profitable market. It was expected that this would require changes in Hygeia's previous marketing approach of adopting a low profile and using 'push' promotional strategy. Hygeia would in the future have to consider whether advertising should be used to promote their products to the end user. In this connection it would be necessary to review advertising used in Ireland and to consider whether adaptation would be necessary for the UK market and, if so, precisely what changes should be made.

In addition Hygeia's large Irish product range had not yet been tested in the UK and, given the extent to which the company had achieved a strong position on the Irish market, further entries to the UK might be considered.

The Future of DDT in Hygeia's Product Line

DDT was an important product in Hygeia's line. However, in 1977 the role which this product should play in the future was very uncertain. The company had a long association with DDT going back to World War II. In the early 1940s the Irish market lacked an adequate supply of pesticides. This situation grew more serious when an infestation of body parasites became almost epidemic. Dr Coyle, Hygeia's founder, saw an opportunity and began manufacturing DDT. Ireland at the time thus became only the second European nation with a market supply of this pesticide. In other countries apart from Switzerland, the supply was being used for the war effort. The patent belonged to the Swiss based Geigy company which formulated the product there. Geigy patented the product in Britain but not in Ireland, presuming that the British patent covered Ireland as well. The error was discovered when production of DDT commenced in Galway. Subsequently, a close relationship developed between the two companies.

The group of products to which DDT belonged consisted of a line of what were by 1977 considered first generation agrochemicals which had become very successful during the immediate post-war era. This success reflected their usefulness in controlling a wide range of insecticides, a generally low handling hazard, and control over a long period of time. They were also cheap enough to be used in both developed and developing nations. Since the mid-1960s, however, the dominant influence on this market sector had been the limitations imposed on use due to long-term effect on the environment. A further concern was that residues of certain products applied early in the season could still be present at harvest giving rise to a possible toxicity hazard in edible crops. In 1970 the Environmental Protection Agency (EPA) in the USA banned the agricultural use of DDT. Other countries followed the example of the USA in imposing similar restrictions on the use of DDT. These included Japan and Germany, where DDT had been restricted to forestry applications since 1974 and would in the near future be banned entirely.

The result of these prohibitions in world markets meant that innovation in the DDT-type group of agrochemicals was limited. USA exports of DDT had fallen dramatically during the 1970s from a figure of 28 million tons in 1968 to 1.8 million tons in 1975. Price trebled in 1975, indicating that a considerable demand still existed for the product worldwide. Indeed, Hindustan Insecticides, an Indian company, had recently invested in new production capacity to supply DDT, confirming that this type of chemical continued to be acceptable in developing countries despite the ban elsewhere. A study by Wood, MacKenzie and Co. on the Agrochemical Industry suggested the possibility that capital investment could be stepped up considerably to compensate for the lack of availability of such materials from traditional sources in the USA and Europe. A further factor to dampen the market was the incidence of resistance to DDT in areas of intensive usage. Insects had been found to develop an immunity to such products where it was used heavily.

In recent years, the original manufacturers had in many cases ceased production of DDT. Those, including Hygeia, who had continued in production, faced a decrease in competition when patents expired. In addition, the versatility of the product combined with its frequent use in mixtures helped maintain its attraction for some manufacturers.

Hygeia was an important supplier of DDT to the UK market where restrictions were not yet as severe as in some other countries. However, the company faced the prospect that UK legislation on DDT usage was also likely to become more restrictive. In the meantime the market was expected to be quite attractive and markets in developing countries were expected to expand. Thus, there were some important strategic questions facing Hygeia in relation to future involvement with DDT, firstly, in regard to future policy on the UK and secondly, on the possibility of entering new markets with a product which many countries had already declared environmentally harmful.

As an indication of the growth in the UK market for Hygeia's DDT Table 19.4 shows trends in their sales.

Table 19.4. Index of DDT Sales by Hygeia in UK*

Year	1974	1975	1976	1977	1978 (forecast)
Index	100	146	1352	468	2563

* figures as supplied by Hygeia Ltd.

Overall, Hygeia management faced some critical and urgent decisions. Success had followed swiftly from the changes in its UK marketing organization. However, this success nurtured the threat of competition. Other markets remained to be explored both in the UK and the rest of Europe. A product of historical significance to the company was now banned in many countries. However, as competitors ceased producing it Hygeia's sales expanded and new markets could open up in developing countries. This posed both ethical and strategic questions for the company. On the domestic front, Hygeia management pondered the efficiency of its Irish marketing system and wondered to what extent UK methods of distribution could be adopted. At this stage only one fact was certain; the agrochemicals market was one of considerable opportunity. For Hygeia, the ability to capitalize on the potential would be largely a test of its marketing organization and strategic choices.

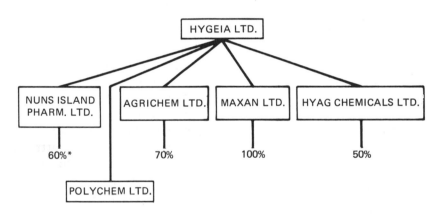

Exhibit 19.1

- *Dairy Detergents*
  Detergent Steriliser No. 1
  Iofor
  Lubine
  Milkstone Remover
  Cold Cleaning Circulation
  Bimasticide

- *Grower and Gardener Products*
  Arbrosan
  Bromotex Emulsion
  Bromotex Seed Dressing
  B.H.C. 50% W.P.
  Capskill
  Captan (50% wettable)
  Chlordane Emulsion
  Caterpillar Spray
  Cosan
  D.D.T. 25%
  Dimethoate
  Dieldrin Emulsion 15%
  Gamagran
  Golden Grain
  Hytin
  Hytox
  Mortweed 'M'
  Sproutex
  P.M.N. 2½%
  Tar Oil

- *Weedkillers*
  Benazolin Plus: (Benazolin with
    2, 4, D, B, and M.C.P.A.)
  Brushwood Killer
  C.M.P.P.
  D.B. Plus
  Dinoseb A
  Dicambone
  Dinitrone
  Hyprone
  Mortone 30% M.C.P.A.
  M.C.P.A. − 25%
  Mortweed
  Morthistle (M.C.P.B.)
  Redshank 'S'
  Hytrol
  Haulmex
  Amizol D

- *Household and Farmyard Products*
  Agro Louse Powder
  Roded
  Flak
  Flak Aerosol
  Flak Fly Strip
  Mosgo
  Hypine
  Hysan Antiseptic

Exhibit 19.2: Hygeia's Domestic Product Range

AGRICHEM
Chlormequat
40

Exhibit 19.3

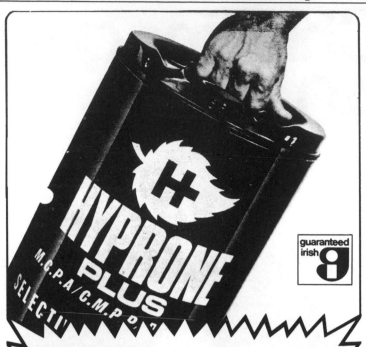

The Strong Answer to Strong Weeds

Hyprone Plus is the strong answer to strong weeds, including chickweed, cleavers, redshank and knotgrass. **Hyprone Plus** contains C.M.P.P., M.C.P.A. and DICAMBA to ensure broad spectrum weed control.

Hyprone Plus is a quality product developed by Hygeia to suit the needs of Irish farming. Hygeia manufacture Ireland's most complete range of selective weedkillers
Dependably good. Dependably Irish.

be selective — choose

HYPRONE PLUS
THE QUALITY HERBICIDE FROM HYGEIA.

Hygeia Ltd.,
Nun's Island, Galway.
Tel (091) 7681.

Exhibit 19.4

is for herbicides.

The Hygeia range of agricultural herbicides are essential to profit-planning on your cereal and grassland projects. Properly applied, Hygeia herbicides will increase your yield per acre, and multiply your profits.

Each Hygeia herbicide is a scientifically balanced formulation, and should be applied in accordance with the directions for best results.

Look for the Hygeia label, your guarantee of satisfaction.

HYGEIA

Hygeia Ltd., Nun's Island, Galway.
Telephone (091) 7681

Hygeia Guide to Weed Control

LOW VOLUME SPRAYING: 15-20 gals.

Weeds	Stage of Growth	Hygeia Weedkiller/Acre	Remarks
Soft Weeds Thistle and Dock	Wheat 5 leaf Oats 2-3 leaf Barley 5 leaf	Hygeia M 25% 4-5 pts. or Mortone 3-4 pts.	Spray as early as possible. Corn Spurry max. rate.
Soft Weeds and Redshank and Chickweed	Wheat 4-5 leaf Oats 3-4 leaf Barley 3-4 leaf	Redshank "S" 4 pts.	If Chickweed severe, use Redshank "S". Spray early.
Cleavers and Chickweed plus Soft Weeds	Wheat 5 leaf Oats 5 leaf Barley 5 leaf	Hyprone Plus 4 pts.	Hyprone best where you have big cover of these two weeds.
Soft Weeds in Undersown Crops	Wheat 4-5 leaf Oats 4-5 leaf Barley 4-5 leaf	D. B. Plus 4-5 pts. Morthistle 4-5 pts.	Spray as early as possible for best results.

MEDIUM TO HIGH VOLUME SPRAYING

Corn Marigold	Wheat 5 leaf Oats 5 leaf Barley 5 leaf	Dinoseb A 3 pts. + Mortone ¾ pts.	Spray as early as possible. Warm moist weather best. Keep pressure low: 30 lbs. sq. inch.
Soft Weeds and Redshank, Chickweed, etc., in Under-sown crops	Wheat 5 leaf Oats 5 leaf Barley 5 leaf	Dinoseb A 4-5 pts.	When clover has developed 2 trifoliate leaves and the grass is established.
Weeds in Cereals before undersowing	Wheat 5 leaf Oats 5 leaf Barley 5 leaf	Dinitrone 6 pts.	Undersow 7 days after spraying.

WEEDS IN PEAS

Weeds in Peas	Peas 2-3 ins. high	Dinitrone 6-8 pts. and ¼ pt. Mortone	Warm moist weather best results.

Exhibit 19.5

GENERAL NOTES

(A) These notes are intended as a guide to treatments, selected from many sources, to assist you in maximising your yield potentials from autumn cereals.

(B) Roberts and Hewett, your Crop Protection Specialists will arrange to steer you through a system most suited to your farm and cropping conditions.

(C) You must commit yourself and ourselves to regular crop inspections so that we can give advice depending on soil, farm, climate and disease conditions that will be changing throughout the season.

(D) Roberts and Hewett's helicopter service will be available to apply herbicides, fungicides, insecticides and trace elements as and when required to your crops.

THE WEST MIDLAND PLAN

An aid to maximise your cereal yields.

1. Draw up a programme and stick to it, allowing for seasonal variations.

2. Regularly inspect your crops as a routine.

3. Choose fields of good fertility status to achieve your optimum yields.

4. Select high yielding varieties with proven vigour seed.

5. Decide on convenient wheel marks to suit both your sprayer and fertilizer working widths.

6. Drill early on a good seed bed.

7. Have the correct seed rate and uniform drilling.

8. Use optimum fertilizer rates especially nitrogen, and split nitrogen dressings to achieve maximum effect.

9. To allow you to get maximum benefit from nitrogen and to ease harvesting use split doses of Chlormequat.

10. Correct weed control is important and you should aim to use autumn applied herbicides.

11. Fungicides should be used regularly as and when you require them.

12. Chelated Trace Elements at ear emergence are beneficial for grain size and weight.

13. Control aphids when necessary.

14. The West Midland Plan has been drawn from many sources including Belgian, German and British systems. These programmes have consistently increased yields by over 25%.

Exhibit 19.6:   Roberts & Hewett Promotional Literature

Biographies

MICHAEL J. BAKER is Professor of Marketing and Dean of the School of Business and Administration at Strathclyde University. Professor Baker is a DBA of Harvard University, and the author of nine books on a variety of marketing topics with a particular emphasis on innovation and new product development.

M. FRANK BRADLEY. After obtaining his PhD from Cornell University, Dr Bradley worked with the Agricultural Research Institute in Dublin. Since 1975 he has been Lecturer in Marketing at University College Dublin where he researches and teaches in the areas of marketing and international business. Dr Bradley is editor of a case book in international marketing and has published articles in such journals as *Irish Journal of Agricultural Economics and Rural Sociology, Journal of Irish Business and Administrative Research, Management Decision* and *Industrial Marketing Management.*

DAVID COOK is Lecturer in Marketing at Bradford University Management Centre. After reading Economics he went on to complete an MBA at Bradford. Subsequently he worked for British Petroleum, English Electric and as a senior consultant with Associated Industrial Consultants Ltd. His current research is in retailing and consumer behaviour where he has published widely.

PETER DOYLE is head of the Marketing Department at Bradford University Management Centre. Previously Professor Doyle has taught at London Business School, and INSEAD (France) and has been Visiting Professor at Stanford, University of South Carolina and the University of Hawaii. He received his PhD from Carnegie-Mellon University, USA, and is a Fellow of the Institute of Marketing and CAM Foundation. Professor Doyle acts as a consultant to a number of companies in retailing, advertising and strategic planning. He has published in many international journals including *Management Science, Economic Journal, Journal of Marketing Research* and the *Journal of Marketing.*

NORMAN A. HART is Director of the CAM Foundation and previously a Unilever Marketing Manager, a publisher and an advertising chief executive. Mr Hart is a Visiting Fellow of Bradford University and holds a Master's Degree in Business Administration in which he majored in Advertising Education. He is the author of a number of books on industrial marketing and advertising, and is a frequent speaker at UK and international seminars.

GRAHAM HOOLEY is Lecturer in Marketing at the University of Bradford Management Centre. After graduation, Dr Hooley joined the Marketing Department of Associated Newspapers Group Ltd as research executive engaged in marketing and advertising research. His doctorate was awarded from the University of Warwick in the areas of market segmentation and product positioning. His current research interests lie in the applications of quantitative techniques to the problems of marketing management.

JAMES E. LYNCH is Lecturer in Marketing at the University of Bradford Management Centre. After graduating from Oxford, he spent several years with Procter and Gamble and subsequently held board-level appointments in the UK textile industry. He consults widely with organizations in the public and private sector. His research interests are in the areas of retailing and corporate planning.

COLIN McIVER has been head of his own marketing and management consultancy firm for the past twenty years. In this capacity he has been responsible for a number of marketing strategy and organizational projects in leading UK banks, insurance companies and other financial institutions. He has written three previous books and a number of articles on the various aspects of marketing.

GEOFFREY K. RANDALL graduated in Law from the University of Oxford and then spent over ten years in business, working in Marketing Research, Marketing, Operational Research and Strategic Planning with a range of UK companies. He is currently Head of the School of Business Administration at Thames Polytechnic. His research interests are in the field of New Product Development and Consumer Decision Models.

JOHN A. SAUNDERS is Lecturer in Marketing at Bradford University. He is a graduate of Loughborough and a Cranfield MBA. His industrial experience is in sales, marketing and planning with Hawker Siddeley Group and as partner in Business Dynamics (Software). Previously he was senior lecturer at Huddersfield Polytechnic. He has completed research and published on teaching in higher education, consumer behaviour and marketing modelling. His current research interest is the design and implementation of computer aided marketing planning systems.

JAMES J. WARD is Bank of Ireland Professor of Marketing at University College, Galway. He received his doctorate in Business Administration from the George Washington University, Washington D.C. in 1971 and taught subsequently at California State University, Hayward. In 1979—80 he undertook a one year assignment with the International Trade Centre, UNCTAD/GATT, Geneva where he has served as a consultant since 1975 on a variety of projects. His publications include a book on The European Approach to US Markets.

RAY WILLSMER is one of the few men to have held Board level appointments in manufacturing, advertising and media. He was Marketing Director of the Grocery Division of J. Lyons & Co, Marketing and Planning Director of The Thompson Organization and had advertising agency experience with J. Walter Thompson, Ogilvy & Mather and latterly his own agency. His is currently Chairman of Ray Willsmer Associates Ltd and Ray Willsmer (Hair Services) Ltd. He has also held a part-time appointment as an Advisor to UNCATD/GATT, is Chairman of the Governing Body of the College of Distributive Trades and lectures regularly for CAM and the Institute of Marketing. He is the author of *Directing the Marketing Effort* and *Basic Arts of Marketing.*

JOHN WILMSHURST is a chemistry graduate of University College, Oxford. He has worked in the Patents Departments of Glaxo Laboratories Ltd and Reed International and later became Group Advertising Manager directing the work of several advertising agencies for Reeds. In 1959 he was invited to become a Director of Roles and Parker Ltd, Europe's largest specialist industrial agency, and was also Director-in-Charge of Stuart Advertising Agency Ltd. He left the agency world in 1971 to work as a consultant and lecturer in marketing topics. He is Senior Lecturer at the Medway and Maidstone College of Technology and is a Course Director and Subject Examiner at the Institute of Marketing. He is also a visiting lecturer at Bradford University.